Introduction to
Masters of American Literature

BY *Henry A. Pochmann* AND *Gay Wilson Allen*

Professor of English,
University of Wisconsin

Professor of English,
New York University

Southern Illinois University Press   *Carbondale and Edwardsville*

Feffer & Simons, Inc.   *London and Amsterdam*

PREFACE

The two-volume Pochmann-Allen anthology entitled *Masters of American Literature* caught the crest of popularity during the late forties when the demand for fewer authors and more complete coverage put the scatter-gun kind of anthology virtually out of business. The wide adoption of this major-authors book underscored the soundness of the idea and, in turn, helped prepare the way for the substitution of inexpensive paperback editions of individual authors or single works for bulky, expensive anthologies. This revolution in the teaching of American literature brought about by paperback texts confirmed the soundness of our design, namely, that the most effective teaching can be accomplished by concentrating on the "literary masters," whose writings are read either uncut or at least in large chunks. Furthermore, the ample selections could be read in the context of the author's whole career and the society in which he lived and for which he wrote. This background information could be supplied by lectures or by introductory essays for reference as needed. The latter method frees the teacher to talk in class about the literary works themselves. Many teachers find this method more stimulating and rewarding than formal lectures. It is for their students that we offer this collection of biographical and critical introductions to the major American authors, which some of our colleagues in the profession have told us have special values of their own.

The two long historical essays (now combined into one) give the backgrounds of American literature from the seventeenth to the twentieth century more coherently and cogently, we believe, than any to be found in the conventional handbook or manual. Each author-essay was written out of as full a knowledge of the author's total work and such a familiarity with biography and criticism as we could command. The care that went into their preparation has been rewarded by praise for their richness of illustrative detail, their impartiality, and their reliability.

If the student wants to do further reading in or about a given author, he can find explicit suggestions in the judiciously critical bibliographical essays in Floyd Stovall (ed.), *Eight American Authors*, orig-inally published in 1956, recently completely revised, brought up to date, and readily available in an inexpensive W. W. Norton paperback edition. The authors covered by this invaluable guidebook are Poe, Emerson, Hawthorne, Thoreau, Melville, Whitman, Mark Twain, and Henry James. A companion volume covering Taylor, Edwards, Franklin, Irving, Bryant, Cooper, Holmes, Longfellow, Lowell, Whittier, Dickinson, Howells, Norris, Adams, and Crane (plus two bibliographical essays on the literature of the Old and the New South) is currently in preparation under the editorship of Robert A. Rees and Earl N. Harbert and scheduled for publication in 1970 by the University of Wisconsin Press in both hardcover and paperback editions. A volume covering twelve twentieth-century American authors, prepared under the editorship of Jackson Bryer, will shortly be published by the Duke University Press. Supplementary, detailed, analytical and critical essays on the total range of American literature are available for the more advanced student in the annual survey of current literary research edited by James Woodress: *American Literary Scholarship . . . 1963* to the present, also published by the Duke University Press.

While most of the existing editions of American authors fall short of meeting the demands of modern scholarship, the following are currently being edited according to specifications laid down by the Center for Editions of American Authors (Modern Language Association): Edwards (Yale University Press), C. B. Brown (Kent State), Irving (Wisconsin), Cooper (Clark), Hawthorne (Ohio State), Emerson (Harvard), Thoreau (Princeton), Whitman (New York University), Melville (Northwestern), Mark Twain (California), Howells (Indiana), Simms (South Carolina), Crane (Virginia), and Dewey (Southern Illinois).

In spite of the great scholarly and critical activity in the field of American literary study since these essays were originally published, it is both surprising and gratifying how few of them have been outmoded by discoveries and reinterpretations. We would like to think that this shows the soundness of our knowledge and judgment, but we are reminded of the fact that for the majority of classic American writers, new discoveries have not essentially affected reputations and values during the past two decades.

Complete coverage of contemporary poets, novelists, and dramatists is beyond our intention or scope. These are adequately, if voluminously, analyzed in readily available article, pamphlet, or book form. Authors not so well covered are the very ones we have treated in our essays, beginning with Cotton Mather and ending with Stephen Crane. Consequently we welcome the opportunity to make these essays once again available to students of American literature.

March 22, 1969

H. A. P.
G. W. A.

CONTENTS

Introduction

Among the numerous problems that confront the student of American literature, one of the most insistent is the question of what makes American literature American. By what factors or stages did it become so? It will become apparent to the student before he proceeds very far that American writings began very early to develop certain uniquely American characteristics. Somewhere, somehow, between the seventeenth-century historians and theologians and the twentieth-century poets and novelists, there was created a distinctively American literature—still possessed of some foreign ingredients but nevertheless distinctively American.

Each student will want to make his own analysis and evaluation, in the process of which he will adopt one or a combination of several points of view. He may, after the example of Vernon Louis Parrington, who viewed American literature as an essentially native phenomenon in which the forces of liberalism oppose those of conservatism, relate all that he reads to this clash of opposing forces. Second, he may find his frame of reference in what Howard Mumford Jones calls the three fundamental impulses that animate American culture: (1) the cosmopolitan spirit, (2) the spirit of the frontier, and (3) the bourgeois or middle-class spirit. Third, he may regard his problem as one that Oscar Cargill has called Ideodynamic, in which Ideas are viewed as "on the March" and "in Conflict." Or he may, following the pattern of Norman Foerster, find in the aforementioned interplay of foreign importations and native conditioning four broad factors: (1) Puritanism, (2) romanticism, (3) realism, and (4) the frontier spirit. But whatever approach he adopts, he will inevitably come back to the basic fact that American literature is the product of the interplay of two basic forces—a foreign tradition and a native environment. It may well be that the beginning student will find the four-fold plan of Professor Foerster most readily adaptable to his immediate purpose. As he proceeds in his study, he will find that no plan yet proposed is entirely adequate for the explanation of a literary culture as complex as ours. Meanwhile the four factors—the Puritan tradition, the romantic revolt, the realistic impulse, and the frontier spirit—will be sufficiently comprehensive to serve many useful purposes.

The first of these four—the Puritan tradition—was transplanted bodily. Early Puritanism, whether we think of it as a theological doctrine or as a general attitude toward life, was, and remained for a long time, basically European; but in submitting to American conditioning, it became increasingly less puritanic as it felt, with ever-increasing insistency, the effects of the romantic, the realistic, and the frontier impulses. The romantic spirit was partially of foreign, partially of native, origin. We admit as much when we speak of Bryant as the American Wordsworth, of Cooper as the American Scott, of Longfellow as the American Tennyson, and so forth for most of the major nineteenth-century exponents of romanticism. These identifications, however superficial, are nonetheless indicative of the debt which Irving owed to Addison, Poe to Coleridge, or of the kinship we discover between the wit of Holmes and that of the Queen Anne writers. When, after the Civil War, the romantic spirit fell before the onslaughts of the disciples of realism, the latter still drew a large measure of inspiration from European sources. One recalls that both Henry James and William Dean Howells freely acknowledged their debts to European realists, and that contemporary naturalists have done no less.

While Puritanism, romanticism, and realism were motivated in varying degrees by European traditions, a more distinctively native impulse, called (for want of a better term) the frontier spirit, was exerting an influence of ever-increasing force upon the American literary consciousness. In so far as this impulse expressed itself in terms of the physical and natural, it began to work upon the earliest immigrants; and the Pilgrim fathers no less than Captain John Smith felt it on stepping ashore. The new land and its products, the forests and rivers and mountains, the wild animals and the Indians exerted molding influences upon the social, economic, and cultural life of the colonists in very real ways. This first phase of the frontier influence upon the European immigrant in America is discernible as much in John Smith's observations as a traveler and explorer of the Atlantic coastal region as in his account of the Pocahontas-Powhatan affair. Similarly, historians like Bradford, Winthrop, and Cotton Mather were acutely conscious of their conditioning by life in a new land, and diarists like Colonel William Byrd and Sarah Kemble Knight left interesting written accounts of frontier society. Crèvecoeur specifically had in mind these effects when, in answer to the question, "What is an American?" he wrote:

He is either an European, or the descendant of an European, hence that strange mixture of blood, which you will find in no other country. I could point out to you a family whose grandfather was an Englishman, whose wife was Dutch, whose son married a French woman, and whose present four sons have now four wives of different nations. *He* is an American, who, leaving behind him all his ancient prejudices and manners, receives new ones from the new mode of life he has embraced, the new government he obeys, and the new rank he holds. He becomes an American by being received in the broad lap of our great *Alma Mater.* Here individuals of all nations are melted into a new race of men, whose labours and posterity will one day cause great changes in the world. . . . The American is a new man, who acts upon new principles; he must therefore entertain new ideas, and form new opinions. . . . This is an American.

Crèvecoeur wrote of a new man who had come into being during the years that led to the Revolution of 1776. This American had become self-reliant, individualistic, independent, and self-assertive. He began by questioning authority alike of church and state; and gradually absolutism, whether theocratic or purely political, fell before the critical rationalism, on the grounds of which this new man based his attack. Deistic rationalism, as an assertion of the right and ability of the individual to deal directly with his God on his own terms, without intervention of church or state, broke the power of the Puritan theocracy. And by 1776, the same spirit of individualism, adapted to the demands of democratic republicanism, declared political dependence upon England at an end. By this time the spirit bred of the frontier had joined hands with romantic ideas derived from Isaac Newton, John Locke, and Jean Jacques Rousseau, and the rise of Unitarian principles in religion and of independent republicanism in politics went forward jointly under the auspices of ideas engendered by the American frontier and others derived from European liberal thought.

During the nineteenth century a form of literary romanticism, as exemplified by the major writers from Irving to Whitman, enjoyed a remarkable efflorescence. At once in revolt against the stern moralism of the Puritanic dispensation and prophetic of the realism of the future, the spirit of the American frontier supplied the chief motivation by which the nationalization of American letters progressed. Thus Emerson, while still powerfully moved in his moral idealism by his Puritan heritage, espoused (in *Nature, The American Scholar, Self-Reliance,* and others of his works) a doctrine of humanistic self-reliance in conjunction with a distinctively American literary nationalism, and warned his contemporaries that no amount of Shakespearizing would produce another Shakespeare. In his essay on "The Poet," he argued that even Milton and Homer were inadequate as models—that "Milton is too literary and Homer too literal and historical." The American poet, he went on to say, must express the American ideal, in terms of what is immediate and indigenous, while sloughing off the distant and the exotic.

Our logrolling, our stumps and their politics, our fisheries, our negroes, and Indians, our boats and our repudiations, the wrath of rogues and the pusillanimity of honest men, the northern trade, the southern planting, the western clearing, Oregon and Texas, are yet unsung.

"America," he concluded, "is a poem," and by way of prophecy he added, "It will not wait long for metres."

Thus wrote Emerson in 1844. In 1855, Whitman printed the first edition of *Leaves of Grass* as if in answer to the call put forth eleven years earlier by Emerson, who hailed the book as signalizing "the beginning of a great career" and the institution of a new and more hopeful era in American literary culture.

Since Whitman's day much has happened to give the methods of the scientist and the findings of the realist a compelling urgency. As the known universe submitted to the processes of the laboratory and observatory, science failed to confirm the faith of the romanticists that nature is vitally concerned with man and his values, and that man is the crowning work of creation. The industrialization and urbanization of a later day and the attendant complexities of life gave rise to a clash of classes and interests, of social stresses and economic strains, that turned a later generation of realists to doubt the large Whitmanesque faith in the future of America. The reservoir of the frontier that had seemed inexhaustible in Whitman's day seemed to them to have run dry; and science, instead of fulfilling its proper purposes of aiding man in his aspirations, seemed to them leagued with the forces of economic determinism to grind him underfoot. Thence arose the strident forms of social criticism manifest in so much of modern realistic and naturalistic writing. The machine age with its manifold social implications, the advance of technology with its indifference to purely human considerations, the rise of Freudian and behaviorist psychologies with their emphasis upon "libidos" and "automatisms," the artificially manipulated financial booms and succeeding economic depressions, the interposition of world-shaking wars with their attendant wholesale dislocations—all conspired to cast doubt upon the humanitarian assumptions and idealistic aspirations of the romantic age. For many, man came to be merely the by-product of vast natural processes—a helpless automaton, controlled by cosmic forces either indifferent or hostile to human hopes and desires. The scientist's telescope, searching Heaven, found nothing but Matter, subject to the same laws that govern matter here on the earth. The realist, concerning himself with material things

—with things as they are—and adopting the painstaking methods of the scientist in drawing his "cross-sections of life"—his pictures of "reality" or "actuality"—found himself becoming (consciously or unconsciously) receptive to the philosophy of scientific determinism, or naturalism. Hence mechanistic materialism came, in writers like Frank Norris or Theodore Dreiser, to be a force vitally affecting their entire outlook on life. But, however responsive writers like Dreiser and Steinbeck have been to these deterministic philosophies, they are often also equally alive to the purely human demands in a contemporary and complex world. It is by no means unusual, therefore, to find underneath this overlay of scientific determinism a fierce spirit of human protest against this bleakly determined universe and a castigation of an order that produces maladjustments leading only to frustration, despair, and tragedy. But whatever the philosophic assumptions or the premeditated techniques of the contemporary writer, he is motivated very largely by the immediacy of the issues in a manner to make many modern books signally alive, compelling, and American. The exotic, the feudalistic, the "unrealistic" or dreamily romantic have been banished.

In the threefold progression of American literature from Puritanism through romanticism to realism, the frontier spirit has exerted an influence of steadily growing vitality and force. For the earliest generations of immigrants to America, bringing a full-blown literary tradition to a new land, the frontier served as little more than a background or backdrop for their writings. This "scenic" concept of America, in terms of the physical and natural features of the land, still chiefly motivated Cooper's Leatherstocking tales; it partially inspired Irving's Knickerbocker stories, Parkman's histories, and Mark Twain's stories of boy life in Missouri or of the scenes sketched in *Roughing It*; it continues vital in our folk literature, in local-color fiction, and in what passes currently for the literature of regionalism.

But as early as the mid-eighteenth century, the frontier spirit began to express itself forcibly in terms of the ideas which a frontier society developed; and these ideas are reflected no less in the religious and political revolutions of the eighteenth century than in the vibrant spirit of literary nationalism that animated American writers from Freneau to Whitman.

Early in the nineteenth century the frontier began a rapid movement westward, and there followed a succession of frontiers, geographical and ideological. As successive waves of scouts, pioneers, and settlers pushed from the Atlantic to the Pacific, mountain ranges, valleys, and deserts alike were crossed and conquered. The spirit of Leatherstocking was transmuted into that of Andrew Jackson; the Daniel Boone of one generation became the pioneer of the next who went "a-westering" in a prairie schooner; and so successions of frontiersmen, including adventurers, traders, trappers, hunters, ranchers, farmers, lumbermen, prospectors, and miners followed until, by the end of the century, the frontier was gone. But its influence lived on. The rugged individualism, independence, self-assertiveness, expansive optimism, vibrant energy, confident resourcefulness, boundless vitality, and what passes among Europeans as "American brawn, brag, and 'know-how' "—all of them traits of frontier character—still operate. The tall tale of the West that infuses so much of American humor is no less a part of it than the demand for bigger and faster automobiles and more of them. The stories of Bret Harte and of Hamlin Garland, the novels of Willa Cather and of Ole Rolvaag, the poetry of Joaquin Miller and of Robinson Jeffers alike are imbued with it. Realism especially has found the West congenial. Long before the physical frontier vanished, the spirit it had fostered reversed its direction and headed eastward, producing what Vernon Louis Parrington called the "Backwash of the Frontier," until New York and even Boston and Hartford felt its impact. And today, a half-century after the "passing of the frontier," we hear more and more about new frontiers—economic, social, scientific, educational, and, most recently, international. This American spirit has become an effervescence in the blood that is loath to admit a possible future when there shall be no new frontiers to conquer.

In short, American culture is not exclusively one thing or another, but an amalgamation of many ingredients that must be viewed in relation to each other. Aside from the accident by which the language of the Pilgrim fathers became the dominant (though by no means exclusive) language of Americans, their chief claim to primacy in America is owing to the fact that they came to these shores relatively earlier than did the Germans, the Norwegians, the Italians, or the Poles. American literary culture is like a large tapestry woven of many threads, exhibiting an intricate pattern of variegated colors; and the critical student who is ambitious to approach the study of it from anything more than a parochial point of view must disabuse his mind of the idea that American literature is an exclusively Anglo-American phenomenon, the product of a peculiarly English tradition that does not in fact exist.

THE PURITAN BACKGROUND

As a matter of fact, even during the seventeenth century, while the Puritans were establishing themselves and their institutions and laying the groundwork for what was to become the basically English tradition of letters in America, they found themslves in contact and sometimes in conflict with the French to the north and west of them, with the Spaniards to the south and southwest, and with the Dutch and Swedes almost in their midst. How they overcame these rival nationalities is a long and involved story that belongs properly to history. Their success was owing in large measure to the permanence of their colonial establishments, aided markedly by the stability of their linguistic and literary traditions. For it is a noteworthy fact that the early Puritans came to stay, and to that end either brought with them a full complement of cultural and institutional heritages or set promptly to work establishing them. For example, lacking an institution for the training of their clergy and for the preservation of the humanistic tradition of education and learning to which they had become accustomed in the old country, the Massachusetts Bay colonists, six years after their arrival, established Harvard College for "the aduancement and education of youth in all manner of good literature, Artes, and Sciences." It may be observed, in passing, that the proportion of university-trained men in America has never been higher than it was among the first generation of Puritans. A printing press came next, and in' 1640 there was issued by the newly established press in Cambridge the first book published in what is today the United States— *The Bay Psalm Book*. Seven years later they passed the Act of 1647 requiring every town of one hundred families or more to provide free common and grammar school instruction, and Connecticut instituted a similar law in 1650. These are but a few of the countless expedients adopted by the early Puritans in their desire to build in the new world another England that should be, except for such modifications as their religion prescribed, as much like the Renaissance England they had left as they could make it.

Indeed, the uniqueness and singularity of the American Puritan have been overstressed. He was not the gaunt, black-clothed, steeple-crowned kill-joy bent on proscribing all the pleasures of life that he is represented to be in the cartoons; he led no crusade against alcoholic beverages; and he was not oblivious to art, beauty, and the satisfactions of gracious living. The architecture of Puritan buildings, the superb lines of their household furniture, and the simple beauty of their pewter and silverware betoken a lively though not ornate or florid aesthetic sense. To be sure, the Puritan preachers fulminated against drunkenness, but they poured no confiscated liquor into the gutters. It was not the drink itself but the abuse of it that Increase Mather warned against in his sermon, *Wo to Drunkards* (1673):

Drink is in its self a good creature of God, and to be received with thankfulness, but the abuse of drink is from Satan; the wine is from God, but the Drunkard is from the Devil.

Actually, wine flowed freely even at such pious ceremonies as the ordination of ministers; nor were other forms of merry-making banned. For example, at the ordination of Jonathan Edwards his father caused a dance to be held in honor of the occasion; while Cotton Mather recommended musical training, especially choral singing, at the same time that he held dancing schools to be a necessary part of a full-bodied system of education. The Puritans' concern, like that of other religious folk, was lest music, dancing, and riotous merriment interfere with Christian observances and duties or lead to licentiousness.

Similarly, the conventional view of the Puritans as harsh, self-centered, and unemotional, as without love for their families or their fellow men, has to be revised in the light of evidence regarding their daily lives as we find it in the letters, diaries, biographies, and histories of the period. It may be presumed that the rigorous exigencies of a frontier existence often bred a harshness not unlike that which Hamlin Garland described in delineating human relations on the great plains while the West was being won. What is more, the rigidity of the Puritan creed often dominated the softer traits of affection and compliance, substituting sometimes a desolate sanctity in the home. But oftener the tenderness of duty, the sense of subordination, the competence of training, and the repose of a clear conscience gave to the Puritan home an atmosphere of serene and equitable joy.

Nor were the Puritans devoid of the spirit of benevolence and charity. To be sure, they had little of the modern spirit of organized alms-giving or wholesale humanitarianism; yet even Cotton Mather, by whose time the originally fine fervor and spiritual idealism of seventeenth-century Puritanism had undergone a certain hardening process, professed a spirit of Christian charity and found no satisfaction so "ravishing" as "relieving the distresses of a poor miserable neighbor" or redressing "the miseries under which mankind is generally languishing." And it is to be recalled that his *Essays To Do Good* were acknowledged by Franklin as the primary inspiration behind his own many-sided humanitarian projects. Theirs was a society in which each man was expected to contribute his full share toward the common goal of establishing religious, political, and social security. Practical or realistic, and endeavoring to promote frugality and self-reliance, they often exercised the strength of will to withhold the "wicked dollar" that Emerson, of a more humanitarian-minded generation, often wished he could muster. Promiscuous alms-giving, they feared, would destroy personal initiative and eventually promote general indigence; but there is no evidence that worthy cases of need among the Puritans went unheeded any more than they do today.

The more we arrive at the facts, the more do we realize that the Puritans of the seventeenth century lived a fairly normal, everyday kind of life, not occupied mainly with marching to meeting, shooting unfriendly Indians by the way, or burning witches. It is a well-established fact that they burned no witches, though they hanged some. While their poor victims were therefore no less dead, the difference in method of execution is noteworthy. Moreover, it is to be remembered that many educated people the world over believed in witchcraft, and that while thirty-four were executed in New England, "half a million" suffered martyrdom in Europe. The Mathers, often singled out as chiefly responsible for the Salem witchcraft delusions, once they saw the thing getting out of control, did as much as anybody toward bringing the tragedies to an abrupt end by counseling moderation and pointing to the inadequacy of the evidence on which the accused were condemned. Professor G. L. Kittredge, after an exhaustive inquiry into the matter, concludes that there was nothing in the tenets of New Englanders by which witchcraft can be ascribed to something peculiar to the religious opinions or the theology of the Puritans.

Thus many of the peculiar and extreme notions which have become attached to Puritanism in the popular fancy fall away as the facts become known, as do also many of the so-called differences by which Puritans are sometimes distinguished from Anglicans and Protestants generally. Actually, they were about ninety per cent in agreement with contemporary Protestants on all social, intellectual, and religious questions. The remaining ten per cent, however, on which there was dispute, made all the difference to them, so much so that they chose to leave their native land for the privilege of starting anew, albeit in a wild country, and of carrying forward their intent of purifying or perfecting the doctrine of the Church of England.

Puritanism had a long history in Europe before it migrated to America. Its origins go back to the protests of Luther and beyond to Wyclif, but more immediately to the break between the Church of England and the Pope of Rome. In seventeenth-century America, Puritanism was nothing more than an extension of the doctrine of reform—the idea that the Reformation remained incomplete, that more abuses remained to be corrected, that the movement for purification should continue until the Church of England should be restored to the "purity" of the Church as originally instituted by Christ. While the Anglicans in general remained content with what was known as the "Elizabethan Settlement" of the Church, the Puritans wanted to proceed with reforms, though there was much difference of opinion among them regarding the means to be employed or the precise ends to be sought. In the main, however, they agreed on certain cardinal points, derived from the institutional theological system of Calvin. These included (1) a supreme triune God as the absolute Creator and Determiner of all things, as infinitely supreme as man is abjectly low; (2) the Holy Scripture as the exclusive revelation of God; (3) man's fall from original righteousness through willful disobedience, hence his loss of all ability of will to do any spiritual good, hence his total depravity and the imputation of Adam's guilt to all his posterity; (4) the "high mystery" of Election and Predestination, by which, through the mediation of Christ, the mercy of God is manifest toward the elect, chosen by His Almighty power of determining them to that which is good, whence it follows that the elect can neither totally nor finally fall from grace, just as the damned cannot attain it; and (5) salvation as dependent upon an inner consciousness of being of the elect, not at all upon outward "good works," although "good works done in obedience to God's commandments are evidences of a true and lively faith."

This last doctrine, which the modern student finds especially puzzling, is explained fully by Cotton Mather in his *Magnalia Christi Americana* (1702), in which he reproduced the Puritan "Confession of Faith" drawn up in 1680. He explains that corrupt man cannot of himself initiate anything good; hence his best works merit neither pardon for his sins nor eternal life. Since through Adam's fall, every man but the elect is damned to eternal torment, it is the duty of everyone to give all diligence to make his calling and election sure by ascertaining introspectively whether his acts are agreeable and in harmony with God's will as revealed in Scripture, for the promise of Christ and salvation by Him are revealed only in and by the word of God. But aside from this outward revelation of the Gospel, there is necessary also an inward conviction—the "effectual and irresistible work of the Holy Ghost upon the whole soul for the producing in man a spiritual life," which may be recognized as something akin to the Quaker conscience and Inner Light. Recognizing the fact that man wages "a continual and irreconcilable war, the flesh lusting against the spirit, and the spirit against the flesh," the Puritan was impelled (1) toward individualistic introspection and diligent soul-searching and (2) toward an eager poring over the will of God as revealed in the Bible.

To the latter end, sound learning, especially linguistic scholarship, was a requisite, for it was well enough understood by the early Puritans that certain passages in the Bible seemed equivocal if taken by themselves or if unchecked against the linguistic transformations which the Bible had undergone at the hands of its numerous translators. "All things in scripture," so they declared officially in 1680, "are not alike plain in themselves, nor alike clear to all. . . . Where there is a question about the true and full sense of any scripture (which is not manifold but one) it must be searched and known by other places that speak more clearly." Inevitably they deferred to the best educated among them, the university-trained clergy, to resolve these questions pertaining to God's will and law; and if anything had been wanting to elevate their respect for their ministers, the resulting growth in their power and influence would have supplied it. For the early Puritans, learned and unlearned alike, came to America for the purpose of establishing there God's ideal state of society. Since they were loyal Englishmen, the English common law was for them the basis of most social and political appointments; but on points not covered by the common law, especially in matters of church government, they zealously searched God's will, i. e., the Bible, for guidance. Accordingly they established a theocracy, in which the government, as the agent of the King, operated under English law, and as the agent of religion, under divine law—which necessarily meant, according to the interpretation of and under the direction of its religious leaders. These leaders proceeded with admirable strategy to charter and incorporate the several settlements under the proper terms, taking care so to restrict the suffrage by religious qualifications as not

to let the power slip from their hands into those of non-church members. To all "right-thinking" Puritans the unity of the church and state was axiomatic for the simple reason that it seemed impossible to them to separate man's spiritual from his earthly estate.

Yet from the first there were dissenting voices, not only from men like the Anglican Thomas Morton of unsavory, worldly reputation at Merry Mount, but also from individuals in their midst, and Governor Winthrop of the Massachusetts Bay Colony found it necessary to defend himself and his policies in court as early as 1645. However, it is worth observing that after securing an acquittal of the charge that he had exceeded his proper authority, he did not let the opportunity slip to inform all and sundry that he intended to enforce the unity of church and state as founded on the principles of morality according to God's word:

Concerning liberty, I observe a great mistake in the country about that. There is a twofold liberty, natural (I mean as our nature is now corrupt) and civil or federal. The first is common to man with beasts and other creatures. . . . This liberty is incompatible and inconsistent with authority, and cannot endure the least restraint of the most just authority. The exercise and maintaining this liberty makes men grow more evil, and in turn to be worse than brute beasts. . . . The other kind of liberty I call civil or federal, it may also be termed moral . . . it is the liberty to do that which is good, just, and honest.

And he went on in a manner to leave no doubt in the minds of his auditors that the determination of what is "good, just, and honest" rested with their betters, i. e., the magistrates, supported and instructed by the learned ministry. Liberty thus defined supplied the foundation for the Puritan insistence upon religious conformity, for there was no doubt in their minds that theirs was the only true and pure religion, and it seemed equally clear to them that they could not willingly countenance people's mistakenly following false religions. Professor Perry Miller puts the matter in the following terms:

The government of Massachusetts, and of Connecticut as well, was a dictatorship and never pretended to be anything else; it was a dictatorship, not of a single tyrant, or of an economic class, or of a political faction, but of the holy and regenerate. Those who did not hold with the ideals entertained by the righteous, or who believed God had preached other principles, or who desired that in religious belief, morality, and ecclesiastical preferences all men should be left at liberty to do as they wished—such persons had every liberty, as Nathaniel Ward said, to stay away from New England. If they did come, they were expected to keep their opinions to themselves; if they discussed them in public or attempted to act upon them, they were exiled; if they persisted in returning, they were cast out again; if they still came back, as did four Quakers, they were hanged on Boston Common. And from the Puritan point of view, it was good riddance.

But this doctrine early came under the attack of Roger Williams, who argued, in a series of pamphlets which he exchanged with John Cotton, for religious toleration and what this principle implied, namely, the separation of church and state. He was banished for his pains. Anne Hutchinson maintained the heretical Antinomian doctrine that she could commune directly with God, that she required no clerical intermediary; and she went on to imply that she was prepared to follow the promptings of the voice within against all the precepts of the Bible, the churches, the voice of reason, the findings of the Biblical scholars, or the combined authority of priest and magistrate in Massachusetts Bay. The magistrates and ministers were not slow to recognize in her doctrine of immediate communion a form of heresy that would quickly destroy their authority and ultimately topple the entire theocratic structure to the ground. Summarily banished, she joined Roger Williams in Rhode Island. Thomas Hooker left peaceably with the larger part of his congregation for Connecticut, where he was free to institute a government which combined church and state less strictly and enjoined religious conformity less severely than was mandatory in Massachusetts.

In 1639 Governor Winthrop admitted the fact in his *Journal* that "the people long desired a body of laws, and thought their condition very unsafe while so much power rested in the discretion of magistrates." What Winthrop did not go on to say is that his setting-up of the first board of Assistants had instituted an oligarchy, with full powers, legislative, executive, and judicial. While the freemen early won the right to elect Deputies to the General Court, they lost their fight against the assumed power of the Assistants to veto the acts of the Deputies, and the Assistants continued to hold the preponderance of political power as long as the General Court merely passed occasional acts and resolutions, leaving the Assistants (as magistrates and judges) to declare the law in all civil and criminal cases and to fix the penalty. The magistrates held (and the logic of the freemen could not gainsay it) that in a Bible Commonwealth the law was God's law as revealed in Scripture; but it became a matter of common observation that the magistrates were clever at finding in the Bible what they wished to find. By 1634 already there was a good deal of agitation among the

Deputies, as the representative body, for the adoption of a published set of laws, wherein every man might read his rights and duties, as well as the penalties for disobedience, thus substituting a government by laws for a government by men. For under the old dispensation, by which the magistrate handed down his decision by right of magisterial discretion, he was free to indulge his personal desire or whim, if he could find a Biblical text to bear him out. It seemed safer to have the laws down in black and white so that there might be no mistaking the terms. There followed a series of agitations that led to the adoption of a written code in 1641 and the Township Act of 1647. The latter is especially significant because by it the General Court gave to non-freemen who were of age, and who took an oath of fidelity to Massachusetts Bay, the right to serve on juries, to be elected selectmen of towns, and what was most important, to vote on all local matters, such as the assessment of taxes, the distribution of lands, the laying-out of highways, the ordering of schools and the herding of cattle. This act, says Professor Samuel E. Morison, was "the entering wedge of democracy in Massachusetts; it gave manhood suffrage in the towns, and opened to non-church members the town-meeting, the most important school of self-government in New England if not in the United States." A still more liberal *Book of the General Lawes and Libertys* was adopted in 1648, and so there followed acts and concessions until toward the end of the century the power of the theocratic oligarchy was seriously damaged.

Many causes contributed to the break-up of the old order. The complexion of the colonies was changing from agrarian simplicity to commercial complexity. Worldly prosperity, founded on the fisheries, the carrying trade, and commerce in rum and slaves, distracted men's attention from religious concern and theological speculation to an ever-increasing attendance upon worldly affairs, while the new royal charter of 1691 struck the power of the clergy a crippling blow by replacing religious tests with property qualifications for suffrage. The theocrats, endeavoring vainly to bolster their position, attempted to arrest the processes of the new order by piling up laws and making new proscriptions, at the same time that they sought to suppress criticism. It fell to the lot chiefly of Increase and Cotton Mather to try to halt the processes of the changing world in New England. Though they labored indefatigably and prodigiously, their best efforts were not good enough, and Increase Mather's removal from the presidency of Harvard College in 1701 and his famous son's failure to secure the appointment for himself signalized the fall of the theocratic state.

Harvard College had become infected with rationalism and wanted no more traffic with the Mathers or with the policy they represented. The orthodox therefore established Yale in 1701, and there, at least through the pulpit-thumping career of "pope" Dwight (terminated by his death in 1817), Calvinism sought to hold its embattled position. A few years after the overthrow of the Mather regime at Harvard, John Wise's *Vindication of the Government of New England Churches* (1717) boldly developed the idea of "the law of Nature" as "the dictates of right reason," and went on to declare that as the people "have a power, every man in his natural state, so upon a combination they can and do bequeath this power unto others, and settle it according as their united discretion shall determine," whence it follows that when the entrusted power is abused, "that power returns to the people again, as to its natural source." From this point onward it was by the most natural progression of ideas that rational principles in religion and the democratic doctrine of natural human rights instead of theocratic ideas in politics should develop. This evolution of radical thought can be traced from Wise's *Vindication*, through such treatises as John Barnard's *Throne Established by Righteousness* (1734) and Jonathan Mayhew's *Discourse Concerning Unlimited Submission* (1750), to the religious and political pronouncements of Thomas Paine and Thomas Jefferson, as incorporated in the Declaration of Independence and put into practice in the American Revolution.

No man or set of men are wholly responsible for the decline of the Puritan theocracy. To be sure, its later defenders often played into the hands of the disciples of rational theology and representative democracy by adopting short-sighted policies and foolish stratagems, or, as in the case of Jonathan Edwards' *Freedom of the Will* (1754), by hammering home their position so heavy-handedly that they defeated their own purposes. But below and behind all this hacking at authority and absolutism lay a deeper cause that would doubtless have asserted itself whatever the men or the times. The spirit of the Reformation, of which Puritanism was born, carried within itself, at least as far as the Puritan theocracy in America was concerned, the germs that were calculated to achieve its undoing. The two intellectual principles enunciated by the Reformation—"the rightful duty of free inquiry" and "the priesthood of all believers"—were always available to be turned against a theological order that threatened to curb

free inquiry or to interpose itself between man and his God. The first of these principles led to liberty; the second, to equality. Both became fecund toward the end of the seventeenth century, and during the eighteenth they became explicit in the growth of Unitarianism in theology and of democratic republicanism in politics.

However, before this twofold revolt was finally consummated, Puritanism had dominated life in New England for upwards of a century. During this time American institutions were in process of formation, and not unnaturally they took on, during this vital period of incubation, a distinctively puritanic stamp which long survived the so-called Puritan age of American civilization.

Two kinds of Puritanism are to be distinguished. One, written with the capital P, has reference to a Calvinistic theology and a theocratic polity that passed as the eighteenth century wore on. The other, written with the small p, insinuated itself into the common life of the people in innumerable, subtle ways. It remains a potent factor today—none more potent. This element of our national heritage, sometimes termed the puritan tradition, as distinguished from historical or theological Puritanism, is less easily defined than the other, partly because Puritanism itself, from which it stems, was of several kinds—seldom quite the same thing at different times or in different places. Even if it had flowed from a single, consistent source, the puritan tradition became mixed up with or influenced by others of the cultural traditions that make up American civilization, so that it is not always clear what is owing to the puritan or to some other strain. For example, we have seen the elements of sobriety, reticence, reserve, self-reliance, discipline, and moral integrity identified with the puritan heritage. Yet sobriety was also a virtue practiced by the Quakers. Self-reliance in the practical affairs of life was bred of the Puritan way of life, but it was no less a trait fostered among all kinds of people on the frontier, whether along the Atlantic seaboard during the seventeenth century, on the mountain ranges during the eighteenth, or on the great plains of the West during the nineteenth. Religious fervor, spiritual faith, and what has been called the "practical idealism" of the Puritans are sometimes designated as marks by which the puritan tradition manifests itself among Americans of later generations. But here again we could point to French Huguenots, Pennsylvania-German Quietists, and Dutch Reformed who have traditionally cultivated the same traits. Nevertheless, among all the various racial, national, or religious groups that went into the making of America, the English Puritans were the earliest and most firmly entrenched, and their cultural influence became the most pervasive. Moreover, the special characteristics developed among groups like the Dutch Reformed, Scotch Presbyterians, or French Huguenots were usually less antipathetic than complementary to the spirit of puritanism, so that they may, for practical purposes, be considered part and parcel of the same impulse. At all events, the listing of such traits of character as moral earnestness, sobriety, reticence, reserve, self-discipline, integrity, practical idealism, godliness, and other-worldliness as we are accustomed to think of them in connection with the puritan spirit is to give them a kind of cumulative cogency that may be helpful to the student in identifying what in Bryant and Emerson or in Emily Dickinson and Robert Frost is owing to this abiding inheritance from our religious-minded forebears.

Yet care must be exercised not to take at face value some of the ready identifications commonly made today between current ideas or attitudes and the spirit of puritanism. Thus, what we know as "fundamentalism," while it may derive in part from the puritan tradition after undergoing the transmutations of time and place, shows also admixtures from other forces and impulses, and is certainly no pure derivative. The Puritans would have been entirely antipathetic to the doctrine that the literal interpretation of Scripture must be maintained in spite of and against all reason, learning, and scientific demonstration. They would not have accepted as valid the evidences of "getting religion" nor approved of the revivalist orgies as these are promoted by the camp meeting; "hitting the sawdust trail" would have seemed abominable to them. Religion with the Puritans was a very serious, complex, and highly intellectual affair, for which they trained their clergy with the same care that our age devotes to the training of its scientific specialists. Again, though they espoused doctrines of practical and Christian humanism, they would have remonstrated against all recent attempts to "humanize" religion—to smooth over hard doctrines, to find easy ways to Heaven, and to introduce sweetness and light at the expense of sound logic and hard-headed realism. Nor would they have taken kindly to such modern efforts as we have witnessed to bring Christ down to earth by making him "The First Great Humanitarian" in the Rotarian sense of the word, or invoking his endorsement of some political party or social doctrine. On the other hand, there are contemporary traits of mind and character that the Puritans would have approved: the sober spirit which still invests a large element of the American populace, the sense of decency and sobriety among common folk, the spirit of keeping the Sabbath, the simple honesty that makes the average man's word as good as his bond, the high moral idealism of an Emerson or the renunciation of an Emily Dickinson, the deferring of immediate sensual pleasure or worldly gain for the more lasting spiritual satisfactions of duty earnestly heeded and labor honestly performed. And these traits, among others, are evidences of the continuance of the puritan tradition in American life.

PURITAN LITERARY THEORY

Aside from this intangible influence that is still very much alive, the Puritans left a written record that is more precise in that it leaves whoever reads himself into it definitely affected, one way or another. The Puritans wrote much, and, on the whole, well. While they had little interest in the cultivation of letters as letters, no generation since them has taken writing more seriously. They were engaged in what they considered the most momentous experiment made during the Christian era to institute God's kingdom on earth, and accordingly they felt divinely impelled to make a full record of the experiment so that men, then and later, might read and go on to do likewise, by building upon the foundations which they were busy laying. They wrote always from conviction, usually with fervor, and often with inspiration—oftener than we realize, because of the difference between their and our concepts of what constitutes inspiration.

They had their own ideas about writing, choosing a simple, direct method of expression in favor of circumlocution or flowery imagery. A Mather's conception of good literature might not coincide with our understanding of the term, but it included a knowledge of the poetry, drama, and history of the ancients and the ability to write a prose sentence that said what the author meant. While great scholars like John Cotton were tempted, as other scholars have been, to affect "florid strains" and a "pompous eloquence," Cotton Mather rated it to his grandfather's credit that he relished "the Words of Wisdom" above "the Wisdom of Words." The Puritan minister was carefully trained in rhetoric and pulpit eloquence, but the "high style" characteristic of Anglican preaching during the early seventeenth century was in disrepute among them. In 1642, for example, John Cotton disparaged "affecting carnal eloquence" in the pulpit, on the ground that "swelling words of humane wisdome make mens preaching

seeme to Christ (as it were) a blubber-lipt Ministry";
while a contemporary put it succinctly by saying,
"Gods Altar needs not our pollishings." Yet they
were not foolishly extreme in this matter of attending
to "Conscience rather than Eloquence, fidelity rather
than poetry," for as Michael Wigglesworth put it,
"Eloquence gives new luster and bewty, new strength
new vigour, new life unto trueth . . . 'tis a fit bait
to catch the will and affections"; and Jonathan
Mitchell stated their position very well when he said,
"Great Truths to dress in Meeter, Becomes a Preacher," adding—

> No Cost too great, no Care too curious is
> To set forth Truth, and win mens Souls to bliss.

Even historians like Bradford and Winthrop sometimes sought to enliven the monotony of their historical prose accounts by breaking into verse, though
it usually turned out to be verse of no very high
order, by either their own or our standards.

The Puritan writer's chief concern was not with
poetic flights of the imagination but with "plainnesse
and perspicuity, both of matter and manner of expression," so that what he said would not "dazzle,
but direct the apprehension of the meanest . . .
and make a hard point easy and familiar in explica-
tion." For the very serious and very practical matter
in hand, he knew very well that the cultivation of
a "studied simplicity" was the proper style, and that
one honest, straightforward prose tract was worth a
hundred poetical effusions. For the common man distrusted fiction and symbolic figures, and wanted none
of them; and the more cultivated, while freely ac-
knowledging the poet's high calling, feared the danger that lay in the magic spell of poetry—feared that
it "might tempt men away from truth to fable."
Not that the Puritans did not write verse. We are
only beginning to discover how much, as considerable
masses of manuscripts come to light. But most of it
was verse, like Michael Wigglesworth's Day of Doom,
designed to lead men in the right way to Heaven.
Whether casting their words into poetic meters or
prose rhythms, the Puritan writers found the chief
inspiration for their writing, as for their thinking,
in the Great Book, which was the Be-all and the
End-all of wisdom. Fortunately it happened that their
model was one of the great masterpieces of English
literature, the King James version of the Bible. They
found in it not only a book of religious instruction
but also a rich repository of history (sacred and
secular), including colorful stories of "intrigue and
adventure, primitive folklore and scandalous anecdote, proverbial wisdom, lyric poetry, and tender

romance." Quite naturally, when they wrote, their
figures and illustrations were drawn from Biblical
stories of the kings and prophets as often as from
ancient history and classical mythology. This being
so, we can understand why their style of writing
should fall, consciously or unconsciously, into the
Biblical cadences and rhythms that distinguish so
much of their poetry and prose.

Still, compared with the full-bodied, myriad-col-
ored richness of English Renaissance literature,
Puritan writings seem didactic, bookish, narrow, and
indifferent to beauty as we conceive beauty. But it is
to be remembered that if their works were didactic,
they were so because of the Puritans' overpowering
desire to live in harmony with God's will; they were
passionately in earnest about spiritual realities; and
in their writings they sought, by every means known
to their rhetoric, to stimulate in their readers or
hearers the elementary and absorbing passion of curiosity concerning spiritual self-preservation. If they
seem bookish, it is because they respected the divine
truth contained in the Bible, and because they sought
accurately to transmit that truth to their readers. The
preface to the Bay Psalm Book (1640) contains an
illuminating statement (well worth careful scrutiny)
by the translators, Richard Mather, John Eliot, and
Thomas Welde, the first two of whom were graduates of Oxford and Cambridge, respectively:

> If . . . the verses are not always so smooth and elegant
> as some may desire or expect; let them consider that God's
> Altar needs not our pollishings: Ex. 20. for wee have re-
> spected rather the plaine translation, then to smooth our
> verses with sweetnes of any paraphrase, and soe have at-
> tended Conscience rather then Elegance, fidelity rather
> then poetry, in translating the hebrew words into english
> language, and Davids poetry into english meetre . . .

Educated and cultivated men as the translators were,
they did not mangle the beautiful King James version
of the Psalms because they were ignorant or because
they lacked good taste; they did it deliberately: to
make a true translation they consciously sought to
make it literal. If, in the process, they lost some or
all of the beauty of the Renaissance rendition, the
loss, they felt, was infinitely compensated for by the
gain in truth. For the Bible represented divine truth
above the need or the possibility of garnishment—
truth which no mere physical or verbal beauty could
enhance. The truth and beauty which the Puritan
chiefly loved were the truth and beauty of holiness,
the result of living in harmony with the will of God
as revealed in the Bible. All other forms of beauty
were inconsequential. If the Puritans were narrow, it
was because their interests were vertical rather than

horizontal; they sought nothing less than moral perfection and spiritual salvation, to which ends all other means and ends were incidental. Thus their literary practice grew out of their literary theory, which, in turn, was a logical development out of their religious theory. Thus, too, their literature developed a consistency of matter and a unity of tone unequaled since in America. As long as the body of their theological theory held together, so long did their style of writing endure. So it came to pass that the Puritan conception of poetry as a means to expressing great truths in exalted moods was not superseded by the urbane appreciation of poetry as a social accomplishment until the eighteenth century was well under way.

COLONIAL WRITINGS

Exploration and colonization have always been conducive to the writing of description, history, chronicles, letters-home, memoirs, biography, and autobiography. John Smith had barely landed his colonists at Jamestown in Virginia, in 1607, when he set to writing his *True Relation of Such Occurrences and Accidents of Noate as Hath Hapned in Virginia since the first Planting of the Colony*, published in London the next year. There followed numerous other writings of his, most notable among which were *A Map of Virginia, the Commodities, People, Government and Religion* (1612) and his more comprehensive, autobiographical work, *The True Travels, Adventures, and Observations of Captaine John Smith* (1630). The founding of Plymouth, thirteen years after Jamestown, was equally well documented. Before landing, the colonists framed the Mayflower Compact, by which they bound themselves into "a civil body politick," the precise wording of which Governor William Bradford took care to reproduce in his *History of the Plymouth Plantation*, begun about 1630, but embracing antecedent events in the form of annals, and terminating about 1647. But long before this extensive work was begun, Bradford, Edward Winslow, and others wrote up the experiences of the colonists from November, 1620, to December, 1621, in a document signed "G. Mourt," and hence known as *Mourt's Relation*, published in London in 1622. Similarly Governor John Winthrop began at the beginning in his diary-like history of the Massachusetts Bay Colony. The first entry reads: "Easter Sunday, March 29, 1630. Riding at the Cowes, near the Isle of Wight, in the Arbella, a ship of three hundred and fifty tons," and so he proceeds to chronicle dutifully every event that

seemed worthy of record, until he reached his last entry in 1649, the year of his death.

These represent but a few specimens of a dozen or more early colonial historians, Northern and Southern. The works of Bradford and Winthrop take on a special significance not only because of their authors' prominence in colonial affairs but also because of their intrinsic merits. Bradford's history, for example, tells an unadorned story of adventure and perseverance, of tenacious idealism that triumphed over reverses and privations, in a homely, lucid style of Biblical simplicity, illustrating that artlessness of great art which comes near making it the literary classic of the American seventeenth century. Winthrop's *Journal*, dealing with the affairs of the far more powerful and numerous Massachusetts Bay settlements, reflects an author of relatively greater learning, wealth, and social standing than Bradford. A veritable compendium of information, it makes a record of official acts and of public as well as private affairs, elections and assemblies, births and deaths, wars and harvests, theological controversies and political contests, visible evidences of God's good will or wrath manifested toward men (termed "Divine Providences"), and a thousand other memorabilia or curiosa—all set down in the order of happening, with little respect for sequence or congruity. Yet so wide is the scope and so faithfully does the book portray the spirit of the times, that Noah Webster, its first editor, had some justification for calling it *The History of New England*.

Other writings there were a-plenty—sermons without number and polemical works chiefly touching theological questions, exegetical tracts, descriptions and accounts of the country, reports to the stockholders and managers of the trading company, or pamphlets designed to attract new settlers. Among the more notable controversial writings are Thomas Morton's irreverently satirical attack upon the Puritan ordering of things in his *New English Canaan* (1637) and the exchange, during the forties and early fifties, of a series of pamphlets between Roger Williams and John Cotton concerning religious conformity and theocratic polity. Nathaniel Ward's *Simple Cobler of Aggawam* of 1647, a notable protest against the doctrine of religious toleration, belongs to the same general category of theological writings, as do most of the titles issuing from the studies of John Cotton (1584–1652), Thomas Hooker (1586–1647), and Thomas Shepard (1605–1652), the three "complete preachers" of the day.

Meanwhile poetry was not neglected altogether—

epigrams, simple·ditties, popular saws, broadsides, and occasional verses of many kinds, including commemorative poems and epitaphs, being especially popular. The deaths of notable persons were special occasions tempting the colonial poetasters to essay new heights of rhetorical splendor and untried figurativeness. Some of the metaphysical similes and metaphors in this type of verse are unmatched for being far-fetched and atrocious; not a few show real ingenuity and wit. The most representative as well as popular of New England poems was Michael Wigglesworth's *Day of Doom* (1652), an extensive and fearful picture of the day when the last trump shall blow and God will judge saints and sinners according to the inexorable law of Calvin. This eminently edifying poem ran its full jigging length of two hundred and twenty-four eight-line stanzas in the old septenary ballad meter with interlinear rhymes, adorned by plentiful chapter-and-verse references in the margin to Biblical authority to authenticate its inviolable orthodoxy. About the same time there appeared *The Tenth Muse Lately sprung up in America, or Several Poems, compiled with great Variety of Wit and Learning, full of Delight* (London, 1650). These early poems of Anne Bradstreet form the first important body of verse written in America that deserves to be taken seriously as poetry, and the new edition (with additions, including her "contemplations"), which appeared in Boston in 1678, added considerably to her poetic stature. New heights were attained shortly after by Edward Taylor (1645?-1729) in his devotional and meditative verse, modeled upon such "sacred poets" as Herbert, Crashaw, and Quarles; but these remained in a four-hundred-page quarto manuscript until 1937, when their publication first made known the figurative brilliance and homely, native coloring of Taylor's poetry. Since then, much other early Puritan poetry has been found, and some of it has been published; but no poet has yet appeared to challenge seriously the position of Anne Bradstreet and Edward Taylor.

By the middle of the seventeenth century the Mather dynasty—Richard, 1596–1669, Increase, 1639–1723, Cotton, 1663–1728, and Samuel, 1706–1785—had their book factory in smooth running order. Richard, the first of the American Mathers, had to his credit sermons, a catechism, a treatise on justification, public letters on church government, several controversial documents, the preface to the *Bay Psalm Book*, and many of the marvels of metrical transliteration contained in that volume. His son Increase outdid the father to the extent that an authentic list of his writings runs to well-nigh one hundred and fifty titles. These sweep the entire circuit of themes, sacred and profane, that employed the thoughts of men in those days—divinity, ethics, casuistry; church government, law, English and American politics, history, heresy, prophecy, demonology, angelology, crime, poverty, ignorance, dancing, the Indian question, earthquakes, comets, winds, conflagrations, drunkenness, and the smallpox. Unfortunately, he is better known today for his *Essay for the Recording of Illustrious Providences* (1684) and *Cases of Conscience Concerning Evil Spirits* (1693), in both of which his scholarship and learning suffer from the credulity of his time, rather than for his histories of the Indian wars or his defenses of the political rights of New England.

His son Cotton, in his turn, outdid the father in like proportion, making good the old epitaph composed for the founder of the clan:

> Under this stone lies Richard Mather,
> Who had a son greater than his father,
> And eke a grandson greater than either.

Of great learning and even greater industry, he wrote prodigiously. His bibliography exceeds four hundred titles, besides other works left in manuscript at his death. Living at a time when it was still possible to take all learning for one's province, his range of interests was truly universal, and it would be difficult to find a field that he did not touch. His monumental *Magnalia Christi Americana* ("Christ's Great Achievements in America"), begun in 1693, completed four years later, and published in two large volumes in 1702, is justly esteemed his greatest work.

The cumulative tendency toward intellectual intensity and literary productivity noticeable in the Mathers was arrested after the first three generations. Samuel achieved respectable fame as an author and Congregational clergyman, but the fire of the Mathers, finding little fuel during the mid-years of the eighteenth century, burned itself out. The new order considered the Mathers anachronistic.

Meanwhile a long tradition of diary-keeping and journal-writing resulted in a series of noteworthy productions in that kind of composition, beginning with Mrs. Mary Rowlandson's *Narrative of the Captivity* (1682), which she suffered at the hands of the Indians in 1675/6, and Sarah Kemble Knight's *Journal*, containing a sprightly account of her experiences and observations during a journey on horseback made through the back country from Boston to New York in October, 1704, and the return trip the following March. But the American classics in this type of writing are the work of Samuel Sewall of Boston, Colonel William Byrd of Virginia, and John Woolman the Quaker.

Samuel Sewall (1652–1730) led a full life as a lawyer, judge, capitalist, and village potentate, but found time to write a number of tracts, including *The Selling of Joseph* (1700), an eloquent protest against slavery. However, it is in his *Diary*, covering, with some omissions, the years from 1674 to 1729, though it was not published until 1878–1882, that he wrote most engagingly. Not designed for publication, his *Diary* is written entirely without pretense, and gives an authentic picture of Puritan society and of the Judge himself as the embodiment of the rising Yankeeism of his day, mercenary but kindly, conventional but vigorous, often short-sighted but always solid.

Down at Westover, Virginia, the courtly Colonel William Byrd (1674–1744) wrote, in *The History of the Dividing Line*, a remarkable and witty account of his experiences while surveying the boundary line between North Carolina and Virginia in 1728, and subsequently, *A Journey to the Land of Eden* and *A Progress to the Mines*, both descriptive of trips which he made to his extensive land holdings in western Virginia. But it is in his diary, or *Secret History*, which has been discovered only recently and parts of which still remain in manuscript, that we get the most interesting glimpses into the life of a cultivated Southern planter and man of affairs, and much else besides of equal interest to the student of literature and of history.

Finally, there is the calm record of the quietist, John Woolman (1720–1772), whose itinerant career as a disciple of the benevolent spirit comes to life in the simple words of his *Journal* (1774). Diary-keeping and autobiographical writing did not end here. Indeed, the records of Sewall, Byrd, and Woolman are but the preludes to the journals and notebooks of Emerson and Thoreau, Hawthorne and Longfellow. The motif persisted through Jonathan Edwards' *Personal Narrative* and Crèvecoeur's *Letters from an American Farmer* (1782), many of which have a distinctively personal and autobiographical tone, to come to full-bodied glory in Benjamin Franklin's *Autobiography*, begun in 1771, and left incomplete at his death. But with Franklin, we reach another phase in the development of American civilization and literary culture, concerning which a few words of explanation are in order.

THE EIGHTEENTH CENTURY: REVOLT AND REORGANIZATION

As the fine fervor of seventeenth-century Puritanism burned low, the process of secularization grew apace. Growing trade and expanding commerce hastened the movement, and stalwarts like Samuel Sewall, while still vitally concerned about insuring for themselves the benefits accruing to the elect in the future life, were nevertheless careful to put money into their pockets for use in this life. The spirit of middle-class mercantilism, sharp trading and hard bargaining, and a preoccupation with worldly affairs bred a spirit of Yankeeism, a practical, realistic concern with temporal affairs that turned men's minds increasingly away from the spiritual promises of Heaven toward the solid remunerations of earthly competence, security, and position. Meanwhile, the hold of the Church on the people fell in proportion as the clergy lost control. The insistence on the part of the British government from the time of William and Mary onward that toleration be extended to all Protestants, and the substitution of property qualifications for church membership as determining citizenship cut the ground from under the theocrats. Still, the old order might have survived even these crippling blows if the people could have been held in line. But the people fell away fast as they took up the infectious ideas of rationalism as these developed under the auspices of Newtonian conceptions of the universe and the Lockean psychology.

Although Cotton Mather testified proudly in 1728, the year of his death, that he did not know "among all the Pastors of the Two Hundred Churches . . . one Arminian, much less an Arian," he neglected to say that while the pulpit was still relatively pure, the subtle poison of rationalism, under the disguise of Arminianism, was spreading rapidly among the masses. The fundamental tenet of Arminianism was to assert that the elect of God are not pre-chosen, but that a righteous life and good works are sufficient to lead men into the way to salvation. Striking, as this doctrine did, at the very taproot of Calvinism by denying the principle of determinism, while insisting on the free will of man, it went even further in its social implications than in its purely theological applications.

It was an expression of the idea of individual responsibility to God—in short, an extension of Luther's doctrine of the right of individual interpretation of the Scripture, to throw upon the individual the whole responsibility of asserting his free will not only in making his peace with God but also in negotiating the terms of government on the earth.

In England, rationalism had already passed from Arminianism through a phase of Arianism, which cast doubt upon Christ as a necessary Savior, to Socinianism, which openly denied his divinity altogether—doctrines that ultimately became popular in America in terms of Tom Paine's brand of deism and New England Transcendentalism. Eventually all religious doctrine that rested on faith, including the superrational, supernatural, and miraculous elements of Christianity as described in the Bible, came under the attack of this critically rational spirit. Wherever English rationalism showed the way, American deism or Unitarianism followed. Even in Cotton Mather's day, incipient rationalism had begun to ask disturbing questions, and Mather himself went to some pains, in *The Christian Philosopher: A Collection of the Best Discoveries of Nature, with Religious Improvements* (1721), to meet the attack of science and reason on their own grounds. By the time of Jonathan Edwards (1703–1758) it had grown aggressive. Dogma was face to face with rationalism; and orthodoxy, definitely on the defensive, was ill-equipped for the impending battle. The man in the street may have known little about the highly technical theological and metaphysical issues involved; but when he came to weigh the assertions of the dogmatic school against those of the rationalists, the latter appeared to have the better of the argument.

The doctrine of total depravity, for instance, seemed not to tally with the daily observations of the common man. In the corrupt world of Augustine or Calvin, the common brutality of the times might have had a reasonable explanation in such a doctrine—namely, that the evils of society originate in the evil hearts of men. But in the village world of New England the doctrine began to lose its social sanction as the honest citizens appraised themselves and their neighbors. Under the spell of a Mather's or an Edwards' Sunday preaching, they may have believed the human heart to be wholly depraved; but in the everyday life of the New England village, dominated as it was by rugged virtues, kindliness, and moral integrity, they were led to wonder whether they and their neighbors were indeed vipers and worms, brutally wallowing in sin, hated of God and man. The conviction grew that they were not altogether vicious; and as they pondered this thought, they experienced mounting difficulties in reconciling their Sunday professions with their week-day experience. Although many continued to repeat their familiar church creed, their sanction of the formal profession of faith was lost as the authority of dogma fell before the voice of experience, reason, and common sense.

Moreover, many of the reading and thinking members of New England society became acquainted with the theories of John Locke, who taught that man, instead of coming into the world freighted with innate or inborn ideas and weighed down by an inherited load of sin, was born with a mind entirely blank. Hence, everything that subsequently entered into man's mind, all his desires, all his acts, were the result of influences upon the human mind after birth. All that man ever learned came to him originally through the five senses—through experience and through the influence upon him of the manifold effects of environment, education, conditioning. If man is born without sin, and becomes a sinner later, it is his environment—earthly institutions and social conventions—that is to be blamed. Thus the idea that "in Adam's fall, we sinned all" became a meaningless one. The natural man, instead of being naturally wicked, is naturally good. This doctrine, supported by the Lockean psychology, received during the eighteenth century an important impetus and support from the ideas emanating from France. Rousseau pictured men as originally and intrinsically good while they dwelt in the original, primitive state of nature, but that they were corrupted through the evils of civilization, which resulted from the perversion of the social contract. This doctrine appealed to men whose daily experience taught them the falseness of traditional dogma. Moreover, Rousseau's ideals of liberty and equality came home with special meaning to men bred in villages and on the frontier. Thus the Rousseauistic glorification of the simple, the primitive, and the natural joined forces with the rationalism of the Newtonian and Lockean tradition to influence the liberalizing trend of American theology, leading, on the one hand, to a romantic concept by which the orderliness of Nature and finally Nature herself become the worshipful objects of man, and reason the proper guide to natural, as opposed to revealed, religion; while, on the other hand, it encouraged opposition to artificial control and traditional authority and thus hastened the American revolution against the governmental absolutism of England.

In a very similar way another cardinal doctrine of Calvinism, that of special election, was discredited. In an aristocratic society it seemed natural to believe that God had set men apart in classes. But as the leveling processes of a democratic land tended to destroy social distinctions, the new individualism undermined the old class psychology. Geographical separation from England favored the development of colonial autonomy and democratic government. Colonial America presents no more consistently straightforward movement than that of self-determinism. As the common man freed himself from political absolutism, he became dissatisfied with theological absolutism; the right to achieve religious salvation is a natural corollary to the right to win social distinction. That one's future lay wholly beyond the reach of one's will, that it rested entirely within the hands of an arbitrary God who gave or withheld salvation at His pleasure, regardless of what the individual might do about it—these were doctrines as utterly at variance with the growing ideals of democracy as was the assumption that Britain had the right to meddle with the internal affairs of citizens in America or arbitrarily to levy taxes and to prescribe rules governing trade.

Indeed, as thinking Americans of the eighteenth century from John Wise, John Barnard, and Jonathan Mayhew to Benjamin Franklin, Tom Paine, and Thomas Jefferson contemplated the issues involved in British sovereignty and absolutism, the divine-rights-of-kings theory, and related principles and theories of state, it became clear that the doctrine of determinism was the crux of their problem, just as the theologians, contemplating the future of the Church, realized that as the decision went for or against determinism, so would the entire metaphysical structure of Calvinism and Puritanism stand or fall.

When the call of distress went out from the churches, and Jonathan Edwards came to the rescue, it was to this problem of a free *versus* a determined will that he directed his mental energies. Edwards' mind, rated by one prominent historian of American philosophy as the finest yet produced in America, focused upon this question, and produced the *magnum opus* of his distinguished career in *The Freedom of the Will* (1754). While he did not prove that the will of man is determined, he demonstrated, by all the laws of logic, that it could not be free, thus leaving no alternative but the conclusion that it must be fixed by the will of God. Starting from the assumptions that he made, and employing the syllogistic method that he adopted, he reached conclusions that seemed irrefutable. But however rigorous his method or unshakable his conclusions, the book failed to achieve its primary purpose of arresting the critically rational tendencies of the age or of re-enthroning God as a sufficient and arbitrary determiner of all things, including the will of man. Logic might be logic, the common people admitted, but they re-

mained unconvinced nevertheless, holding instead with Dr. Samuel Johnson that while all logic and philosophy were against the theory of a free will, all experience and common sense were for it. Edwards made a last-ditch stand for the conservative forces of Puritanism. It proved incapable of arresting (1) the progress of the Newtonian concept of an orderly, systematic universe, governed by immutable natural laws, to the discovery of which the reason was considered a sufficient index; (2) the deistic criticism of revealed religion as distinguished from natural religion; (3) the Unitarian deposition of a personal, triune God for *one* God, synonymous with order, harmony, reason, or moral law; (4) the attendant French romantic doctrines of the natural man and of the state of nature as naturally good; and (5) the corollary doctrine of the inherent natural rights of all men as distinct from the special privileges of the elect, as predetermined by divine ordinance. In drawing lightning from heaven, to demonstrate that it was electricity, Franklin robbed God of much of His awe-inspiring quality among men—lightning was no longer a manifestation of God's wrath, but a perfectly natural phenomenon. The eighteenth-century man, searching for the religious and practical principles that should guide him, became convinced that God worked less by special providences than by general laws, and that His wishes were more readily ascertainable by the simple laws of logic than by the mysterious edicts of revelation. The idea gained ground that God Himself was order and law, Himself subject to His own ordained natural and moral laws.

Thus faith and revelation fell before the attack of reason and nature, and liberal individualism triumphed over theological authoritarianism. The next point of attack was political authority. For, as the seventeenth century was predominantly concerned with theological issues, the eighteenth (especially the latter half) turned with all-absorbing interest to political issues. To contrast Jonathan Edwards with Benjamin Franklin is to illustrate the change that took place in the temper of men's thinking. Edwards failed to save Calvinism, and 1754 signalized the end of the religious era. Franklin, as one of the prime movers behind the establishment of political independence and democratic republicanism, came to be known as the "First American." His success illustrates the triumph of the eighteenth-century temperament over that of the seventeenth—the assertion of natural rights over inherited rights, of Yankeeism over Puritanism, of this-worldliness over other-worldliness.

To be sure, Franklin did not win the victory single-handedly. Behind Franklin there stood more than two centuries during which a tradition of local self-determination had developed. The practice of self-government had evolved during the early seventeenth century among colonists who could not, and would not, send three thousand miles for royal sanction every time some local crisis arose. This long schooling in local self-government and the attendant development of independence of thought and action in a frontier and democratic society had, by the middle of the eighteenth century, bred a spirit of self-reliance and self-assertion among the colonies that would have balked at a Stamp Act and other arbitrary decrees even if they had never heard about the abstract theories of the natural rights of man. As it was, the home-grown tradition of freedom and liberty to arrange their own affairs combined with English and French ideas of political liberalism to raise voices in support of Franklin—men like the Adamses, James Otis and Patrick Henry, John Dickinson and Francis Hopkinson, Tom Paine and Thomas Jefferson. Among them, they produced a literature of political dissent and revolt that often rises above the usual literary level of purely polemical writing.

Soon after independence was won, Hamilton, Madison, and Jay penned The Federalist (1787–1788), a series of essays on the proposed Constitution of the United States that not only turned the tide to win its adoption by a majority of the states but demonstrated to the world that "Americans could write prose as well as any English-speaking people in the world."

The chief penman of these papers was Alexander Hamilton (1757–1804). After a brilliant career as pamphleteer and soldier during the Revolutionary War, he took a prominent part during the period between the Peace and the formation of the Union in the government of the states under the Confederation. The loose organization of the Confederation and the attendant dissension, turmoil, and insecurity intensified his advocacy of a strong centralized government. As a member of the Constitutional Convention, he was dissatisfied with the document as drawn, but in the Federalist papers he strongly advocated its ratification as the best Constitution possible at the time. A disciple of law and order, he set himself, as first Secretary of the Treasury, to institute principles and procedures to insure regularity, strength, and stability of government. In a series of cogently written reports he advocated (1) the federal assumption of state debts, (2) the refunding of

both national and state debts at par, (3) the levying of an excise tax to provide revenues for the government, (4) the establishment of a bank of the United States, modeled on the national Bank of England, and (5) the imposition of a protective tariff for military self-sufficiency, for the preservation of a home market, for agrarian products, and for the encouragement of American manufacturing. These measures, known as the Hamiltonian system, tended toward the strengthening of the federal government at the expense of state governments and toward the alliance of the government with the moneyed interests. Opposed to these principles were the agrarians, the disciples of state rights, and the more politically and social liberal elements of American society whom Jefferson sought to organize into an effective party of opposition to the Hamiltonians, or Federalists.

Like Tom Paine, Jefferson was the advocate of liberty, natural rights, and the common man; but unlike him, he retained his influence to the end, becoming the visible embodiment of the democratic ideal and the leader of the masses, who elevated him to the presidency of the United States in the faith that he would curb the growth and power of aristocracy and special privilege in the new democracy. A man of extraordinary breadth and versatility, he was alive to all the interests of his time. A Virginia gentleman of culture and attainments, he won distinction as a lawyer, agriculturist, inventor, educator, writer, architect, philologist, scientist, philosopher, economist, historian, sociologist, diplomat, and statesman. During his lifetime he disputed with Hamilton the empire of American political opinion; he was in his time the acknowledge head, as he remains today the perpetual symbol, of the democratic spirit of America.

From the beginning of his legislative career in Virginia he sided with the patriot party and led the protest against British-colonial policies. As lawmaker and later as governor of Virginia (1779–1781), he pushed a broad program of reform, designed to put into practice the broad principles which, in 1776, he incorporated in the Declaration of Independence. His codification and modernization of the laws of Virginia included legislation designed to make impossible the maintenance of a landed aristocracy and an established church. He advocated reforms in education and the establishment of a complete state free-school system, wrote the statute for religious freedom in Virginia, sponsored measures designed to promote economic equality, agitated for the abolition of slavery, and advocated other humanitarian principles.

At the age of thirty-two he became, in June of 1775, the youngest member of the Continental Congress. While he seldom spoke on the floor of Congress, he established himself at once as being always "prompt, frank, explicit, and decisive upon committee and in convention," and within five days of taking his seat, he was chosen, with Benjamin Franklin and John Adams, to draft a reply to Lord North. Next, he was appointed, with John Dickinson, to draw up a *Declaration of the Causes and Necessity of Taking Up Arms*. And when it became apparent that the Congress would soon be debating the momentous resolution—"that these United Colonies are, and of right ought to be, free and independent States; that they are absolved from all allegiance to the British crown; and that all political connection between them and the state of Great Britain is, and ought to be, totally dissolved"—young Jefferson, receiving the largest number of votes, was put at the head of a committee to draft the Declaration of Independence. Associated with him were Benjamin Franklin, John Adams, Roger Sherman, and Robert Livingston. The actual writing was done by Jefferson, although corrections were made by Franklin, Adams, and the Congress at large.

During the war years Jefferson devoted himself mainly to the government of Virginia. During 1783–84 he was a delegate to the Congress of the Confederation. From 1784 to 1789 he served as American minister to France, succeeding Franklin, and in 1784 he printed (in Paris, for private distribution) his *Notes on the State of Virginia*. He traveled extensively in Europe, associated with moderate leaders of the French Revolution, and studied the temper of the French people. As a man who declared, "I have sworn upon the altar of God eternal hostility against every form of tyranny over the mind of man," he watched with sympathy the mounting spirit of freedom and republicanism among the French, meanwhile gathering lasting impressions and forming political opinions which his Anglophile, or pro-English, opponents later attacked as Galliophile, or pro-French, and therefore subversive and anarchical.

Returning to America in 1790, and becoming Secretary of State during Washington's first administration, he was alarmed to see that during his absence movements and tendencies had developed which ran counter to the spirit for which the Revolution had been fought. Under the influence of Alexander Hamilton as Secretary of the Treasury, Jefferson saw vast powers being centralized in the federal government and a rising power of aristocracy and privilege developing among those in control. Fearing that the United States was "galloping fast into monarchy," he openly and secretly opposed Hamilton until, at the meetings of Washington's Cabinet, the two resembled "two cocks in a pit." The feud at length grew even beyond Washington's power to curb, and Jefferson withdrew from the Cabinet in 1793 to organize the people's party of opposition to Hamiltonian Federalism.

Having an implicit faith in the common man, the efficacy of a democracy resting on a free yeomanry, and an economy based on the produce of labor in the earth, Jefferson was a disciple of the Physiocratic school of social economics, emphasizing the principle of *laissez faire* and an agrarian, instead of a capitalistic, economy. He was little concerned about stable government, but was anxious that government should be responsive to the popular will. He denied the right of the past, in terms of tradition, or form, or money, to rule the present. He asserted that government, like all institutions, must accommodate itself to the demands of modernity, lest it become ossified and tyrannical. For the maintenance of good government, he believed that a bit of blood-letting could be very efficacious: "What signify a few lives lost in a century or two? The tree of liberty must be refreshed from time to time, with the blood of patriots and tyrants." He held that a government grown strong and enriched by excessive revenue will only encourage ambition in its administrators in a way eventually to endanger the rights of men. He saw in the capitalistic order of Hamilton a nursery of potential plutocrats, and he remarked acidly that he had never observed "men's honesty to increase with their riches." As he watched Chief Justice John Marshall, who regarded the Supreme Court as an instrument of national unity and of federal power above state rights, handing down decisions and judicial interpretations that nullified the laws passed by Congress, thus giving the judiciary extensive legislative powers, Jefferson repudiated the idea of a strong Supreme Court as necessary for the preservation of justice. What was needed to cure the ills of democracy, he believed, was not more power in high places, but more democracy.

Seeing in the Hamilton program only "Toryism in disguise," ambitious to build a rigorous federal machine by which to establish monarchical absolutism, and thus to override and nullify the democratic will and to destroy the common interests, Jefferson proceeded so well in his organization of the opposition party that by 1796 he narrowly missed defeating John Adams for the presidency. Having received the second highest number of votes, he became Vice-President. Four years later, after a campaign of unequaled bitterness and acrimony, the powers of an insurgent democracy swept the Federalist party aside, and Thomas Jefferson became the third President of the United States.

During Jefferson's two terms in office (1801–1809) the territorial area of the United States was doubled by the purchase of the Louisiana Territory, the national debt was reduced while taxes were decreased and the internal prosperity of the nation mounted manifold, the Lewis and Clark expedition explored the West, the menace of the Tripolitan pirates was eliminated, and a war with France was honorably averted. He was also responsible for the Non-Importation and Embargo Acts which, though designed to prevent foreign depredations against American industry and commerce, worked disastrous hardships in some quarters of the country. However, he succeeded in keeping his party in power through the administrations of Madison and Monroe, while making himself as thoroughly hated among Federalists as Lincoln was ever despised by Southerners during the Civil War.

In 1809 he retired to private life at Monticello to devote himself to scientific and philanthropic pursuits and to the cultivation of the arts. The sale in 1812 of his library of 10,000 choice volumes to the government resulted in the establishment of the Library of Congress. While opposing the encroachments of governmental power in all other respects, he urged an extension of state powers to provide a system of public education, and he devoted the years from 1814 to 1819 principally to the establishment of the Virginia school system, taking especial interest and pride in the building and establishment of the University of Virginia. He died on July 4, 1825, the fiftieth anniversary of American Independence. On his tombstone is inscribed the epitaph (found among his papers) attesting his three great services to the cause of freedom and democracy:

Here lies buried
THOMAS JEFFERSON
Author of the Declaration of Independence,
of the Statute of Virginia for Religious Freedom,
and Father of the University of Virginia.

The opposition between Hamiltonian and Jeffersonian, between Federalist and Republican, forces provoked a gigantic struggle that ran its rancorous course throughout the nineties and well beyond. Both parties solicited the ablest and most practiced pens available. In the flood of polemical satire, harangue, and invective which the controversy engendered, many an inexperienced writer learned to

sharpen his wit. The contest produced few significant examples of writing that exhibit a high degree of purely literary excellence, and it diverted a number of men from the gentler pursuit of polite literature into that of controversy. Trumbull and Dwight, for example, could not resist entering the fray on the side of conservatism and Federalism, while Freneau was in the thick of it from the very beginning on the side of Jefferson and republicanism. But once the issues were decided, the air was cleared, and writers with literary inclinations returned to pursue a more distinctively literary vein. The Hartford Wits, for example, resumed their ambitious designs of creating a body of national poetry. All too often this desire to write verse that should be commensurate with the grandeur of the new nation turned out to be ponderous and grandiloquent. Meanwhile Freneau retired to Mount Pleasant, rededicated himself to the poetic muse, and prepared a collected edition of his poems, which won him the title of "First American Poet." As a transitional figure between the Age of Reason and the Romantic Age, he wrote much poetry that still expresses the concepts of eighteenth-century rationalism in the language and conventions of a neoclassical era; but his best work looks forward to the Romantic Age that came to fruition, about the time of his death, under the aegis of poets like Bryant, Poe, Emerson, and Longfellow, and prose writers like Irving and Cooper.

LITERARY NATIONALISM
AND THE RISE OF ROMANTICISM

As would be expected, the development of political nationalism following the Revolution was attended by a rapidly growing consciousness of literary nationalism, the cumulative tendency of which can be traced throughout the writings of the men who are today accounted the leading spirits of the time. The tendency is notable in the ambitious and concerted efforts of the Hartford Wits to cultivate polite literature. They were often deflected from the course of pure literature by the clash of social forces and conflicting political ideas of the day, but their interminable epics were nevertheless ardently nationalistic attempts to provide their country with a body of epical poetry befitting the birth of a great nation. As the poet of the American Revolution, Philip Freneau devoted much of his time to satire directed against the British, and during the Hamilton-Jefferson debate his productions were heavy with political controversy. But aside from this and his tendency toward rational moralization, he often turned to the purer strain of *belles-lettres*, and with such pieces as "The

Wild Honeysuckle" and his Indian poems earned the title of "Father of American Poetry." Besides these versifiers, there were others who chose the drama and the novel as their media by which to help America to literary maturity.

The drama, formally introduced in 1752 by Lewes Hallam's professional company brought over from London, made its way only slowly against religious and temperamental opposition to playhouses and actors, and the production of original plays in America was retarded not only by the common colonial tendency of depending up the mother country but also by the difficulty that native playwrights experienced in trying to compete with the established European dramatists. The interposition of the long and all-absorbing Revolutionary War years interrupted the progress that had been made; for the Continental Congress, in its efforts to "encourage frugality, economy and industry, and to promote agriculture, arts and manufactures," found it expedient to "discountenance every species of extravagance and dissipation, especially all horse-racing, and all kinds of gaming, cock-fighting, exhibitions of shews, plays, and other expensive diversions and entertainments." Even after the war, restrictions and proscriptions of one sort or another operated to keep acting companies more or less in the status of vagrancy until, toward the end of the century, the construction of the first permanent theatres gave them a home and some professional stability. Even so, plays like Othello and The School for Scandal had to creep in surreptitiously under the disarming guise of "moral lectures" or "concerts," while the theatres themselves were ingeniously called by such names as "Historic Academy" or "Academy of Music." In Pennsylvania the law prohibiting plays remained in effect until 1787, and the order of the General Court of Massachusetts in 1750 against play acting stood until 1781, after which time it became safe openly to enact plays in moral Boston.

Under such circumstances it is surprising that the first regular American play, in the sense that it was written by an American and produced by a professional acting company, should have been written as early as 1759 and enacted for the first time in 1767. This was The Prince of Parthia, a romantic tragedy, rather exotic in theme and derivative in inspiration, by Thomas Godfrey of Philadelphia. The first regular comedy followed in 1787—a play by Royall Tyler, entitled The Contrast. Besides being a play of considerable dramatic merit, its contrast of Englishmen and Americans to the advantage of the latter makes it a notable expression of the rising tide

of national literary consciousness of that day. William Dunlap (1766–1839) catered to the same taste in The Father; or, American Shandyism (produced in 1788), and his Andre (produced in 1798) is a play utilizing events of the Revolutionary period of American history. Talented as a writer and especially as an adapter of plays, Dunlap was also a capable theatre manager. Although he went bankrupt in 1804, he left the American theatre in a position beyond which his successors, generally less capable than he, were enabled to carry on in good style.

The novel encountered many of the same obstacles that the drama had to overcome, and at approximately the same time. Aside from the general cultural lag in America, native novelists had to compete against the better productions of European novelists, whose works, in the absence of international copyright, could be pirated and consequently sold for greater profit than could the native product. But it was the prejudice of the piously moral and realistically frugal-minded populace that was chiefly to be overcome, as well as the wealthier and more influential Tory-minded group of Americans who withheld their support of a native art when, as they argued, they could have better reading by importing their novels from abroad. America, they held, contained no fit material for literary treatment: the country was too young, too raw; the democratic way of life put everything and everyone on a dead level of mediocrity; there were no romantic legends, no age-old superstitions, no "high-life" for the novelist to portray. To be sure, there were the Indians, but, as one critic put it, "a novel describing these miserable barbarians, their squaws and papooses, would not be very interesting." Hence, until the program of literary nationalism got fairly started, some of the earlier novelists felt themselves called upon to apologize for using native characters, scenes, and events.

As would be expected, the first American novels were highly imitative of the novels of Richardson, whose Pamela (1740) had set the pattern for the epistolary form, its sentimental motivation, and its stilted and florid elegance of style. The first noteworthy American novel is The Power of Sympathy (1789), long ascribed to Sarah Wentworth Morton, but now generally attributed to William Hill Brown. It follows rather precisely the vain sensibility, high-flying sentimentality, and moralizing tendencies of Richardson, involving an attempted seduction, a change of heart, and an eminently satisfying marriage. Charlotte Temple: a Tale of Truth (1704) by Susannah Rowson is, like The Power of Sympathy, a tale of seduction, but it adds also the theme of desertion, following which there are dire results for all concerned. It was particularly designed "for the perusal of the young and thoughtful of the fair sex." Its tremendous popularity, indicated by the 161 editions through which the book has gone, was owing largely to its reputation as a true story. All early novelists made a great point of the truth of their stories. Fiction, they knew, was inadmissible and banned. The third notable example of the American novel is Hannah Foster's anonymously published *Coquette* (1797). Epistolary in form, like the others, it is, like them also, reputedly a true story, based on the life of a distant relative of the author, named Eliza Wharton, who was allegedly seduced by Jonathan Edwards' son Pierrepont. Still conventionally moral, it is less sensationally sentimental than its predecessors, and excels them also in character portrayal.

Such was the state of the American novel when Royall Tyler, following his success in the drama with native materials, turned his attention to fiction in *The Algerine Captive* (1797), written in a more realistic tone, using native matter, and pointedly insisting, in the preface, upon a substitution of "home-spun" materials for the supernumerary horrors of the Gothic novels and the moral sentimentality of the school of sensibility. Henry Hugh Brackenridge (1748–1816), the author of several long poems designed to demonstrate the rising glory of America, also wrote a satirical back-country novel, called *Modern Chivalry* (1792–1805), to inculcate principles, manners, and mores consonant with his ideas of a democratic society. Even Charles Brockden Brown (1771–1810) turned aside, for the better half of his novels, from the Gothic and sentimental motifs prescribed by English and Continental models, to work on indigenous materials. And Noah Webster (1758–1843), the "Schoolmaster to America," devoted his linguistic talents to justifying and standardizing the American language as distinct from English precedent. He campaigned for the right of Americans to develop their own linguistic tradition, insisting that "America must be as independent in *literature* as she is in politics, as famous for *arts* as for *arms*." This argument was carried forward by William Ellery Channing in his *Remarks on American Literature* (1830), Emerson's call for literary independence a few years later, Lowell's reinforcement of the same idea, and Whitman's illustration in 1855 of what could be done in that direction.

During the early decades of the nineteenth century the United States of America were experiencing the pangs of growing pains. Expansion came so fast that it left Americans, no less than Europeans, gasping. Between the adoption of the Constitution in 1789 and the close of the century, three new states—Vermont, Kentucky, and Tennessee—were added to the original thirteen. In 1802 Ohio was admitted to the Union, and the next year the vast Louisiana Territory was acquired. Louisiana became a state in 1812, and during the six years between 1816 and 1821 six more states were incorporated—Indiana, Illinois, Mississippi, Alabama, Maine, and Missouri. The acrid factionalism represented by the Hamiltonian and Jeffersonian parties, while not forgotten, however much transmutation and realignment the parties had undergone, was appreciably toned down as the strength and promise of the new country gained on the imagination of the people. Rivalries and jealousies, hangovers of the old colonial exclusiveness and provincial economy, grew weaker as the idea of state sovereignty faded before the larger conception of a great republic already well on its way to stretch from sea to sea. The opening of the fertile Mississippi Valley vastly enlarged the national agricultural productivity, which, in turn, reacted on trade and manufacturing, not only in the old settled regions but in the new West. Bostonians, recalling that it had required two centuries for their native city to grow from fifty inhabitants to thirty thousand, were amazed to see Cincinnati after a scant half-century of existence, very nearly equal the population of the Hub of the Universe of some one hundred and seventy thousand in 1860. The vision of a Manifest Destiny, to which the Lewis and Clark expedition of 1804–1806 had given a new impetus, became a reality far more quickly than even the most exuberant expansionists had anticipated. Internal canals, railroads and highways, the steamboat, and new inventions like the reaper, the cotton gin, and the telegraph, put to speedy use by an eager, pushing, progressive spirit, helped create a new empire out of the vast West, South, and Southwest. By the thirties, thoughtful men were warning that material growth was outrunning cultural development, that things were in the saddle riding mankind, and that the new nation was fast becoming, in Irving's phrase, the "Land of the Almighty Dollar."

All however, was not given over to quantity. Some there were who stressed quality. The public-school system was extended as fast as the concentration of population permitted, and often liberal appropriations of land were made to support popular education. Educators like Horace Mann and Henry Barnard were beginning to put order into instructional methods. To the thirty colleges existing in 1810, seven permanent institutions were added by 1821.

and before 1830 twelve more were founded. Outmoded curricula were revised, and the advantages of a collegiate education were made more readily available to all classes. Outside the colleges considerable progress was made in the popularization of knowledge. The three hundred printing presses existing in 1800 were more than trebled during the first quarter of the nineteenth century, to supply American readers with approximately thirty per cent of their current books, the others being imported chiefly from England. Despite this large dependence upon Europe, it is estimated that some 50,000 titles of all kinds bearing an American imprint were issued from American presses during the first three decades of the century. Whereas 376 newspapers in 1810 circulated 22,321,000 copies annually, by 1828 some 850 periodicals boasted an annual issue of 68,117,971 copies, thus increasing the copies per person from 3.8 to 13.8. Intellectuals and writers were beginning to find some popular support, and the government notably during the administration of John Quincy Adams, began to advocate governmental support to intellectual interests, although it was long before anything much more substantial was done than to reward literary ability with custom-house positions or diplomatic appointments. Meanwhile institutions like the Massachusetts Historical Society (founded in 1791), the American Academy of Arts in New York (1802), the Boston Athenaeum (1807), the American Antiquarian Society (1812), the Library of Congress (1815), mercantile and apprentices' library associations, museums, and art galleries were being instituted; magazines like the *North American Review*, founded in 1815, exerted a powerful cultural influence; and the popular lyceum, combining entertainment with instruction, was well on its way to success by 1825. By that time Irving had scored a popular success with *Knickerbocker's History of New York* in 1909, while *The Sketch Book* ten years later made him a literary figure of international reputation. Cooper had published *The Spy* in 1821 and *The Pilot* in 1824; *The Pioneers*, the first of the Leatherstocking Tales, had made its appearance the year before. Joseph Rodman Drake's promising poetic career had come to an untimely end by his death in 1820, but Fitz-Greene Halleck's *Fanny* (1819, expanded 1821) was a popular hit, and *Alnwick Castle* followed soon after. Bryant's "Thanatopsis" had appeared as early as 1817, and most of his best-known poems were familiar to many by 1825, when he went to New York City, soon to start his long and distinguished editorial career on the *New York Evening Post*.

American literary culture, it seemed to many, had come of age. Having twice defeated the British in trials at arms, Americans (so thought and said many of the more enthusiastic literary nationalists) would have no difficulty demonstrating their supremacy over effete Europeans if it came to a contest in the arts. This attitude bred a form of provincial bumptiousness and chauvinism which took extreme offense at the criticism and condescension displayed by British observers and travelers. Ill-feeling between Englishmen and Americans had mounted steadily since the days of the Revolution when Dr. Samuel Johnson, while avowing his readiness "to love all mankind, *except an American*," believed and said that Americans were "a race of convicts," who "ought to be thankful for anything . . . short of hanging" that the British chose to allow them. Americans like Charles Brockden Brown could say without fear of being misunderstood, "The cause why the intellectual soil of America is comparatively sterile . . . [is that] we do not cultivate it"; but any such opinions expressed by Englishmen were promptly ascribed to British envy or malice. The long-standing attitude of disdain and resentment expressed in British reviews and travel accounts was fanned to new intensity when America declared war on England at the very height of her struggle against Napoleon. The Americans, in their turn, considered the scurrilous attacks as evidence at once of a desire for revenge and of a wish to belittle everything American in a desperate attempt to stave off reform at home, to check further immigration to America, and to protect British markets against the competition of American enterprise. American charges that characterized British culture as decadently feudal goaded the British into charging Americans with execrable taste, unbounded vulgarity, unlimited bigotry, colossal ignorance, and to characterizing them as slave-flogging, materialistic, gross, undisciplined people, devoid of all elements of greatness. British criticism reached a new high in 1820, when Sidney Smith, writing in the *Edinburgh Review*, charged that "during the thirty or forty years of their independence" the Americans had done "absolutely nothing for the Sciences, for the Arts, for Literature, or even for the statesmanlike studies of Politics or Political Economy." He wound up his tirade saying that he wanted to know—

In all the four quarters of the globe, who reads an American book, or goes to an American play? or looks at an American picture or statue? What does the world yet owe to American physicians or surgeons? What new substance have their chemists discovered? or what old ones have they analyzed? What new constellations have been discovered by the telescopes of Americans?—what have they done in the mathematics? . . . Finally, under which of the old tyrannical governments of Europe is every sixth man a Slave, whom his fellow-creatures may buy and sell and torture? When these questions are fairly and favourably answered, their laudatory epithets may be allowed.

In his high conceit the Reverend Sidney Smith could not have known (or he would hardly have laid himself open to becoming the laughing stock of later generations of Americans) that at that very moment a young man named Washington Irving was seeing through the press a series of papers called *The Sketch Book*, which not only Englishmen but all men were soon to read. While it may be freely admitted that there are elements of greatness in passages of the Declaration of Independence which men like Sidney Smith were congenitally incapable of appreciating, all Englishmen were prompt to recognize in *The Sketch Book* an account of old England ideally calculated, for both matter and manner, to find a warm place in their affections. William Godwin found in it everywhere "the marks of a mind of the utmost elegance and refinement," though he admitted that he had not been "exactly prepared" to look for those virtues in an American. Irving himself wrote, in the introduction to his next book:

It has been a matter of marvel to my European readers, that a man from the wilds of America should express himself in tolerable English. I was looked upon as something new and strange in literature.

What is fully as important as the excellent quality of Irving's writings is that he was the first man to inject good humor and common sense into the British-American cultural relations of the day. Himself the embodiment of geniality and graciousness, his book contained, besides its idyllic sketches of merry England and his inimitable Knickerbocker stories, an essay entitled "English Writers on America," in which he urged both sides to exercise fairness and forbearance, pointing out that no good could come from a continued literary animosity, fed by accusations and recriminations. Fond as he was of the old-world culture, he was also a patriotic American who did not neglect to tell the British that while they might be right in many of their charges, they were not very wise if they persisted in building up resentment against them among the people of a new nation who had all the good will in the world to be friendly. He reminded the British that while "the present friendship of America might be of little moment" to them, there could be no doubt about the future destiny of the new democracy, while over

England he saw lowering "some shadows of uncertainty." No intellectual giant and little given to worrying himself about public affairs, Irving nevertheless went on to add words strangely prophetic of what has twice happened, within the first half of the twentieth century, when Americans went to the rescue of England.

Should, then, a day of gloom arrive; should these reverses overtake her, from which the proudest empires have not been exempt; she may look back with regret at her infatuation, in repulsing from her side a nation she might have grappled to her bosom, and thus destroying her only chance for real friendship beyond the boundaries of her own dominions.

At the same time he told his own countrymen that the continuation of the quarrel was as senseless as spitting into the wind. American criticisms, he pointed out, never reached their mark because they were never republished in England, and accordingly served no other purpose than to foster a querulous and peevish temper among American writers, making "sour the sweet flow of our early literature." "What," he asked, "have we to do with national prejudices? They are the inveterate diseases of old countries, contracted in rude and ignorant ages, when nations knew little of each other, and looked beyond their own boundaries with distrust and hostility." Instead, he urged Americans freely to acknowledge European leadership in cultural attainments, while keeping England especially before their eyes as "a perpetual volume of reference" from which to derive valuable lessons. Thus, while taking care to "avoid the errors and absurdities which may have crept into the page, we may draw thence golden maxims of practical wisdom, wherewith to strengthen and to embellish our national character."

As the Ambassador of Good Will from the New to the Old World, Irving achieved a notable success in removing a good deal of the rancor and acrimony from the Anglo-American cultural controversy, but the ruffled temperaments of both nations were not calmed at once. English travelers continued to find us boorish in some ways; some of the remarks of Charles Dickens' *American Notes* of 1842 or of Matthew Arnold's *Impressions* of 1888 were hard to swallow. And as late as 1862, when the British-threatened intervention in the Civil War strained relations anew, Lowell complained, in the second series of the *Biglow Papers*, of the British facility "for the minding of other people's business." However, it is worth observing that by this time, although the matter in hand was one of deadly seriousness, Lowell's tone is that of raillery rather than rancor. Americans had got over carrying chips on their shoulders and daring Europeans to knock them off. As solid artistic accomplishment allayed the discomfiture felt by earlier generations when weighing their achievements against their intentions and public professions, the self-conscious straining to realize at once their full, national, cultural potentialities subsided; the high-tension phase of forcing the artistic impulse passed, the overweening claims of the swaggerer and the braggart disappeared, and a natural efflorescence of American art followed.

Not the least of the causes contributing to this healthy change of attitude was the emergence of an American school of criticism. The most notable among the earlier native critics who judged American productions dispassionately, while criticizing sharply and insisting upon ever-higher standards of literary excellence was Edgar Allan Poe, editor of the *Southern Literary Messenger* in Richmond during the mid-thirties. He declared war on mediocrity, exposed it wherever and whenever he detected it, and deflated many literary personalities and reputations which American self-consciousness and an unacknowledged sense of cultural inferiority had overrated. He exposed imitation and plagiarism and demanded originality of conception and execution. He insisted upon the divorcement of aesthetics and morality and refused to regard as literary such productions as were avowedly didactic. By the time of his death in 1849, other critics were prepared to speak with assurance and authority, and writers and critics alike deferred less and less to foreign opinion and more to their own.

When Thoreau professed to having a greater desire to see Oregon than to visit Europe, and when Whitman disdained the "feudalistic" impulse that he saw expressed in Shakespeare, neither of them was directing any oblique remarks at England. Both were making simple statements of individual preference and of American self-sufficiency. In the further cultural development of America, England and Europe generally came to be relatively unimportant. Having all but come of age, America was deciding for herself, for better or worse, what her literary course should be. Today, knowing that she has nothing to fear from any comparison of her artistic creations with contemporary British productions, the condescending or supercilious comments a Somerset Maugham, for example, may choose to make (if only to show that old John Bull still affects the vacant stare that he cultivated in an earlier day when he could afford to be blunt or insular or insensible to the

feelings of others) create not a ripple in the American reviews; while the raillery of a George Bernard Shaw, however pointed the hit, is hugely enjoyed.

The history of this spirit of literary independence in America is no simple one. Artistic endeavor began exuberantly and boisterously soon after the Treaty of Paris. By 1800 it began to falter and show signs of discouragement, first, at the failure of America actively to support an incipient art, and, second, in the face of foreign criticism. During the first two decades of the new century it passed through an awkward, hobbledehoy stage, uncertain of its own ability, half afraid to exert its own strength in opposition to convention and tradition, at one time deferring reverentially to authority, and at the next kicking fiercely at all restraint. During the twenties it began to get rid of its adolescence and the attendant growing pains, writers like Irving, Cooper, and Bryant showing the way. The thirties saw Emerson established as an essayist and lecturer, Longfellow as a poet, Poe as a poet and short-story writer and, what is more important for the development of the American literary temper, as a critic bent on enforcing high literary standards. By the forties the literary climate was prepared to entertain and accommodate the intellectual and social ferment that stirred men and women during the two decades immediately preceding the Civil War.

The result was what has been termed the American Renaissance of the mid-years of the nineteenth century—not so much a rebirth of what had previously existed in America as a birth, *i.e.*, the American way of producing a renaissance, "by coming to its first maturity and affirming its rightful heritage in the whole expanse of art and culture." We might designate the half-decade from 1850 to 1855 as marking the climax of this efflorescence. During that short period appeared a remarkable procession of books by five American writers then at the height of their powers—Emerson, Hawthorne, Melville, Thoreau, and Whitman. The books are *Representative Men* (1850), *The Scarlet Letter* (1850), *The House of the Seven Gables* (1851), *Moby Dick* (1851), *Pierre* (1852), *Walden* (1854), and *Leaves of Grass* (1855). Together they form a collection so distinguished for imaginative vitality that the whole range of American literature does not exhibit anything approaching it in any period of time twice as long. In searching for causes for this extraordinary flowering of literary art, we may consider the coming to fruition of romanticism, transcendentalism, and humanitarianism as among the major contributory factors.

As has been indicated, the American renaissance

under the guise of literary romanticism may be thought of as coming to a climax during the fifties, just before the dark clouds of the Civil War cast their shadows over America. But it must be borne in mind that this romanticism as a motivating force had a long history, going back to Irving, and beyond. Irving still stood half-way within the neo-classical tradition of the eighteenth century, while, for the other half, he followed in the wake of romanticism as exemplified by the antiquarianism of Scott, the popular lore of Germany, the Arabesque legends of Spain, and the localism of his own Knickerbocker region. By birth and rearing a patrician aristocrat, Cooper, too, retained many of the characteristics of the eighteenth century, but his investiture of the frontier and of Leatherstocking in an aura of myth and romance is a major contribution to the literature of romanticism. Bryant, in spite of his inevitable moralizing and frigid formalism, was the first in America to find the indwelling spirit in flower, stream, and forest, at the same time that he dwelt with romantic reverie and feeling on the themes of mutability, transience, and death. With the generation of Poe, Emerson, Margaret Fuller, Longfellow, Lowell, and Thoreau, the romantic spirit in America came to maturity.

Romanticism in the United States, as elsewhere, drew inspiration from many sources and manifested itself in numerous ways. In Poe's poems and stories, where the emphasis is less upon ideas, or intellectual content, than upon artistry, or literary execution, romanticism had its finest purely literary exemplification in America. Avowing the doctrine that the literary artist confines himself to the province of beauty and the cultivation of taste, he sought to create a poetic "ideality" in terms of mood, tone, impression, and atmosphere that included the singular, the bizarre, the grotesque, and the arabesque, and created a slender but successful body of lyric verse that remains unique and in many respects unrivaled.

On the other side were those who were more profoundly attracted to the ideas, the programs, and the reforms that were identified with romanticism. Their approach to romanticism, too, already had a long history, for it is to be recalled that ideologically the romantic temperament had drawn sustenance from Newton and Locke no less than from Rousseau and Paine. The revolt against theocracy dating back to the early years of the eighteenth century, when John Wise had argued the cause of independency and autonomy of separate church organization to establish the principle of Congregationalism, may be taken as the focal point from which to trace, through the regular processes of descent, a romantic revolt by which Unitarianism grew out of Congregationalism, and Transcendentalism, in its turn, became the left-wing development of Unitarianism. In very much the same way the principle of political liberalism that fostered the American Revolution was extended, during the early years of our national life, into the political principles of the Jeffersonian party, and eventually into the Jacksonianism of the West. This twofold revolt in theology and in political theory antedated the romantic revolt in literature, while laying the foundations or groundwork that would nurture it, for it drew a large measure of support from both. But it derived also from other quarters—from the Wordsworthian concept of nature and the Coleridgean world of the visionary and the supernatural, from German transcendental thought and from French social theory, from American nationalism and from the spirit of humanitarianism that expressed a wide sympathy for all living things. Romanticism insisted on individualism, democracy, and the worth of the common man. It avowed the will of man to be free, the human heart essentially good, and human perfectibility possible. It glorified the simple, the elemental, and the natural. It sought expression in a liberation of the imagination, relief of the emotions, and freedom and variety of poetic form as a means to securing more adequate self-expression. It emphasized the very near and the far distant, the common and the exotic. It explored personality in terms of the subconscious, the dreamy, and the visionary. It saw each in all, and all in each; the miraculous in the common, and the divine in the human. It abominated scientific analysis, cold logic, and sterile formality; it aimed at color, warmth, sympathy. It extended tremendously the range of matter and form of poetry and gainsaid the traditional laws of restraint, decorum, and verisimilitude. It was for some a religion, for others a philosophy, or a social theory, or a literary creed. For some it was all these at once.

In New England, Transcendentalism became the philosophy and religion of romanticism. As first expounded by Immanuel Kant, Transcendentalism was a rigorously logical criticism of metaphysical method designed to explore the mental faculties of man and to mark the limits and validity of human knowledge. Of this epistemological system, most of the American Transcendentalists understood little and wanted less. But they appropriated the transcendental terminology and the transcendental definition of ideality, rejecting the knowledge of the Understanding as supplied by sensation and logic, meanwhile accepting the Ideas of the Reason, intuitively or immediately conceived. Into American Transcendentalism went portions of

Kant as well as of Plato, of Cousin no less than of Swedenborg, of Schleiermacher no less than of Dr. William Ellery Channing, of Quakerism and of Puritanism—with the result that the ideas of no two Transcendentalists were quite alike. Transcendentalism was liberal enough to include anybody who distrusted Lockean sensationalism and denied the efficacy of the human understanding to satisfy man, while affirming that the Reason, usually intuitively (or morally) interpreted, led directly to philosophical reality or spiritual verity. For many, Transcendentalism was mainly and primarily a form of idealism designed to halt the all-engrossing materialism to which America seemed on the verge of surrendering. They agreed with Emerson, the high priest of New England Transcendentalism, when he complained—

> Things are in the saddle,
> And ride mankind;

or when he went on to explain that—

> There are two laws discrete,
> Not reconciled,—
> Law of man, and law of thing;
> The last builds town and fleet,
> But it runs wild,
> And doth the man unking.
>
> Let man serve law of man; . . .
> The state may follow as it can.

Emerson put it simply when, in 1842, he sought to explain himself and his associates by saying, "What is popularly called Transcendentalism among us, is Idealism; Idealism as it appears in 1842." Though he sought all his life long to regularize his ideas and to make the several parts of his philosophy cohere, he never added significantly to this first definition. Others commonly referred to New England Transcendentalism as the New Views or the Newness, and let it go at that. Lowell, himself a votary during his earlier years, called it "simply a struggle for fresh air, in which, if the windows could not be opened, there was danger that panes would be broken, though painted with images of Saints and martyrs."

Lowell here hints at an important aspect of the Transcendental movement; for aside from its ideological and religious aspects, it had its practical or (shall we say?) iconoclastic sides. It often opposed the existing order of things and endeavored to reform men and the institutions of men in conformity with its idealistic and humanitarian programs. High thought, Emerson held, was worthless unless translated into action. Accordingly Transcendentalists

organized themselves into clubs, associations, or communities like the Brook Farm Association for Agriculture and Education, and they founded journals of propaganda like the *Dial* and the *Harbinger* to propagate their views. They adopted and practiced a philosophy of "plain living and high thinking" in degrees that sometimes ran to what the man in the street considered idiosyncratic or eccentric. Emerson himself was too much devoted to his doctrine of individualism to participate actively in Brook Farm, which he characterized as "a perpetual picnic, a French Revolution in small, an Age of Reason in a patty-pan." He did not join whole-heartedly in the organized movement for reform; nevertheless he attended the Chardon Street Convention in Boston during 1840. Though he did not speak, he sat on the platform, and studied the faces before him. Hither had come disciples of many kinds, representative of all the forms of religious, philosophical, and social unrest of the time—some of them of the wildest type. Among them, his practiced eye recognized "Madmen, madwomen, men with beards, Dunkers, Muggletonians, Come-outers, Groaners, Agrarians, Seventh-day Baptists, Quakers, Abolitionists, Calvinists, Unitarians, and Philosophers." All came successively to the top to seize their moment, or their hour, wherein to chide or pray or preach or protest. Surely, contemplated Emerson, these were wild and "transcendental" times!

Lowell, too, commenting on the eccentric or comic side of the reform movement associated with Transcendentalism, observed:

Every possible form of intellectual and physical dyspepsia brought forth its gospel. Bran had its prophets, and the presartorial simplicity of Adam its martyrs. . . . Plainness of speech was carried to a pitch that would have taken away the breath of George Fox; and even swearing had its evangelists, who answered a simple inquiry after their health with an elaborate ingenuity of imprecation that might have been honorably mentioned by Marlborough in general orders. Everybody had a mission (with a capital M) to attend to everybody else's business. No brain but had its private maggot, which must have found pitiably short commons sometimes. Not a few impecunious zealots abjured the use of money (unless earned by other people), professing to live on the internal revenues of the spirit. Some had an assurance of instant millennium so soon as hooks and eyes should be substituted for buttons. Communities were established where everything was to be common but common sense. Men renounced their old gods, and hesitated only whether to bestow their furloughed allegiance on Thor or Budh. Conventions were held for every hitherto inconceivable purpose. The belated gift of tongues, as among the Fifth Monarchy men, spread like contagion, rendering its victims incomprehensible to all Christian men. . . . Many foreign revolutionists out of work added to the general misunderstanding their contribution of broken English in every most ingenious form of fracture. All stood ready at a moment's notice to reform everything but themselves. The general motto was:—

> "And we'll *talk* with them, too,
> And take upon 's the mystery of things
> As if we were God's spies."

These represent some of the ways by which the general quickening of the romantic spirit during the first half of the nineteenth century expressed itself. While this flowering was especially luxuriant in New England (notably among the groups of writing men and women in the vicinity of Boston, Cambridge, and Concord), other sections of the country also felt its effects. Philadelphia, where so many of the stirring events of the Revolution had been enacted, had been among the first to dispute with Boston the literary and intellectual leadership, but after we have named the essentially eighteenth-century figures of Benjamin Franklin and Thomas Paine, Pierre S. Du Ponceau and Benjamin Rush, Francis Hopkinson, Charles Brockden Brown, and Joseph Dennie, the list of nineteenth-century men grows markedly meager. Meanwhile New York had gathered a notable literary colony, called the Knickerbocker group, including the Irving brothers, Paulding, Brevoort, Verplanck, the Duyckincks, and Cooper. Bryant, editor of the *New York Evening Post* from 1830 to 1876, and Horace Greeley, the reforming editor of the *New York Tribune* from 1841 to 1872, were no less influential, but not strictly speaking members of the group. In the South, there was Charleston, South Carolina, with William Gilmore Simms, Paul Hamilton Hayne, and Henry Timrod taking the leadership; while Virginia boasted men like John Pendleton Kennedy, William Alexander Caruthers, John Esten Cooke, and Edgar Allan Poe. Nor was romanticism in America a peculiarly Anglo-American manifestation. The French of Louisiana developed between 1830 and 1860 an *esprit* of racial and cultural solidarity that expressed itself in the remarkable body of literature with which the names of Gayarré, Testut, Cononge, Dugué, Roquette, and Mme. la Houssaye, among others, are linked. Another considerable literature was produced among the numerous though widely scattered German groups. Much of it dealt with the common themes of immigration, settlement, repatriation, and acculturation, but they also developed their own forms of romanticism, including nostalgia for the old country as well as romantic glorifications of the new home, accounts of their

wanderings forth, which already lay sufficiently in the past to be idealized or embroidered, or romantic tales of adventures on the frontier. Occasionally they produced a professional man of letters like Charles Sealsfield (Carl Postl), who wrote a series of notable American ethnographic novels which seem at once to reflect the literary method and saga-like manner of a Cooper and to foreshadow the scope of a Rolvaag, who belongs to a much later wave of European immigration.

But it was chiefly in New England, among the coteries of Concord and Cambridge, that we see the romantic spirit at its best and fullest development. In his study and on his quiet walks about Concord, Emerson pondered the idealistic thoughts which he incorporated in his lectures, essays, and poems. Nearby was Henry David Thoreau, who could be counted on to test Emerson's theories by putting them into practice. Intent on living life as daintily as one would pluck a flower, but even more bent on living so that it would not be said of him, when he came to die, that he had spent all his time merely preparing to live, Thoreau seemed to make an art of living, even while people stood a little in fear or awe of him. A long stone's throw away was Amos Bronson Alcott, the Orphic Sage, who expounded neo-Platonic mysticism and experimented with educational theories, communal living, and vegetarian diets. Close by, in his little study at the Old Manse, brooded Nathaniel Hawthorne while he plumbed the psychological and moral depths of man in his tales and romances. The mystic Jones Very and the eccentric William Ellery Channing the Younger were in Concord much of the time, and Margaret Fuller, apostrophized by Emerson as the greatest woman of ancient and modern times, though a storm center wherever she appeared, was a frequent visitor. Not many miles away, at Brook Farm, were the Ripleys and two or three score of other spiritually minded individuals bent on working out, on a cooperative basis, a satisfactory combination of spiritual effort and physical labor. George Ripley's fourteen volumes of *Specimens of Foreign Standard Literature* (translations chiefly from German transcendental literature and French eclectic philosophy) provoked a spirited controversy during the forties over the latest form of infidelity currently being proclaimed in such addresses as Emerson's before the Divinity School in Cambridge. The flames were fanned to new heat when Theodore Parker, proceeding on the bases of conclusions derived from German biblical critics, sought to say "a higher word" on the controversy in a pamphlet, in which he tried to segregate the transient from the permanent elements of Christianity. During the years while Poe gravitated between Baltimore and Richmond, Philadelphia and New York, while Melville in New York pondered the tragedy of the human mind and made a Promethean assault on the inscrutability of the universe in *Moby Dick* and *Pierre*, up to the time when Whitman first sounded his "barbaric yawp over the roofs of the world," the atmosphere in the vicinity of Boston was supercharged with ideas and theories that transformed reasonable men into enthusiasts. Perfectionism and idealism joined hands with humanitarianism to engender a reform movement that included women's rights, universal suffrage, temperance, prohibition, abolition, and many more.

The movement to abolish slavery profoundly stirred individuals like John Brown, William Lloyd Garrison, Harriet Beecher Stowe, and John Greenleaf Whittier from the first. Originally suspect, the movement gradually gained momentum and respect, as Daniel Webster learned to his cost on falling from the position of a New England deity who could do no wrong in 1830 to the inglorious position of "Ichabod" in 1850 because he had dared to compromise over the issue of slavery. The abolition agitation provoked the young Lowell, a scion of one of the old, staid families, to go crusading for human rights, redressing wrongs, and overthrowing tyrannies of all kinds. It drove the gentle Alcott into a fine frenzy and the recluse Thoreau to attempt a one-man revolution against the United States government for conducting an unjust war with Mexico in order to extend the boundaries of slavery; and it succeeded in drawing even the Jovian Emerson sufficiently away from his individualistic and humanistic way of life to speak publicly in behalf of John Brown while the latter was under sentence of death as a "new saint awaiting his martyrdom, who, if he shall suffer, will make the gallows glorious like the cross."

Thus the renaissance of the forties and fifties ran full blast into the catastrophic war years, during which the prewar idealisms were tried by fire, and out of which emerged a chastened consciousness, a revaluation of human aspirations, and a reorientation of national destiny that led by slow degrees to the critically realistic temperament of modern America.

EXPANSION AND CRISIS

In 1850 the United States stretched from the Atlantic to the Pacific coast, but the nation had been continental for only a few years. Texas had been acquired in 1845, New Mexico, Arizona, and California in 1848. In 1846 Great Britain had finally agreed to a settlement of the Oregon dispute, establishing the new boundary at the 49th parallel, the present dividing line between the northwestern United States and Canada. In the summer of 1845 an imaginative newspaper editor had discovered the phrase "Manifest Destiny" for the impending territorial expansion, and most American citizens had caught the shining vision of a great, utopian, and irresistible empire in North America.

Some conscientious moralists in New England condemned the war with Mexico and tried to oppose the greed of the expansionists. Thoreau went to jail rather than pay a poll tax to the government that supported such unholy rapacity (the fact that the tax went to the state of Massachusetts and not the federal government made no difference in his mind). Lowell wrote the first series of the *Biglow Papers* as his contribution against war, imperialism, and slavery. Emerson prophesied that "The United States will conquer Mexico but it will be as the man swallows the arsenic which brings him down in turn. Mexico will poison us." Yet despite their moral scruples over the means by which the new territory was being added to the Union, the Transcendentalists also romanticized the West and the frontier. Even Thoreau felt the gravitational pull westward:

Eastward I go only by force; but westward I go free. Thither no business leads me. It is hard for me to believe that I shall find fair landscapes or sufficient wildness and freedom behind the eastern horizon. I am not excited by the prospect of a walk thither; but I believe that the forest which I see in the western horizon stretches uninterruptedly toward the setting sun, and there are no towns nor cities in it of enough consequence to disturb me. Let me live where I will, on this side is the city, on that the wilderness, and ever I am leaving the city more and more and withdrawing into the wilderness. I should not lay so much stress on this fact if I did not believe that something like this is the prevailing tendency of my countrymen. I must walk toward Oregon, and not toward Europe.

To the literary mind Texas, Oregon, and California were thus becoming symbolic. Not only did they suggest, as to Thoreau, wildness, adventure, and freedom, but to the average, more practical mind, they held out vast opportunities for immense wealth, especially during and immediately after the discovery of gold in California in 1848 and the mad "gold rush" of '49. Horace Greeley, the enterprising editor of the New York *Tribune*, sent Bayard Taylor to observe and report this social phenomenon. Taylor called the book which he wrote *Eldorado* (1850), and the title did not exaggerate the contents. He saw in the gambling, speculation, and mad inflation an epic splendor symbolic of the natural resources, scenery, and future development of the country. He subtitled his book "Adventures in the Path of Empire." The work was reviewed in *Harper's Magazine* with the prediction: "We shall yet have the poetry, the romance, the dramatic embodiment of the strange life in the country of the yellow sands." Four years later Bret Harte was in San Francisco, and within two decades he, Joaquin Miller, and Mark Twain were fulfilling the prophecy.

Regional literature, however, was not the most important or lasting product of this epoch of national expansion. The literary imagination of a whole generation of writers was affected by the space-conquering exploits of the soldiers, miners, explorers, adventurers, and, finally, settlers, of the decade and a half preceding the Civil War. In *Mardi* Herman Melville satirized such rabid imperialists as Senator Allen of Ohio ("Alanno of Hio-Hio"), but, as De Voto has remarked in *The Year of Decision: 1846*, Melville's Polynesian utopia "opening to the westward, though built of dream, is also part of expansionism . . ." And in 1855 Walt Whitman envisioned a bard commensurate with the continent, who would incarnate "its geography and natural life and rivers and lakes." Such a "bard" would be able to tally the physical growth of the young nation: "When the long Atlantic coast stretches longer and the Pacific coast stretches longer he easily stretches with them north or south." Space, plenitude, and fecundity supplied Whitman's primary imagery, and no other aspect of his thought or style was more typical of the times than his attempt to symbolize the whole North American continent.

Whitman was also characteristically American in his belief that his country's expansion meant the spreading of democratic freedom to less fortunate people. While still editor of the Brooklyn *Eagle* he declared:

We pant to see our country and its rule far-reaching, only inasmuch as it will take off the shackles that prevent men the even chance of being happy and good—as most governments are now so constituted that the tendency is very much the other way . . . [But] the mere physical grandeur of this Republic . . . is only desirable as an aid to reach the truer good, the good of the whole body of the people.

Americans of all sects and creeds believed that God had permitted their forefathers to people the wilderness in order that a world-regenerating political theory and practice might develop for the benefit of all mankind. On the very brink of the Civil War President Lincoln, stopping for a few hours in Philadelphia on the way to his inauguration, reiterated this idealistic faith:

I have often inquired of myself what great principle it was that kept this confederacy so long together. It was not the mere matter of the separation of the colonies from the mother land, but something in that declaration giving liberty, not alone to the people of this country, but hope for the world for all future time It was that which gave promise that in due time the weights should be lifted from the shoulders of all men, and that all should have an equal chance. This is the sentiment embodied in the Declaration of Independence. . . . I would rather be assassinated on the spot than surrender it.

Lincoln's democratic idealism rested on three basic assumptions. The first was that God had created an absolute moral law, which all men recognized through their consciences and could apply through the use of reason. The second was that man, possessing a conscience and the ability to reason, was innately good and intelligent. The third was the belief that the best of all economic systems was capitalism, or the private ownership and control of property, with the rôle of government being confined to that of umpire, so that each individual might have a fair chance to acquire as much property as his ability permitted. Wages and prices were determined entirely by supply and demand. In the words of Lincoln, "We propose to give all a chance; and we expect the weak to grow stronger, the ignorant wiser, and all better and happier together."

There were two threats, however, to this national dream. One, the rapid industrialization of the Northern cities with the increasing concentration of power and wealth in the hands of a few, was not generally recognized in the North as a threat, for it was still too new for most men to see its consequences. The Hoe rotary press, making possible high-speed printing, and the Howe sewing machine, harbinger of the garment industry, were recent inventions. The McCormick reaper works were established in Chicago in 1849. Two years later William Kelly invented a method of making steel that anticipated the Bessemer process. A pooling of the Kelly and Bessemer interests made possible the rapid mechanization of the United States. Railroads were still being built, but the Northeast had a good transportation system by 1860. In this year the total annual value of manufactured goods was nearly two billion dollars, almost double the value for 1850. The North manufactured four times the value of goods produced in the slave states, a potent factor in the defeat of the South in the ensuing war.

The other danger to Lincoln's dream was, of course, the increasing antagonism between the slave and the free states. The rapidly growing population of the Northern states, partly through European immigration to the factory towns and to the new territories which the North was determined to keep free of slavery, and the ever-increasing industrial power of the Northern cities, had long ago threatened to overbalance the political strength of the South. Of all Southern statesmen, the one with the most carefully thought-out philosophy of government was John C. Calhoun, of South Carolina, whose *Disquisition on Government* was published in 1851, a year after his death. Like Northern political theorists, he also believed in a fundamental, God-given moral law. Like them, too, he thought that the purpose of society was "to preserve and perfect our race." But he saw in majority rule a threat to the personal liberty of the South—assuming always, of course, like most slave owners, that the Negroes were inferior creatures without rights to freedom.

In 1850 the abolitionists in the North were a small, noisy, and unpopular minority. Many thoughtful men, like Lincoln himself, believed slavery was in a moribund condition and would eventually die of its own inefficiency. But the passage in 1854 of the Kansas-Nebraska Act, which permitted slaveholders to transport their property to the Kansas and Nebraska territories, aroused Lincoln to the danger.

He was still not an abolitionist, but he was resolved to confine slavery to the South, because he saw in its extension a threat to the free labor of the North and the principle of majority rule. The existing political parties, however, failed to meet the issue. The Democratic party was in control of the slavocracy. The Whig party compromised itself out of existence. In 1856 men who shared Lincoln's point of view organized the Republican party, and as a result of the resounding Lincoln-Douglas debates, chose Lincoln in 1860 as its candidate for the Presidency. Lincoln wanted only to preserve the Union, and the utopian dream, but the defenders of slavery knew that the majority rule of the united nation would encroach upon what they believed to be their personal and sectional freedom. To Lincoln's consternation, they chose to secede from the Union.

The emotional tension engendered by these years of heated debate, political intrigue, the inflation at the beginning of the decade, and the depression in 1857, stimulated literary production also. The reading public had suddenly become larger, and the growth of the Lyceum Lecture Bureau brought authors before audiences in all parts of the Northeast and as far west as Wisconsin. The high hopes for a native literature which Americans had clung to for half a century at last bore fruit. Aside from such unquestioned classics of American literature as *The Scarlet Letter* (1850), *Moby Dick* (1851), *Walden* (1854), and *Leaves of Grass* (1855), before the end of the decade other notable works appeared, among them Whittier's *Songs of Labor* (1850), Emerson's *Representative Men* (1850), Hawthorne's *The House of Seven Gables* (1851), Parkman's *The Conspiracy of Pontiac* (1851), Harriet Beecher Stowe's *Uncle Tom's Cabin* (1852), Longfellow's *Hiawatha* (1855), Irving's voluminous *The Life of George Washington* (1855-59), Motley's *Rise of the Dutch Republic* (1856), Holmes' *The Autocrat of the Breakfast-Table* (1858) and *The Professor at the Breakfast-Table* (1860). It is safe to say that no other decade in American literature down to the present time can match the 1850's in number of masterpieces. After the Civil War there was not another comparable period of literary activity until the 1920's.

The 1850's also witnessed the rise of "best sellers" in the modern tradition, *i.e.*, works which so accurately echoed the popular sentiments, thoughts, and prejudices of the times that they promptly sold thousands of copies—in some cases, eventually several millions. It is significant, too, that the majority of these writers of best sellers were women. Whittier and Longfellow were read widely, but not even they

could compete in sales with Maria S. Cummins, who at the age of twenty-four wrote *The Lamplighter* (1854), a pious novel that sold 70,000 copies the first year and continued to sell for decades. Hawthorne read it and wrote bitterly to his publisher in 1855 that, "America is now wholly given over to a d——d mob of scribbling women." Other successful "scribbling women" were E. D. E. N. Southworth, called "Queen of the Killers," who published seventy novels containing approximately 200 melodramatic villains and 500 heroes and heroines; and Mary J. Holmes, known as "Queen of the Tear Compellers," whose *Tempest and Sunshine* (1854) sold over two million copies. Perhaps the earliest "best seller" in American fiction, however, was Susan Warner's *The Wide, Wide World* (1850), an extremely sentimental story of the moral development of a teen-age girl. Some light is thrown on these literary phenomena by the experience of Alice and Phoebe Cary, homely sisters who first attracted attention with poetry and prose sketches which they wrote on an isolated Ohio farm and published in popular magazines. In 1850 they settled in New York, being able in 1853 to buy a house on Twentieth Street, where they were visited by nearly everyone of importance in the city. Alice's greatest success was with *Clovernook, or Recollections of Our Neighborhood in the West* (1853). It was bare, almost realistic in detail, but appealed to the thousands of lonely, emotion-starved women who had found a narcotic for their loneliness in *Jane Eyre* and *Wuthering Heights*, and American imitations.

One of the most successful magazines of the period was also edited by a woman for women, the famous *Godey's Lady's Book*, which attained a circulation of 98,000 before 1860. *Godey's* was published in Philadelphia, as were also *Sartain's* until its failure in 1852 and *Graham's Magazine* in 1858. In the absence of an international copyright law, American authors were at a great disadvantage when Dickens and Thackeray could be pirated at will. *Graham's*, however, had paid well, and *Sartain's* had encouraged American writers. In New York *Knickerbocker's Magazine* continued, and *Harper's* was founded in 1850. The latter was on a higher level than the Philadelphia magazines, but also printed Dickens and Thackeray and pandered to popular taste. *Putnam's*, under the able editorship of C. W. Curtis, printed American material, but lasted only four years. In Boston the *North American Review* had become moribund, but after the founding of the *Atlantic Monthly* in 1857 the best New England authors had a distinguished periodical. In the South the *Southern Literary Messenger*, which Poe had once edited, continued in Richmond. In Charleston W. G. Simms struggled with the *Southern Quarterly Review* until its failure in 1857. For three years thereafter another Charlestonian, Paul Hamilton Hayne, attempted bravely to create a Southern literary tradition in *Russell's Magazine*, which was well edited and which printed distinguished writing, but there was no market for a literary magazine in the South.

Yet there were promising authors in the South, especially the four poets, Simms, Timrod, Hayne, and Chivers. The last is thought by some critics to have been plagiarized by Poe, and by others to have himself imitated Poe. However, it seems probable that Chivers was more influenced by Swinburne and Rossetti, in such poems as "Avalon," "Rosalie Lee," and "To Allegra Florence in Heaven." He published two books in the early fifties, *Eonchs of Ruby* and *Virginalia*. Simms also wrote prose romances with Southern historical settings, as did John Esten Cooke in *Leather Stocking and Silk* and *The Virginia Comedians* (1854). Cooke attempted, in his own words, "to do for the Old Dominion what Cooper had done for the Indians, Simms for the Revolutionary drama in South Carolina, Irving for the Dutch Knickerbockers, and Hawthorne for the Puritan life of New England." The war interrupted these experiments in literary regionalism.

CIVIL WAR AND DECADENCE

Perhaps it is idle to guess what might have happened to American literature if war had not shattered the romantic dreams of the literary optimists, but there are signs that the vigor which produced *Walden* and *Moby Dick* and the first edition of *Leaves of Grass* was diminishing even before Fort Sumter was fired upon. True, Melville and Whitman lived on until the last decade of the century, but Melville became more brooding and introspective and finally wrote only for himself, and Whitman lost some of his cosmic breadth in his briefer, more disciplined war lyrics—though his best single poem, aesthetically, was to be his great elegy for President Lincoln, "When Lilacs Last in the Dooryard Bloom'd." But both Melville and Whitman were exceptional, we might almost say—despite their many native characteristics—anomalous, in nineteenth-century American letters. Melville's pessimistic conviction that evil was the chronic malady of the universe, and that the mystery of life could not be unveiled, so shocked his contemporaries in the optimistic 1850's that they stopped reading his books, and a revival of his reputation had to wait for the disillusioned period that followed World War I. Walt Whitman

had as much faith in the meaning of life and the cosmic purpose as the idealistic transcendentalists, but he anticipated the realists and the naturalists in his frank treatment of all aspects of human experience, including sex, and his discarding conventional style for a symbolic crudity. Though he owed a great debt to Emerson, he did not fit into the pre-Civil War literary traditions.

Certain minor poets who began to publish in the fifties and came to their maturity during the next three or four decades were more typical, and more widely appreciated in the United States than either Melville or Whitman was during his life. One of these was Richard Henry Stoddard, whose *Songs of Summer* appeared in 1857. He wanted to be a reincarnated Keats and wrote not from depth of experience but in feeble imitation. Another was Thomas Bailey Aldrich, whose *Ballad of Babie Bell* caught the popular fancy in 1855. After some years of journalism in New York, during which he associated with the would-be Bohemians who gathered at Pfaff's Cellar, he moved to Boston in 1865, where he wrote graceful short stories, trivial verse, superficial novels, and venerated the New England writers. Bayard Taylor was a good journalist, but he continued to write derivative "pastorals" and "romances" in verse and travel books in prose which had a contemporary appeal but no lasting vitality. There was a certain superficial brilliance in this minor group, especially in the chief of the Bohemians, Fitz-James O'Brien, but they lacked sincere convictions and depth of understanding. They were symptomatic of the literary debility already creeping upon the nation in 1860—not to be shaken off until Mark Twain, William Dean Howells, and Henry James had reinvigorated the national letters.

During the war and for some years following, American literature suffered a marked decline. Much of the poetry written was simply propagandistic, and little survives in modern anthologies. Though Whittier's strongest abolition poems preceded the war, he published *In War Time and Other Poems* in 1864. Lowell revived *The Biglow Papers*. E. C. Stedman published *The Battle of Bull Run* in 1861, and both Melville and Whitman produced collections. Whitman's *Drum-Taps* (1865), reflecting the poet's intimate knowledge of soldier life and his compassion for the fighting men of both sides, easily surpasses all other Civil War poetry. In the South, Timrod, Hayne, and Margaret Preston were active in eulogizing Confederate heroism and sacrifice for the cause which they believed to be just.

One branch of literary activity which the war stimulated was that of humorous writing. In addition to Lowell's dialect satires, Charles Farrar Browne, as "Artemus Ward" the circus proprietor, commented shrewdly on national affairs, and Henry W. Shaw as "Josh Billings" did the same. One of the most active propagandists for loyalty to the Union was David Ross Locke, who wrote under the name of "Petroleum V. Nasby," from Findlay and Toledo, Ohio. "Nasby" lived in a region where the "Copperhead" movement was strong, and to counteract the influence of these traitors to the Union he started his ironical letters supposedly written by a Confederate scoundrel. These letters quickly achieved fame throughout the North and were read eagerly by Union troops and President Lincoln himself. In the South the satire of Charles H. Smith ("Bill Arp") was a great aid in maintaining morale during the war and in the trying days of Reconstruction. He used both Negro and Georgia "cracker" dialect and is said to have influenced Joel Chandler Harris. After the war C. G. Leland also became famous for his dialect humor, and George W. Harris as "Sut Lovingood" capitalized on blackguard farce. In 1865 Mark Twain's "Jumping Frog" yarn became a national sensation and prepared the way for the author's second book, *Innocents Abroad* (1869). These humorists were the first to record American speech with accuracy and understanding. Since satire is always critical, they also prepared the way for realistic treatment of native manners and customs.

Most of the numerous novels written about the war were absurdly romantic. Especially was this true of the Confederate romances of John Esten Cooke, such as *Surry of Eagle's Nest* (1866) and *Hilt to Hilt* (1869), with their archaic chivalry. The chief weakness of the Southern writers was their obsession with an outmoded literary feudalism, faults that the South's greatest poet since Poe, Sidney Lanier, never outgrew. But even in Lanier's amateurish novel, *Tiger Lilies* (1867), there were passages of accurate description of war hysteria and the recording of actual East Tennessee dialect. In the North, writers were also observing speech and conduct with greater attention. Oliver Wendell Holmes' awkward "medicated" novels, *Elsie Venner* (1861) and *Guardian Angel* (1867), contained detailed observations of the petty lives of back-country New Englanders. Whittier's most famous poem, *Snow-Bound* (1866), gave an authentic picture of home life on an isolated farm. Americans were beginning to write with their eyes and ears fully open, though true realism would have to wait for other hands.

Meanwhile several poets were turning to transla-

tion, Longfellow to the *Divina Commedia* (1867), Bryant to the *Iliad* (1870) and *Odyssey* (1871), Bayard Taylor to Goethe's *Faust* (1870), and Christopher Cranch to the *Æneid* (1872). Translation requires high linguistic and literary skill, but it is likely to appeal to a writer in his less creative periods. Perhaps it is significant, too, that these romantic authors were turning back to the great classics of the past. Romanticism would continue to linger on, but it had lost its dominance.

For the South the decade and a half following the close of the Civil War was the most discouraging period in its history. For the North it was a time of great economic and industrial expansion, though interrupted by a financial panic in 1873. After the assassination of President Lincoln in 1865, the "radical" Republicans pushed through Congress a series of "reconstruction" measures far more harsh than the wartime President had planned. Meanwhile most of the Southern states were ruled by military government, and in many sections civilians were terrorized by Northern "carpet-baggers" and uneducated Negroes suddenly elevated to political power. The South struck back by organizing the secret Ku Klux Klan, meeting violence with violence—which soon got out of control of the leaders. Finally by 1870 the South was officially "reconstructed" and most Federal troops were withdrawn. But financial recovery was painfully slow, and the psychological scars would remain for generations.

By 1870 the total population of the nation had reached 38,500,000, though of course the growth was in the North and West. The territories beyond the Mississippi were filling up at the rate of 100,000 a year. These regions needed transportation, and Congress encouraged the construction of railroads by granting free lands to private investors for rights of way, sale of the lands to help bear the expense of construction. This practice led to bribery, graft, and colossal swindling, but the railroads were built. Patents were also being taken out for new inventions which would revolutionize the life of the country: the typewriter in 1868, the refrigerator car in 1875, the telephone in 1876, the phonograph in 1877, the "gasoline carriage" in 1879. Men like Carnegie, Rockefeller, Fisk, and Gould were becoming millionaires by stock manipulation, cutthroat competition, organizing trusts, and establishing monopolies. But despite the growth of capital and speculative wealth, the price level began a decline in 1865 that lasted until the end of the century, and the recurrent "boom and bust" about every ten years brought suffering to industrial workers and small farmers. Under these conditions labor unions grew. In 1869 an Eight Hour League was organized in Boston—and ridiculed by conservatives as a sign of the increasing laziness of working men. The same year garment workers in Philadelphia started the Noble Order of the Knights of Labor, which held a national convention in 1875, and reached the height of its power by 1880. The bloody railroad strike in 1877 prejudiced the average citizen against the organization, and in the eighties it lost its power through a series of blunders on the part of its leaders. But in 1886 a number of craft unions combined to form the American Federation of Labor.

The collapse of farm prices in the depression that began in 1868 also resulted in an agrarian movement, led at first by Oliver H. Kelley, who founded the Patrons of Husbandry, and through this society the Grange. In 1870 there were Granges in nine states, and by 1875 there were 20,000 Granges, mostly in the Middle West and the South, with a combined membership of over 800,000. At first the Grange was social in function, providing lectures, picnics, and entertainment for farm families, but in the Middle West, especially, it gradually entered politics, agitating for financial relief through railway and warehouse regulation. Many Granges also established cooperative stores, factories, creameries, elevators, warehouses, and even insurance companies. Most of the political reforms were in the long run ineffective and many of the cooperatives failed through poor management. Nevertheless, the attempt to work together was undoubtedly beneficial to the farmers, and the Grange did help save some money. With improvement in farm prices, however, the membership declined to around 100,000 by 1880. The Grange then gave way to the more aggressive Northwestern Alliance in the West and the Farmers' Alliance and Industrial Union in the South. The Alliance supported the Populist Party in 1890-92, and then, after the failure of Populism, returned to its social gatherings and cooperative enterprises. If they accomplished nothing else, these farm organizations made rural life less dreary and frustrating. The heroine of Hamlin Garland's A Spoil of Office (1892), a novel written to support the Populist Party, expressed the new vision:

I see a time when the farmer will not need to live in a cabin on a lonely farm. I see the farmers coming together in groups. I see them with time to read, and time to visit with their fellows. I see them enjoying lectures in beautiful halls, erected in every village. I see them gather like the Saxons of old upon the green at evening to sing and dance. I see cities rising near them with schools, and churches, and concert halls and theatres. I see a day when the farmer will no longer be a drudge and his wife a bond slave, but happy men and women who will go singing to their pleasant tasks upon their fruitful farms. When the boys and girls will not go west nor to the city; when life will be worth living. In that day the moon will be brighter and the stars more glad and pleasure and poetry and love of life come back to the man who tills the soil.

This was truly an age of contradictions: unparalleled industrial growth, exploitation of natural resources at a rate that would soon make the United States the wealthiest nation in the world, and a constant rising of the standard of living, accompanied by increasing social unrest, political ineptitude, and moral and aesthetic degeneration. Able critics of these conditions were not wanting. In 1871 Henry Adams complained in an article in the North American Review that in the years following the war the United States had witnessed "some of the most remarkable examples of organized lawlessness, under the forms of law, which mankind has yet had an opportunity to study." He continued:

Single men have controlled hundreds of miles of railway, thousands of men, tens of millions of revenue, and hundreds of millions of capital. The strength implied in all this they wielded in practical independence of the control both of governments and of individuals; much as petty German despots might have governed their little principalities a century or two ago.

The same year Walt Whitman admitted in Democratic Vistas that "Our New World democracy," despite materialistic achievement, "is, so far, an almost complete failure in its social aspects." Two years later Mark Twain, in collaboration with Charles Dudley Warner, gave a name to this disgraceful period in the satire of The Gilded Age. J. W. De Forest made an ironical attack on the corrupt politician in Honest John Vane (1875). In "The Symphony" Sidney Lanier cried:

O Trade! O Trade would thou wert dead!
The Time needs heart—'tis tired of head . . .

Henry George argued in Progress and Poverty (1879) that in American society as currently organized the poor would continue to get poorer in inverse ratio to the accumulation of wealth by the few. Ambrose Bierce declared acidly in 1881:

The frosty truth of the situation is that we are a nation of benighted and boasting vulgarians, in whom the moral sense is as dead as Queen Anne, at her deadest; that we are hopelessly floundering and helplessly floundering in a sea of public and private corruption as offensive as that upon which the Ancient Mariner saw the shiny things that "did crawl with legs"; that we are a laughing stock to Europe and a menace to civilization.

Thus spoke many literary minds.

But these were voices crying in the wilderness. Other voices preached more loudly the gospel of wealth. A Baptist minister named Russell H. Conwell gave a popular lecture, *Acres of Diamonds*, six thousand times. "To secure wealth is an honorable ambition," he preached, "and is one test of a person's usefulness to others." Protestant churches accepted the argument that "Money is power. Every good man and woman ought to strive for power, to do good with it when obtained." And the "robber barons," as they were later called by the debunkers, were generous in endowing universities, hospitals, and other public institutions. Said another faithful Baptist, John D. Rockefeller: "The good Lord gave me my money, and how could I withhold it from the University of Chicago?" The eloquent pleas for this new "Gospel" were climaxed by Andrew Carnegie's article on "Wealth" in the June, 1889, issue of the *North American Review:*

The laws of accumulation will be left free; the laws of distribution free. Individualism will continue, but the millionaire will be but a trustee for the poor. . . . Such, in my opinion, is the true Gospel concerning Wealth, obedience to which is destined some day to solve the problem of the Rich and the Poor and to bring "Peace on earth, among men good-will."

After the financial geniuses had accumulated their fortunes, they began yearning for "culture." Where was it to be found? Not, they thought, in their own raw country. These men who themselves, or their fathers, had come to the United States only a generation or two earlier as poor immigrants, longed for the art and traditions of the long-established nations of Europe. Carnegie, for example, planned to retire in his early thirties to Oxford or some other small, cultured town of England, though when the time came he could not give up the pursuit of money. What many of the newly-rich families of America did instead was to make fashionable the annual tour of Europe, with pious visits to old cathedrals and famous art galleries. Then with their ever-increasing wealth they began to buy paintings by the old masters, tons of sculpture, and sometimes even a whole building, such as a medieval abbey. These were transported to American museum-homes, later (in most cases) to be installed in endowed art galleries.

This attempt of the millionaires to buy a past and an embalmed culture had pervasive effects upon the intellectual life of America. Henry James, the novelist, described the attitude of many of his contemporaries in this personal recollection:

I saw my parents homesick, as I conceived, for the ancient order and distressed and inconvenienced by many of the immediate features of the modern, as the modern pressed upon us, and since their theory of our better living was from an early time that we should renew the quest of the ancient on the very first possibility, I simply grew greater in the faith that somehow to manage that would constitute success in life.

Out of his search for "ancient order" grew James' incomparable studies of American character in contact with Europe, and they were not divorced, as early critics thought, from contemporary reality. There were Americans, like Christopher Newman in *The American*, who went searching in Europe for the "best" after accumulating a fortune in their native country—and like Newman, too, they often failed to obtain it, or found its value synthetic. Henry Adams, in a similar dissatisfaction with "the immediate features of the modern," retreated to the thirteenth century for vicarious certainty and stability, though he did not publish *Mont-Saint-Michel and Chartres* until 1905.

PRAGMATISM AND SCIENCE

William James, however, turned his back not only on Europe but on all metaphysical attempts to find absolute truth. Both as evolutionist and American he knew life to be experimental, and he regarded mind and its results as biological instruments useful in the struggle for existence. He was not the first pragmatist, but his use of the word in his lectures and books gave it currency, and through the works of William James and John Dewey it has become known as the typical American philosophy. James himself, however, called it not a philosophy or a doctrine but a method for testing ideas and experience. Truth he conceived to be not an eternal verity but a working hypothesis for achieving "practical" results. He even defined truth as something the mind carves out for itself. "Reality," he said, "is still in the making and awaits a part of its complexion from the future."

William James was strongly individualistic, a trait that contributed to the formation of his doctrine of pluralism. He came to believe that there was no underlying *unity* (monism) in man's universe but a rich diversity or plurality. This extreme individualism is thought by some critics to be a major weakness in James' philosophical thought. Dewey's pragmatism, on the other hand, emphasizes social responsibility, though his theory of education is also individualistic

—extremely so in the "progressive" or "child-centered" schools founded on Dewey's theories. Critics have been quick to denounce the lawlessness and "expediency" (James liked the word) of these two philosophers. But no matter what one thinks of their ideas, it must be agreed that in their love of freedom, change, and variety of experience they reflect the national contempt for tradition and for the past and the well-known American fondness for activity and rapid growth.

The final decade of the nineteenth century is known in song and nostalgic memoirs as "the gay nineties," but many an average citizen lived through it with anxiety and little gaiety. The eighties had ended in turmoil and conflict—riots, strikes, and violence. During 1886 there were fifteen hundred strikes. In March much property was destroyed in the course of a strike on the Southwestern railroads. On May 4 several Chicago policemen were killed during a mass demonstration in Haymarket Square when someone—no one yet knows who—threw a bomb. Suspected anarchist internationalists were arrested and four were executed after a trial that William Dean Howells, Frank Harris, and other liberals believed to be a travesty of justice.

After a boom in the cattle business, the market collapsed because of the influx of homesteaders and consequent overexpansion. The dissatisfaction of farmers and industrial workers contributed to the bitterness of the political battles of the nineties over "free silver," protective tariff, and the Sherman Anti-Trust Law, which was intended to break the monopolies of the powerful corporations. Acute economic distress resulted in the panic of 1893—the year, ironically, of the World Fair in Chicago. Banks were closed and many businesses were ruined. Drought and crop failure in the West increased the suffering and discontent. Labor agitators were active, increasing the dissatisfaction of labor and the alarm of capital. President Cleveland broke the Pullman strike by calling out Federal troops. But after the election of 1896, when William McKinley defeated William Jennings Bryan, conditions improved, gold was discovered in Alaska, and the nation recovered its confidence. In the war with Spain in 1898 America won an easy though bungling victory and acquired new territory. The United States had become a world power.

The material growth of America during the latter part of the nineteenth century influenced writers to examine more closely various phases of the national life. As early as the seventies William Dean Howells and Henry James were advocating and practicing in the novel a fidelity of truth similar to the realistic

movements in France and Russia, though without the sordidness of Balzac and Zola or the morbidness of Dostoevsky. James' realism consisted in the faithful recording of the nuances of consciousness and the interaction of one character on another, while Howells represented the average American in all his tiresome inanity. In a more literal realism Edward Eggleston in *The Hoosier Schoolmaster* (1871) described life in the back-country district of the Western States, and E. W. Howe in *The Story of a Country Town* (1883) anticipated Sinclair Lewis by depicting the mean, narrow life of a small Midwestern settlement.

The "local color" movement, which flourished from around 1870 to well into the twentieth century, also contributed to the understanding of American life, though it usually idealized the quaint and picturesque features of the region, both in human conduct and natural scenery. The most synthetic "local color" came from California, where Bret Harte and Joaquin Miller romanticized frontier lawlessness and primitive emotion. Constance Fenimore Woolson treated with greater accuracy the local types of the South, Mary Murfree (Charles Egbert Craddock) the mountaineers of Tennessee, George W. Cable the Creoles of New Orleans, and Sarah Orne Jewett coast-country New Englanders. Joel Chandler Harris wrote stories about Georgia "crackers," but will be longest remember for his "Uncle Remus" tales, which have become classics in the literature of Negro life on the Southern plantations.

The social unrest of this period also gave rise to the problem novel and the use of literature for propaganda. Thomas Bailey Aldrich in *The Stillwater Tragedy* (1880) and John Hay in *The Bread-Winners* (1884) attempted to show the damage of strikes and labor violence. Hay's novel was answered in a parody by Henry F. Keenan called *The Money-Makers* (1885). Edward Bellamy in *Looking Backward* (1888) and Howells in *A Traveler from Altruria* (1894) accused capitalism of waste, cruelty, and obsolescence, and projected a utopian socialistic state. Albion Tourgée, in *Bricks Without Straw* (1880), pleaded for education of the Negro. Helen Hunt Jackson, in her sentimental *Ramona* (1884) and articles in the *Nation*, helped create popular sympathy for the plight of the American Indian.

The full impact of new scientific thought was not felt by American writers until toward the end of the century. Whitman had attempted to be the poet of science along with his other poetic rôles, but his democratic idealism reflected the national temper of the forties and fifties before the United States had made any significant contributions to science. The "Father of American Anthropology," Lewis Henry Morgan, began his researches before the Civil War by investigating the ethnology of the Iroquois Indians. Unlike Darwin, he was interested not in biological but social evolution, and his studies led to an attempted formulation of a science of man. In *Systems of Consanguinity and Affinity of the Human Race* (1871) he argued that all peoples were related, and in *Ancient Society; or Researches in the Lines of Human Progress* (1877) he outlined the steps of development through savagery, barbarism, and civilization. But he did not think mankind had reached the peak of social development; there would be a fourth stage surpassing any civilization hitherto known. Meanwhile John Wesley Powell explored the Grand Canyon in the sixties, and in subsequent writings laid the foundations of American geology. He thought—like the professional "freethinker" Robert G. Ingersoll—that science had displaced religion, and looked forward to a new "scientific ethics." John Fiske, lecturer and writer, popularized the theories of Darwin and Herbert Spencer in several books, including *The Outlines of Cosmic Philosophy* (1874), *Darwinism and Other Essays* (1879), and *The Destiny of Man Viewed in the Light of His Origin* (1884). Lester Ward believed that man, scientifically educated, could become complete master of his own destiny and continue his evolution indefinitely. Ward advocated these ideas in *Dynamic Sociology* (1883) and *The Psychic Factors of Civilization* (1893). Most of these theories were optimistic and democratic, looking forward to a Golden Age to be created by scientific progress. William Graham Sumner believed in progress and wanted to hold on to democracy, but he was a determinist, and he rejected the utopias of the social planners, declaring that man "is in the stream and is swept along with it. All his sciences and philosophy come to him out of it. Therefore the tide will not be changed by us."

In 1890 Captain Alfred T. Mahan of the United States Navy published a book which received wide attention throughout the world. It was called *The Influence of Sea Power in History*, and could hardly have been published at a more opportune time. Eight years later President McKinley crushed Spain, once a mighty naval power, with two fleets. In 1901 President Theodore Roosevelt began building a more powerful navy. Sumner, along with William Vaughn Moody, Mark Twain, and a few others, raised his voice in protest against expansion and imperialism, but he did not expect to influence the course of history. Like Melville, who had declared half a century

earlier that "evil is the chronic malady of the universe," Summer acknowledged that "war always has existed and always will." But he saw in nationalism the greatest danger to democracy, and looked upon the future as darkly as did Henry Adams.

PESSIMISM AND DETERMINISM

Despite the fact that the nineties saw a flare-up of escapist romances, such as those of F. Marion Crawford and Lew Wallace, and a great public demand for the sentimental verse of James Whitcomb Riley and the *Songs of Vagabondia* of Bliss Carmen and Richard Hovey, the decade belonged to the pessimists. Mark Twain was sinking deeper into his bleak determinism. Henry Adams was skipping from continent to continent, fleeing his own dark thoughts. When Emily Dickinson's eccentric poems finally reached the public between 1891–96, most readers (if they were at all interested) found them charming in a naïve way, but later critics have perceived in their broken rhythms and ironical images the mind of another disillusioned idealist.

Emily Dickinson was not herself a "naturalist," but it is significant that one of the earliest Americans to write in the naturalistic tradition, Stephen Crane, composed his first free verse poems after hearing William Dean Howells read her poetry. Naturalism, both in France and in the United States, was the offspring of post-Darwinian science. In France Zola declared, "We naturalists, we men of science, we must admit nothing occult; men are but phenomena and the conditions of phenomena." Crane evolved his own theory and practice independently, but he was entirely in agreement with other naturalists in his attempt to be objective and completely truthful. His ironical, pessimistic detachment came from his own temperament. The pessimism of the naturalists is shown in the selection of details to prove that life is mean, or that life is a trap (determinism or fatalism), and the irony arises from a sense of man's anomalous position in a hostile world. In Crane's *The Open Boat* nature is "flatly indifferent" to man. In *The Red Badge of Courage* (1895) the strongest instinct is self-preservation, though in the heat of battle the hero eventually discovers a maniacal will to fight and endure pain. When he came close enough "to touch the great death" he "found that, after all, it was but the great death. He was a man."

The stoical will was so emphasized by Frank Norris and Jack London that their theory became an inverted romanticism. London wrote semiautobiographical stories in which the hero demonstrated his fitness to survive in brutal conflict with men and nature. In his earlier novels Norris gloried in situations that aroused in the "primitive man, the half-brute of the stone age." In later works, especially *The Octopus* (1901) and *The Pit* (1903), he turned socialistic and humanitarian and attacked the greed of capitalism. He had shifted his emphasis from the individual to the race. Jack London also passed through the same general development, though fitfully and inconsistently. Both his own temperament and his reading of Nietzsche influenced him to exalt the "old law" that improves the species by eliminating the weak and unfit. In *Martin Eden* (1909) he agreed that "it is too bad to be slaves," but "slaves dream of a society where the law of development will be annulled, where no weaklings and inefficients will perish. . . ."

Admiration for power, and men strong or clever enough to acquire it, may likewise be seen in Theodore Dreiser's captains of industry in *The Financier* (1912) and *The Titan* (1914), men whom the author both envied and condemned. Dreiser confessed in his autobiography, *A Book About Myself* (1922), that in youth his body "was blazing with sex, as well as with a desire for material and social supremacy—to have wealth, to be in society." All his books, in fact, have been more or less personal confessions, giving vent to his resentment against his father's religion, the poverty of his own youth, and the repression of the individual by the conventions of society. But to Dreiser man was not merely a victim of social conventions; he was also controlled "by the inescapable chemicals and physical reactions and compulsions of seemingly blind forces" operating mechanically within him. Thus man is not morally responsible for his conduct. Clyde Griffiths in *An American Tragedy* (1925) committed murder because of his own "chemic compulsions" in social relationships not of his own choosing. Dreiser called man "an orphan in space."

The pessimistic determinism of Dreiser was not, however, typical of American life between the Spanish-American War and World War I. Though this was an age of the consolidation of "big business," with consequent social maladjustments, reform sentiment was very strong. For all his intense nationalism and high-handed methods of acquiring rights and building the Panama Canal, Theodore Roosevelt was a tireless fighter for the rights of the average citizen through his "trust busting," court reforms, and social legislation of various kinds. He inconsistently branded as "muckrakers" some of the journalists who exposed graft and corruption, but the most prominent muckrakers, particularly Lincoln Steffens and Ida Tarbell,

had much in common with the dynamic "T. R." Steffens' sensational revelation of municipal graft in *The Shame of the Cities* (1904) shocked decent, law-abiding Americans, but it also gave a great impetus to political movements for reform. Ida Tarbell's *The History of the Standard Oil Company* (1904) revealed how monopoly was created and maintained. Upton Sinclair's novel, *The Jungle* (1906), exposed the danger to public health of the insanitary conditions in the packing plants.

These muckrakers deserve a great deal of the credit for such legislation during the first decade of the twentieth century as pure food acts, workingmen's compensation for industrial injury, and the first—though largely unsuccessful—attempts to eliminate child labor. Roosevelt's successor to the Presidency, William Howard Taft, proved to be so conservative that he soon alienated the liberals who had supported him. In 1912 Theodore Roosevelt, convinced that both the Republicans and the Democrats had become hopelessly reactionary, bolted his party and ran for the Presidency on the "Bull Moose" ticket, using for his platform many of the "socialistic" ideas of Robert M. La Follette. But another reformer, Woodrow Wilson, won, and under his leadership the Underwood Tariff Act (liberalizing the tariff restrictions) was passed, and the Federal Reserve banks and the Federal Trade Commission were established. Likewise under him the corporations were brought under closer federal control by the Clayton Anti-Trust Act. Despite two little skirmishes with a Mexican revolutionist in 1914 and 1916, during which United States Home Guard troops were marched into Mexican territory, the dominant mood of the nation was confident and optimistic. Even the war that engulfed Europe in 1914 seemed remote to most Americans, and in 1916 they re-elected Wilson because "he kept us out of war."

THE "LOST GENERATION"

When the United States was finally drawn into the European conflict in 1917, President Wilson made it a holy crusade to end all wars. The country united behind him as it had probably never been united before in its history. Without waiting to be drafted, thousands of young men marched off voluntarily to "save Democracy." At home atrocity stories whipped up a furious hatred for the uncivilized "Hun." In the trenches of France some American soldiers lost their enthusiasm, but the fresh strength and vast material resources of the United States soon brought victory to the Allies. The whole world then looked to this young nation for spiritual guidance. President Wilson became an international hero. In America the moral crusade turned domestic and was directed toward granting suffrage to women and passing the Volstead Act prohibiting the sale of alcoholic beverages. At the peace conference in Paris President Wilson was forced to compromise. Then at home the "isolationists" thwarted his plans for American participation in the League of Nations. Some historians think Wilson's defeat in the United States Senate made World War II inevitable. At any rate, Woodrow Wilson soon died a broken, rejected leader in the crusade for permanent peace. What followed was more disgraceful than the Gilded Age itself. With President Harding the country lost interest in world problems and attempted to return to "normalcy." The scandals of his administration did not die down before the nation swung into the speculative, boom years of Calvin Coolidge—which ended with the world-shaking crash of the stock market in 1929.

American literature did not parallel these events year by year, but it was nevertheless profoundly affected by the emotional experiences through which the country passed between 1914 and 1929. Henry James' disciple, Mrs. Edith Wharton, daughter of a New York society family and wife of a Boston banker, lived in Europe after 1907, but she continued to write novels about the narrow and superficial lives which she had known in the United States. She wrote about the war, too, but her best works were *The House of Mirth* (1905), concerned with a tragic victim of class snobbery in New York's "Four Hundred," and *The Age of Innocence* (1920), a mildly ironical revelation of the mores of Victorian Manhattan. In Virginia another lady novelist with an aristocratic family background, Ellen Glasgow, was continuing to write realistically of life in the tradition-ridden South, as in *Barren Ground* (1925) and *The Romantic Comedians* (1926). Another Virginian, Willa Cather, moved to Nebraska when she was a child and discovered in the lives of the immigrant settlers of the prairies subject matter for some of her best novels, like *O Pioneers!* (1913) and *My Ántonia* (1918). She had a romantic love for youth, the land, and simple people, but she could describe the hardships of the immigrants and first-generation Americans with convincing authenticity.

For outright rebellion against the narrowness of American life, however, we must turn to other authors. Although revolt against the small Midwestern town began as early as Eggleston's *The Hoosier Schoolmaster* (1871), it became a literary movement only in the first two decades of the twentieth century.

In 1915 Edgar Lee Masters published his free-verse epitaphs, *Spoon River Anthology*, on the tragic failures of an Illinois village, the poet's own home town. A few of these characters led normal, happy lives, but the general tone of the book was elegiac and tragic. Another Midwestern poet, Vachel Lindsay, tried to start a poetic "Village Improvement" crusade, but he attracted no followers. As civic leader he was as eccentric as Oscar Wilde lecturing in Nebraska with the sunflower in his buttonhole. Lindsay himself was a victim of the cultural barrenness which Masters attacked. Sherwood Anderson in *Winesburg, Ohio* (1919) wrote stories without plots about the groping, neurotic inhabitants of an Ohio village in their more intense moments of awareness of their own frustrations. Anderson's men and women lacked cultural roots. They felt separated and longed inarticulately for a spiritual home. Like Mark Twain in his later pessimism, both Lindsay and Anderson regarded life as a dream. This sense of the unreality of their own existence was a subjective form of social criticism. Anderson shared the conviction of John Ruskin that the factory system had deprived men of the pleasure of creating with their own hands and skill. Consequently Anderson's semiautobiographical characters sought emotional compensation in sex, alcohol, and fantasy.

Disillusionment with twentieth-century American life was not confined, however, to the village or the Midwest. The village was small enough to be placed under the literary microscope; its tone, accent, and manners could be more readily and convincingly mirrored than the heterogeneous metropolis. Sinclair Lewis, the most successful of all the satirists of the small Midwestern town, wrote about the wage slave in Manhattan (*The Job*, 1917) before he discovered "pay dirt" in *Main Street* (1920). While Harding exalted "America first" and the politicians distracted sympathy from war-ravaged Europe, literary minds in the United States became increasingly rebellious against nearly all the ideals which the nation had previously cherished. Edmund Wilson has remarked that "never in all history . . . did a literary generation so revile its country." In literary criticism this rebellion became a thesis, represented in Van Wyck Brooks' *The Ordeal of Mark Twain* (1920) and *The Pilgrimage of Henry James* (1925). The thesis was that America was no place for an artist. In his Foreword to *Jurgen* (1919) James Branch Cabell accused Philistia (the United States) of having starved Edgar, made a paralytic of Walt, and frightened Mark "into disguising himself in a clown's suit."

What was wrong with America? The more vigorous

of the young critics agreed that there was: (1) no culture in this land of machine-minded money-grabbers; (2) no personal freedom because of too much moral inhibition; (3) no courage, the average citizen being afraid to think or act independently of the herd; (4) no true cosmopolitanism, but narrow provincialism in taste and conduct. What did these critics propose as remedy? Most of them were not seriously concerned with economic or political reform. Some thought T. S. Eliot and Ezra Pound had been wise to flee to England. Gertrude Stein was in France, where several expatriates—notably E. E. Cummings and Malcolm Cowley—joined her. Back home Sinclair Lewis shocked and entertained the country with his heavy-lined caricatures of the business man, the Protestant minister, the doctor, and other typical Americans. In the *American Mercury* and his series of books labeled ostentatiously *Prejudices*, H. L. Mencken cudgeled the middle class for its traditional morality and intellectual mediocrity. He translated Nietzsche, whose doctrine of the "Superman" he distorted into a version which anticipated Hitlerism, and advocated a society ruled by an "intellectual minority." In literature he praised only the realists, the satirists, and the aesthetes like Cabell, Hergesheimer, and Thomas Beer.

Cabell, convinced that this is the worst of all possible worlds, and that the wisest thing man can do is to escape into an ideal dream world of art and romance, created an imaginary medieval land which he called Poictesme and peopled it with semimythological characters. His ingeniously contrived romanticism was a pose. Behind his mask of irony and satire lurked one of the most disillusioned men since Jonathan Swift. Hergesheimer also turned to the past, though a past slightly resembling periods and places in American history, for his exotic character portraits. Beer's relation to these conscious stylists can be seen in the urbane irony of his *Stephen Crane* (1923) and the *Mauve Decade* (1926), the latter an impressionistic study of the late nineteenth century in America.

In the United States disillusionment with World War I was so great that writers and publishers avoided the subject until John Dos Passos started a new vogue in 1921 with his *Three Soldiers*, an acrid revelation of the debasing effects of army life. The following year E. E. Cummings published his brilliant psychological narrative, *The Enormous Room*, about life in a military prison. In 1924 Laurence Stallings and Maxwell Anderson attacked war in their sensational drama, *What Price Glory?*, one of the most successful plays of the decade. The hero of Ernest Hemingway's *A Farewell to Arms* (1929) experienced, like the author himself, the disintegration of the Italian army and lost all faith in patriotism and moral idealism. He retained belief only in the integrity of his own emotions and the English nurse whom he came to love. But when she died in childbirth, life no longer held any meaning for him. These writers of the twenties were truly, as Gertrude Stein called them, the "lost generation." Hemingway lived to find a new faith during the thirties in the cause of the Loyalist side in the Spanish civil war, but the career of another "lost" writer, the gifted novelist, F. Scott Fitzgerald, ended in unfulfilled promise. Perhaps no one else better expressed in imaginative literature such as *This Side of Paradise* (1920) and *The Great Gatsby* (1925), or better exemplified in his own life, the economic extravagance, the moral corrosion, and the dissipation of intellect during the "jazz age."

The twenties were, nevertheless, one of the most stimulating decades in American literary history. One evidence of this was the fruitful experimentation in style and technique—usually a sign of vitality and growth. Gertrude Stein's attempt to find new values in words influenced both Anderson and Hemingway in evolving styles unique for their particular needs. In England T. S. Eliot and Ezra Pound continued their innovations in poetic form. Dos Passos made his own adaptation of James Joyce's stream-of-consciousness technique, combining it with devices invented on the analogy of American newspaper headlines and the flowing imagery of the movies. In the thirties William Faulkner perfected a flamboyant rhetoric suitable for his Poesque horrors in settings of decayed Southern aristocracy. In the drama O'Neill continued to experiment with dramatic techniques for revealing the inner lives of his characters. Maxwell Anderson, on the other hand, tried with some success to restore blank verse to the stage.

HUMANISM AND NATURALISM

In 1930 the publication of a book called *Humanism and America* stirred up a violent controversy among the literary critics for two or three years. The book, edited by Norman Foerster, was a collection of essays written by Paul Elmer More, Irving Babbitt, and their disciples. They believed life to be a dualism between the natural and the supernatural. Man himself, they said, contained a dualism between the animal and the human. His animal nature gave him his sensual appetites; his human nature gave him a moral will and "ethical" imagination. These critics laid great stress upon the conscience, or the "inner check," for moral control over man's animal impulses and passions. The human side of man should check him not only against physical overindulgence but also against sentimentalism and vague, uncritical humanitarianism. These neo-humanists were thus classical in literary taste; they must have specific critical and ethical standards, and for these they searched the cultural traditions of the past. For contemporary American writers, these new humanists had little use, though they were tolerant of the milder realists such as Howells, James, Mrs. Wharton, and Willa Cather. Literature, like ideal human life, they taught, should be sane, ethical, and well-balanced.

In placing man above and beyond nature, the humanists came into direct conflict with the naturalists, who insisted that man is *in* nature. Although a considerable number of the important twentieth-century American writers cannot be classified as consistent naturalists, the over-beliefs of naturalism have been major literary influences in this country since Stephen Crane, Frank Norris, and Theodore Dreiser began in the 1890's to accept the scientific theories which reduced man to a mere speck of protoplasm in a universe indifferent to his existence. The new humanism was too rational for the average religious American and too inhibiting for the typically individualistic artist, author, and literary critic. Humanistic influence has lingered on in academic halls, but as a literary movement it was stillborn in 1930.

At the very time when this critical debate was taking place, American literature was already beginning to decline in both productivity and quality. The depression marked the end of a literary epoch, not only because it curtailed publishing but even more because it shook the personal convictions of authors. Many of the naturalists turned Marxist, or at least became propagandists against capitalism. John Steinbeck's *Grapes of Wrath* (1939) aroused the social conscience of the nation. Hemingway's *For Whom the Bell Tolls* (1940) recorded the first round of war between democracy and fascism. Even Thomas Wolfe began to discover a social philosophy not long before his death in 1938. Carl Sandburg asserted his faith in the soundness of the American way of life in *The People, Yes* (1936), and completed his monumental biography of Lincoln. Robert Sherwood dramatized the life and philosophy of Lincoln. Archibald MacLeish turned to immediate social issues in his verse drama, *Panic* (1935), and his poem, *America Was Promises* (1939). In Vermont, Robert Frost be-

came more speculative on the meaning of human existence, but changed none of his fundamental attitudes toward either life or art, continuing in his common-sense, Horatian manner to observe the world with the eyes of a shrewd farmer.

Whether or not naturalism and materialism have reduced American literature to near stagnation in the 1940's, as the new humanists would maintain, it is a fact that most of the vigorous writing has come from the "Cult of Cruelty," the continued grotesqueries of Faulkner, the descriptions of Georgia "cracker" degenerates by Erskine Caldwell, the odysseys of Chicago slums by James T. Farrell, and the melodramatic realism of Steinbeck's California and Southwest stories. Another Californian, Robinson Jeffers, also continues to write his poetic prophecies of the doom of Western civilization.

So far World War II has found little expression in literature that promises to endure. The disillusionment that followed World War I aroused both a militant pacifism and a hedonistic rebellion that acted as a powerful stimulant on writers. In the age of the atom bomb and East-West rivalry, pacifism has little meaning. And instead of rebelling against tradition, most literary minds seem homesick for the less complicated past. The fiction writers are reviving the historical novel. Van Wyck Brooks in *The Times of Melville and Whitman* (1947) has traveled so far away from his early conviction that the artist cannot live in America that he is now painting with loving care static portraits of nineteenth-century authors and thinkers, being especially devoted to Emerson and the Emersonian tradition. Melville and Whitman lived through tumultuous experiences too, but Brooks now evidently hates conflict so much that he even seems to remove these authors from the tragic times in which they wrote. Though naturalism in fiction still continues to come from the presses, poetry shows indications of returning to something resembling classical form, especially in the works of Karl Shapiro and Robert Lowell. Critics are also beginning to write once more about the English Victorian poets and novelists, and efforts have already been made to resuscitate the reputation of Longfellow in America.

In a recent essay on the "Dilemma of the Modern Poet in a Modern World," Stephen Spender, now living in America, declared that events have taken place so rapidly in the experiences of the present "generation" of poets that they "find themselves separated by the overwhelming circumstances of their particular phase of the struggle from all that has gone before and has gone after them." Consequently:

The modern poet is in the dilemma that he wishes to create a poetry of the modern world but cannot find in contemporary religion, science, philosophy, politics or psychology attitudes capable of giving external events the kind of order of the imagination which we find, for example, in Shakespeare, Racine or Dante. In being modern he risks being artistically destroyed by the modern world (in the manner of the "social realists") or else having to declare unremitting spiritual war on the modern (in the manner of Baudelaire and Rimbaud).[1]

[1] Quoted by permission of the author and the New York *Times Book Review.*

Literature, not only in America but in other countries as well, seems, therefore, to be at a new crossroads. What direction it will follow depends, ultimately, upon the solution—or the mere prospect of solutions—to international political and social problems. In other words, it depends upon whether the literary mind can foresee the continuance of mankind upon this planet on a human level of existence. Meanwhile, there is no better time for exploring and evaluating the contributions of the literary masters who have helped shape and perpetuate the cultural traditions of the United States of America.

Introduction to

Masters of American Literature

COTTON MATHER (1663–1728)

Although Cotton Mather is today considered a greater man than his father Increase, during his lifetime fate played him a shabby trick by arranging affairs in such a way as to make him stand always a little in the shadow of his illustrious father, whom he outlived by only five years. Increase Mather served as pastor of old North Church in Boston from 1664 to his death, his son having to content himself with the position of teacher, so that on numerous occasions great opportunities passed him by to go to his senior, in a manner seriously to restrict the scope of Cotton's genius if not of his productivity. His father's forced retirement from the presidency of Harvard College in 1701 was a serious blow to Increase, but it was catastrophic for his son, who, at thirty-eight, had still a long life-expectancy. Although he yearned for the post, the trustees of Harvard thrice passed him up to elect men who he had every reason to believe were not his equals in intellectual attainments or pious orthodoxy. By 1723, when Increase Mather went to his well-earned reward, the opportunities which Cotton might have seized triumphantly if they had presented themselves earlier came too late. A generation that wanted none of the father wanted less of his son, and it fell to the unhappy lot of Cotton to preside at the fall of the Mather dynasty which Richard had established and Increase had sought to maintain. Even in death the hand of Increase remained on the son. When, about 1723, the offer of the rectorship of Yale came to Cotton, he felt bound to put aside this tempting offer to go over to the rival of his Alma Mater, which had treated him so shabbily. He chose to remain with his father during his last years, to minister to his beloved congregation in Boston, and to preside in the pulpit which had been for so many years the stronghold of the Mathers.

Destined by birth and motivated by ambition to perpetuate and glorify the orthodoxy of his father and his grandfathers (Richard Mather and John Cotton), Cotton Mather developed the precocity that sent him to Harvard College in 1675 when he was barely twelve, and that enabled him to take his first degree in due course. At eighteen he held a second degree and preached his first sermon; but being afflicted by a grievous habit of stammering, resolved to give up the ministry for medicine, when a friend suggested that his trouble could be remedied if he would remember always to speak "with a dilated deliberation." He tried it and was cured. At the age of twenty he was ordained, and two years later was formally installed as the associate of his father in the most influential pulpit in America at the time. Here, in ceaseless prosecution of almost incredible labors —ministerial, literary, civic, philanthropic, oratorical, political, scientific, and social—he continued to the end of his sixty-five years of life.

Intensely emotional, introspective, serious-minded, and ascetic, his long "scholar's day" was packed with pastoral duties, study, domestic cares, fasts, and prayers, besides many midnight vigils devoted to soul-searching analyses of his heart and mind, during which he lay on his study floor alternately writhing in agonies over his "vileness" or reveling in spiritual ecstasy in moments of exaltation. Enormously read in many languages, encyclopedically learned, proud, pedantic, fantastic, he labored ceaselessly, preaching thousands of sermons, engaging in time- and energy-consuming public and political affairs, keeping some four hundred fasts, and publishing four hundred and forty-four books and pamphlets, besides leaving a number of extensive works in manuscript at his death. "In a single year," says Moses Coit Tyler, "besides doing all his work as master of a great metropolitan parish, and besides keeping sixty fasts and vigils, he published fourteen books." Small wonder that he wrote over his study door, as a reminder to himself and a warning to his visitors, "Be Short." He kept before him constantly the admonition that the work required by the Lord was great, and that the time to do it was brief. On his deathbed he gave this final charge to his son Samuel, "Remember only this one word—'Fructuosus.'" It was the hereditary motto of the Mathers, descriptive of their passion for mighty labor and achievement.

Proud of his birth and heritage and addicted to vanity and an excessive consciousness of his high calling, he was ambitious to achieve sainthood; he was also often intemperate in denouncing his enemies

3

and all too eager for controversy with those who opposed him. Impulsive, nervously sensitive, and lacking in a sense of proportion in matters that touched his family or his personal pride, he was often dogmatic, dictatorial, overbearing, and querulous.

The record of his prodigiously fruitful life is all the more remarkable because it was made under very trying circumstances. Besides suffering much from poor health, perhaps partly self-induced by his over-wrought, introspective, and acutely ascetic nature, he suffered much unhappiness in his private and domes-tic life. Burdened all his life by financial worries, he buried two of his wives early; his third wife became insane and caused insufferable domestic difficulties; a scapegrace son added special torments; nine of his children died in childhood; and when, in 1728, he himself gave up the ghost, only two of his fifteen chil-dren survived him. Yet through it all, he carried on to provide for his time and place the leadership to which he felt his high office called him, ministering to the spiritual wants of his people, endeavoring to educate and guide them in every detail, reproving them for their shortcomings or inspiring them to a greater service of God, and devoting much time and energy to organizing societies and public services among them.

With his father he was chiefly responsible for the overthrow of the hated Governor Andros, the restora-tion of a charter that had been revoked in 1684, and the appointment of Sir William Phips—revealing ac-counts of which affairs he subsequently incorporated in his laudatory *Life of Phips* (1692), also included in the *Magnalia Christi Americana* (1702), and in the appreciative life of his father which he published under the title of *Parentator* in 1724. About 1690 the Mathers were riding the crest of the waves of influ-ence and power; but their successes were short-lived. The modified charter which Increase Mather secured did not win general approval in New England, and some of the policies and acts of Governor Phips backfired. The Mathers were blamed, and they suf-fered a decline in popularity. About the same time the Salem witchcraft troubles came to a head, and again they did not go unscathed. In this matter the mind of the Mathers found a congenial area, accept-ing with alacrity the challenge to delve into the world of spirits, in which they, along with the rest of the world, had implicit faith. Both took an active part in the trials, and Cotton especially sought to make fundamental inquiries into the problem by taking into his own home one of the bewitched children in order to study the manifestations of witchcraft at first hand. With his father, he distrusted the validity of accepting "spectral evidence," but allowed his scruples to be overborne. What is more, his interest was less in securing convictions in court than in dis-covering curative measures, chiefly through prayer and fasting; and when it became evident that witch-craft was getting out of hand, Cotton Mather, more than anybody else concerned in the affair, was respon-sible for stopping the Salem delusions of 1692. But having participated in the trials, and being congeni-tally incapable of graciously admitting himself in error or inconsistent, he maneuvered himself into a position of defending the methods and judgments of the magistrates. The acrimonious pamphlet warfare that he carried on with Robert Calef did nothing but harm his cause, himself, and his father; and together they were singled out as chiefly responsible for the miscarriage of justice in Salem, while Samuel Sewall, another of the hanging judges, having the good grace to stand up in public meeting and to acknowledge his mistake, went unscathed. Cotton Mather, self-right-eous and orthodox, and convinced that as one of the elect of God he could not have done wrong, never yielded an iota.

A few years later the Overseers of Harvard, respon-sive to the liberal rationalism to which the College had gone over, invoked an old law by which the presi-dent was required to live in Cambridge. Increase Mather, whose church and home were in Boston, was declared ineligible and forced to resign. When the trustees went on to appoint Samuel Willard, another nonresident, thus pointedly blinking the law which had served to rid them of the Mathers, it became clear to them how the wind was blowing. In the western part of the Bay Colony, Solomon Stoddard of Northampton inaugurated policies abhorrent to them; while in Boston itself Elisha Cooke, the one-time associate of Increase Mather in making repre-sentations against Andros to King William, turned against them to become the leader of the political opposition. Another blow that was especially hard to bear was the establishment of the Brattle Street Church in Boston under Benjamin Colman in 1699, and the institution in that church of liberal beliefs and practices against which the Mathers had held the line all along. While their power and influence were thus severely curtailed, they remained prominent fig-ures, fighting a courageous though losing battle, but still attaining occasional triumphs, as in their success-ful scheming to secure the appointment of Joseph Dudley as governor. But once Dudley was in office, he repudiated them and their policies, thus forcing them into new schemes and intrigues to effect his removal.

Shorn of much of his hold on the public by the failure of his father to maintain his political dominance, Cotton turned his abundant energies and versatility more and more into purely intellectual pursuits and to the preparation of his more substantial books. Following his *Memorable Providences, Relating to Witchcraft and Possessions* (1689) and *The Wonders of the Invisible World* (1693), both reflecting the issues that culminated in the sad affair at Salem, he wrote the *Magnalia Christi Americana: Or, the Ecclesiastical History of New England* (1702), a compendium of history, theology, science, politics, diplomacy, and every other subject vitally affecting seventeenth-century America. His *Angel of Bethesda* is a medical manual, and *The Christian Philosopher* (1721) is a summary of the scientific knowledge of the day, in which the facts of science are used to support religion. As an attempt to reconcile religion and science and as an anticipation of the Emersonian dictum that "the religion that is afraid of science dishonors God and commits suicide," it demonstrates the catholicity of Mather's interests and disproves the traditional concept of him as a man whose mind was closed to all innovation. A presentation of the world as well planned, ordered, and beauteous, an enforcement of the idea that to study nature is to realize God's benevolence, and an argument for the idea that man can appreciate his Maker by the exercise of his observation and reason, this book presents ideas well advanced over those espoused by him earlier in his career, and furnished proof that, far from representing a Puritan type of mind that had become "ossified," Cotton Mather was capable of entertaining new ideas and developing intellectually even in his old age.

His *Psalterium Americanum* (1718) is an experiment in translating the Psalms while adapting them to metrical rendition. *Bonifacius: An Essay upon the Good that is to be Devised and Designed* (1710), better known as *Essays to Do Good*, remains one of the classics in that type of ethical writings. Another of his works distinguished for "practical piety" is the *Manductio ad Ministerium. Directions for a Candidate of the Ministry* (1726), a very comprehensive manual or guidebook for young men preparing for the service of the Lord, offering sound advice on social and aesthetic as well as on spiritual and professional matters. It is written "heartily, with real enthusiasm for the subject and with greater directness and simplicity of style" than his other works exhibit. Among the biographies of the 114 men and 20 women that he wrote, *The Life of Phips*, while one of the most entertaining, illustrates some of his greatest faults as a biographer. It poses, as Professor Kenneth Murdock has observed, the interesting and insoluble question "of how far the book was written to exalt himself and his father and to defend their political tenets, and how far it was designed as a tribute to Sir William Phips." All in all, his *Parentator: Memoirs of Remarkables in the Life and Death of Increase Mather* (1724) is his most satisfactory biography. Despite its obviously favorable picture of his father, it stands in no bad light when compared with English works of the same type produced during the same period.

Besides these books, he kept an elaborate *Diary* (published in volumes VII–VIII of the *Massachusetts Historical Society Collections* for 1911-2), wrote numerous reports of his scientific observations for the Royal Society of London, penned his skillful *Political Fables*, and recorded his extensive biblical learning in the six ponderous folio volumes, entitled *Biblia Americana*, that are still preserved in manuscript by the Massachusetts Historical Society, besides numerous lesser works left in manuscript at his death.

In the *Manductio*, *The Christian Philosopher*, and the *Political Fables*, Mather illustrates the fact that he could write simply and directly, without the pedantry, show of erudition, circumlocution, and allusiveness of the "fantastic school" that overload the style of his biographical and historical writings with the surplusage of a "book-suffocated" mind.

Despite its faults of style and its numerous instances of special pleading, the *Magnalia Christi Americana* remains his most important book and provides his chief claim to a position of prominence as a writer. Ambitious in scope and purpose, its two bulky volumes are divided into seven books: (1) a history of the settlement of New England; (2) "the lives of the governors and magistrates of New England that have been shields unto the churches of New England"; (3) "the lives of sixty famous divines by whose ministry the churches of New England have been planted and continued"; (4) the history of Harvard College and of "some eminent persons educated therein"; (5) "the faith and order of the churches"; (6) "many illustrious discoveries and demonstrations of the Divine Providences in remarkable mercies and judgments"; and (7) "a book of the wars of the Lord," including "the afflictive disturbances which the churches of New England have suffered from their various adversaries," such as the Devil, Separatists, Familists, Antinomians, Arminians, Arians, Socinians, Quakers, clerical impostors, and Indians.

However circumscribed Mather's political and theological influence became during his later years, he continued active in founding organizations for social betterment, including proposals for the education of Negroes and missions to the far corners of the earth. His correspondence in the interest of these public-spirited measures was voluminous, and the names of his foreign correspondents read like a roster of all the learned men of the world, regardless of nationality, language, or distance. He braved unintelligent popular opinion that regarded diseases like the smallpox as a visitation from God, not to be interfered with by scientific or any other earthly measures, by introducing inoculation in Boston, despite threats of personal violence and a bomb hurled through his bedroom window with this note attached: "Cotton Mather, you Dog; Dam you: I'l inoculate you with this, with a Pox to you." In recognition of his learning and scientific attainments, he was elected a Fellow of the Royal Society in 1713, to join the exceedingly small number of Americans similarly honored.

Bookish, but no mere bookworm, instructive and pious but also an engaging conversationalist, Cotton Mather was more than an ordinary man. A vast reader, he contrived somehow or other to lay his hands on virtually all the significant books of the world. His manner of riding posthaste through an author, penciling as he went along, and reducing the whole substance of a book to two or three sentences, which he transcribed into his book of "Common Places" of "Quotidiana," whence they could be revived at his leisure, was something to behold. It was what enabled the Reverend Joshua Gee, in his sermon on the Death of Cotton Mather, to pay tribute to "the capacity of his mind, the readiness of his wit, the vastness of his reading, the strength of his memory . . . the tenor of his most entertaining and profitable conversation." Few men of his generation, or of later generations, could, with equal justice, say of themselves what he said of himself: "I am able with little study to write in seven languages. I feast myself with the sweets of all sciences which the more polite part of mankind ordinarily pretend to. I am entertained with all kinds of histories, ancient and modern. I am no stranger to the curiosities which, by all sorts of learning, are brought to the curious. These intellectual pleasures are far beyond any sensual ones."

JONATHAN EDWARDS (1703–1758)

Jonathan Edwards, the greatest of American theologians, was the last great champion of Calvinism. When he was born in 1703, at East Windsor, Connecticut, liberalism at Harvard had already driven Increase Mather into retirement; and Cotton Mather, exerting every effort to stave off the further decline of orthodoxy in New England, was working with might and main to serve the best interests of Yale, established in 1701 as a bulwark of defense against the rising tide of rationalism. Edwards came to play a very similar rôle for his generation to that which fate decreed for Cotton Mather in his time and place. For Yale, too, became infected with the new views shortly after Edwards' graduation in 1720, so that the Calvinists soon chalked off Yale as an asset to their cause, and in 1746 founded the College of New Jersey, later Princeton University, to stem the tide. Shortly after his *Freedom of the Will* (1754) established Edwards as the greatest living defender of the Calvinist faith, the trustees of Princeton called him from his obscure missionary post among the Indians at Stockbridge, Massachusetts, to assume the presidency of "Old Nassau." Whatever he might have done there for the cause was stopped in 1758 by his sudden death, brought on by inoculation against smallpox, within a few months after his inauguration.

Edwards, the fifth of eleven children and only son of a Calvinist preacher, was of orthodox ministerial ancestry. His father's service for more than sixty years in one congregation bespeaks his worth. For lack of good schools at East Windsor, young Edwards' schoolroom became his father's study, where he progressed so well under his father's direction that he entered Yale in 1716, during his thirteenth year. Already as a boy he was passionately fond of study, not only acquiring a knowledge of Latin, Greek, and Hebrew writings, but being especially interested in the pursuit of abstruse subjects. He early trained himself to read with pen or pencil in hand, and not only to think as he went along, but to put his thoughts into exact language, with the result that he early acquired an extraordinary perspicacity of mind.

Moses Coit Tyler relates the following story to illustrate the lad's unusual sagacity at the age of twelve.

Hearing that an older boy in the neighborhood held the opinion that the soul is material, and that it remained in the body until the resurrection day, young Edwards, instead of debating the question in the typical boyish fashion, wrote his friend a playful letter, ironically professing to be on the point of adopting the same opinions, but humbly submitting for solution a number of questions which served most ingeniously and effectively to expose the absurdities of his friend's doctrines. Here already are evident the peculiarities of Edwards' mind—a keenness of analysis, a faculty for discovering the absurdities involved in a false proposition, an unusual ability to set forth these absurdities in a manner at once fair and irresistible, an engaging sense of raillery, freedom from any arrogance of tone, and an adroit use of the Socratic strategy of a deferential manner in debate.

As an undergraduate at Yale (hence before his eighteenth year) he began the keeping of a notebook in which he tried to put into precise form the thoughts that came to him on subjects like being, cause, space, time, motion, matter, consciousness, union of mind and body, and personal identity. The following notation under the heading of "The Place of Minds" illustrates the nature of these early intellectual interests.

Our common way of conceiving of what is spiritual, is very gross, and shadowy, and corporeal, with dimensions, and figure, and so forth. If we would get a right notion of what is spiritual, we must think of thought, or inclination, of delight. How large is that thing in the mind which they call a thought? Is love square, or round? Is the surface of hatred rough, or smooth? Is joy an inch, or a foot, in diameter? These are spiritual things; and why should we then form such a ridiculous idea of spirits, as to think them so long, so thick, or so wide, or to think there is a necessity of their being square, or round, or some other certain figure?

Already as a lad of sixteen or seventeen he worked out for himself a system of idealistic philosophy that is essentially the same as Berkeley's. For example, at the end of his notes on "Being," while considering the relation between ideal reality and material existence, he asked:

What, then, is to become of the universe? Certainly, it exists nowhere but in the Divine mind. . . . Those beings which have knowledge and consciousness are the only proper, and real, and substantial beings; inasmuch as the being of other things is only by these. From thence we may see the gross mistake of those who think material things the most substantial beings, and spirits more like a shadow; whereas spirits only are properly substance. . . . The material universe exists only in the mind. . . . All material existence is only idea.

No wonder that with a mind so inclined he should devour eagerly the metaphysical books which he found in the Yale library. As a sophomore he discovered Locke's *Essay Concerning Human Understanding,* and fell upon it, he tells us, with a greater delight "than the most greedy miser finds when gathering up handsful of silver and gold from some newly discovered treasure."

While he continued to pursue philosophical inquiries with a passion, he was also interested in scientific questions. Already as a boy at East Windsor, he had indulged his curiosity about things in the realm of natural science. Out of this interest grew his composition on spiders, which his father encouraged him to write and to send to a learned correspondent in Europe with whom the elder Edwards was in the habit of exchanging intelligences and letters on scientific, metaphysical, and religious topics. In the resulting essay on spiders, Edwards detailed with great precision of statement and with equal cogency of reasoning his own observations, in a manner to make spiders as interesting as, many years later, Darwin was to make earthworms. Some years after, as a tutor at Yale, he pursued his scientific researches with great diligence, especially in physics and astronomy; and original notes of the time reveal that his acute, ingenious, and original mind anticipated a number of important scientific theories and discoveries. He did enough in mathematical investigations, in the physical sciences, and in linguistic studies to show that, given adequate outward facilities, he might easily have acquired the same fame in these areas that his contributions to mental science and divinity merit.

The intense intellectual training to which he subjected himself as a student was accompanied by equally rigorous moral and spiritual discipline. Much troubled about his own faith and salvation, he made, between 1720 and 1723, a series of seventy resolutions by which to regulate his life. The following are typical: "To live with all my might, while I do live." "To do whatever I think to be my *duty.*" "Never to do any thing which I should be afraid to do, if it were the last hour of my life." "When I feel pain, to think of the pains of Martyrdom, and of Hell."

"Never to do any thing for revenge." "Never to speak anything but the pure and simple verity." "Never to give over in the least or slacken my fight with my corruptions, however unsuccessful I may be." On September 23, 1723, he made the important observation that "old men seldom have any advantage of new discoveries, because they are beside the way of thinking to which they have been so long used," and accordingly he resolved, "If ever I live to years, that I will be impartial to hear the reasons of all pretended discoveries, and receive them if rational, how long soever I have been used to another way of thinking."

Thus he sought to develop alike in scientific knowledge and moral perfection during the years between his graduation in 1720 and his becoming in 1726 the colleague of his grandfather Solomon Stoddard in the Northampton parish. Yet, through the earlier of the intervening years, two of which were devoted to studying divinity at Yale, another as pastor to a Presbyterian congregation in New York City, and the last two to tutoring at Yale, he felt the lack of a third element in his soul—the sense of religious perfection, the development of his religious affections toward an exalted, mystical sense of sweet and absolute dependence on God's sovereignty. His struggles came to a head in 1721, when he felt a conversion, described in the following terms:

From my childhood up, my mind had been full of objections against the doctrine of God's sovereignty, in choosing whom he would to eternal life, and rejecting whom he pleased; leaving them eternally to perish, and be everlastingly tormented in hell. It used to appear like a horrible doctrine to me. But I remember the time very well, when I seemed to be convinced, and fully satisfied, as to this sovereignty of God, and his justice in thus eternally disposing of men, according to his sovereign pleasure. . . . But I have often, since that first conviction, had quite another kind of sense of God's sovereignty than I had then. I have often since had not only a conviction, but a *delightful* conviction. The doctrine has very often appeared exceedingly pleasant, bright, and sweet. Absolute sovereignty is what I love to ascribe to God. . . .

The first instance, that I remember, of that sort of inward, sweet delight in God and divine things, that I have lived much in since, was on reading these words, I Tim. i. 17. *Now unto the King eternal, immortal, invisible, the only wise God, be honour and glory for ever and ever, Amen.* As I read the words, there came into my soul, and was as it were diffused through it, a sense of the glory of a divine Being; a new sense, quite different from anything I ever experienced before. Never any words of Scripture seemed to me as these words did. I thought with myself how beautiful a Being that was, and how happy I should be, if I might enjoy that God, and be rapt up to him in heaven, and be as it were swallowed up in him forever! I

became wholly absorbed in the question of the determined *versus* the free will. Unless the doctrine of necessity could be established, he admitted, "it is, to me, beyond doubt, that the friends of those great gospel truths [i.e., the Calvinists] will but poorly maintain their controversy with the adversaries of those truths [i.e., the Arminians]. They will be obliged often to dodge, shuffle, hide, and turn their backs: and the latter will have a strong fort, from whence they never can be driven, and weapons to use, which those whom they oppose will find no shield to screen themselves from; and they will always puzzle, confound, and keep under the friends of sound doctrine, and glory and vaunt themselves in their advantage over them; and carry their affairs with a high hand, as they have done already for a long time past." Ready to admit that if the opposition could prove the will to be free, the Calvinist position would be utterly lost, he devoted his full energies to the establishment of the doctrine of necessity, calling it "one of the most important truths of moral philosophy that can ever be discussed, and most necessary to be known."

His contribution to this high philosophical problem appeared in 1754 as *A Careful and Strict Enquiry into the Modern Prevailing Notions of that Freedom of Will which is supposed to be Essent.' to Moral Agency, Vertue and Vice, Reward and Punishment, Praise and Blame.* In this book he is not content merely to establish the sovereignty of God according to the time-hallowed practice of the Calvinists, *i.e.*, by referring the matter to the proofs of Scripture; but he chose to meet the opponents on their own ground and with their own weapons by proving it on the bases of logic and metaphysics. His rigorously reasoned book falls naturally into two parts: the first containing his positive argument for the principle of necessity, together with his definitions of the terms "liberty" and "freedom," and the second, his answers to the objections raised by the Arminians. Both rest upon one fundamental postulate: "I assert that nothing ever comes to pass without a Cause," and the corollaries (1) that it is the strongest motive that moves the will, and (2) that man is always moved in the direction of what seems to him most agreeable. Careful to exclude any notion of independent activity on the part of the will, he considered the will as purely passive. That is, the will is always of necessity drawn in the direction of the greatest apparent good, which is to say that the actions of the will are necessarily determined by something outside itself. Thus the will itself appeared to have no *freedom*, while man still retained *liberty*; for *liberty* he defined as "the

power, opportunity, or advantage that any one has to do as he pleases, or conducting in any respect, according to his pleasure, without considering how his pleasure comes to be as it is." The question, as Edwards sees it, is: Can a man do what he wills? Not, Can he will as he wills? As long as man is able to *do* what he chooses, he is free, although he may not be able to choose his choices. Having defined liberty as the ability of man to do as he wills, Edwards went on to assert that no higher liberty than this could be conceived, but this liberty did not presuppose that man's will is able to modify the desire or choice that, in the first instance, determined the will. Thus Edwards does not so much deny the freedom of the will as define it in such a way as to limit it to the power of acting solely upon impulses from outside itself, in the generation of which the mind, or will, is wholly passive.

In the second part of his treatise he took up the objections of the opposition to the doctrine of necessity, disposing of them one by one by bringing them to their *reductio ad absurdum*, at the same time that he traced back, through the labyrinth of causation, all effects to an all-inclusive, all-enduring First Cause, which itself is uncaused, and hence superhuman, or supernatural, or from God, since in the purely human realm an uncaused effect is inconceivable.

While thus arguing quite logically from his original assumptions, Edwards succeeded in proving to his satisfaction the central doctrine of his faith—the absolute dependence of man on the absolute sovereignty of God. His book remains the most original contribution of colonial America to philosophic thought. But Edwards did not succeed in saying the last word on the subject and settling the matter for all time, for the perennial philosophic controversy regarding free will and determinism still goes on among theorists with some slight shifts in the grounds and methods of debate.

By the irony of fate Edwards' championship of revivalism and his insistence on "conversion" as the sole ground of salvation supplied the final blow to destroy the theocratic system that he later labored to uphold. And in this later effort, beginning with *The Freedom of the Will*, to restore Puritanism to its pristine glory, the rigor of his systematic philosophical writing served only to expose in stark and naked relief the humanly intolerable grotesqueries of the Calvinistic dogma, in a way effectively and finally to doom it.

Edwards' crowning work on the freedom of the will failed to achieve the high purpose for which he designed it. It brought the theoretical philosopher very little nearer the solution of his problem; while the ordinary man commonly contents himself with Dr. Samuel Johnson's dictum about the free will when he observed that "all theory is against it, all experience for it." Or he may take the position of Dr. Oliver Wendell Holmes, who observed (possibly with Edwards' logical argument in mind) at the end of his poem on "The Wonderful One-Hoss Shay," which was built to outlast eternity, only to collapse—

> All at once, and nothing first,—
> Just as bubbles do when they burst.
>
> End of the wonderful one-hoss shay.
> Logic is logic. That's all I say.

After *The Freedom of the Will*, Edwards produced several more important treatises: (1) *The Nature of True Virtue*, (2) *Concerning the End for which God Created the World* (both written in 1755 but first published posthumously as *Two Dissertations* in 1765), and (3) *The Great Christian Doctrine of Original Sin Defended* (1758), thus rounding out and unifying his system.

Readers of Edwards often encounter difficulties trying to reconcile his earlier transcendental tendencies as expressed in the *Personal Narrative* and *The Treatise Concerning Religious Affections* with his later Calvinistic position as promulgated in *The Freedom of the Will* and *The Great Christian Doctrine of Original Sin Defended*. The *Personal Narrative*, for example, abounds in moods of exalted rapture during which the virtue of holiness appeared to him as bright, charming, and serene; religion was a joyful experience, and the things of the spirit were "immensely and most exquisitely beautiful." Edwards, almost alone among Puritan theologians, succeeded in transmuting religious experience into forms of lofty and enduring beauty; and the *Personal Narrative* is excellent even when judged by the aesthetic standards of pure literature. Though his words are sometimes incapable of carrying the burden of his ecstatic vision, he nevertheless possessed, as Professor Walter F. Taylor says, "the romantic gift of suggesting far reaches and overtones of experience that words, by their very nature, cannot fully convey," and his mysticism appeals to human traits that are immemorial and enduring. "No religious autobiography in English," concludes Professor Taylor, "is so rich in poetry as the *Personal Narrative*."

To the younger Edwards, feeling his way along the path of mysticism and transcendentalism, rediscovering the doctrine of the inner life, the subjection of will to the natural desires of man was not a fearful and horrible thing; for they had led, in his case at least, to that sweet inwardness of affection that found extreme pleasure in "taking a trembling walk with God." And the first flush of his tremendous success as an evangelist, when hundreds professed themselves "converted" to God by his excitation within them of the religious emotions, supplied him with confirmatory faith in the efficacy of the affections. However, subsequent events, attended by the growing responsibilities and severe trials of life that he experienced and the sobered reflections of maturity, led him to re-examine the psychological bases of his thinking and eventually to doubt whether the emotional man were quite worthy of implicit trust. And as he questioned his earlier faith in the free exercise of the affections, he placed greater emphasis on rational restraint. There was no complete change of front, but a shift of emphasis from faith in the heart to a trust of the head.

This very complex development of his mind, too involved to be stated here, is treated excellently in the Introduction by Professors Clarence H. Faust and Thomas H. Johnson to their book of *Selections from Jonathan Edwards* (New York, 1935). It is indicated summarily by their comments on the complex of ideas that welled up in New England under the guise of humanitarianism during Edwards' younger years. Humanitarians emphasized "the belief that man in the savage or 'natural' state is a better creature than when he is educated. Under theocracy sound learning was assumed the root of true religion, but for the humanitarians too much learning was a dangerous thing; for them the inner light needed not training but release, that the splendor might escape."

These doctrines, taught later in various forms by Rousseau and the French Revolutionists, had earlier found expression in the philosophy of the deists and the Quakers, and indeed by such leaders as John Wesley and George Whitefield—itinerant exhorters whose stress upon their faith that conversion, or the conviction that a "new light" had shone upon them, gave rise to a tide of revival meetings which Edwards supported.

Incompatible as these philosophies are, we see Edwards trying to reconcile them as their vectors cut through his career, and the tragedy that overtook him may be perceived more clearly if the student watches their intersections without losing sight of their direction. It is in moments when Edwards attempted to bring his theocratic and humanitarian principles together, when he sought to establish in logical relationship the intellectual love of God with human emotions, that his mysticism is most evident—as, for example, in the *Treatise concerning Religious Affections*. The tragedy inherent in the *Farewell Sermon* is that Edwards's earlier support of emotional relief, his devotion to 'New Lightism,' had been lessons too well learned by his congregation. His effort to re-assert theocratic government came tardily, and the casuistry to which he resorted in an attempt to reconcile the eternal antinomies passed over the heads of his pastoral children. Thus he was compelled to abandon his pulpit.

Jonathan Edwards never abandoned his fundamentally psychological approach to the problems of theology and philosophy, as first outlined in the *Treatise Concerning Religious Affections,* or changed his terminology, or admitted that he had been wrong in his defense of the Great Awakening; but after that upheaval he was impelled, by natural causes, to fight henceforth for the logical and rational re-establishment of Calvinism in terms of determinism, depravity, and election.

Edwards' position in the history of American literature rests not merely on the cogency of his logic or the systematic structure of his philosophy. He is a man of letters in his own right and in the full meaning of the terms. Following his thought, especially in his more technical works, is often hard work; but it is so because his matter, not his manner, occasions the difficulty. His style does not get in the way of his ideas, as does that of Cotton Mather. His manner of writing is direct and precise, dignified but clear. Often he is graphic in his representations, and not infrequently his sentences are illuminated by telling figurativeness, though never remotely resembling the pedantic allusiveness or fantastic imagery of Cotton Mather. He is notably free from clichés and jargon. His style becomes the perfect medium of the quiet, unostentatious ebb and flow of his serious and profound thought in a manner to make him a great artist and a master of English prose writing.

BENJAMIN FRANKLIN (1706–1790)

Franklin, only three years younger than Edwards, outlived the defender of Puritanism by thirty-two years. As Edwards' order passed, Franklin became the champion of a new order, that of the Enlightenment, scientific deism, political liberalism, and humanitarian progressivism. While "Edwards' conversions at Northampton were reckoned as thirty a week, Franklin was selling 10,000 copies of *Poor Richard's Almanac*." And when, after three months as president of Princeton, Edwards died in 1758, Franklin, having already "drawn lightning from heaven," was preparing soon to "snatch the sceptre from tyrants." While Edwards devoted his life to "exploring the fearful mysteries of God," Franklin was "making himself thoroughly at home with Man"; for as Edwards incorporated in his large nature the religious experience of his times, so Franklin represented the secular experience of the eighteenth century. During his life, which all but spanned the century, Franklin's industrious versatility touched every important movement of the age. He was active as a tradesman, printer, publisher, publicist, propagandist, economist, public official, diplomat, statesman, philosopher, man of letters, philanthropist, inventor, scientist, moralist, scientific deist, and man of the world. His copious mind and industrious versatility furnished him points of contact with men as various as Increase and Cotton Mather, the Puritan priests, Whitefield the Methodist, Rush the physician, West the artist, Webster the lexicographer, and Jay, Adams, Jefferson, Washington, and a host of other American statesmen; while abroad he met the deist Voltaire, the leveler Tom Paine, the celebrated North, the ministerial Pitt, the chemist Priestley, the statesman Burke, the despotic minister Vergennes, and the aristocrats of Louis' court in France. In his youthful years he set type in the London of Pope and Swift's day and talked with Bernard Mandeville, author of *The Fable of the Bees; or, Private Vices Public Benefits* (1723). In middle life he associated with the members of the Royal Society in London and the Physiocrats in France, while submitting to Parliamentary examination in London and winning diplomatic triumphs in Paris. He was as capable in affairs of state and diplomacy as he was gracious in high social circles or honored among learned groups, employing his pen with equal finesse, whether writing documents of state or exchanging billets-doux with the ladies of the French court. In his old age he read the tidings of the Fall of the Bastille; he heard the wranglings of the Constitutional Convention, throwing his wisdom and influence on the side of adoption; and he lived to see the United States of America established.

Franklin's *Autobiography* has made the details of his earlier life a matter of common knowledge. The fifteenth of seventeen children of a thrifty tallow chandler of Boston, sprung from humble, sturdy stock, he inherited from his father not only his strong physical constitution but also "solid judgment in prudential matters." On his mother's side he was descended from Peter Folger, one of the early New England settlers, of whom Cotton Mather thought well enough to commemorate him in the *Magnalia* as "a learned and godly Englishman." He had enjoyed only about two years of schooling when his father put him to work cutting wicks, filling candle molds, boiling soap, and running errands—work very little to Benjamin's taste, which turned more to books. He soon exhausted the slender stock of his father's library, which consisted chiefly of the New England historians and theologians. With his first money he bought a copy of Bunyan's *Pilgrim's Progress*, and after he had thoroughly digested it, traded it for Burton's *Historical Collections*, a class of writings for which he had a special fondness.

A new period of his life began when, at the age of twelve, he was apprenticed to his brother James, a printer and the editor of the *New-England Courant*. His mind profited by the information he gathered from the material he set to type; and, what is equally important, his training as a typesetter and proofreader taught him accuracy and dexterity in handling words precisely. Later he freely acknowledged, "It has ever since been a pleasure to me to see good workmen handle their tools; and it has been useful to me, having learned so much by it as to be able to do little jobs myself." That is, he came to look upon words like tools; and while he escaped becoming a poet, as he laughingly admitted, his use of words in much the same way that a master workman handles the implements of his trade led to his development of an effective, workmanlike prose style that eventually became his most useful accomplishment and the principal means to his advancement.

Meanwhile he steadily added to his self-acquired store of knowledge, passing from Plutarch's *Lives* to Defoe's *Essay on Projects*, from which he doubtless gathered early a good deal of the inventive zeal that he later displayed. Cotton Mather's *Essays to Do Good* set his mind in the direction of the humanitarian purposefulness for which he became distinguished. Careful reading of Shaftesbury and Collins made him "a real doubter" in many points of religious doctrine, while Xenophon's *Memorable Things of Socrates* led to his adoption of the Socratic strategy in argumentation, even to making himself a nuisance to people by leading them into confusing and contradictory positions in theological questions. Locke *On the Human Understanding* prepared his mind for the acceptance of the experimental, empirical, and inductive method of studying the physical world; while his exercises in turning the *Spectator* papers into his own words (both prose and verse) and then back into Addisonian prose were all-important for the development of his clear and effective prose style.

Contact with printer's type and ink exerted another influence on young Franklin—an itch to see his writing in print. In the *Autobiography* he relates how, fearing that his brother would not print any of the writings of his apprentice if his authorship were known, he contrived to slip one of his anonymous compositions under the door, taking care himself to be present when it was discovered.

It was found in the morning, and communicated to his writing friends when they call'd in as usual. They read it, commented on it in my hearing, and I had the exquisite pleasure of finding it met with their approbation, and that, in their different guesses at the author, none were named but men of some character among us for their learning and ingenuity.

Thus were initiated the series of fourteen *Dogood Papers*, printed anonymously in the *New-England Courant* during 1722.

Soon thereafter, young Franklin found his apprenticeship under his brother getting more and more intolerable, and in 1723 he resolved to run away. His entry into Philadelphia as described in the *Autobiography*, however humble and poor a figure he cut at the time, turned out to be only the first step in a long triumphal march through competence and achievements, to successes and honors such as no earlier American had won. It can hardly be doubted that Franklin's going to Philadelphia was one of the most fortunate events in his life, for in that relatively cosmopolitan and genuinely friendly city, opportunities for advancement were offered to the runaway apprentice that might never have come to him in his native city. Thus Franklin's case becomes an early illustration of the quipster's remark that "Boston is a good place to be *from*."

In Philadelphia, while working for the printer, Samuel Keimer, he prospered, even to being patronized by Governor Keith, who sent him to England on a commission to buy type and a printing press to be set up in his behalf by Keith. When Keith's promised credit did not arrive, Franklin, thrown on his own resources for a livelihood, found work in the large printing establishments of London. Alert to learn the latest improvements of the trade, he turned his disappointment to advantage, and when he returned to Philadelphia, he was a far more experienced and efficient printer than when he had left eighteen months before. During his stay in London he also expanded his knowledge of men and of books, while moving in the infectious atmosphere of liberal thought represented by Henry Pemberton and Bernard Mandeville.

Pursuing his frugal, prosperous career, he set himself up in 1729 as an independent printer in Philadelphia. The next year he tucked away in his pocket a nice contract by which he became the printer for the Pennsylvania Assembly for the next thirty-four years. He became prominent in the Masonic lodge and began to engage in civic and philanthropic enterprises while forming profitable printing partnerships and other business alliances as he progressed, with the result that in 1748 his industry, thrift, and foresight had rewarded him with a safe competence. He was thus enabled, at the age of forty-two, to retire from the active management of his business and to devote, for another forty-two years, all of his time to those public, philanthropic, and scientific affairs which had come to absorb more and more of his time, and which he preferred to the acquisition of greater wealth.

Franklin's well-known advocacy of the prudential virtues of thrift and industry is often stressed in a way to suggest that he was motivated solely by self-interest. He was, it may freely be admitted, a practical moralist, a successful tradesman and printer, a shrewd propagandist and financier, a clever diplomat, and a disciple of efficiency, but he was also a disinterested inventor who refused to take out patents for his contrivances, a philanthropic humanitarian, and a scientist, philosopher, and statesman who gave of himself with the liberality of a prince in the service of his fellow men. He had a true passion for scientific and philosophical inquiries, and throughout his young manhood and middle life he complained that business, public and private, prevented his pursuing his "philosophical amusements" and scientific investigations. In 1765, upon completing his negotiations in England in behalf of the Pennsylvania Assembly, he promised Lord Kames that he would engage in no other political affairs; but year after year his people called upon him for services which only he could render; and in 1785, in his eightieth year, when he entertained the hope that his countrymen would grant him rest and leisure during the few years that remained after his ceaseless efforts in their behalf, he was drafted to serve for three years as President of the commonwealth of Pennsylvania. He could only comment:

I have not firmness enough to resist the unanimous desire of my country folks, and I find myself harnessed again to their service. . . . They engrossed the prime of my life. They have eaten my flesh, and seem resòlved now to pick my bones.

In his public life he rose from the position of justice of the peace to clerk of the Pennsylvania Assembly in 1736, postmaster of Philadelphia in 1737, deputy postmaster-general to the colonies in 1753, and so on to commissioner from Pennsylvania to the Albany Congress in 1754, where he proposed the Albany Plan of Union. As supervisor of the construction of forts in the province of Pennsylvania, he aided General Braddock in getting supplies and transportation during 1755 and unsuccessfully urged the General to adopt the methods of frontier warfare that might have averted his defeat. He became colonial agent in London for Pennsylvania in 1757 and again in 1764; by 1770 he represented also Georgia, New Jersey, and Massachusetts. He was Postmaster-General under the Confederation. In 1775 he was a member of the Philadelphia Committee of Safety, a delegate to the Second Continental Congress, and a member of the Committee of Secret Correspondence. In 1776 he was commissioner to Canada, president of the Constitutional Convention, one of the committee to frame the Declaration of Independence, and commissioner of Congress to the French court. He became the chief arbiter and signer of the commercial treaty and of the alliance for mutual defense with France, signer of the Treaty of

Paris in 1783, negotiator of treaties with Sweden (1783) and with Prussia (1785), president of the commonwealth of Pennsylvania from 1785 to 1787, and finally, delegate from Pennsylvania to the Constitutional Convention. Among all the illustrious men of his time he is the only one whose name is affixed to all four principal documents of the Revolutionary period: the Declaration of Independence, the treaty of alliance with France, the treaty 'of peace with Great Britain, and the Constitution of the United States.

Franklin's passion for service manifests itself nowhere more tellingly than in his educational and generally philanthropic projects. As a man who in his youth had lacked social advantages and a proper education, he made up these wants as best he could through self-study. He read assiduously during hours stolen from sleep or recreation, confessing that his "only recreation" for many years after his return from England in 1726 was his reading. He found time somehow to make himself one of the best-read men of his time, even to acquiring Latin and the modern languages of French, Spanish, Italian, and German at a time when the classical languages were considered the only linguistic requirements of a scholar. But his zeal for education did not stop with himself, although such organizations as the Junto and the Philadelphia Library Company were certainly partially motivated by his own desire for self-improvement. His first major educational project was the formation in 1727 of the Junto, or Leather Apron Club, which became in its day "the best school of philosophy, morality, and politics that then existed in the province." Recalling Defoe's proposals for the formation of Friendly Societies and Mather's urging, in his *Essays to Do Good*, the formation of mutual improvement societies, Franklin also took a cue from the organization of Masonic lodges as he had observed them in London. The members of the Junto were urged to communicate to one another everything significant "in history, morality, poetry, physics, travel, mechanic arts, or other parts of knowledge." Their utilitarian object was equalled only by their humanitarian purposes. The members were sworn to "love truth for truth's sake," but also to be "serviceable" and "to love mankind in general, of whatever profession or religion soever," and to oppose persecution "for mere speculative opinions, or external ways of worship." They cultivated a rigorous ethical program, and members were encouraged to report not only "unhappy effects of intemperance" and of "imprudence, or passion, or of any other vice or folly," but also the "happy effects of temperance, of prudence.

of moderation." Thus they encouraged tolerance, the empirical method, scientific disinterestedness, and humanitarianism.

Out of the Junto grew the Philadelphia Library Company in 1731 to become "the mother of all the North American subscription libraries." It grew rapidly, and an inventory of 1757 shows that by that time it owned what was necessary for an alert mind to discover all the theses and their implications— philosophic, religious, political, scientific, and social —that were needed to overthrow priest and king, dogma and authority. Franklin also played a prominent part in the founding of the American Philosophical Society in 1744, becoming its first secretary and subsequently its president. In 1749 he founded the Philadelphia Academy, later the College, and eventually the University of Pennsylvania. In his *Proposal for Promoting Useful Knowledge among the British Plantations in America* (1743) and the *Proposals Relating to the Education of Youth in Pensilvania* (1749) he urged the necessity of supplying "the succeeding Age with Men qualified to serve the Publick with Honour to themselves, and to their Country." Designed for the citizenry rather than for the clergy, offering instruction in English and the modern foreign, as well as the classical, languages and literatures, in physical culture, natural history, mechanics, mathematics (especially arithmetic), and gardening, rather than sectarian theology, Franklin's academy was more utilitarian and secular than any other school then existing in the colonies.

But no amount of learning or theorizing, unless it could be turned to use, was worth much to Franklin: "I have always set a greater value on the character of a *doer of good* than on any other kind of reputation." Less concerned about the golden pavements in Heaven than that the cobblestones on Chestnut Street should be evenly laid, less troubled about saving his soul from burning in Hell than that there should be a fire company in Philadelphia to protect his own and his neighbor's house, less interested in the light that never was on sea or land than that there should be street lamps to light the belated wayfarer to his home—Franklin set about, with true Yankee practicality, to put theory to use. His inventive ingenuity resulted in many improvements in the techniques of printing, his perfection of the stove that bears his name, and the invention of the lightning rod. He inquired into the causes and cure of smoky chimneys. He instituted a better system of paving, cleaning, and lighting the streets of Philadelphia, methods that were widely adopted elsewhere; he organized the first regularly paid police force in

the colonies; he founded the first fire insurance company in Philadelphia; he organized an efficient fire-fighting company in Philadelphia; he established the first charity hospital in the city; and he inaugurated a postal system in his city and for the colonies without which they could hardly have developed the cohesion necessary to fight and win the war for independence.

Beyond these more practical applications of his desire to improve the lot of mankind on this earth, he turned his curiosity to the realm of natural philosophy, and in 1752 demonstrated the identity of lightning and electricity, going on to a variety of investigations into such subjects as evaporation, ocean temperatures, the course of storms over the Atlantic, the distillation of sea water, the sources of springs, the cultivation of grass, the effects of the sun's rays on cloth, and the efficiency of various mediums for sound. On the strength of his accomplishments in these experiments he was elected a Fellow of the Royal Society of London in 1756 and to membership in other learned or scientific societies of Edinburgh, Göttingen, Rotterdam, Paris, Padua, Madrid, Lyons, Orleans, Manchester, Milan, London, and St. Petersburg, while collecting honorary degrees from Harvard, Yale, William and Mary, the University of St. Andrews, and Oxford, besides numerous medals and awards in honor of his contributions to knowledge. In the end, his international fame rested as much on his character as a statesman, diplomat, and economist as on his scientific and philosophic enquiries. However, in a conversation reputed to have taken place between Joseph II of Austria and himself, he said, "Necessity . . . made me a politician. . . . I was Franklin the *Philosopher* to the world long before I had in fact, become Franklin the *Politician.*" His prior and real interest lay in scientific research and speculation, and there can be little doubt that "his doctrine of scientific deism antedated and conditioned his political, economic, and humanitarian interests."

In his case, science and philosophy reinforced each other in the determination of his religion and in the regulation of his entire outlook on life. For one thing, his fame as a scientist preceded him wherever he went, and in the course of his wide travels in Europe he found himself openly welcomed by, and invited to exchange ideas with, the great savants of England, Holland, Germany, France, Italy, and Spain. In England he associated with liberals like Richard Price, lodged with the philosopher Hume, consulted with Adam Smith, and was on intimate terms with the chemist and political liberal, Joseph Priestley. In

France he knew Voltaire, Turgot, Buffon, Mirabeau, Quesnay, Lavoisier, Robespierre, D'Alembert, Condorcet, La Rochefoucauld, and the Abbé Raynal, besides many others hardly less prominent. While there were great differences among them, they possessed minds that were alike "free, liberal, and inquiring"; and Franklin found in them all confirmation for the rational views and enlightened cast of mind that his early reading had inspired in him.

Following an early reading of Locke, doubts raised concerning the Calvinism in which he had been reared set his mind off on a series of questions from which there was no return to bibliolatry. Passages like the following in Locke induced an *odium theologicum* at the same time exalting the reason as the only proper and efficacious medium for religious inquiries:

> Since . . . the precepts of Natural Religion are plain, and very intelligible to all mankind, and seldom come to be controverted; and other revealed truths, which are conveyed to us by books and languages, are liable to the common and natural obscurities and difficulties incident to words; methinks it would become us to be more careful and diligent in observing the former, and less magisterial, positive, and imperious, in imposing our own sense and interpretations of the latter.
>
> Nothing that is contrary to, and inconsistent with, the clear and self-evident dictates of reason, has a right to be urged or assented to as a matter of faith, wherein reason hath nothing to do.

By the time he reached sixteen, his reading of some of the Boyle lectures (presumably Bentley's *Folly of Atheism* of 1692 and Derham's *Physico-Theology* of 1711-1712), of Anthony Collins' *Priest-craft in Perfection* (1710) and *Discourse of Free-Thinking* (1713), and of Shaftesbury's *Inquiry Concerning Virtue or Merit* and his *Characteristics* had effected a conversion, and he avowed himself a "thorough Deist." In London, while setting up Wollaston's *Religion of Nature Delineated*, he was inspired to write his *Dissertation on Liberty and Necessity, Pleasure and Pain* (1725), which led to an acquaintance with Lyons, author of *The Infallibility of Human Judgement* [*sic*]—a connection which in turn led to an intimacy with Dr. Henry Pemberton, then assisting Newton in the preparation of his third edition of the *Principia*. Thus he came close to the fountain-head from which scientific deism derived its basic principles, and it is not surprising that in 1728 he incorporated the fundamental deistic ideas in his *Articles of Belief and Acts of Religion*—a statement of principles from which apparently he never swerved in any essentials during his natural life. This creed is notable as allowing for only one God and for its

assertion that proper worship of God consists primarily in the cultivation of virtue and the doing good to man. There is no hint of a Christ as a necessary redeemer, of Scripture as the sole revelation, or of atonement for sin by repentance. Fundamentally this is the creed that he reiterated sixty-eight years later in his famous letter to Ezra Stiles:

> Here is my Creed. I believe in one God, Creator of the Universe. That he governs it by his Providence. That he ought to be worshipped. That the most acceptable service we render to him is doing good to his other Children. That the soul of Man is immortal, and will be treated with Justice in another Life respecting its Conduct in this. These I take to be the fundamental Principles of all sound Religion, and I regard them as you do in whatever Sect I meet with them.
>
> As to Jesus of Nazareth, my Opinion of whom you particularly desire, I think the System of Morals and his Religion, as he left them to us, the best the World ever saw or is likely to see; but I apprehend it has received various corrupting Changes, and I have, with most of the present Dissenters in England, some Doubts as to his Divinity; tho' it is a question I do not dogmatize upon, having never studied it, and think it needless to busy myself with it now, when I expect soon an Opportunity of knowing the Truth with less Trouble. I see no harm, however, in its being believed, if that Belief has a good Consequence, as probably it has, of making his Doctrines more respected and better observed. . . .
>
> I shall only add, respecting myself, that, having experienced the Goodness of that Being in conducting me prosperously thro' a long life, I have no doubt of its Continuance in the next, though without the smallest Conceit of meriting such Goodness. . . .

Although his death was hardly more than a month off, Franklin was still the prudential man, and consequently added this characteristic postscript:

> I confide, that you will not expose me to Criticism and censure by publishing any part of this Communication to you. I have ever let others enjoy their religious Sentiments, without reflecting on them for those that appeared to me unsupportable and even absurd. All Sects here, and we have a great Variety, have experienced my good will in assisting them with Subscriptions for building their new Places of Worship; and, as I have never opposed any of their Doctrines, I hope to go out of the World in Peace with them all.

Franklin's creed is a succinct, though moderate, statement of scientific deism as formulated during the seventeenth and eighteenth centuries on the bases of Newtonian science and Lockean psychology. It represents an assertion of the rational credo of Newton, Diderot, and Voltaire over the religious concepts of Luther, Calvin, and Edwards—an Age of Enlightenment superseding an Era of Faith.

Motivated by the amazing discoveries of Newton

respecting the operation of universal laws throughout the cosmos, the men of the Enlightenment came to regard the universe as one gigantic machine, controlled by harmonious, changeless laws, behind which stood an impersonal Creator, who instituted the laws and set them in motion, but who then withdrew himself from his creations, to stand aloof merely to observe their operation. He no longer interferes in the affairs of the world, or changes the laws by which it operates, or works any special providences. The remarkable success of Newton in formulating the laws of motion led the disciples of the Enlightenment to believe that man might penetrate the secrets of nature, that human reason might ultimately "read the thoughts of God." For the attainment of this goal, they argued, man would do better to study the entities of mind and matter in time and space than to quarrel over the meaning of the equivocal terms of the Scriptures. With infinite faith in the benevolence of nature and the ability of man's reason to penetrate to the core of rationality underlying all nature, the scientific rationalist assumed that natural laws are designed to afford man all the happiness he is capable of, provided man brings himself into harmony with those eternal, natural laws. As part of this natural universe, man originally shared in its benevolence, and accordingly the deist had faith in man's goodness as opposed to the Calvinist's belief in man's natural depravity. He was ready to admit the evils of tyranny, priestcraft, poverty, and inequality in the world, but these he referred to long accretions of traditionalism and superstition by which man had fallen from his harmonious adjustment to this divine, universal law and order. What was desired was a rededication of the human reason to the search for this orderliness and a readjustment of man's life and of his environment to the findings of the enlightened reason.

Corollary with these principles deduced from Newtonianism was the psychology and sociology of John Locke, the close friend of Newton, with whom the great mathematician had discussed his theories in detail. Locke had denied innate ideas and all inherited traits supposedly setting men apart from each other. He had affirmed the all-importance of a proper education according to logic and natural principles and the readjustment of man's environment in accordance with those principles by the removal of institutions and conventions inimical to the full, natural, free development of human potentialities. The evils of society could be abolished, it was argued, by a return to the rationally ordered life of the natural man and the overthrow of unnatural or unreasonable conventions and institutions, whether social or economic, throne or altar. Hence the men of the Enlightenment became critics of the *status quo*, breakers of idols, and disciples of progress, professing and practicing humanitarian principles. Doing good to one's fellow man became a satisfactory substitute for an unreasoned worship (or idolatry, as they called it) of God. A religion of practical morality based on rational principles replaced a worship by adoration of a deity resting on faith or authority. "The most acceptable service of God," said Franklin, "is doing good to man." Thus it came to pass that while the Enlightenment sanctioned "a radical attack on ancient wrongs," it also sanctioned a program that had special American connotations—"the ideal of a larger, more satisfactory life for the common man." Franklin, standing squarely in this tradition of the Enlightenment, illustrates its manifold program in (1) his satirical attack on irrational and traditional policies and institutions, (2) his practical humanitarianism, (3) his absorbing interest in scientific inquiries and philosophical liberalism, and (4) his rational and prudential moralism.

Franklin's ethical system is based on human reason and prudential wisdom rather than on religious authority or transcendental duty. The thirteen virtues, as set down in the *Autobiography*, in which he schooled himself, include only four—Temperance, Sincerity, Justice, and Humility—that derive purely or largely from a love of righteousness for its own sake. The other nine must be referred to more worldly considerations—either his love for a systematic and industrious conduct of business or his passion for living on good terms with his fellow men. There was for him no great difference between *moral* virtue and *prudential* wisdom. His form of morality based on rational conduct left far more freedom for the desires of the natural man than did the older systems based on revealed religion. All he desired was rational, temperate self-control, and he was not squeamish about the precise means best designed to achieve that end. The best expression of his practical morality appears in his two *Dialogues* between Philocles and Horatio, written to show that the proper object of conduct is a temperate pleasure. True pleasure, he pointed out, depends upon the conscious choice of what is moral or right, and right is determined by the human reason studying "the Sacred Book of Nature."

It is in connection with his desire to teach his lessons of prudential morality to the common man of his day that we come (after his earlier *Dogood* and *Busy-Body* papers) upon the first significant work of Franklin the writer, or man of letters. Himself a self-made man and a disciple of economic individualism, he was firm in his faith that what was most needed by his clientele of mainly middle-class readers was practical advice on how to develop economic independence in terms of moral integrity and prudential wisdom. Accordingly he set about instructing his fellow men on these heads in *Poor Richard's Almanac*, which circulated annually many thousand copies. Poor Richard, or Richard Saunders, became the purveyor of the sugar-coated pills of pointed jest, witty sayings, popular saws, and prudential preachments which Franklin inserted wherever there was a bit of space in the calendar not filled with other matter. *Poor Richard's Almanac* thus became, during the years from 1732 to 1757, a miscellany of both useful and entertaining knowledge, liberally besprinkled with the sayings of Poor Richard—some new, some old. In 1757 Franklin very cleverly wove these pungent epigrams and proverbial gems into a connected essay, called *The Way to Wealth*. Among typical ones are the following: "Keep your eyes wide open before marriage, half shut afterwards." "He that can have patience can have what he will." "Three may keep a secret if two of them are dead." "God heals, the doctor takes the fee." "Plough deep while sluggards sleep, and you shall have corn to sell and to keep." "Many a little makes a mickle." "Beware of little expenses, for a small leak will sink a great ship." "It is hard for an empty sack to stand upright." "Get all you can, and what you get, hold." "Diligence is the mother of good luck." "God helps them that help themselves." "Dost thou love life, then do not squander time, for that's the stuff life is made of." "The sleeping fox catches no poultry." "There will be sleeping enough in the grave."

The Way to Wealth emphasized individual enterprise in a way that appealed to people just embarking on the exciting adventure of exploiting the vast resources of a new land. The industrial revolution, a machine age, and the complexities of modern urban life had not yet cast any doubts upon the faith that a man's future could be assured by the labor of his own hands. Franklin's *Way to Wealth* put in trenchant words what thousands of Americans were thinking, and to the many others who had not yet advanced to grasp this ideal of American self-sufficiency and self-reliance, Poor Richard became an inspired and revered tutor. The tremendous effect of his philosophy of thrift, industry, and prudence on a young nation during its period of tutelage can hardly be overestimated. Nor was its influence confined to America. By the beginning of the current century

The Way to Wealth had gone through seventy-five editions in English, fifty-six in French, eleven in German, and nine in Italian; was translated also into Spanish, Danish, Swedish, Welsh, Polish, Gaelic, Russian, Bohemian, Dutch, Catalan, Chinese, and modern Greek; and was put into phonetic writing and into Braille. It has been printed at least five hundred times and is today as popular as ever.

Although Franklin never thought of himself as a literary man, in the course of his long career as publisher, statesman, publicist, and diplomat, he tossed off either as by-products or as calculated means to some immediate and practical end hundreds of pamphlets, reports, proposals, articles, essays, letters, dialogues, dissertations, allegories, apologues, fables, and bagatelles, besides lampoons and burlesques, emblems and epigrams. Of them all, his *Autobiography* is the most important single document entitling him to a place of prominence as a writer of *belles-lettres*. A classic of its kind, reaching "virtual perfection in graceful clarity of style," it merits the popularity which it enjoys the world over as a purely literary work. But even it was written, so he declared, less at his own instance than at the ceaseless importunities of friends and strangers, so that he determined it would be a saving of time and energy to himself if he wrote his life down in simple terms that all might read rather than to answer all individual persons who desired information about him, or to give reasons and detail excuses to all and sundry explaining why he had not written his autobiography. Begun in 1771 and added to from time to time until 1789, the *Autobiography* remained incomplete at his death, tracing his life to 1757 only. Remarkable as it is for clarity, it leaves out much of importance even for this first half of his life, before he entered upon the most successful and celebrated part of his career, so that it must be supplemented by others of his numerous writings before anything like a full-bodied picture of the many-sided Franklin emerges. Aside from its stylistic excellence and the great importance of the subject itself, the book is notable for its near approach to true autobiography—its numerous "little, nameless, unremembered" but nonetheless authentic and influential episodes of life, and especially its accuracy and fidelity. He is not the successful man intent on covering up those acts of his that in retrospect he would rather have left undone or those episodes that he preferred neither to remember nor to perpetuate for the delectation of posterity. Franklin blinked none of these unpleasant aspects of his life, but set down with frank fidelity his major "errata" as well as his lesser vices, not neglecting to point out that, his program of self-discipline notwithstanding, he was often disorderly and unmethodical, not always scrupulous in his business, and sometimes overindulgent and immoral. But through it all appears the portrait of a man that is authentic because it is stripped of all pretense and defense, and a character who is lovable because he is human. It cannot be said of Franklin, as it can of Mark Twain, who tried equally hard to write true autobiography, that he "never came within shouting distance of self-revelation."

At the beginning of his long career as an occasional essayist Franklin wrote the fourteen *Dogood* papers which he printed anonymously in his brother's *New-England Courant* during 1722. The six numbers of *The Busy-Body* papers that he wrote in Philadelphia during 1729 are in all essentials a continuation. From time to time he wrote other informal essays, dialogues, and other forms of polite discourse dealing playfully with the vices and follies of men, but, as he grew in age and influence he turned more and more to serious ethical and religious matters, aspects of current political and economic issues, scientific and philosophical investigations, the treatment of Indians and Negroes, colonial defense and military preparedness, forms of government (colonial and intercolonial), and the relations of the colonies to the mother country and to the other European nations. Never ambitious to build for himself a literary reputation, he took no care of his writings, and usually sent them forth to take their chances without so much as affixing his name. When Lord Kames asked him for copies of all his writings, he had to say that he had not kept copies, but would see what could be collected from among his friends. He allowed even his scientific and philosophical opinions to shift for themselves; and once, when his invention of the lightning rod was attacked in print, and friends urged him to publish a rejoinder, he said, "I have never entered into any controversy in defence of my philosophical opinions, I leave them to take their chance in the world. If they are *right*, truth and experience will support them; if *wrong*, they ought to be refuted and rejected. Disputes are apt to sour one's temper and disturb one's quiet. I have no private interest in the reception of my inventions by the world, having never made, nor proposed to make the least profit by any of them." Believing that "there never was a good War, or a bad Peace," he preferred peace to disputation, and his usual manner, when dealing with controversial matters, as he explained in the *Autobiography*, was to say "I conceive," "I apprehend," "I imagine," or "It so appears to me at present" rather than "I declare" or "I assert." Often

he was strongly provoked to take a less deferential line of attack, but he persevered in his resolution, while admitting:

. . . this mode, which I at first put on with some violence to my natural inclination, became at length so easy, and so habitual, that perhaps for these fifty years no one has ever heard a dogmatical expression escape me. And to this habit (after my character of integrity) I think it principally owing that I had early so much weight with my fellow-citizens when I proposed new institutions, or alterations in the old, and so much influence in public councils when I was a member; for I was but a bad speaker, never eloquent, subject to much hesitation in my choice of words, hardly correct in language, and yet I generally carried my points.

But if Franklin took little care of his writings, his friends did it for him. Thus it happened that the reports of his electrical experiments first came to be published, not at his own instigation, but because a correspondent to whom he had communicated his findings, published them in London, without Franklin's knowledge, in 1751 under the title *Experiments and Observations on Electricity, made at Philadelphia in America, by Mr. Benjamin Franklin, and Communicated in Several Letters to Mr. P. Collinson, of London, F. R. S.* This booklet was enlarged in 1752 and again in 1754, and was soon many times republished, in English, Latin, French, German, Dutch, Italian, and other languages. His fame spread, and among common folk in Europe he came to be regarded as a kind of arch-magician, whose renown as an electrician threw an exaggerated and somewhat weird light upon his accomplishments and prestige as a statesman. The vision was made complete by pictures circulated throughout Europe and America showing him seated in an arm chair, with flashes of lightning playing about his head, while underneath appeared a subscription to the effect that he had "seized the lightning from heaven and snatched the sceptre from tyrants." Even the hard-fisted Dr. Johnson professed to believe Franklin the "master-mischief, who has taught his countrymen how to put in motion the engine of political electricity . . . and to give the great stroke by the name of Boston," while lesser people felt that things in the British colonies were well enough were it not for Dr. Franklin, who had, "with a brand lighted from the clouds, set fire to all America."

His stature as an economist and political thinker is revealed in his numerous pamphlets and dissertations in these areas. Ordinarily they are done in a straightforward, expository style of argumentation, a manner calculated to add little to his literary renown. But there are exceptions, notably when he employed satire to subserve his political and diplomatic pur-poses. Like Swift, he enjoyed the practical joke done with a straight face, especially if it could be made to carry a pointed allegory. He scored several highly successful hits in this Swiftian technique of ridiculing an opponent's position by pretending to support it but managing so subtly to distort it as to render it absurd or foolish. For the reception of the first of these successes the ground had been prepared by his admirable *Examination of Dr. Benjamin Franklin in the British House of Commons relative to the Repeal of the Stamp Act* (London, 1766). Its tact, good humor, and lucidity recommended it to many Englishmen as the most informative document of the day, and succeeding straightforward pleadings of the American cause in other pamphlets heightened the impression that Franklin was a reliable reporter. At the psychological moment he published in the *Gentleman's Magazine* for September, 1773, his *Rules for Reducing a Great Empire to a Small One*. His readers were prompt to see the parallelism between his "rules" and British colonial "policies," and many Englishmen were won over to the colonial point of view. The next month he published, in the same magazine, his *Edict of the King of Prussia*, and had himself the great good fortune to see how some of his British friends were taken in by the hoax which represented the King of Prussia, as patron to Britain, adopting the same tone in his edict toward England that the British were employing in their pronouncements toward the American colonies. His satirical letter in 1777 "From the Count De Schaumbergh to the Baron Hohendorf" on the sale of Hessian troops used during the Revolutionary War was hardly less effective; and even in the last year of his life, while serving as president of the Pennsylvania Society for the Abolition of Slavery, he employed this technique with telling effect. In the last piece of writing published during his lifetime he represented one Sidi Mehemet Ibrahim, a member of the Tripolitan divan and a professing African Mohammedan, defending the practice of enslaving Christians, by employing all the arguments current among American defenders of the Negro slave trade—with the notable difference that they were used by the heathens against Christians.

Finally, it remains to mention the most delightful of Franklin's miscellaneous and more trifling writings as an eighteenth-century wit and accomplished man of the world, as typified by his ephemera-like "Bagatelles." Most of these graceful letters and familiar essays, varying from the light, urbane meditations of a *bon vivant* to the clever gallantry of a courtier,

were written during his years at Passy for the diversion of his French friends. These "Bagatelles," as he called them, reflect the French elegance of the *salons* of Madame Brillon and Madame Helvétius. Among the best known of these trifles is "The Whistle," a moralized anecdote, and the most graceful is "The Ephemera," a parable on the brevity of life. As Stuart Pratt Sherman has remarked, the tallow chandler's son who entered on the cycle of his development by cultivating thrift with Defoe, continued it by cultivating tolerance and philanthropy with Voltaire, and completed it by cultivating "the graces" with Lord Chesterfield. Franklin himself was aware of this remarkable progression, resulting largely from his long residence abroad; for it is a noteworthy fact that he spent practically the whole of the Revolutionary War period away from America in the diplomatic and political interests of his country. Writing home in his seventy-second year, he said, "Figure to yourself an old man, with gray hair appearing under a marten fur cap, among the powdered heads of Paris. It is this odd figure that salutes you with handfuls of blessings."

Yet, extensive as were his education and experience, his mind was focused on "useful attainments." He had little of what is called poetry in his soul. His writings, filling ten stout volumes, contain few references to the theater, fiction, music, painting, sculpture, or architecture. He does not instinctively resort for the illustrations of his writings to the illuminating facts of history; he seldom explores the broader reaches of philosophy; only occasionally does he touch upon the wider and larger implications of science. As Sainte-Beuve once observed, "There is a flower of religion, a flower of honor, a flower of chivalry, that you must not require of Franklin." One needs to go no further than to compare him with his townsman Francis Hopkinson or his compatriot Thomas Jefferson to realize how relatively limited he was in point of cultural variety. Throughout his life he sought for and won other, simpler, and more substantial goals, which, at least according to his way of thinking, were equally honorable. Yet in dedicating his life to the service of his fellow men, he achieved, more or less incidentally, certain priorities at which he had not aimed at all, but which posterity gratefully acknowledges. He was the first to offer "a widely influential challenge to the religious life by the secular life," in the sense that he is the first important American writer to break with Puritanism; he was the "first genuinely international figure" to emerge in America; and he was the first American to achieve "solid permanence in literary fame."

THOMAS PAINE (1737–1809)

Variously apostrophized as the "Author-Hero of the American Revolution," "the ragged philosopher," "the Creator of Independent Democracy in America," and "a drunken infidel," Thomas Paine is "the epitome of a world in revolution." No American author did more for America by his writings than he, and none of his generation suffered greater ingratitude and calumny at the hands of his fellow citizens. A citizen of three nations, he came to be a man without a country. His native England outlawed him; as a citizen of France, he was imprisoned and long in danger of execution; the United States of America, which no one labored more than he to bring into being, subsequently denied him citizenship and heaped obloquy upon him. Yet his writings, which netted him little profit, were the most influential in the era of the American Revolution, and he must be rated as one of the three or four most powerful propagandists of ideas in the history of the world. His philosophy was as simple as it was broad: "The world is my country; to do good, my religion." Republicanism and deism have had more erudite, profound, and subtle proponents, but they never had a more eloquent, forthright, and sincere advocate than Tom Paine. Much of the odium that still attaches to his name and memory is owing to his religious creed, enunciated in *The Age of Reason* (1794–1795). Published at the height of the conservative reaction against the French Revolution, its outspokenly deistic attack on Christianity alienated the conservatives; his name became anathema to succeeding generations who were led by prejudice or ignorance to repeat with John Adams and Theodore Roosevelt the charge of "filthy little atheist." Actually his religion was no more reprehensible than was Franklin's. Both were scientific deists who derived their religious beliefs from the scientific principles current in their day. Their chief difference lay in the fact that Franklin prudently kept his religious opinions private, while Paine, bent on converting mankind to what he conceived as the true religion, boldly published his views and drew upon himself the hatred of "right-thinking Christians," Franklin, for his part, becoming enshrined in their memories as a saint.

When, on the last day of November, 1774, Thomas Paine arrived in Philadelphia, he was (except for Franklin's letter of recommendation that he carried in his pocket) far worse off than Franklin had been some fifty years earlier when he walked down Market Street with a roll of bread under each arm. Nearly thirty-eight years of age, he was already what the world called a failure. Since his birth in 1737, the son of a poor stay-maker in Thetford, England, Paine had encountered little good fortune in life beyond acquiring from his Quaker father and Anglican mother "a good moral education" and picking up "a tolerable stock of useful learning," though he knew no language but his own. Born a Friend, he became an independent rationalist and humanitarian, practicing Quaker doctrines. Although he laughed when he thought of the sad world the Quakers would have made of the creation if they had been consulted, and reproved them for their pacifistic refusal to fight for principle, his last will requested that his body be interred in a Quaker burying-ground if they would admit "a person who does not belong to their society."

Tiring of his father's trade of corset-making, and lusting for adventure, he tried, as a lad of seventeen, to enlist on Captain Death's privateer, the *Terrible*; but this first independent venture ended ingloriously when he was nabbed by his father just before the ship could sail and put back to stay-making. Shortly thereafter, however, he shipped on the *King of Prussia*, but one cruise on a licensed pirate ship was enough for him, and disconsolately he settled back to making stays.

He pursued the trade for several years at various places with indifferent success, while devoting his leisure time to studying philosophy and astronomy. In 1759 he married Mary Lambert, only to lose her by death the next year. Again tiring of stay-making, he secured a government appointment as an exciseman in 1764, and two years later was dismissed, reputedly for neglect of duty. Next he turned schoolteacher, served as usher in an academy, practiced stay-making for brief periods, turned an honest penny by occasionally ascending some pulpit or other to preach his gospel to such saints and sinners as would hear him, and at one time considered taking holy orders. After a prayerful petition and a promise to do better, he was reappointed to the excise in 1768. In 1771, still an exciseman, he married Elizabeth Ollive, a young lady with whom he was already in partnership as grocer and tobacconist. Three years later he was again dismissed from the excise on the charges that he had neglected his duties without leave of the Board, and that he had not paid his debts. Another complication appears to have been his writing in 1773 of an appeal addressed to Parliament asking better pay for excisemen. A few days after his dismissal, all his effects personal and otherwise, were sold at auction for the benefit of his creditors; and about the same time he signed papers of separation from his wife, the arrangement apparently being entirely amicable, since neither party had found their union either profitable or particularly happy.

A disconsolate bankrupt, he betook himself to London, where he consulted with Franklin about prospects in America. Something in the young man impressed Franklin sufficiently to give him a letter of introduction commending Paine as "an ingenious and worthy young man" and recommending him as "a clerk, or assistant in a school, or assistant surveyor." Franklin's letter opened to him pleasant relations with some of the best people in Philadelphia. He went to work for Robert Aitken, then about to launch the *Pennsylvania Magazine or American Museum*, and soon became its editor. A complete failure in England, he resolved to make something of himself in America. He worked diligently as a journalist, haunted the bookshops, adroitly pushed his way into an acquaintance with the leading citizens just then congregating in Philadelphia, and kept eyes and ears open to gather all facts, impressions, and opinions then being generated by the quarrel between his native country and the land of his adoption. His contribution to the first number of the *Pennsylvania Magazine* started him on his successful career as a propagandist, the collected results of which fill ten volumes. His essays soon established him as one of the moral pioneers of his generation. He advocated international arbitration, attacked dueling, suggested rational ideas of marriage and divorce, pleaded for mercy to animals, argued for the need of international copyright, demanded justice for women, and assailed Negro slavery. His articles against slavery are reputed to have led directly to the formation of the first antislavery society in Philadelphia. Indeed, the abolition of slavery was a cause for which he fought constantly; and when, years later, he became the target of religious persecution, it was in their dual capacity as Christians and slaveholders that Americans reviled him.

Keeping his finger on the pulse of the people and training his ear to catch the shifting winds of popular feeling and opinion, he guardedly kept his peace until he was sure of himself and of the people whom he hoped to lead if given half a chance. He familiarized himself with what James Otis had said in opposition to the Writs of Assistance in 1762, and he reviewed the legalistic arguments of John Dickinson and of Samuel Adams protesting the Stamp Act while taking care not to deny the right of Parliament to levy taxes. He familiarized himself with the issues involved in the Declaratory Acts of 1766, the Boston Massacre (March, 1770), the Boston Tea Party (December 16, 1773), the acts and resolutions of the First Continental Congress (1774), and the flood of pamphlets, essays, and public letters that followed in their wake. He carefully gauged the rise of feeling following the skirmishes at Lexington and Concord on April 19, 1775. He watched the Second Continental Congress, which began its session on May 10; he tried to interpret the effect of the Battle of Bunker Hill (June 17), of the selection of Washington as commander of the Army (June 15), and of the final breakdown of arbitration when England rejected American petitions and the colonies refused proffered compromises during the latter part of 1775. Six months after the fiery Virginian, Patrick Henry, made the speech about "Liberty or Death" (urging armed resistance but saying nothing about independence), Tom Paine had made up his mind to take the next step, highly treasonable though he knew it to be. He would propose not merely resistance, but independence. On October 18, 1775, writing in the *Pennsylvania Journal*, he said: "I hesitate not for a moment to believe that the Almighty will finally separate America from Britain. Call it Independence or what you will, if it is the cause of God and humanity, it will go on." This was nine months before the Declaration of Independence.

Few were ready for the idea of separation. The revolt had begun with a limited object. Very few realized whither they were heading; none knew what the outcome would be. They still argued over legalities and constitutional rights and loyalties. It would require a severe jolt to jar them out of their accustomed modes of thinking. Paine had had enough experience as a propagandist to realize, as he said, "It is necessary to be bold. Some people can be reasoned into sense, and others must be shocked into it. Say a bold thing that will stagger them and they will begin to think. . . . I deal not in hints and intimations. . . . I bring reason to your ears, and in language as plain as A, B, C, hold up truth to your eyes."

Lexington and Concord had prepared the people to be receptive and ready for anything, and Paine, waiting just so long as was necessary but no longer, seized exactly the right moment to publish *Common Sense* on January 10, 1776, to show that any man who used his common sense could do nothing other than demand separation and fight for independence. The time had come to act.

Friends and enemies agree in ascribing to Paine's pamphlet an unexampled effect. In three months, 120,000 copies were sold—an event hitherto unequaled in the history of American printing. So that it might have the widest possible circulation, Paine put the price of *Common Sense* so low that while some 500,000 copies were disposed of, he found himself in the end indebted to the printer. But he achieved his purpose: the little pamphlet inspired a rebellion and created a nation.

The essay is happily entitled *Common Sense* because that was all Paine had to bring to bear on the subject, concerning whose legal points he knew nothing. Instead of arguing the legalistic issues involved in the contest, he brushed aside as irrelevant all technical questions and appealed his case to the tribunal of common sense—to the rank and file who knew no law, but who felt nonetheless strongly. He always maintained, law or no law, that what a whole people chooses to do it has a right to do. While professing to address only the common sense and reason of men, he never lost an opportunity to rouse also their feelings and passions. Employing exaggeration, misrepresentation, invective, and satire, Paine used all the tricks of the political agitator to break down traditional loyalty to England and to build up a spirit of active rebellion. It was ridiculous, he argued, for free men in America to remain any longer bound subjects of Great Britain: that they were free men and should assume the rights of independent American citizens, and that nothing stood in their way but the trash of a few pedants like John Dickinson, who still argued about legalities and constitutionality, and other timid souls who still respected the authority of certain ruffians and brutes called kings.

Accordingly Part I of his epoch-making pamphlet begins with a rhapsodical and sword-rattling overture of sweeping affirmations and pungent observations concerning government in general and of the English government in particular—all intended to rid the colonial mind of any undue reverence it still had for

organized or legal authority and to convince the people that the hour had arrived "to legalize disobedience to law."

"Society is produced by our wants," Paine begins, "and government by our wickedness. . . . Society in every state is a blessing, but government, even in its best state, is but a necessary evil; in its worst state, an intolerable one. . . . Government, like dress, is the badge of lost innocence; the palaces of kings are built on the ruins of the bowers of paradise." Such, says Paine, is the origin of government. Its objects are twofold: freedom and security. But the British government affords us neither.

Part II is a discussion of monarchy and hereditary succession. In reply to the query about the true form of government, Paine answers that whatever it is, it is not monarchy. The government which rests on "the distinction of men into kings and subjects" is one for which no "natural or religious reason can be assigned."

Male and female are the distinctions of nature, good and bad, the distinctions of heaven; but how a race of men came into the world so exalted above the rest, and distinguished like some new species, is worth inquiring into, and whether they are the means of happiness or misery to mankind. . . . The nearer any government approaches to a republic, the less business there is for a king. . . .

In England a king hath little more to do than to make war and give away places; which in plain terms is to impoverish the nation and set it together by the ears. A pretty business indeed for a man to be allowed eight hundred thousand sterling a year for, and worshipped into the bargain! Of more worth is one honest man to society, and in the sight of God, than all the crowned ruffians that ever lived.

Part III presents some "thoughts on the Present State of the American Affairs" to show that "the period of debate is closed. Arms as the last recourse, must decide the contest. . . . All plans, proposals, &c. [for reconciliation] prior to the nineteenth of April [1775], i. e., to the commencement of hostilities [at Lexington and Concord], are like the almanacs of the last year."

Aside from the fact that America has nothing to gain by her continued connection with England, but much to lose, Paine argued that it is "repugnant to reason, to the universal order of things, to all examples from former ages, to suppose that this continent can long remain subject to any external power." There is something preposterous in the idea that a great nation on one side of the Atlantic shall remain in a state of permanent vassalage to a small island on the other side; while to be "always running three or four thousand miles with a tale or a petition, waiting four or five months for an answer, which, when obtained, requires five or six more to explain it in, will in a few years be looked upon as folly and childishness. There was a time when it was proper, and there is a proper time for it to cease."

> Small islands not capable of protecting themselves are the proper objects for governments to take under their care; but there is something absurd in supposing a continent to be perpetually governed by an island. In no instance hath nature made the satellite larger than its primary planet; and as England and America, with respect to each other, reverse the common order of nature, it is evident that they belong to different systems. England to Europe: America to itself.

After offering a plan by which the thirteen colonies can effectively unite in a representative democratic form of government, Paine proceeds to the fourth and last part, "On the Present Ability of America, with Some Miscellaneous Reflections," designed to convince the people that armed resistance will be attended by success. "Nothing," he concludes, "can settle our affairs so expeditiously as an open and determined DECLARATION OF INDEPENDENCE." "O ye that love mankind! Ye that dare oppose, not only the tyranny but the tyrant, stand forth!" In an appendix added to later editions, Paine closed with the declaration: "We have it in our power to begin the world over again. . . . The birthday of a new world is at hand . . . the FREE AND INDEPENDENT STATES OF AMERICA."

Paine's challenge at the strategic moment "proved to be the deciding word." Dr. Benjamin Rush acknowledged the pamphlet's effect such as had been "rarely produced by types and paper, in any age or country." Major General Lee, writing to Washington, called it "the *coup-de-grace* to Great Britain"; and Washington himself, fighting an undeclared war since June of the preceding year and wanting a decisive declaration, wrote on January 31, 1776:

> A few more such flaming arguments as we exhibited at Falmouth and Norfolk, added to the sound doctrine and unanswerable reasoning contained in the pamphlet *Common Sense*, will not leave numbers at a loss to decide on the propriety of a separation.

The separation came five months later, on July 4, 1776.

Despite its crudities of thought, its superficiality, its rashness of assertion, the pamphlet was a masterstroke. Its smattering of historical lore, its cheap display of statistics, and its clumsy attempts at a political philosophy were no deterrents either to Tom Paine or to the people, who just then cared more about imperiled rights than about either learning or philosophy.

Not content to fight with his pen alone, Paine shouldered a musket as a private and was soon raised to the position of aide-de-camp to General Greene. The fortunes of war turned against the patriots. By the end of 1776 the desertion of soldiers, encouraged by short-term enlistment, had grown to alarming proportions, and Washington's retreat across the Delaware seemed catastrophic. General Washington himself confided to his brother on December 18, 1776: "Between you and me, I think our affairs are in a very bad situation. . . . If every nerve is not strained up to the utmost to recruit the new army with all possible expedition, I think the game is very near up."

Again, Paine's pen came to the rescue. In January he had opened the immemorial year of '76 with *Common Sense*, a call to decision; in December, he closed the year with the first of a series of sixteen papers called *The Crisis*, a call to action. It opened with the stirring lines:

> These are the times that try men's souls. The summer soldier and the sunshine patriot will, in this crisis, shrink from the service of his country; but he that stands it *now*, deserves the love and thanks of man and woman. Tyranny, like hell, is not easily conquered; yet we have this consolation with us, that the harder the conflict, the more glorious the triumph.

The first of the *Crisis* papers attempts to reconstruct American confidence in its own powers. It stimulated enlistment in the new army, and Washington ordered a copy read to every regiment. By January 13, 1777, the second installment appeared in the form of a letter to Lord Howe, commiserating with the noble lord, enumerating his insuperable difficulties in attempting a conquest of a vast country with a handful of soldiers. Next he charges Howe with being a wanton marauder and pillager, and returns to sympathize with him in the hopelessness and folly of his undertaking—mocking, advising, and blasting him all at once. It is good propaganda, and it provoked many a chuckle round the campfires of weary, disheartened American soldiers. The third paper, issued on the anniversary of Lexington and Concord, returns to a discussion of the principles at stake in the contest, and so on until the last number appeared on December 9, 1783, seven years (lacking a day) from the time No. 1 had appeared.

The sixteen papers fall into three time groups: seven in the first two years, three between March and October, 1780, and six in the last twenty-one months of the war. The first are divided between defiance of British power and denunciation of political doctrine. The middle three aim at discouraging the British and inspiring Americans with renewed zeal and effort. The last six press the offensive and lead up to the discussion of peace. Thus he kept up, throughout the war years, his incessant harangue and irresistible bombardment of the American conscience (military and civilian), playing with matchless skill and power upon all the springs of human anxiety, resolution, anger, fear, contempt, hatred, fortitude, duty, honor, patriotism, self-interest, and love of fame. How he found time to do it remains a mystery, for during the early years of the war he shared every service, action, and privation of the army, even to enduring the winter at Valley Forge with Washington.

In 1777 he was elected secretary to the Committee of Foreign Affairs of the Continental Congress, a post which he resigned in 1779; and later in the same year he was elected clerk of the Pennsylvania Assembly. During 1781 he sailed for France and successfully negotiated a large loan for the American cause. For his services as penman, soldier, and diplomat, he was awarded several sizable gifts of money and a confiscated Royalist estate at New Rochelle, N. Y. At the conclusion of the war he went to Bordentown, N. J., to devote himself to his inventions, which included a smokeless candle and the perfection of an iron bridge without piers.

But these were tame pursuits. Franklin had declared, "Wherever is liberty, there is my home"; Paine countered, "Wherever is not liberty, there is my home." Accordingly, when the political struggle for greater liberty in France and England became intense, Paine, having fomented one rebellion by a pamphlet, and looking for a new revolution, hied himself off to France in 1787. During 1787–1792 he shuttled back and forth between Paris and London, arranging for the patenting and building of his bridge and promoting political rebellion. Shortly after the fall of the Bastille, he went to Paris to observe the Revolution. It was then that Lafayette entrusted to him the key of the Bastille, bidding him to bear it safely to America as a symbol of despotism overthrown in France as it had been in America. Paine became the natural link of the revolutionary spirit that had already succeeded in the New World, that was in progress in France, and, as was ardently hoped, that would soon sweep England also. Back in London by February of 1791, he published the first part of his *Rights of Man*, in reply to Burke's *Reflections on the French Revolution* (1790), followed by a second part a year later. Both breathed political radicalism of a kind not countenanced in England, just then experiencing a strong feeling of revulsion at the excesses of the French Revolution. Paine was summoned to stand trial as the author of a libelous work. During the ensuing delays and postponements, he made good his opportunities to make his way secretly to France—and none too soon, for a half hour after he sailed from Dover the order for his arrest arrived.

In France he was welcomed warmly. He was chosen as a representative from Calais in the General Assembly, and the title of Citizen of France was conferred upon him. In the meantime he enjoyed informing the London judges, who had ordered him to return and stand trial, that he was too busy in Paris with important matters to accommodate their wishes, but that they might proceed against him during his absence—which is what they did, and would have done in any case.

A leader from the first, he exercised a powerful influence for moderation while the Girondin party was in power, speaking against the guillotine and holding out for humane and just procedures. In the end, however, as the power passed more and more into the hands of the more radical Jacobins and the mob, he lost influence. His valiant efforts to save the life of the King and Queen brought him under suspicion, and on December 23, 1793, he was confined in the Luxembourg Prison.

Seeing atheism making great gains on every hand in France, and having conceived the idea of checking it by giving the French people his rationale of a deistic, moral, and natural religion, he wrote furiously to complete Part I of *The Age of Reason*, and a few hours before he was carted off to prison he managed to put the manuscript into the hands of Joel Barlow, who arranged for its publication in January, 1794. Declaring his American citizenship, he demanded to be released, but the American government did nothing to help him, and he languished in prison until after the fall of Robespierre. He was marked for the guillotine several times. Once he escaped because the guard chalked the mark designating him for execution on the inside of his cell door while it stood open. Paine lost no time erasing the fatal mark. At another time he was saved because when the guards came to carry him before the tribunal, he was lying in a state of insensibility from fever occasioned by poor care and prison food. On November 4, 1794, James Monroe, the American Ambassador to France, finally secured his release, and took him into his home for the next eighteen months to give him a chance to recuperate. During the ten months that he had lain in prison he had employed his time, whenever he was able, to write portions of Part II of *The Age of Reason,* published in 1795. This book brought down upon him the attacks of the orthodox, and the ill will toward him was intensified in 1796 when he published his *Letter to George Washington,* upbraiding him for folding his arms as President in America while his erstwhile comrade-in-arms languished in prison in France.

Paine's truculent attack upon the British had endeared him to all patriots in America, but when he turned to attack Christianity with the same ferocity, many of his friends shrank from him. And it must be admitted that he drove his points home with reckless abandon, as when, on the first page of *The Age of Reason,* he wrote:

> I believe in one God, and no more. . . . I do not believe in the creed professed by the Jewish church, by the Roman church, by the Greek church, by the Turkish church, by the Protestant church, nor by any church that I know of. My own mind is my own church.

Part I is a destructive inquiry into the bases of Christianity, its theology, its mysteries, miracles, prophecies, and revelations; and Part II is a critical examination of the Old and New Testaments to support the negative conclusions and inferences of the first part. Concluding that the "Word of God is the creation we behold," he reiterates the charge that "the bible and testament are impositions and forgeries," and that "of all the religions that ever were invented, there is none more derogatory to the Almighty, more unedifying to men, more repugnant to reason, and more contradictory in itself, than this thing called Christianity."

> Too absurd for belief, too impossible to convince, and too inconsistent for practice, it renders the heart torpid or produces only atheists and fanatics. As an engine of power, it serves the purpose of despotism; and as a means of wealth, the avarice of priests; but so far as respects the good of man in general, it leads to nothing here or hereafter.

Despite all its shortcomings, weaknesses of argument, and crudities of style, the writing of *The Age of Reason* was the bravest thing Paine ever did, for he must have known that it would gain him nothing. On the other hand, he must have known that his "going through the Bible," as he put it, "as a man would go through a wood with an axe on his shoulder to fell trees," would bring down upon him the wrath

of orthodox Christendom. Slaveholders, royalists, and fanatics of orthodoxy combined to condemn the man who had dared to deny the inspiration of the Bible, while the grandsons of Puritans who had hanged witches and flogged Quakers denied him a place on the stagecoach lest an offended God should strike it with lightning. Bishops in England and "Pope" Dwight at Yale fulminated against him. The consternation became complete when in 1802 Jefferson dispatched a man-of-war to France to conduct this arch-infidel safely to America, where he got a sorry reception indeed. Fanatics accosted him and damned him in public, and in 1805 an attempt was made on his life at New Rochelle, where he was denied the right to vote on the ground that he was not an American citizen.

Yet all this hubbub was beside the point. Thomas Paine's work was done. Ostracized, broken in health, and in desperate financial straits, he died on June 8, 1809. A few days later a funeral cortège of six persons, including a Frenchwoman and her two sons, a Quaker, and two Negroes, accompanied his remains and laid him away where he would do no more harm.

But, as Tom Paine himself had observed, "reason, like time, will make its own way," and the passage of the years has brought him justice and renown. Not many years after his death, in a log hut out in Illinois a lad named Abe Lincoln sat up all night to read *The Age of Reason* by the flickering light of the fireplace, and trudged twelves miles the next morning to return the book to its owner; today no other American of the Revolutionary age is so much the object of biographical and historical research as Tom Paine; and the world is coming to realize that in an age of bold men he was the bravest. He could rouse the passions, and he could brave them. He used his gifts not only in defense of democracy, but also for women, slaves, and animals. Poverty never left him, for though he made fortunes by his pen, he gave everything to the great cause he served. His fault as a man was a kind of naïve vanity that often dogs men of large mold. In a fight he often forgot the principle he recommended to all others—common sense. No half-way measures served him. It was his fate to escape the gallows in England and the guillotine in France, and either would have supplied the crown of martyrdom that he merited. Certainly a better democrat never fought tyranny, and a better Christian never assailed orthodoxy.

PHILIP FRENEAU (1752–1832)

The title-makers have done so well by Philip Freneau that he passes today as (1) poet of the American Revolution, (2) journalist of Jeffersonian and French Democracy, (3) apostle of the Religion of Nature and Humanity, and (4) the father of American poetry. Aside from the fact that he merits these fine titles, they are important as indicating the wide range of his interests and as suggesting that, like other writers of his day, the times made him a propagandist first and a poet afterwards. Like Trumbull, Dwight, and Barlow, or David Humphreys, Lemuel Hopkins, and Francis Hopkinson, he lived in an age of political and social turmoil, and like them, he could not avoid the burning issues of the day. Three-fourths of his energy went into crusading, and only a fourth was available for the cultivation of the purer poetic vein.

Born of French Huguenot parents in New York on January 2, 1752, he enjoyed the advantages of a genteel rearing and a good education; for when the boy was ten, his father inherited an estate at Mount Pleasant, New Jersey, of a thousand acres, spacious buildings, and slaves. When Freneau entered Princeton in his sixteenth year, his knowledge of the English poets and the classics elicited a letter of congratulation from President Witherspoon.

Like the Hartford Wits at Yale, Freneau and his Princeton friends, who included Henry Hugh Brackenridge, Aaron Burr, Henry Lee, William Bradford, Henry B. Livingston, and his roommate James Madison, set themselves to cultivating polite letters. Like them, too, they turned rather too much toward the exotic and the grandiloquent, choosing historical subjects of the antique world or the epical themes of Holy Writ.

During his freshman year Freneau wrote a lengthy poem in well-turned rhymed pentameters on the discouraging subject, "The Prophet Jonah," followed the next year by a dramatic fragment in blank verse on "The Pyramids of Egypt." With Brackenridge he wrote several chapters of an unfinished, fantastic novel entitled *Father Bombo's Pilgrimage to Mecca in Arabia*. But, as at Yale, liberal, not to say deistic, currents were coming into vogue among the students

at Princeton. Freneau's "Power of Fancy," written in 1770 and reminiscent of Miltonic phraseology, reflects not only incipient romantic characteristics of fanciful figurativeness and musical elasticity of form but also Freneau's early deistic faith in nature as a divine revelation, by which the planets, suns, moons, and stars are regarded as—

> But thoughts on reason's scale combin'd,
> Ideas of the Almighty mind!

Again, as on other college campuses of the day, the political opinions current among the students reflected the rising tide of colonial opposition to British measures, and Princeton especially acquired the reputation of being a "hotbed of Whiggism." In a letter written in 1770, Madison described a vivid night scene in the college yard where students, robed in black gowns, burned, amid the tolling of bells, the letters of merchants who had failed to keep their non-importation agreements. The Commencement poem on "The Rising Glory of America," in which Freneau and Brackenridge collaborated, is an expression of the same emerging spirit of independence and national self-consciousness that brought on the Revolution, and that inspired the epic flights of Trumbull and Dwight and the dramatic independence of Royall Tyler and William Dunlap.

Following his graduation in 1771, Freneau taught school on Long Island and in Maryland, and wrote poems like "The American Village" (in "rocking horse" Popean couplets), which was "damned by all good and judicious judges," but which foreshadows many of his poetic characteristics, such as his love for nature and for indigenous, rural themes, his kinship with Goldsmith, with "heav'nly Pope" and with "godlike Addison," as well as his scorn for luxury and civilization and his naturalistic glorification of primitive life and the noble savage.

In the summer of 1775 he appeared in New York to win fame through eight satirical verse pamphlets turning upon the battles of Lexington and Bunker Hill and the fate of Generals Gage and Howe, breathing defiance to British tyrants and marauders, and ending with the prayer:

29

Libera Nos, Domine.—Deliver us, O Lord, not only from British Dependence, but also,

. . . From a kingdom that bullies, and hectors, and swears,
We send up to heaven our wishes and prayers
That we, disunited, may freemen be still,
And Britain go on—to be damned if she will.

Antedating as these do the Declaration of Independence by a full year and the first version of Trumbull's hit in *M'Fingal* by six months, Freneau's satires did in verse what Paine's *Common Sense* did in prose.

This marks the beginning of Freneau's rebellious career as "a volunteer in two revolutions"—in which he was judged patriotic or seditious depending on whether he was with or against the victorious party. In 1776 he fought with Hamilton, John Adams, and Washington for national independence, and won high praise from them and all other patriots. But in the revolution of 1793, breaking with Hamilton, Adams, and Washington, he joined Jefferson in the fight to hold the advantages won in '76 against the forces of special privilege, aristocracy, and monarchy, which he and Jefferson believed to be threatening republicanism in America. For him it was no new cause, but merely a continuation of the old fight for democratic liberty and individual freedom; but in his former friends' eyes it allied him with Jeffersonian democrats, insubordinate levelers, and Jacobin radicals, and it brought upon him the odium attaching the Federalist mind to a vulgar democrat and a rascally infidel that threw an ugly shadow over his old age.

But during the earlier revolution he was an honored compatriot, although he spent most of the war years in the West Indies, where the exotic luxuriance of the land and the tropical atmosphere of the sea stirred his fancy to the writing of such poems as "The Jamaica Funeral," "The Beauties of Santa Cruz," and the weird "House of Night." On his second return trip in 1778 he was captured by the British but was set free after a short detention, and upon his arrival in America he published a belated poem, "America Independent," celebrating the Declaration of Independence and calling upon his countrymen to avenge the "hell-born spite" of British bondage. On a third voyage to the West Indies he was again captured, after a bloody fight between the American *Aurora* and the British *Iris*, an engagement in which he participated as a civilian. He was kept for a while on a British prison ship, the *Scorpion*, and later transferred to the *Hunter*, a hospital ship lying in New York harbor. The brutal treatment which he experienced

there drove him to that frenzied hatred of everything British as expressed in his poem on "The British Prison Ship," written just after his release, when he tells us he "came home round through the woods, for fear of terrifying the neighbors with my ghastly looks had I gone through Mount Pleasant." Henceforth he devoted himself to war propaganda, sharpening and letting fly his "best arrows at these hell-hounds," as he came to characterize the British. His "wrathful muse" breathed defiance and hatred, sarcasm and invective, in hundreds of poems that were widely circulated and read, as were Paine's *Crisis* papers, at army campfires and wherever else patriots gathered. From 1781 to 1784, while employed in the Philadelphia Post Office, he became the leading contributor, if not editor, of the *Freeman's Journal*, and published in its columns such well-known paeans as "The Memorable Victory" of Paul Jones and "To the Memory of the Brave Americans" who died at Eutaw Springs, while mercilessly ridiculing the British in "The Fall of General Earl Cornwallis" and in "The Political Balance."

The sea, for which he developed a fondness during his first trip to the West Indies, and which supplied him with some of his best images and motifs ever afterwards, called him again in 1784. He sailed the Atlantic and Caribbean as captain of a brig until 1790, when he married Eleanor Forman, of a distinguished family, and left the sea to become editor of the New York *Daily Advertiser*. A year later he was mentioned by Aedanus Burke to James Madison as "struggling under difficulties," whereupon Jefferson, then Secretary of State, appointed him to a clerkship in his department on August 16, 1791. Nine days later Freneau announced his intention of publishing the *National Gazette*. It appeared on October 31, 1791, and lasted until October 23, 1793.

The first number of the *National Gazette* praised Thomas Paine and the French Revolutionists, and succeeding issues left no doubt that Freneau's periodical was the organ of Jeffersonian views designed to counteract the *United States Gazette*, the partisan organ of the Hamiltonian party.

Ever distrustful of a plutocratic aristocracy and alarmed at the centralizing powers of the government which Hamilton was building up, Freneau, with Jefferson, fought with all the means at his command to combat Hamilton's measures in public as Jefferson opposed them in Washington's Cabinet. It was a "grim, unsparing, deadly" battle of ruthless partisanship in which nothing less than scurrilous lampoon and sledge-hammer invective served the purpose. Freneau's training in that department during the war period had made him a master of intense attack, and the Federalists were soon smarting under his whiplash, despite the able defense of Federalism as promulgated by John Fenno, the editor of the *United States Gazette*.

Hamilton early recognized that the chief business of the *National Gazette* was to destroy him, and he resolved on desperate measures. Blinking the fact that Fenno and the *United States Gazette* were subsidized by the government in the form of fat printing contracts many times more lucrative than the annual salary of $250 which the Secretary of State paid Freneau as Clerk for Foreign Languages, he published an anonymous attack in Fenno's *Gazette* for July, 1792, charging Jefferson with having "hired" Freneau to "bite the hand that puts bread in his mouth" and of using the patronage of his Federal office to encourage an anti-government periodical. Freneau was hamstringing the Federalists at every turn, rousing popular opposition to the funding scheme, the bank, the excise, the tariff, the ceremonialism in high places, and the drift toward monarchical forms and practices. He publicized every known case where a Federalist had toasted the King of England, and he recorded numerous instances when they had spoken contemptuously of "the people." He supported the popular Jacobin demonstrations following the execution of Louis XVI, and in the Genêt affair, he defended Genêt, while reminding President Washington, since he was only a "public servant," he should remember that "the people are sovereign in the United States."

It was more than even Washington could bear. He sent for Jefferson and charged him with employing "that rascal Freneau" who had abused not only him but every branch of the government, adding (according to Jefferson's account), "By God, he had rather be in his grave than in his present situation." Jefferson refused to fire Freneau, for he believed that his paper "saved our Constitution, which was galloping fast into monarchy." The question of whether Freneau was actually employed by Jefferson is still being debated, but there is no longer any question about Freneau's being as effective as was Jefferson himself in arousing the popular opposition to Federalist measures that destroyed the party a few years later. But his partisanship also served to break Freneau. Championing the cause of democracy and the principles of French republicanism at a time when the reaction against the excesses of the French Revolution had provoked a strong revulsion of feeling among conservatives in America, Freneau also advocated lesser causes, among them deism, Unitarianism, hu-

manitarian reforms (notably antislavery), and Americanism in education; and these, as much as his partisanship for Jeffersonian democracy, brought down upon him the resentment of the powerful forces of conservatism. In the rough work that he engaged in, he forsook poetry to turn journalist and to heap abuse and scurrility upon the men whom he believed to be the enemies of the people. They retaliated in kind, calling him "a hireling mouthpiece of Jefferson," "a writer of wretched and insolent doggerel," "a vulgar democrat," and "a disseminator of insubordination and infidelity." Timothy Dwight lectured his boys at Yale that Philip Freneau was no better than Tom Paine—"a mere incendiary, or rather . . . a despicable tool of bigger incendiaries, and his paper . . . a public nuisance." Even the gentle Irving, who took his Federalism in moderate doses, spoke of him as "a barking cur"; while the saintlike Washington, forgetful of the time when Freneau had been more essential to his cause, seemed, to a people who adored him, to give everybody leave to dub Freneau "that rascal." From this heaping up of abuse, his name and fame did not recover until the dawn of the twentieth century.

When Jefferson, his patron, left Washington's Cabinet, Freneau resigned his secretaryship and gave up the *National Gazette*. Discredited and disgusted, he retired from "knaves and fools" to Mount Pleasant, now reduced to "a couple of hundred acres of an old sandy patrimony," to reflect that he had reposed his trust too blindly in the faith that the age of reason had already arrived, and that the overthrow of tyranny in government and religion would follow as soon as men were shown the way to do it.

For a year (1795-96) he edited the *Jersey Chronicle*, "a free, independent, republican paper," devoted to "the natural and political rights of nations." In June of 1795 he printed, with his own hands, his collected poems, the first edition to receive his own supervision, for the two earlier ones (1786 and 1788) had been printed by a friend while he was at sea. After various changes of work and residence, poverty drove him back to his old calling as master of coast-line freight vessels during 1803–1809. In 1809, back at Mount Pleasant, he prepared the 1809 edition of his poems, in two volumes. The War of 1812 revived his old rancor against the British, and he wrote another notable series of spirited satirical and patriotic poems. The burning of his old home in 1815, poverty, foreclosures and mortgages, and a weakness for "the tavern and the flowing bowl" completed his misery; and one night, just a week before the Christmas of 1832, while going home, the old man of eighty lost his way in a snowstorm and was found the next morning dying of exposure.

Freneau's literary output falls roughly into three classes: (1) his patriotic and political satires, songs, and invectives; (2) his fanciful or imaginative verse, lyrical, descriptive, or reflective; and (3) his prose writings. The last have been too much neglected and remain still largely uncollected. During the course of his long and active career as a journalist, he wrote countless editorials, attacks, commentaries, reports, and essays of many kinds. Like his poems, these are uneven in composition and worth, often hastily written (as they had to be), and colored by the party spirit of the times. But in a number of his familiar essays, a form to which he especially devoted himself after his retirement from Washington, he achieved often a pleasing combination of sentiment, humor, and discernment. One of his most successful essays is his characterization of Tomo Cheeki as a commentator on the white man's way of life. Among the more personal of his familiar essays is "A Speech on a New Subject," presenting an unforgettable sketch of a retired sea captain; while among his essays commenting on the follies and foibles of human nature there are several that Addison could readily have accepted for the *Spectator*.

Freneau's later verse of propaganda—whether patriotic, political, or religious—suffered no diminution of forcefulness. His poetic fame during his own day rested almost wholly upon his polemical verse, and it is freely admitted that in that genre he excelled all of his contemporaries. His moralizing verses on matters of general philosophical import and his poems on natural or universal religion are all good in their way, several of the latter being little behind Alexander Pope's famous "Universal Prayer" in quality.

But it is upon what he called his "Poems of Romantic Fancy" that his more enduring fame as a poet must rest—poems like "The Power of Fancy," "The Beauties of Santa Cruz," "The Indian Burying Ground," and "The Wild Honey Suckle." In these, he is the poet of the transition between the old neo-classic conventionality and the new romantic imaginativeness. His fondness for moralizing, his rationalism, his addiction to the pastoral and the sentimental, and his use of personification and poetic diction ally him with the school of Gray, Collins, and Cowper, whose inspirations in some of his verses are not hard to discover. His youthful poem on "The Power of Fancy" appears to have derived at once from Milton's "L'Allegro" and "Il Penseroso" and from Joseph Warton's "Ode to Fancy"; while "The House of

Night" shows parallelisms with the "Induction" to *Mirror for Magistrates* no less than with the graveyard poetry of Blair and Gray, at the same time that it foreshadows the Gothic vein of Mrs. Radcliffe and Charles Brockden Brown or the funereal morbidity of Edgar Allan Poe. In his Indian poems he exhibits some similarities to the antiquaries and the primitivists of the late eighteenth and the early nineteenth centuries, and in his lighter, brighter lyrical mood he reminds the reader of Marvell and of Herrick. His perfect combination of the wistful mood of transience with a rich coloration of the beauteous forms of nature in "The Wild Honey Suckle" produce a really fine poetic expression that reaches a climax in the closing lines:

> The space between, is but an hour,
> The frail duration of a flower.

Often his excellence lies in individual lines or short passages, of the kind typified by "The Indian Burying Ground":

> The hunter still the deer pursues,
> The hunter and the deer, a shade!

He was to be followed by many American poets who possessed a surer touch, a finer taste, and a firmer power; but it is to his credit that he could, on occasion, turn aside from rancorous political factionalism to write verse that is of value as poetry, rather than for what it theologically preaches, historically illustrates, or politically argues. He realized that in the America of his day—

> Low in the dust is genius laid,
> The muses with the man in trade;

for

> An age employed in edging steel,
> Can no poetic raptures feel.

As a wit who might have learned to restrain his muse in a way to develop his best powers under the stimulation of sympathetic criticism and the friendly rivalry of fellow poets, he had cause to complain—

> Thrice happy Dryden, who could meet
> Some rival bard in every street!
> When all were bent on writing well,
> It was some credit to excel.

In the America of his time there was not that incentive. Moreover, he had the misfortune in his later years to see younger men like Halleck, Drake, and especially Bryant, writing under more favorable circumstances, surpassing him in his own lifetime—a fate that the novelist Brown and the dramatist Dunlap happily escaped.

Nevertheless, he cultivated his faculty for pure poetry in a degree to produce the first considerable body of authentic verse in America and to make him, rather than Michael Wigglesworth or Edward Taylor or John Trumbull, the Father of American Poetry.

JAMES FENIMORE COOPER (1789-1851)

Cooper has been interpreted variously by different generations. By the time he went abroad in 1826, his first half dozen novels had made him an international figure. His stories were republished in England and translated in France, Germany, Italy, Sweden, and Denmark almost immediately. He was widely applauded as the American Scott. During the years that he spent in Europe (1826-1833), he became a critic of European civilization, and immediately upon his return home, he became thoroughly disliked by large segments of American society for his frank criticism of life as he found it in the United States. Following his death in 1851, his position became secure as the great prose poet of the frontier and as the annalist of American naval history. The twentieth century is inclined to find his social criticism most significant. He was at various times novelist, romancer of the frontier and of the sea, chronicler and historian, commentator on civilizations and governments, and critic of society.

Motivated as he was throughout his life by what he called his "American principles," and living in a time when the United States was struggling through schisms and conflicts to attain national harmony and cultural homogeneity, it was inevitable that he should have been more than a mere practitioner of *belles-lettres* or a spinner of pleasant yarns. During the years when Cooper grew to manhood, America was divided politically between Federalists and Republicans, socially between aristocrats and democrats, religiously between Congregationalists and Unitarians, philosophically between idealists and materialists, and economically between agrarians and industrialists. The party spirit of Hamilton and Jefferson's day developed into the factionalism of Jackson's time. Men like Cooper felt that these divergencies and conflicts must be synthesized by a unifying body of principles before national and cultural unity could be achieved. All of his writings are therefore in greater or lesser degree activated by his so-called "American principles," which have been analyzed by Professor Robert E. Spiller as (1) a belief in liberty as a moral force, (2) a social structure with private property ownership as its base, (3) an aristocracy of worth, instead of

blood or wealth, and (4) a strong sense of nationality and cultural solidarity. These principles and their implications animate much of Cooper's works. Their injection into his writings removes his books from the narrow realm of polite literature into that broader concept by which American literature is conceived as an expression of the whole of American experience. Literature, he held, should not exist as an end in itself, and the social novel as he wrote it he considered to be a consciously purposive but nevertheless legitimate form of art. Aside from his great saga of Leatherstocking on the frontier and of his notable sea stories, Cooper's greatest service as a literary man is his enlargement of the scope of American letters.

Born at Burlington, New Jersey, in 1789, Cooper spent his boyhood at Otsego Hall, Cooperstown, New York, where his father, a judge and owner of a large estate in what was still essentially a frontier country, lived in gentlemanly and patriarchal state. It has been suggested that here already were brought to bear upon the boy the two dominant, often rival, forces of his character: (1) the inherited gentility of family, aristocratic bearing, and patrician way of life and (2) the republican sympathies inherent in the frontier conditions of central New York. Following his preparation for college by an Anglican clergyman of Albany, he entered Yale in 1802, but failed to distinguish himself as a student, meanwhile acquiring a settled distaste for New England and a decided prejudice against all Yankees. Cashiered for a student prank during his junior year, he was articled by his father to the captain of a merchant vessel sailing for England, and during 1808-1811 he served as a midshipman in the United States Navy and saw duty chiefly on the Great Lakes. Following his marriage in 1811 to Susan Augusta De Lancey of an old Tory family, he resigned from the Navy and settled down to the pleasant life of a country gentleman in Westchester County, where he was near enough to New York City to attend the theatre and to enjoy social and literary contacts.

Up to this time he had given no indication of being interested in writing; but one day, while reading aloud to his wife an English novel, and growing impatient with its insipid nature, he remarked that he could write a better book himself. Challenged by his wife to try, he wrote *Precaution*, published in 1820. It is a conventional novel of English society, about which Cooper knew nothing at first hand; but its poor success aroused Cooper's fighting instincts to write a book that would command the attention of readers. Ashamed of having "fallen into the track of imitation" in his first work, Cooper later explained, "I endeavoured to repay the wrong done to my own views [his American principles], by producing a work that should be purely American, and of which love of country should be the theme." The result was *The Spy* (1821), which established his reputation as a novelist, and which marks, according to Carl Van Doren, the coming of age of American fiction. A cursory comparison between this novel and the best of Charles Brockden Brown's hot-house products should serve to illustrate the truth of Mr. Van Doren's observation.

The action of the story is localized in Westchester County, the Neutral Ground between the two armies of the Revolutionary War, which his long residence had made thoroughly familiar to him. For his hero he chose Harvey Birch, a spy, who had served General Washington with extraordinary fidelity, and an account of whose exploits he had heard years before from John Jay.

Although the language is somewhat stilted and affected, the story itself is vigorously narrated. It introduces us to Cooper's device of flight and pursuit, which he was to repeat many times in his later novels. It contains, besides, a surprising variety of characters drawn from all stations of life, and it develops and maintains suspense admirably through rapid action, sharp contrast, and mental tension. Three editions of *The Spy* were called for during the first year of its appearance, and Cooper was gratified to find popular support for his idea of employing familiar American scenes, interests, and characters for literary treatment. The success of the book had the added effect of heightening or confirming the ideas slowly forming in his mind of his so-called American "opinions" or "principles."

His next novel, *The Pioneers* (1823), was an extension of these same principles with the difference that for its material he turned to another great source-area of American fiction—the settlement of the frontier. The novel introduces us not only to Natty Bumppo, the Leatherstocking, who was to become his greatest fictional creation, but also to his successful portraiture of that vast movement by which the

wilderness was conquered by the American people. Here he was in his native element, having to draw only upon his own knowledge of the frontier society in which he had grown up. This familiarity with the variety of scene and character and his matchless skill of infusing vitality into it account for the remarkable success which the book enjoyed. Thirty-four hundred copies were sold 'on the first day of its publication.

Before he went on with this theme, he wrote *The Pilot* (1824, but dated 1823), a patriotic romance of the sea during Revolutionary days. The book was prompted by his dissatisfaction with Scott's *Pirate*. Believing that Scott as a landsman had failed to make the best of his opportunities, Cooper aimed to show in *The Pilot* what a man who had sailed the high seas might do with a sea tale. The story is notable as a thrilling account of sea battles, of flights and pursuits, in which John Paul Jones as the pilot figures prominently. But his best creation is the salty old sailor, Long Tom Coffin, who is on the sea what Leatherstocking is in the forest. The book is the first of a notable group of American sea stories, to which Cooper himself later added, among others, *The Red Rover* in 1828, *The Wing-and-Wing* in 1842, and *Afloat and Ashore* in 1844, and to which belong such classics as Dana's *Two Years before the Mast* (1840) and Melville's *Moby Dick* (1851).

Following these three successes, Cooper became the leading literary personality in New York City. He founded and dominated the famous literary society, the Bread and Cheese Club, took an active part in such public affairs as the welcoming of Lafayette on his return to America, and received an honorary degree from Columbia. About this time he planned a series of thirteen historical and patriotic novels, one for each of the original states, but only one was written—*Lionel Lincoln* (1825), an accurate but rather dull account of Bunker's Hill. The next year he returned to Leatherstocking in *The Last of the Mohicans*, to write what is generally considered his best novel. In it Natty Bumppo reappears as Hawkeye, now in the prime of manhood, as a scout in the frontier warfare between the English and the French and Indians. The book introduces also the Indian chiefs, Chingachgook and Uncas, distinguished for their noble, cunning, and romantic characters, as Magua, the Iroquois chieftain, is notable for the opposite qualities. The book is devoted to an epic-like portrayal of the vanishing Indian race, in a setting of the changeless majesty of the forest that sharpens, by contrast, the restless sense of danger and death.

In 1827 Cooper published *The Prairie*, portraying Leatherstocking in his extreme old age, compelled to retreat before the encroaching westward movement of the settlements. It completes the saga of the pioneer. Years later, after much had intervened to take his mind away from Chingachgook and Uncas, Magua and Hawkeye, he wrote two more novels, *The Pathfinder* in 1840 and *The Deerslayer* in 1841. These supply, as it were, the third and first acts, respectively, to make the five novels an epic of the frontier in a kind of dramatic progression of five acts. The order in which they should be read to illustrate what Cooper himself referred to as "a drama in five acts" is as follows: *The Deerslayer* (1841), *The Last of the Mohicans* (1826), *The Pathfinder* (1840), *The Pioneers* (1823), and *The Prairie* (1827). Leatherstocking is the unifying character, shown in five successive stages of his long and hazardous life. In *The Deerslayer*, laid in the time between 1740 and 1745, he is a young woodsman, on his first warpath. *The Last of the Mohicans* and *The Pathfinder* both belong to the period of the French and Indian wars—1756-1757, to be precise—when Leatherstocking, now aged about forty, is at the height of his strength and prowess. In *The Pioneers*, we are carried forward to 1793. The old scout is already past his prime. The country is being rapidly settled; and the old hunter and pathfinder, as he is compelled to retreat before the successive waves of settlers, grumbles that he loses himself in the clearings which the settlers' axes have made. In *The Prairie*, which represents the dénouement, we have arrived at the year 1804, just after the Louisiana Purchase. The frontiersman, fleeing before the encroachments and restraints of the settlements, finds himself an old man—no longer the deerslayer and pathfinder, but a trapper. His former friends are all dead; and his famous rifle Killdeer is now out-of-date and ready, like its owner, to be laid aside. Such are his thoughts as he watches the emigrant trains typifying the westward surge of civilization in which there is no place for his free life.

Like Daniel Boone, Leatherstocking is a heroic figure symbolizing a momentous epoch in American history. He is a highly romanticized figure, too much the poet of fine moral sentiment and the philosopher of deistic altruism to be quite convincing as a man drawn entirely from frontier life. Similarly Cooper's "noble red men" are idealizations of dignity, self-control, tribal loyalty, and reverence, which identify them more with Christian than pagan ethics, and suggest that, like Leatherstocking, they derive as much from French theories of the noble savage as from Cooper's own observations among the characters of the frontier. The polished British and French officers and gentlemen who move across the scenes are too much the "fine flowers of civilization" to be quite alive. Finally, his "females" (for that was the term used in Cooper's day, when "lady" was still reserved for women of social or class distinction) are conventional figures possessing tender hearts, graceful forms, and a superabundance of "sensibility," so that Lowell had some justice on his side when he wrote in *A Fable for Critics*:

> And the women he draws from one model don't vary,
> All sappy as maples and flat as a prairie.

There are other flaws. The language is often stilted and verbose. Evidences of hurried and careless writing are everywhere. Words are often ill-chosen, attempts at dialogue are sometimes amateurish, and pseudo-archaisms detract from the total effect of naturalness and simplicity that he aimed at. He shows little skill in anything more than the simplest plot; his handling of a complex situation is always confusing or cumbersome. Some of his stories open languidly, and others spin themselves out needlessly after the main business of the story has been transacted. Instead of carefully working out proper motivations, he resorts too frequently to stock devices; and some of his most thrilling narratives and his most exciting episodes—a battle, a pursuit, a capture, an escape, or a hand-to-hand conflict—are all too often prepared by some trifling accident or coincidence of the sort that led Mark Twain to rename the Leatherstocking tales the "Broken-Twig Series."

Nevertheless, as Percy H. Boynton has observed, few who came to scoff could have remained to rival or surpass Cooper as a story-teller. His accounts of deadly struggles and hairbreadth escapes have thrilled millions of readers at home and abroad, and his novels were long the most potent inducements to lure weary Europeans to the new land. In Europe, as in America, he remains perennially popular, and few ask or care how accurate his details of frontier existence or how authentic his characterization of woodsmen and Indians are. His saga-like portrayal of the frontiersman received eloquent expression in the remark of a French statesman in the spring of 1917, when the American national spirit was at length roused to enter the world conflict, "Thank God, the spirit of Leatherstocking is awake." Meanwhile, a hundred years after their appearance, Cooper's novels continue to sell in a way to gladden the heart of many a contemporary novelist and to prove the justice of Cooper's remark late in his life, "If anything from the pen of the writer of these romances is to outlive himself, it is unquestionably the series of 'The Leatherstocking Tales.' "

Long before the epic of the frontier was told, Cooper turned to new scenes and other books. In 1826 he received a nominal appointment as consul in Lyons, France, and for seven years (1826–1833) he lived in Europe, traveling a good deal in England, Holland, Germany, France, Switzerland, and Italy, and meeting many European notables. This experience vastly widened his outlook and turned his mind in new directions. His travels made him see his own country in a different light and to appreciate anew her virtues; and while he was made aware of the graces and dignities of aristocratic countries, he also appraised the social oppressions on which they so often depended. His nationalism thus intensified, he resented the ignorance everywhere shown by Europeans regarding America, and set himself to educating them in sounder views and attitudes toward his native land. It was a hopeless and thankless task, as Franklin or Irving could have told him—especially for one as unabashedly outspoken as Cooper was. His *Notions of the Americans* (1828), too frankly partisan to convince Europeans, served only to annoy them; and his three novels—*The Bravo* (1831), *The Heidenmauer* (1832), and *The Headsman* (1833), designed to "debunk" the glamour of aristocratic and feudal traditions in Italy, Germany, and Switzerland, respectively—further antagonized his European readers. An unprofitable controversy in Paris over the relative costs of the French and American governments into which he allowed himself to be drawn pleased neither nation. His residence in Europe served only to precipitate the conflicts long brewing within him between his innately aristocratic social sensibilities and his republican convictions and to engender the critical temperament that embittered the rest of his life.

But before his comparative studies of European and American society completely absorbed him, he wrote three more novels that are innocent of social and political criticism. *The Red Rover* of 1827 is a notable sea tale in which the ocean plays the same role in disciplining man that the frontier and later the prairie play in the life of Natty Bumppo. In *Wept of Wish-ton-Wish* (1829) he wrote a historical romance of New England around an episode of King Philip's War that was more successful than *Lionel Lincoln* had been, despite his apparent dislike of the Puritan characters whom he portrayed. *The Water Witch*, which followed the next year, and which

Cooper regarded as the most imaginative of his books, is another story of the sea, including an account of a spirited naval battle; but his attempt to localize a supernatural legend in New York harbor, he admitted a few years later, proved "a comparative failure."

When he returned to New York in 1834, he was met by an attack upon his conduct as a critic of Europe. *A Letter to His Countrymen* (1834) was his prompt reply, explaining that his books on Europe were motivated solely by his desire to set aristocracy in its proper relation to democracy and to bring "American opinion . . . to bear on European facts." But he went further to explain that while he espoused republican as against aristocratic principles, he was not prepared to join whole-heartedly in the American chorus of self-approval just then sounding on every hand. He discovered that during the seven years of his absence the American temper had undergone a sweeping change, and he did not like what he saw of the political demagoguery, the social leveling rampant under the new Jacksonian spirit of frontier democracy, and the rising power of the masses unless they were prepared to wield that power wisely.

A careful reading of the passages in *The American Democrat* (1838) in which he distinguished between "the aristocrat" and "the democrat" will indicate why, though he considered some of the popular fruits of Jacksonian democracy to be vicious, breeding a greedy, ignorant, and contentious spirit, he could admire the sterling qualities of Old Hickory himself, and vote for him. It was not democracy that he attacked, but what he considered the abuse of it. Accordingly he lashed out at every group or agency which he sensed to be dangerous to true democracy —whether these represented entrenched conservatism or unbridled innovation. He particularly deplored the factionalism which party spirit seemed to him to breed. Himself nominally a member of the Democratic party (although he did not subscribe to all its tenets), he repeatedly declared that he "belonged" to neither of the two great American parties, and that if he had his way, he would do away with parties altogether. While his European novels attacked political corruption and feudalistic survivals in old-world governments and society, pointed to the dangers inherent in the assumption by government of infallibility or arbitrary power, and illustrated the baneful effects of special privilege, they were intended also to warn Americans that watchful vigilance was necessary to prevent the perversion of republicanism into tyrannical absolutism. And he made it clear that the tyranny of the masses could be as devastating as the tyranny of a single despot.

In *The Monikins* (1835), a thinly veiled and incredibly dull satire on England and the United States as the Leaphigh and the Leaplow of the story, he made his views more explicit: European civilization fails because of "caste, corruption, and insusceptibility to social change"; American, because of "party vulgarity and money madness." While he believed firmly in a widely extended suffrage and in the equality of democratic opportunity, he doubted that the new Jacksonian democracy, as exemplified by the mobs of bustling, ill-bred, contentious partisans and opportunists who attached themselves to the Jacksonian movement, was quite the proper medicine for American ailments. The popular demonstrations of Jacksonian democracy seemed to him ill-suited to advance the graciousness of cultivated living or to enhance the cumulative values of the humanistic traditions that Americans stood in need of learning; his innate Toryism asserted itself in his refusal to admit the extreme premises on which the social equalitarianism of Jacksonian democracy was based. The obligation of leadership, he felt, rested with the class who were endowed by wisdom, manners, and possessions to lead—rather than with upstarts, demagogues, and coonskin democrats. So, while he raised a voice of warning in *The American Democrat* against "the narrow and selfish dogmas of those who would limit power by castes," he also condemned in uncompromising terms "the cant of demagogism" and "the impractical theories of visionaries." He questioned "the scheme of raising men very far above their natural propensities," and in the preface made the ill-advised admission that since he aimed at "correction," he wrote the book "more in the spirit of censure than of praise." Not unnaturally, the rank and file of the new Democrats resented his finding them composites of "intelligence, kindness, natural politeness, and vulgarity." Always hot-headed in controversy, he fulminated against "the coarse-minded and ignorant," while "the mass of the nation" retaliated in kind. An agrarian, sharply critical of the methods of commerce and trade, he alienated the tradesman, manufacturer, and financier no less by his strictures on their money-grubbing ways than he angered the backwoods people by his calling them low-born and vulgar. And as the abuse against him piled up, he concluded that the tyranny of an autocrat was no worse than the tyranny of public opinion. "As the press of the country now exists," he wrote in 1838, "it would seem to be expressly devised by the great agent of mischief, to depress and destroy all that is good, and to elevate all that is evil in the nation."

In *Homeward Bound* and *Home as Found*, both of 1838, he contrasted the glories of American civilization, as he envisaged them after his disillusionment over European society, with the offensive manners, shoddy social pretenses, questionable political practices, and shifty business methods, as he found them on their return. He offered Aristabulus Bragg as the typical product of this new democracy: "a compound of shrewdness, impudence, common-sense, pretension, humility, cleverness, vulgarity, kind-heartedness, duplicity, selfishness, law-honesty, moral fraud, and mother-wit, mixed up with a smattering of learning and much penetration in practical things . . . in short, purely a creature of circumstance." It was a round indictment in which, however well-founded his criticisms or laudable his purpose, he nevertheless allowed a rancorous tone and an ill-manered censoriousness to destroy whatever chance he had of exerting a good influence. Lowell summed up the matter rather well in *A Fable for Critics*:

> There is one thing in Cooper I like, too, and that is
> That on manners he lectures his countrymen gratis;
> Not precisely so either, because, for a rarity,
> He is paid for his tickets in unpopularity.
> Now he may overcharge his American pictures,
> But you'll grant there's a good deal of truth in his
>   strictures;
> And I honor the man who is willing to sink
> Half his present repute for the freedom to think,
> And, when he has thought, be his cause strong or weak,
> Will risk t' other half for the freedom to speak,
> Caring naught for what vengeance the mob has in store,
> Let that mob be the upper ten thousand or lower.

Indeed, one of the besetting faults of Cooper was that he was so right. He was always right. He became embroiled in various controversies, first, with his neighbors at Cooperstown over a picnic ground which they thought was theirs, and the relinquishment of which would certainly not have impoverished him. However, he chose to fight a long legal battle that proved he was right, but that lost him much good will. *Homeward Bound* and *Home as Found* provoked a flood of attacks upon him, which he seemed to delight in meeting with libel suits. He fought at one time a dozen law suits and won them all; but while he always won his points, he usually won only nominal damages and empty glory. In the process of elevating "a succession of newspaper editors into the honorable guild of the sued," he himself became one of "the most vilified men in America."

Personalities loomed large in these legal battles; but Cooper was really interested in larger issues and broader principles. These have been conveniently summarized by Professor Robert E. Spiller as a set of ideals: (1) "a class consciousness in America founded on a flexible principle of moral worth and individual ability, but controlling social life, as in Europe, through education, wealth, and property," (2) "an American press, freed from imitative servility to foreign presses and foreign political interests, and guided by high moral and patriotic ideals," and (3) "an American literary criticism, freed from personal abuse, and consciously fostering a national literature." Naturally his adversaries lost sight of these more general objects, and, while attributing his quarrelsomeness to personal vindictiveness, put him down as a common scold. These embroilments continued to embitter his later years, during which he found himself distracted and confused by issues that carried him further and further from his more rewarding career as a novelist.

Indeed, in 1834 he swore that he would write no more novels for an ungrateful world unprepared to profit by good advice; but once fairly launched on his controversial career, there was no withdrawing from social criticism, and after six years he returned to the novel as such, finishing out in 1840 and 1841 the Leatherstocking series. He began in 1836 a series of five volumes of *Gleanings in Europe*—critical travel sketches of France, England, Switzerland, Italy, and Germany, that irritated the people of two continents; in 1839 he published an admirable *History of the Navy of the United States of America*, the real value of which long remained obscured by a controversy that had no direct bearing on the merit of the book; and he wrote also various stories and books of a miscellaneous character. So he proceeded, in the midst of vilification and controversy, to produce a shelf of fiction, history, and social criticism.

One important group of these later works is a series of sea stories. *Mercedes of Castile* (1840) deals with the first voyage of Columbus. *The Two Admirals* (1842) contains one of his best accounts of a naval battle, and *Wing-and-Wing* (1842), a romantic story of the Mediterranean, ranks high among his sea tales. *Afloat and Ashore* (1844), dealing with the evils of impressment, is no less powerful in its description of naval engagements than were his earlier sea stories, and *Jack Tier* (1846–48) is a lurid tale of piracy during the period of the Mexican War.

During 1844–46 he published also a series of novels dealing with the theory of property rights as the basis of American civilization. *Afloat and Ashore* (1844) is properly a kind of introduction to the so-called Littlepage trilogy: *Satanstoe* (1845), *The Chainbearer* (1845), and *The Redskins* (1846). In these novels he treated three generations of a New York family with some of his old skill, but more immediately they were Cooper's contribution to the Anti-Rent War of 1839–46, affording him an opportunity to promulgate his ideas of the inviolability of property rights as affecting his "American principles" of democracy, and providing future generations with a fine piece of social documentation for up-state New York for the period covered.

In 1846 he brought out the *Lives of Distinguished American Naval Officers*, to clinch his position as historian of the United States Navy. Thereafter came various novels and even a comedy called *Upside Down, or Philosophy in Petticoats*, which was produced in New York in 1850, but never published. Among his more notable later books were *The Crater* (1848), a social allegory relating the fate of a colony founded on a volcanic reef, and *The Ways of the Hour* (1850), a satire on trial by jury designed "to draw the attention of the reader to some of the social evils that beset us, more particularly in connection with the administration of criminal justice." The conclusion is the melancholy reflection of Cooper, within a year of his death, that after his long struggle for his "American opinions," the vulgar were still occupying the seats of the mighty, the press still used its power indiscriminately, and the demagogue still went unchecked, while the law and the courts were in the employ of those who planned the destruction of stability and the rights of property. Chaos—domestic, economic, national—threatened. His conclusion is that of an irreconcilable Tory commenting on past times when "in the days of the monarchy, in truth, greater republican simplicity really reigned among us, in a thousand ways" than reigns in the degenerate, decadent days of 1850. In the last days of his life he reaffirmed his distaste for the America of his later days and of the future toward which he saw America rushing, by forbidding any biography of his to be authorized.

While to most readers Cooper is the creator of the nearest approach Americans have to a national epic, and his Leatherstocking series undoubtedly remains his greatest contribution to American literature, he is coming to be viewed as essentially greater than a mere *belles-lettres* writer. For over and above the narrator of thrilling stories of the frontier and of the sea, he was a conservative patriot—none more sincere and none more indefatigible in urging his countrymen to adopt noble principles while sloughing off shabby ones. If his patriotism led him into endless controversy with his countrymen, it was this same love of country that made him the creator of Harvey Birch, Long Tom Coffin, Chingachgook, and Leatherstocking. His native qualities of character and the native quality of his books are what give him enduring worth.

WILLIAM CULLEN BRYANT (1794–1878)

Identified for the sake of convenience with the Knickerbocker group of writers, who dominated the American literary scene from the War of 1812 to the rise of the Transcendentalists during the thirties, Bryant was a New Yorker by adoption only. Upon going to New York in 1825 (aged thirty-one), he shared with Cooper and Irving the literary leadership, and for the next fifty-three years he was a commanding figure as editor, publicist, essayist, critic, orator, and poet. But while he was identified, during most of his mature life with New York City, he belongs to New England by birth, by inheritance, by early associations, by almost every shaping influence on his literary personality. Maturing early and changing little afterwards, the Bryant who left his native regions to become one of the most influential editors of the century was already, in all essentials, the Bryant whom we know best today. His first volume of forty-four pages of 1821, contains most, and the second, of 1832, contains almost all, of what is essential in Bryant's poetry. In the half-century during which he added considerably to the bulk of these early volumes, he varied his emphasis, constructions, and forms, but added virtually nothing basically new to the content of his poetry. There was little change in what he valued in nature and in human nature, how he envisaged it in his imagination; or how, after it had passed through the alembic of his mind and character, he gave it expression. Although he subsequently published several more volumes of verse (including many fine poems), they contain few revelations and no radically new forms. His life, however busy and fruitful, was relatively calm and uneventful. It included, neither during his middle nor later life, many soul-stirring or deeply humanizing experiences. As the editor of one of the most influential newspapers in America, he was stirred by portentous events and important social issues to write pungent editorials, but they seldom touched his poetic nature and evoked few poems in him. European travel, while producing several series of travel letters, came too late to effect such a marked intellectual change in him as it made in Emerson, or to give him a new poetic outlook, as it did for Longfellow. The death of his wife, in 1866, profoundly stirred him, but at seventy-two he could turn his grief into the quiet channel of translating Homer. In short, what had been needful for the development of his poetic personality happened to him before he left the haunts of his boyhood, and accordingly his early life is of particular importance by way of explaining the content and form of his poetry.

Born November 3, 1794, at Cummington, in the Berkshire hills of western Massachusetts, Bryant was the son of genteel parents who traced their descent directly to the Mayflower pilgrims. The father was a kindly, cultivated physician, staunchly orthodox in his religion, and Federalist in his political views. When Dr. Peter Bryant, himself fond of poetry, heard his precocious son praying that he "might receive the gift of poetic genius and write verses that might endure," the father undertook to introduce the lad to "Johnson deep," "Addison refined," and especially "Pope's celestial fire." Under promptings such as these, the lad of nine began to versify after the manner of the pseudo-classical English poets, and in 1804 he had the satisfaction of seeing his "Description of a School" published in the *Hampshire Gazette* of Northampton. Four years later his proud father caused to be published in Boston young Bryant's satirical poem on Jefferson, *The Embargo, or a Sketch of the Times*. Besides illustrating his thorough schooling in the conventional couplets of Pope, *The Embargo* contains evidence of the lad's complete indoctrination in Federalist principles by his father. Occasioned by the unpopularity of Jefferson's Embargo of 1807, the poem voices all the negative aspects of the Federalist attack upon the stupidity of all Democrats, the vileness of the "French intrigue," and the alleged villainy of President Jefferson, to whom the young Federalist issued the following invitation:

Go, wretch, resign the presidential chair,
Disclose thy secret features foul or fair,
Go, search, with curious eyes, for horned frogs,
'Mongst the wild wastes of Louisianian bogs;
Or where Ohio rolls his turbid stream,
Dig for huge bones, thy glory and thy theme; . . .
But quit to abler hands, the helm of state,
Nor image ruin on thy country's fate!

Just as he absorbed his political opinions from his
father, so he took the impress of religious orthodoxy
from his elders of the Cummington community,
when he wrote in 1807:

> Then let us tread, as lowly Jesus trod,
> The path that leads the sinner to his God;
> Keep Heaven's bright mansions ever in our eyes,
> Press tow'rds the mark and seize the glorious prize.

All these juvenile poems illustrate the ready dependence of the young poet for his measures upon
the eighteenth-century wits of Queen Anne's England. As yet utterly unmindful of the revolution that
was going forward under the auspices of Wordsworth
and Coleridge, Bryant set himself to write—

> With classic purity, unstudied ease,
> To sense instructive, pleasing to the ear,
> Correct, yet flowing, elegant and clear.

That is, his early verse was all written from a Federalist, Calvinist, and classicist point of view. There was
as yet nothing to suggest the turn he was to make
within the next decade toward Democratic, Unitarian, and romantic principles.

Most prominent among the agencies influencing
his conversion from conservatism to liberalism was his
contact with rational currents of thought fashionable
among the students of Williams College, whither he
went in 1810 as a sophomore. The break with the
religious orthodoxy of his youth is announced in
"Thanatopsis," the first draft of which was written in
1811, shortly before he reached his seventeenth birthday. The subject itself, Death, or more particularly,
How shall a man approach the grave? was not new.
Bryant had himself encountered it in the poems of
Henry Kirke White, Robert Blair, and others of the
"graveyard" school of English poets. Their influence
on the poem is marked. What is new is its unortho-
dox, that is, un-Christian, approach to death. Instead
of any reference to the conventional doctrines of
election or of rewards and punishments, of Calvin or
of Christ, the young rebel offers the stoical view of
death as a welcome release from the miseries of
human existence. Instead of the usual consolatory
assertion of the soul's immortality and the perpetua-
tion of individual being or of death as a progression
to the eternal bliss of Heaven, there is only the deistic
doctrine that the grave ends all:

> Earth that nourished thee, shall claim
> Thy growth, to be resolved to earth again,
> And, lost each human trace, surrendering up
> Thine individual being, shalt thou go
> To mix forever with the elements,
> To be a brother to the insensible rock
> And to the sluggish clod . . .

The only consolation offered is that this is the fate
of all men. Since none can escape it, it behooves a
man to make the most of it by meeting death heroically, that is, stoically.

By 1817, when he wrote "To a Waterfowl," he
had moderated his views to an expression of faith in
a supernatural power above, who could be relied on
to lead man's steps aright just as God guides the
waterfowl from "zone to zone" in its flight; and in
"The Forest Hymn" of 1825 the groves are called
"God's first temples." Although he often employed
familiar religious imagery in his later poems, he never
returned to the Calvinist faith of his youth, but
adopted the naturalistic philosophy of the Unitarians.
Unable to accept the Trinity, he identified God with
the "Great First Cause" in "An Evening Reverie"
(1841) and with the "Great Movement of the Universe" in "The Flood of Years" (1876). He worshipped a God who was spiritual rather than anthro-
pomorphic—who typified universal love and benevolence among men, and who could be contemplated
in the universality of the visible creation.

In his political views he experienced a similar conversion. Among the first causes leading to an examination of the Federalism inherited from his father was
the hot sectionalism engendered by the War of 1812.
He was himself ready at one time to enlist in the
Massachusetts militia and to resist forcibly federal
usurpation. But just about the time he attained his
majority and set out to practice law, the once powerful Federal party went into a decided decline, and
party alignments grew more indistinct. In the meantime, Bryant had been disappointed, after his year at
Williams College, in not being able to continue his
education at Yale. Instead he turned to studying law
in several lawyers' offices at Worthington and Bridge-
water. Admitted to the bar in 1815, he practiced first
at Plainfield and from 1816 to 1825 at Great Barring-
ton. During these years his reading in the law and in
history, together with what he saw of the practice of
political principles, made him dissatisfied with the
parochialism of his inherited political views. Before
he removed to New York City in 1825, he had become a liberal devoted to a broad program of reform,
including world peace, emancipation from slavery,
free trade, and democratic principles of government.
In short, he was prepared, in all essentials, for the
great role that he was to play for the next fifty years
as a liberal and democratic editor of the influential
New York *Evening Post*.

No less radical than the change in his religious and
political thinking was his conversion from classicism
to romanticism in his literary theory and practice. It
went forward as an attendant development with his

political and religious liberalism. Although he vowed in 1815, when he was admitted to the practice of law, that he would devote himself entirely to the work of his profession, and that he would "tune the rural lay no more," he admitted also—

I cannot forget with what fervid devotion
I worshipped the visions of verse and of fame.

However determined his resolution, poetry was an irresistible effervescence in his blood that would not be denied. Immediately upon writing the first draft of "Thanatopsis" in 1811, he made the discovery of Wordsworth and Coleridge's *Lyrical Ballads*. "A thousand springs," he said, "seemed to gush up at once into my heart and the face of Nature, of a sudden, to change into a strange freshness and life." "The Yellow Violet," written in 1814, and "Inscription for the Entrance to a Wood," of the next year, bear witness of how the earlier influences of White, Blair, Cowper, and Thomson (as these are manifest in "Thanatopsis," for example) were transmuted into the fullness of a romanticist's worship of nature under Wordsworthian influence. This new love of nature "in all her visible forms" led him often to forsake his Coke and Blackstone for ramblings among the hills and in the valleys—

Till I felt the dark power o'er my reveries stealing,
From the gloom of the thickets that over me hung,
And the thoughts that awoke, in that rapture of feeling,
Were formed into verse as they rose to my tongue.

A few years later he recalled how he had sought to break the spell that held him long, "the dear, dear witchery of song," resolved that "the poet's idle lore" should waste his "prime of years no more," forgetful that wheresoever he looked he saw "Nature's everlasting smile" recalling him to "the love of song." Thus Wordsworth and nature reclaimed him to the sweet uses of poetry.

In the meantime his earliest compositions under the new impetus of nature had been acclaimed notable successes. The reception of "Thanatopsis" itself had been flattering. When the verses were first sent by Bryant's father to the editor of the *North American Review*, the latter, doubting their authenticity, read them to his associate, who told him, "You have been imposed upon; no one on this side the Atlantic is capable of writing such verses." Upon being assured that they were indeed Bryant's own, they were printed in the *North American Review* for September, 1817, together with the "Inscription for the Entrance to a Wood," with its new Wordsworthian notes. "To a Waterfowl" was no less popular on its first appear-

ance in 1818. Shortly thereafter Bryant fell in love with Fanny Fairchild, whom he apostrophized, after the manner of Wordsworth's Lucy poems, in "Oh Fairest of the Rural Maids" (written in 1820). From now on, nature worship, love, and poetic inspiration went forward hand in hand under romantic auspices. Like Wordsworth, he felt himself a "dedicated spirit," seeking emanations of the indwelling life of nature. Like Wordsworth, too, he found in nature forces to stimulate and delight as well as to soothe and heal the spirit of man. He began to show the typical romantic interest in simple types of humanity and to regard the Indian as an example of "the noble savage race." The prairie and the pioneer fascinated him, and he became an ardent literary nationalist. Like a romantic antiquary, he searched for traditions, superstitions, and legends of the past to romanticize, even to dabbling in the horrible, the terrible, and the grotesque. New themes needed new forms, and he early began his experimentations in metres and genres that made him eventually one of the most various and versatile of American versifiers. Most important of all, he insisted that while poetry at its best aims to promote "the virtue and welfare of society" by inspiring and perfecting moral character, it originates in the feelings and operates through the imagination. The true office of poetry, he said in an essay on "Early American Verse," published in the *North American Review* for July, 1818, is to "touch the heart"; and in a series of four "Lectures on Poetry," delivered in 1826 before the Athenæum Society of New York, he expounded this theory at greater length. While insisting that "to write fine poetry requires intellectual qualities of the highest order," its humanized moral teachings are not to be presented barefacedly but imaginatively and in terms of beauty: "The most beautiful poetry is that which takes the strongest hold on the feelings, and, if it is really the most beautiful, then it is poetry in the highest sense. . . . The great spring of poetry is emotion. . . . Strong feeling is always a sure guide. It rarely offends against good taste, because it instinctively chooses the most effectual means of communicating itself to others." Forty years later he repeated the same creed in "The Poet" (1864). "The framing of a deathless lay," he observed, is not "the pastime of a drowsy summer's day," but requires a gathering of all the poet's powers, intellectual and emotional:

The secret wouldst thou know
  To touch the heart or fire the blood at will?
Let thine own eyes o'erflow;
  Let the lips quiver with the passionate thrill;
Seize the great thought, ere yet its power is past,
And bind, in words, the fleet emotion fast.

In 1821 Bryant published the first collection of his verses under the simple title of *Poems*. Despite its slender bulk of forty-four pages, it was the most important body of original verse published in America up to that time. During the same year he was invited to read "The Ages" as the annual poem of the Phi Beta Kappa Society at Harvard. The years 1824–25, while he was actively writing for the *United States Literary Gazette* of Boston, represent his most creative period as a poet. Long desirous of moving to Boston, he found no good opportunity there, but in 1825 he accepted the co-editorship of the *New York Review*, and immediately became a member of the literary group forming Cooper's Bread and Cheese Club. Before the year was out he went over as assistant editor of the New York *Evening Post*, whose full editorship he assumed in 1829.

His translation to New York marks the beginning of a new period in his life. Although he continued to write poetry, publishing important collections in 1832, 1844, and later, the poet in him was henceforth subordinate to that of the editor, critic, orator, and man of public affairs. Besides making the *Evening Post* the greatest newspaper of the time and acquiring a considerable private fortune, he spoke with conviction and authority to become one of the most influential voices in the land advocating freedom of speech, the principle of collective bargaining and the right of workmen to strike, free trade, reform legislation for crime and punishment, sound currency and banking methods, and the liberation of subject peoples abroad and of slaves at home. Forthright and vigorous in the statement of his views on such subjects as slavery and workingmen's rights, he was considered by his contemporaries as an aggressive, not to say violent, editor. Indeed, it is said that for many years the *Post* suffered financially because New York businessmen withheld their advertising from the paper on the ground that its editor, in supporting labor, was opposed to their interests. A supporter of Andrew Jackson because of Old Hickory's "simplicity and frankness . . . incorruptible honesty . . . and fearless directness," he was no uncritical follower of party. When Harrison's log-cabin, hard-cider campaign got under way, he was disgusted by what he considered its fraudulent character, and he mercilessly ridiculed coonskin democracy. As the struggle over slavery became acute, he denounced the Fugitive Slave Law as "the most ruffianly act ever authorized by a deliberative assembly." The cause of the Free-Soil men he called "great and righteous"; the Dred Scott decision, a "disgrace"; and John Brown a "martyr and hero." In 1855, having decided that the Democratic party was no longer true to its ideals, he

became active in the organization of the Republican party in the East. From the beginning he was vehement in his denunciation of the doctrine of nullification. When secession came, he said fearlessly and uncompromisingly, "If a state secedes, it is rebellion, and the seceders are traitors." Once war became inevitable, no one was more insistent than he on a vigorous prosecution of the bloody contest, or in the suppression of such disrupting forces as the draft riots in New York City during 1863, himself resolutely braving the unbridled mob violence that convulsed the city for three days. When the Republican party openly allied itself with post-war capitalism, his suspicion and opposition were aroused. Whatever his party allegiance, he was a democrat from principle, demanding tolerance and fairness, championing unpopular causes, and defending the rights of free men.

In the end he came to have less faith in outward than in inward reform. As a progressive utopian during his middle years, he often joined whole-heartedly in efforts to remake society through local and national reform; but fundamentally he was a humanist rather than a humanitarian, holding to the simple faith of his New England rearing that as the perfect state of society is reached only through the emancipation and perfecting of individuals, so the liberty of the individual is the only infallible cure for all ills. In his old age, too, he submitted to the Christian rite of baptism, by a Unitarian minister, and he became a member of the Unitarian church. It is sometimes said that his translation of Homer, after his wife's death in 1866, was a capitulation to classicism. But these modifications of the old Bryant in his political, religious, and literary views constitute not so much a reactionary reversion to conservatism as a moderation or mediation, occasioned by the wisdom of a long life of rich and varied experience.

Despite the wealth and fame that crowned his old age, he continued to live simply and to work earnestly for the cause of liberty. His last public performance, one that hastened his death, was to speak at the unveiling of Mazzini's statue in Central Park. His speech was a plea for human liberty and "the rights and duties of human brotherhood." Throughout his long career, as editor and critic, he was indefatigable in his desire to raise the level of American literature by urging American authors to adopt simplicity, integrity, and freedom as their guiding principles. No one worked more earnestly than he in discovering new talent and encouraging young writers.

His numerous volumes of later verse are all distinguished for evenness and dignity. Occasionally, as in "The Prairie" (1832), "The Battlefield" (1842), and "The Death of Lincoln" (1865), he matched his earlier performance; but he had no markedly new themes to add to the few elemental ones of his youth: the beauty and beneficence of nature, the sacredness of human freedom, the ebb and flow of human existence, and the dignity and abiding influence of goodness. His last long poem, "The Flood of Years," in 1878, is in the same lofty mood of meditation as is "The Ages" of 1821. His range was narrow, but within its confines he was a master. There is in his poetry no pagan luxuriance and no riot of colorful sensuousness; instead, the ethical idealism of his New England conditioning gives stately, restrained form to his passionate righteousness and his high seriousness. The austerity and frigidity of his verse, popularized by Lowell's humorous lines in "A Fable for Critics," proceed not from a cold heart or an illiberal brain, but from a noble reserve and the fine poise of a mind that lives contentedly within its own resources.

The poet's was for Bryant the highest calling. It proceeded, he said in "The Poet," from

> . . . feelings of calm power and mighty sweep,
> Like currents journeying through the windless deep.

He allowed "no empty gusts of passion," no merely "fluent strains" or "smooth array of phrase," no emotional crotchets or erratic sensibilities, to distract him from his high purpose of clothing—

> . . . in words of flame
> Thoughts that shall live within the general mind.

Not one of the world's master poets, because he was not pre-eminently endowed with intellectual intensity and imaginative concentration, yet he remains unequaled among American poets as leaving a record markedly true to his poetic aims.

A Puritan-liberal, as Parrington has called him, Bryant, the journalist and critic who sat for fifty years in judgment on matters political and economic as well as cultural, and who reflected in the *Evening Post* a refinement of taste and dignity of character unequaled in earlier American journalism, performed an important service for America quite apart from his contribution to our incipient poetry. He was at once the father of nineteenth-century American journalism and the father of nineteenth-century American nature poetry.

WASHINGTON IRVING (1783–1859)

Washington Irving enjoyed the signal honor of becoming the first American author to be widely appreciated abroad. The popular success of *The Sketch Book* in England at precisely the moment when British-American animosity had reached a new high made him doubly dear to Americans who had long waited for a native writer capable of scotching the superciliously contemptuous attitude of English critics toward American productions of the spirit. The honor was all the more phenomenal because it was won on purely literary merit. Intellectually, Irving was a lesser man than the more notable of his predecessors. He lacked the high seriousness of a Mather, the philosophical acumen of an Edwards, the versatility of a Franklin, the statesmanship of a Jefferson, and the profundity of a Dwight. Yet he has overshadowed them all and continues today as a more significant figure in the history of American letters than any of them. Relatively unconcerned with great ideas and lacking in emotional intensity or imaginative power, Irving nevertheless possessed a temperament and a style the combination of which enabled him to vary his tone from sentiment and romance to wit and urbanity in a manner which left no doubt that here at last was an American whose gentlemanly geniality was as authentic as his elegant good taste was instinctive. To be sure, his endowments were not prodigious, but they were sufficient to establish him as a man of parts. Far from being a bumptious provincial, he was a cosmopolite, speaking a language of suavity and gentility universally recognized and understood in polite and cultivated circles.

In the attainment of the graces of living he was naturally conditioned by the circumstances surrounding his earlier years. Born in New York City on April 3, 1783, the favorite and last of eleven children of an austere Presbyterian father and a more genially-minded Anglican mother, young Irving grew up in an atmosphere of indulgence. A disposition toward frailty and sensitivity got for him the best that family competence and brotherly favoritism could supply. After eleven years of elementary schooling, he escaped the regularity of a collegiate education which his father had prescribed for his older sons. But because

it was still customary for a gentleman to have a profession, even though he might not practice it, he read intermittently at the law for a half-dozen years in several law offices of New York, notably in that of Judge Josiah Ogden Hoffman, with whose pretty daughter Mathilda he early fell in love. His "inveterate enemies, the fathers of the law," did not, however, prevent his participation, as a gay young man-about-town, in the social whirl of the city or his hobnobbing with a knot of gay young men, known as the "Nine Worthies of Cockloft Hall," who were bent, like himself, on enjoying life in terms of conviviality, feminine society, theatrical entertainment, and literary amusement. Association with literary-minded young dandies like Peter and Gouverneur Kemble, Henry Brevoort, Henry Ogden, James K. Paulding, and his own brothers, William, Peter, and Ebenezer, led to his writing a series of whimsically satirical essays over the signature of "Jonathan Oldstyle, Gent.," published in Peter Irving's paper, the *Morning Chronicle*, during 1802–03. This youthful playing with the pen was interrupted by several trips up the Hudson, another into Canada in the interest of his health, and during 1804–06, an extended tour of Europe. Although the captain of the ship on which he sailed said, when young Irving first came aboard, "There's a chap who will go overboard before we get across," his health was markedly improved during the two years in Europe, which served also to give his manners a brush, and to fill several notebooks with experiences picked up in a constant round of sight-seeing, flirtatious pleasantries, and frivolous entertainment.

Upon his return to New York, he passed the bar examination late in 1806, "by the grace of God and Josiah Hoffman," the chief examiner, and in the following February he set up as a lawyer, at least to the extent of moving into the office of his brother John, at No. 3 Wall Street. But he argued no more cases than Oliver Wendell Holmes later healed broken bodies. During 1807–08 his chief employment was to collaborate with James K. Paulding and his brother William in the writing of a series of twenty periodical essays, entitled *Salmagundi*. To secure variety, they followed the Addisonian scheme of having the several subjects dealt with treated by several gentlemen, each reminiscent of the members of the Spectator Club. The department of society was under the direction of Anthony Evergreen, Esq.; that of criticism was the special province of William Wizard, Esq.; poetry came from Pindar Cockloft; and the better to motivate their instructions, the authors presented characters and family relationships reminiscent of Addison's Distaffs. Facetiously posing as "critics, amateurs, dilettanti, and cognoscenti," the editors proceeded, in true *Spectator* fashion, "to instruct the young, reform the old, correct the town, and castigate the age." All was in good humor and fun, for, as they declared, "While we continue to go on, we will go on merrily; if we moralize, it shall be but seldom; and on all occasions, we shall be more solicitous to make our readers laugh than cry; for we are laughing philosophers, and clearly of the opinion that wisdom, true wisdom, is a plump, jolly dame, who sits in her arm-chair, laughs right merrily at the farce of life—and takes the world as it goes." So they proceeded to satirize the ways of the fashionable world, ridiculing the pretensions of political upstarts and social climbers, inserting squibs on the theatre, occasionally mixing a little pointed political satire, waging war against boorishness and mediocrity, "folly and stupidity," while teaching "parents . . . how to govern children, girls how to get husbands, and old maids how to do without them."

Salmagundi made an impression, created a stir, and became a mild terror in certain quarters of the town. While the editors were concerned primarily with passing phases of contemporary society, some of the numbers retain significance even today as an index to the social milieu in which young Irving moved so easily. One of the most vital features is the series of nine letters of Mustapha, Captain of a Ketch of Tripolitan prisoners, now waiting in New York to be returned to his country, employing his leisure to observe men and manners in the United States, and reporting his observations to Asem Hacchem, Principal Slave-Driver to His Highness the Bashaw of Tripoli. His commentary on American customs and institutions is all the more pointed, coming as it does from a barbarian; his observations on American democracy and his characterization of leading "republicans" like Paine and Jefferson are edged and barbed. Mustapha descants upon the nature of the American government:

To let thee at once into a secret, which is unknown to these people themselves, their government is a pure unadulterated *logocracy*, or government of words. The whole nation does everything *viva voce*, or by word of mouth; and

in this manner is one of the most military nations in existence. Every man who has what is called the gift of gab, that is, a plentiful stock of verbosity, becomes a soldier outright; and is forever in a militant state. The country is entirely defended *vi et linguâ*; that is to say, by force of tongues . . .

In this logocratic country, civil wars of great violence, as Mustapha regards election campaigns, are carried on every so often. One is now reported in progress— "a conspiracy, among the higher classes, to dethrone his highness, the present bashaw, and place another in his stead." A good deal of fun is poked at Jefferson's affection for red breeches, his "enlightened" religious opinions, his philosophical pretensions, and his fondness for a certain "professed antediluvian from the Gallic empire"—Tom Paine, of course—who is said to have illuminated two continents "with his principles—and his nose." Throughout the seven years that the present bashaw has been in office, the entire nation has been kept in a blaze, for every slang-whanger has resorted "to his tongue or his pen" to set the country by the ears. Thus did the young Federalist authors proclaim their inherited dislike of insurgent republicanism. Thus, too, Irving the lawyer (although he continued for a while longer to share his brother's office) fades into the background as Irving the writer emerges directly out of the social milieu of early nineteenth-century New York.

His next book owes its inception to the same love of fun-making and the same social background, except that the materials are not of contemporary Manhattan but of the New Amsterdam of the Dutch regime. Begun as a *jeu d'esprit*, in collaboration with his brother Peter, and intended merely as a parody of Dr. Samuel Mitchell's guide-book to New York City, it was expanded by Washington, after Peter withdrew to Liverpool in the interests of the Irving importing business, into a comic history of the Dutch settlements of New York. Like *Salmagundi*, it embodied a great deal of contemporary personal and political satire, born of youthful exuberance, effrontery, and bravado, and it introduces us to Irving the antiquarian—an impulse that played henceforth an increasingly prominent part in his literary development. Aside from its criticism of Jeffersonian democracy and its whimsical satire on pedantic historians and literary classicists, *Diedrich Knickerbocker's History of New York* is "the first great book of comic literature written by an American."

The composition of the book was interrupted in April of 1809 by the sudden death of Mathilda Hoffman. Grief incapacitated Irving for a while; but in the end the hard work necessary to complete *Knicker-*

bocker, the success of the book upon its appearance in 1809, and his transfer in 1811 to the newer and wider scene of Washington as a lobbyist in the interests of the Irving brothers' hardware importing firm helped relegate his grief to the realm of memory. The sentimental story woven by Pierre M. Irving round his uncle's undying and undivided love for Mathilda Hoffman is overdone. Irving was drawn to attractive women all his life, as much after Mathilda's death as before, and there is a long succession of beautiful women in his life to whom he paid court in cavalier phrases and with gallant address, while steadily refusing to accommodate the romantic match-makers who never gave up hope of marrying off one of the most eligible young bachelors of two continents, until he settled down at Sunnyside to bask in the smiles and under the care of his numerous nieces.

Irving's gallantry was of a piece with his gentlemanly, essentially aristocratic, bearing in all other relations of life. Belonging by birth, rearing, and inclination to the well-to-do and aristocratic circle of New York Federalists, he came to hold, more or less unconsciously, their principles of class privilege, class interests, capitalism, stability, and centrality of governmental power. Disliking money-getting and commercial pursuits, he developed into an urbane New Yorker neither personally nor vitally interested in the economic ideals or the political principles of either party. Mechanics and yokels, tinkers and tradesmen, of whatever party, left him cold; and he had little interest in their so-called Rights, abstract or otherwise. One electioneering experience in city politics, shortly after he hung out his shingle, destroyed his taste for the ruck of practical politics, and he concluded, "Truly this saving one's country is a nauseous piece of business, and if patriotism is such a dirty virtue—prithee, no more of it." A gentleman could not meddle with it without getting his fingers soiled. While he was never disdainful of any rich political plum that might fall into his lap, he could not "run with the hungry pack of office-seekers," and he gave up all ideas of saving his country on a government salary. Subsequently, especially after he was thrown upon his own resources, he repeatedly angled for a good political appointment, and eventually he was rewarded with several good diplomatic assignments. He could have had better posts, including the mayoralty of New York City and a cabinet post under Van Buren, but he was neither politician nor statesman. He was a detached, amused observer of life, of the old gentlemanly school, looking about him with genial eye, resolved to make of

life an art, content to leave to "abler heads" the making of converts in religion or politics. Such matters he professed to find "full of perplexity"; so he stuck to his idea that for himself he could do more good to men by entertaining them and thus "keeping mankind in good humor with one another" than by instructing or lecturing them.

It was this same spirit of geniality which led him to say that as a traveler, when he found it impossible to get a dinner to suit his taste, he endeavored to get a taste to suit his dinner. It was this geniality of temperament more than anything else that enabled him to captivate readers of many countries and to get along famously with men of opposing parties or philosophies. He was less interested in the political issues, of which the embroilments of politicians are only the external signs, than in the thing itself—the Federalist attitude toward life as an ideal of living, so that in spite of his indifference to party, he was really more Federalist than the Federalists themselves. Without comprehending all the implications, he was keenly aware of a change coming over the country under Jeffersonian auspices, and he was plainly disturbed by the rebellious and discontented elements among the common people who, in their determination not to remain common, seemed to him to be losing all respect for their betters. He cast his eyes lovingly back toward the good old days when everybody knew and kept his place, and he viewed with suspicion the tendency to forget the graces of living in the grasping for power and money, privileges and rights. Hence *Salmagundi* is an onslaught upon the vile manners of a mercantile, middle-class seaport town; and *Diedrich Knickerbocker's History of New York,* in its Dutch aspects, is a satire upon their sluggish bourgeois nature, their lack of grace, and the "happy equality" of their earth-creeping minds, while, in its attacks upon the Yankees, it is a satire on their ungainly manners and their odious practices of pilfering and money-grubbing. Similarly, in his next books, *The Sketch Book* (1819–20) and *Bracebridge Hall* (1822), the life of a "gentleman," in the eighteenth-century sense of the word—whether the urbane man-of-parts or the eccentric but worthy country squire—is lovingly idealized; while tradesmen, demagogues, upstarts, innovators, levelers, and dullards alike are ridiculed. In Book IV of *Knickerbocker,* the reign of William Kieft serves admirably for Irving's clever satirization of Jefferson and of Jeffersonian democracy. The same motive animates his sympathetic delineation of Rip Van Winkle in *The Sketch Book*— the picture of Rip and his cronies, humorous, honest, and happy in their lethargic contentment, contrasted with the cantankerous demagoguery of the shabbily pretentious and slatternly democratic village to which Rip returns after his long sleep. *Bracebridge Hall, Tales of a Traveller* (1824), and *The Alhambra* (1832), alike, are tinged with the melancholy nostalgia for a beautiful age that has departed—rich in loyalty, solidity, human worth, instead of human rights, in contrast with the present, given over to innovation, social mediocrity, and material acquisitiveness.

Following *Knickerbocker* in 1809, Irving was for ten years more or less at loose ends. Having been made a profit-sharing but generally inactive partner in his brothers' business, he did a small chore of lobbying in Washington in the interests of the firm, but he was more assiduous in attendance upon the White House levees of Dolly Madison than upon the debates in Congress. During 1812–13 he did some editorial work, notably as editor of the *Analectic Magazine*. He wrote some biographical sketches of popular naval heroes of the War of 1812, and in 1814 he himself did a little soldiering as aide-de-camp to Governor Tompkins; and though he saw no action, he annexed the rank of colonel. The next year he sailed for Europe to aid in the conduct of the Liverpool branch of the Irving firm, which, despite his manful efforts, went from bad to worse during the depression that followed the war. In 1818 the firm went into bankruptcy, and Irving was, for the first time in his life, thrown upon his own resources to earn a livelihood.

Turning down several lucrative editorial offers, he chose to rely upon his pen. Contact with Scott and most of the literary people of Edinburgh and London, including the stimulating people who frequented Murray's drawing-rooms in London, put him in a mood to resume writing after a ten-year interval. The result was *The Sketch Book*, originally published serially in America and England in 1819–20 and reprinted in book form in 1820. Compounded of some thirty separate essays, sketches, and stories, it is a miscellany. About half of the pieces are based on observations of English life and customs, towns, estates, and places rich in legendary lore and tradition. Six are roughly classifiable as literary essays, four are in the nature of traveling reminiscences. Three others—"Rip Van Winkle," "The Legend of Sleepy Hollow," and "The Spectre Bridegroom"—are short stories. Two deal with the American Indian. The remaining three are so miscellaneous as to defy classification.

One of the most noteworthy essays in *The Sketch Book* is entitled "English Writers on America." It represents the first sane and effective word spoken on the long and rancorous literary controversy between England and America, and it did much to allay the senseless animosity between the two nations. In it, Irving urged his countrymen to forget their resentments, to overcome their inferiority complex, to rise above petty parochialism, and to start thinking like generous-minded, independent Americans. Carefully avoiding all semblance of truckling obsequiousness, he appealed to the British sense of decency and fair play, reminding the English that all they needed to do to retain American good will was to show a mutual spirit of conciliation. He went on to tell Englishmen that it was of comparatively little importance "whether England does us justice or not; it is, perhaps, of far more importance to herself." And suggesting that in the history of the world's great empires, none has yet been exempt from decline and decay, he pointed out that the future destiny of America is as assured as that of England is insecure, adding that if England persists in her short-sighted policy, she may come to rue the day when she repulsed from her side a young nation that has every wish to be friendly, thus destroying "her only chance for real friendship beyond the boundaries of her own dominions." This was good-natured plain-speaking that John Bull could appreciate.

The three tales in *The Sketch Book* are the first examples of what Poe later called the American short story. They represent Irving's most popular contributions to American literature. Essentially re-workings or transcriptions of old German legends (to which Scott first called his attention), they are as original in treatment as they are old in subject matter; for in transferring Germanic *motifs* to the Sleepy Hollow locale and reinvesting German legendary figures in Knickerbocker characteristics, he unconsciously invented a new genre. The success of *The Sketch Book* was so great that it set him off on a series of travel stages in the hope of exploring and capitalizing more fully upon the traditions to be picked up and reworked in that way. His mind was receptive rather than creative, and he had to rely upon what he came across in his travels or in his reading to set his pen to work. Describing his faculties as "desultory" and lacking command of his talents, he admitted that he had to write when he could, not when he would, adding, "I shall occasionally shift my residence and write whatever is suggested by objects before me . . ." His extensive travels and protracted stays in Germany, Austria, France, Spain, and England were the result; and these in turn explain why his pictures are transcripts rather than conceptions; his characters are such as have lived and moved among men rather than creatures of his imagination. They are derived from his travels or assimilated from books or from fragments of old legends, and they were built up by the memory and the fancy, which patch or combine rather than create. They are given cogency by certain attributes of his mind, the combination of which enabled him to achieve that delicacy of style by which Irving lives today. On this head may be enumerated (1) an inborn, somewhat incalculable feeling for sentiment and, particularly after *Knickerbocker* (1809), sensibility, (2) an equally natural feeling for the Federalistic attitude toward a gentlemanly way of living—geniality, graciousness, urbanity, tastefulness, (3) a feeling for romanticism, imbibed partly from Scott and German literature, and first markedly apparent in *The Sketch Book* (1819), (4) an inherent love for the method of the literary antiquary, especially from *Knickerbocker* onward, (5) an extraordinary sensitivity for sense impressions from without, and (6) a remarkable facility for form within the limits of short units, especially the essay and the short story.

Whether writing Knickerbocker sketches, Moorish legends, banditti stories, or Gothic tales, it was the style that chiefly interested him.

I consider a story merely as a frame on which to stretch my materials. It is the play of thought, and sentiment and language; the weaving in of characters, lightly yet expressively delineated; the familiar and faithful exhibition of scenes in common life; and the half concealed vein of humour that is often playing through the whole—these are among what I aim at, and upon which I felicitate myself in proportion as I think I succeed. . . . I believe the works I have written will be oftener re-read than any novel of the size that I could have written. . . .

I have preferred adopting a mode of sketches & short tales rather than long works, because I chose to take a line of writing peculiar to myself; rather than fall into the manner or school of any other writer: and there is a constant activity of thought and nicety of execution required in writings of this kind, more than the world appears to imagine. . . . In these shorter writings every page must have its merit. The author must be continually piquant—woe to him if he makes an awkward sentence or writes a stupid page; the critics are sure to pounce upon it. Yet if he succeed: the very variety & piquancy of his writings; nay their very brevity; makes them frequently recurred to—and when the mere interest of the story is exhausted, he begins to get credit for his touches of pathos or humour; his points of wit or turns of language. . . .

Indeed, Irving's attempts at the novel were abortive. He lacked the requirements of a good novelist—sustained concentration, searching analysis of character, strict construction of plot, and fine adjustment of numberless details into a continuous fabric. The best of his original works are brief, and he showed a good deal of acumen when he observed, "If the tales . . . should prove to be bad, they will at least be found short." Even *Knickerbocker* is more an aggregate of tales by chapters than a continuous history; while his biographies, which required a minimum of invention, exhibit no great structural skill. His most successful biography, *The Life of Goldsmith* (1849) is good because, aside from his felicity of style, he is in perfect sympathy with his subject. He was unable himself to write a good play, but was excellent in collaboration, and with John Howard Payne he scored a great hit in the comedy, *Charles II* (1824).

Following *Bracebridge Hall* (1822), a kind of sequel to *The Sketch Book*, Irving spent 1823 in Germany, where he planned a German Sketch Book, which appeared in much-modified form as *Tales of a Traveller* in 1824. After periods in London and Paris, he went to Madrid on the invitation of Alexander H. Everett, minister to Spain, to join the American Legation in a purely nominal capacity, for he intended to devote himself to translating a recent Spanish biography of Columbus. There followed a remarkably fecund period, for the Spanish sojourn furnished him with the materials for *The Life of Columbus* (1828), *The Conquest of Granada* (1829), *The Companions of Columbus* (1831), *The Alhambra* (1832), *The Conquest of Spain* (1835), and eventually *The Life of Mahomet* (1850).

In 1832, having been continuously abroad since 1815, he returned to the United States. Like Cooper, he was very much surprised at the altered social, economic, and political complexion of the country; but more readily adaptable than Cooper, he made up his mind to like what he found. All reports that he had while still in Europe had led him to suspect Jackson and Jacksonianism; but when he met Old Hickory, he took a liking to his "rough chivalry" and accordingly came easily to the position of saying, "The more I see of this old cock of the woods, the more I relish his game qualities." He became known as a mild Jackson man, and he resolved to familiarize himself with the new America, especially with the vast, new frontier. An extended tour of the West resulted in three books on the frontier: *Astoria* (1834), a romanticized account of Astor's fur empire, *A Tour of the Prairies* (1835), and *The Adventures of Captain Bonneville* (1837). Moving easily and agreeably among the prophets of the new day, whether John Jacob Astor or Andrew Jackson, he was readily accepted by them. Eager to make capital of his literary reputation, they courted his favor, urging upon him various offices, all of which he had the good sense to decline until, in

1842, he took the ministership to Spain. Following the distinguished diplomatic service which he rendered his country during the difficult years of 1842-45 in Spain, he returned to New York and soon thereafter settled at Sunnyside, in Sleepy Hollow. Here he was near enough to his beloved city to enjoy the theatre and to participate in literary and social affairs. Here he lived the retired life of a country gentleman, devoting himself to the collection of several volumes of miscellanies, *The Life of Mahomet* (1850), and the five-volume *Life of Washington*, which he just lived to complete in 1859.

Irving was no great man. He was not bursting with big ideas or burning messages. He regarded life not from a philosophic, religious, or political, but from a literary, point of view. He never caught the restlessness of the century, and he embraced no schemes for the reformation of mankind. He was content to be a mere *belles-lettres* writer. As early as 1823 he resolved that he must make his way in the literary world on his own terms:

One must take care not to fall into the commonplace of the day. Scott's manner must likewise be widely avoided. In short, I must strike out some way of my own, suited to my own way of thinking and writing. I wish, in everything I do, to write in such a manner that my productions may have something more than the mere interest of narrative to recommend them, which is very evanescent; something, if I dare to use the phrase, of classic merit, *i.e.*, depending upon style, etc., which gives a production some chance of duration beyond the mere whim and fashion of the day.

His style became part of himself. He had learned, as a young gentleman of fashion, how to turn a pretty phrase; he continued for the rest of his life to write wittily and gracefully—like a gentleman. And since the world does not willingly forget a stylist if he is fortunate enough to find even a few themes that summon all his powers, Irving has outlived men who were intrinsically greater than he. He very wisely calculated that a Washington Irving who would take sides in public arguments and political controversies was less serviceable than a Washington Irving who would portray for the American and for all people the illuminating life of a Washington or the endearing qualities of a Goldsmith. He believed he could do his countrymen a greater service chronicling Hudson River legends and bringing to them a touch of merry England and of romantic Spain than by misapplying his slender genius and tiring his reader's patience with theological disquisitions. He calculated correctly that as an intermediary between old-world culture and new-world rawness, and as a romancer of the romantic and the picturesque in the sphere of *belles-lettres*, he would write to better purpose than as politician or moralist.

NATHANIEL HAWTHORNE (1804–1864)

In spite of his detachment from the tumultuous America of his day, Hawthorne's immersion in the past of his country made him one of the most deeply-rooted of American writers and enabled him to record with singular clarity the subterranean history of American character. Sprung from a long line of Puritans who had lived in Salem without interruption since the founding of the colony, he dwelt with something like the old Puritanic introspection upon the race and place that had bred him. New Englander that he was, he shared fully in the New England provincialism, and until he was fifty never got farther away than Niagara Falls. New England, he said, was as large a lump of earth as his heart could readily take in. Few of his contemporaries studied more intently the pages of Puritan history; none knew more intimately that stern Puritan conscience or the hard Puritan character. He was, at various times, both attracted and repelled by Puritanism, but he never got wholly outside its influence.

A psychologist and a moralist, concerned with human problems and spiritual effects, he probed and analyzed the inner recesses of mind and conscience to illustrate the subtle relations between men and, quite as often, between man and his Maker, or between man and his own humanity. The characters, action, and setting of his stories exist primarily to give body to some allegory, to enforce some moral, or to illustrate some abstraction. The narrative, often satisfactory enough in itself, is never an end in itself, but rather the illustration that a preacher employs to elucidate or enforce his text. Yet his moral, however direct, is never the barefaced preachment; and Poe, who found writers less purposeful than Hawthorne guilty of the "heresy of the didactic," never specifically attacked Hawthorne on this head, though he criticized him for other real or fancied faults, while praising him for his pure style, fine taste, delicate humor, touching pathos, radiant imagination, and consummate ingenuity. What Poe missed in Hawthorne, probably because it did not accord with Poe's own idea of what a short story should be, is Hawthorne's greatest contribution to the genre as Irving had left it: that is, Hawthorne's investiture of the story with an idea. Thus he gave the American short story carrying power and made of it something more than the mere vehicle of entertainment as Irving had conceived it.

Foremost in importance as explaining the uniquely somber, contemplative cast of Hawthorne was his Puritan descent. In the preface to *The Scarlet Letter* he recalled, with mingled feelings of pride and apprehension, the American founders of his race who were invested by family tradition with "a dim and dusky grandeur." First, there was the "grave, bearded, sable-cloaked and steeple-crowned" Major William Hathorne (the *w* was first added to the family name by Hawthorne himself during his college years), who, as "soldier, legislator, judge, and ruler in the church," had all the Puritanic traits, "both good and evil." Like the first, the second Hathorne stood high in the Puritanic hierarchy. He was Colonel and Judge John Hathorne, and like his father, a good persecutor of Quakers and other dissenters. Mindful of the Biblical text on the sins of the fathers being visited on successive generations of their children, Hawthorne's Puritanic conscience impelled him to write in 1850:

I know not whether these ancestors of mine bethought themselves to repent, and ask pardon of Heaven for their cruelties; or whether they are now groaning under the heavy consequences of them, in another state of being. At all events, I, the present writer, as their representative, hereby take shame upon myself for their sakes, and pray that any curse incurred by them—as I have heard, and as the dreary and unprosperous condition of the race for many a long year back would argue to exist—may be now and henceforth removed.

Closely associated with these family ties was the old town of Salem itself, that remarkable old Puritan hive, where he was born, and where he dwelt all but a few of the first forty years of his life. Years later he testified that though he had been invariably happier elsewhere, he still possessed "a feeling for old Salem," which for lack of a better phrase he had to call "affection." Salem, he said, drew him like a magnet, and remained for him "the inevitable center of the universe." There all the descendants of Major Hathorne had been born, and there they died, to mingle "their earthly substance with the soil," until, as Hawthorne put it, in typically Hawthornesque terms, "no small portion of it must necessarily be akin to the mortal frame wherewith, for a little while, I walk the streets."

In part, therefore, the attachment which I speak of is the mere sensuous sympathy of dust for dust. Few of my countrymen can know what it is; nor, as frequent transplantation is perhaps better for the stock, need they consider it desirable to know.

This passage, together with the reference to the "dreary and unprosperous condition" of the Hathornes following the two earliest generations, introduces us to another family influence that preyed on Nathaniel Hawthorne's mind. The Hathornes had fallen through the centuries from the position of colonel, priest, and judge to that of sea captain. For many generations they had been sea-faring men, "a gray-headed ship-master, in each generation, retiring from the quarterdeck to the homestead, while a boy of fourteen took the hereditary place before the mast, confronting the salt spray and the gale, which had blustered against his sire and grandsire." Thus, while they still carried on in the vigorous tradition of activity, they had left behind them much of the glory, honor, wealth, and position of the earlier day. Closely associated with this loss of influence was the once large estate in Maine which had slipped through their fingers, until, by Hawthorne's time, only a few acres remained. Given as he was to brooding on family fortunes and the past, he could not but reflect on the grandeur that was gone; and, as might be expected, certain aspects of this loss of estate appear in his stories, notably in *The House of the Seven Gables*; while the attempts of one generation to secure for its progeny earthly wealth and position form a common motif in his short stories as well as in several of the four romances which he left incomplete at his death. It was a recurring and absorbing theme, of which, like so many others, he could make neither head nor tail. The older he grew, the more did he encounter problems of life that seemed unaccountable and irresolvable.

Hawthorne's generation did not suffer actual poverty, but when, in 1808, Mrs. Hathorne's husband died in Dutch Guiana, she was left with very little with which to rear her two daughters and one son, and an uncle had to lend his assistance to give Hawthorne a college education. But here again, Bowdoin College, then a struggling little freshwater college, was the best that was available to him, while the earlier Hathornes had enjoyed the best educational advantages of the land.

These circumstances doubtless encouraged what may have been an innate tendency in Hawthorne to ponder the somberness and transitory nature of life. His mother's retirement from the world upon her husband's death was another formative factor. She affected widow's weeds, dedicated the rest of her life to mourning, and spent weeks on end in her room. During his ninth year Hawthorne was struck on the ankle by a ball. This accident left him lame for several years, and robbed him of the opportunity of indulging in the rough-and-tumble of boyish play during these most impressionable years of a boy's life. The result was to accentuate his tendency toward retirement, introspection, and a generally sedentary life, which naturally sought an outlet in reading. And his reading, since it was done chiefly in allegorical literature like Spenser's *Faerie Queene* and Bunyan's *Pilgrim's Progress*, tended to develop still more this inwardness of temperament. During 1816–18 he spent portions of each year with his uncle Richard Manning, near Lake Sebago at Raymond, Maine, on what was left of the family estate; and during 1818 his mother, partly to live more cheaply, moved her family thither. Here Hawthorne spent a year entirely to his heart's content, running quite wild, hunting and fishing, but reading a good deal, too, especially during the rainy seasons and during the long winter. Years later he told his friend J. T. Fields, "There I lived . . . like a bird of the air, so perfect was the freedom I enjoyed. But it was there I first got my cursed habits of solitude."

In 1819 Mrs. Hathorne returned to Salem to put her children to school. Nathaniel would have preferred his father's calling, but Mrs. Hathorne, having taken an extreme aversion for the sea, insisted that he prepare himself for college. He spent the years from 1821 to 1825 at Bowdoin, where he submitted to the educational process only half-willingly, at all events, unenthusiastically; but he was hail-fellow-well-met among his classmates, and graduated about the middle of his class. Here he formed lasting friendships with Horatio Bridge, Franklin Pierce, and Henry Wadsworth Longfellow.

Already before going to college, the choice of a calling had troubled him, and writing to his mother he admitted that while he was "quite reconciled to going to college," he still considered that "four years of the best part of my life is a great deal to throw away." Knowing very well that his uncles wished him to choose one of the regular professions as the more promising and remunerative, he already found reasons why none of them was altogether acceptable, and ended the letter on this note: "Oh that I was rich enough to live without a profession! What do you think of my becoming an author, and relying for support upon my pen? Indeed, I think the illegibility of my handwriting is very author-like." Four years later, when he was about to graduate, without having prepared himself for anything in particular, he again wrote:

> I do not want to be a doctor and live by man's diseases, nor a minister and live by their sins, nor a lawyer and live by their quarrels. So I don't see that there is anything left but for me to be an author. How would you like to see some day a whole shelf full of books written by your son, with "Hawthorne's Works" printed on the backs?

Thus it was that he returned to Salem ill prepared to add much to the family income. Whatever hopes he had about the money to be made by his writing must have been considerably dashed by the failure of his first novel, entitled *Fanshawe* (1828), which he recognized as a failure the moment it appeared in print, and which accordingly he did his best to withdraw from circulation by buying up all copies that he could find. Nevertheless, he persevered, and during the twelve years that he spent in his "solitary chamber under the eaves," he used up reams upon reams of paper, burning, rewriting, and polishing away at his style. All this was without the least recognition or applause. It was a self-imposed period of rigorous literary discipline during which Hawthorne the writer was born, but during which Hawthorne the man suffered irreparable harm from the virus of solitude, isolation, enervation, and distrust of his own abilities. The lack of wholesome human contacts wore on him. The household to which he had returned in 1825 was drearier than ever, the mother's way of living having been adopted by his sisters also, so that, as he observed, "We do not even live at our house!" He seldom left the house except to go on a solitary ramble in the woods, and during the summer, to enjoy a daily swim early in the morning, before anyone else was astir. Consequently he could write in 1837 that though he had lived in Salem almost all his life, there were not a score of people in the town who so much as suspected his existence. During the twelve years between his graduation from college and the publication of *Twice-Told Tales* in 1837 (arranged for by his friend Bridge), he published twenty-five of his tales and sketches in various periodicals, mainly in *The Token*, an annual edited by S. C. Goodrich; but these were published anonymously. They brought him no fame and almost no financial reward.

The modest title of *Twice-Told Tales*, while appropriate to the tone of the stories, was really a misnomer, for as far as the public was concerned they were entirely new. But their appearance in collected form over his name in 1837 was an event of no small importance to the life of Hawthorne the writer as well as of Hawthorne the man. The book elicited several appreciative reviews, including a very favorable one by Longfellow in the *North American Review*, and Hawthorne himself admitted, "I was compelled to come out of my owl's nest and lionize in a small way." But, as he went on to admit to Longfellow, he had by now so long secluded himself from society, or rather permitted himself to be carried so far apart from the main current of life, that he found it impossible to get back again.

> I have secluded myself from society; and yet I never meant any such thing, nor dreamed what sort of life I was going to lead. I have made a captive of myself, and put me in a dungeon, and now I cannot find the key to let myself out,—and if the door were open, I should be almost afraid to come out. You tell me that you have met with troubles and changes. I know not what these may have been, but I can assure you that trouble is the next best thing to enjoyment, and that there is no fate in this world so horrible as to have no share in either its joys or sorrows. For the past ten years, I have not lived, but only dreamed of living. . . . As to my literary efforts, I do not think much of them. They would have been better, I trust, if written under more favorable circumstances. . . . There has been no warmth of approbation, so that I have written with benumbed fingers. I have another great difficulty in the lack of materials; for I have seen so little of the world that I have nothing but thin air to concoct my stories of, and it is not easy to give a lifelike substance to such shadowy stuff. Sometimes through a peep-hole I have caught a glimpse of the real world, and the two or three articles in which I have portrayed these glimpses please me better than the others. . . .

Hawthorne's latest biographers minimize his hermit-like, retiring existence, emphasizing instead his extrovert, gregarious nature. The truth doubtless lies somewhere between these two views. Both as boy and man, he often showed mental independence and physical vigor. All his life he enjoyed good conversation and convivial companionship; while his talk was characterized by a variety and raciness of speech that does not harmonize with the picture of Hawthorne as a secluded, delicate aesthete, lacking all contact with life. But however much he expanded the scope of his experience after he left Salem, in his writings he seldom got very far outside himself or outside the manner which had become instinctive. The somber tone had become too definitely fastened on his mind to be dispelled. While attempting to write *The Dolliver Romance* he said, "I wish God had given me the faculty of writing a sunshiny book"; and while he was preparing a new edition of the *Mosses from an Old Manse* in 1854, during the busy period of his consulate in Liverpool, he confessed to his publisher, "I am not quite sure that I entirely comprehend my own meanings, in some of these blasted allegories; but I remember that [when I wrote them] I always had a meaning, or at least thought I had." Four years later, he wrote to Fields, "My own individual taste is for quite another class of works than those which I myself am able to write. If I were to meet with such books as mine, by another writer, I don't believe I should be able to get through them." Shortly after completing *The Marble Faun* (1860), he said, "I will try to write a more genial book; but the Devil himself always seems to get into my inkstand, and I can only exorcise him by pensful at a time." No sunshiny book was to come from his pen; the last four separate attempts that he made at writing a more cheerful romance all turned out to be abortive.

The preface to the *Twice-Told Tales* contains a remarkably accurate piece of self-criticism, indicative of the fact that Hawthorne early learned what he was about stylistically. The stories, he says, have

. . . the pale tint of flowers that blossomed in too retired a shade,—the coolness of a meditative habit, which diffuses itself through the feeling and observation of every sketch. Instead of passion there is sentiment; and, even in what purport to be pictures of actual life, we have allegory, not always so warmly dressed in its habiliments of flesh and blood as to be taken into the reader's mind without a shiver. Whether from lack of power, or an unconquerable reserve, the Author's touches have often an effect of tameness; the merriest man can hardly contrive to laugh at his broadest humor; the tenderest woman, one would suppose, will hardly shed warm tears at his deepest pathos. The book, if you would see anything in it, requires to be read in the clear, brown, twilight atmosphere in which it was written; if opened in the sunshine, it is apt to look exceedingly like a volume of blank pages.

The stories, except for several descriptive sketches, are either searching psychological analyses or illustrations of some abstract or philosophical question of the type that he jotted down in his notebooks for literary elaboration: "A hint for a story,—some incident which should bring on a general war; and the chief character in the incident to have something corresponding to the mischief he had caused." "A well-concerted train of incidents to be thrown into confusion by some misplaced circumstance, unsuspected till the catastrophe, yet exerting its influence from beginning to end." "Cannon transformed into church-bells." "To make one's own reflection in a mirror the subject of a story." "Every individual has

a place to fill in the world, and is important, in some respects, whether he chooses to be so or not." "A snake taken into a man's stomach and nourished there from fifteen to thirty-five, tormenting him most horribly. A type of envy or some other evil passion." "A lament for life's wasted sunshine." "What were the contents of the burden of Christian in the 'Pilgrim's Progress'?" "Trifles to one are matters of life and death to another." "A person to be in possession of something as perfect as mortal man has a right to demand; he tries to make it better and ruins it entirely." "To make a story out of a scarecrow, giving it odd attributes . . ." "Curious to imagine what murmurings and discontent would be excited, if any of the great so-called calamities of human beings were to be abolished,—as, for instance, death."

Following the success of *Twice-Told Tales*, Hawthorne made renewed efforts to break through the walls of his self-imposed prison. Through the instrumentality of Elizabeth Palmer Peabody, an enthusiastic Transcendentalist, who kept an up-to-date bookshop in Boston, he saw something of literary society and came to know the other Peabody girls, who lived in Salem. Mary Peabody was to become the wife of Horace Mann, the educator, and Sophia, an artistically inclined invalid, eventually became Hawthorne's wife. They became engaged in 1838, but the marriage was deferred, at first, presumably because Hawthorne lacked the means and possibly also because of Sophia's ill health. But even after her health improved, Hawthorne still held off. Something is doubtless attributable to the timidity and hesitation of a bachelor who has lived too much to himself. For even after Elizabeth Palmer Peabody had helped him to the post of weigher and gauger at the Boston Custom House, where, during 1839–41, he saved a thousand dollars, instead of marrying Sophia, he took the extraordinary step of investing all his savings in the Brook Farm Association for Agriculture and Education near Roxbury, Massachusetts, a Transcendentalist experiment in communal living designed to combine ideal proportions of physical, intellectual, and artistic endeavor. Considering his inherent distrust of reformers and his lack of enthusiasm for Transcendentalism, no good reason remains but that he hoped to find in Brook Farm a place where he might cultivate his starved sense of sociability; and since he bought two shares of stock, it seems likely that, if he found life congenial at Brook Farm, he planned to bring his bride there.

The *Notebooks*, kept during the six months of 1841 while he lived there, and *The Blithedale Romance*, written a decade later and based on his experiences in the Roxbury community, record his growing disillusionment with the program of Brook Farm and his disaffection for some of its inmates and visitors. He experienced trouble retrieving his $1,000 investment in the enterprise; but his good fortune in securing rent-free the Old Manse in Concord doubtless facilitated matters; and in July of 1842 he finally terminated his four-year engagement to Sophia Peabody by marriage.

They were poor but altogether happy in Concord. In the preface to *Mosses from an Old Manse* (1846) Hawthorne wrote an appreciative sketch of the old house that had never been profaned, as he said, by a lay occupant until the memorable summer when he entered it as his home.

A priest had built it; a priest had succeeded to it; other priestly men from time to time had dwelt in it; and children born in its chambers had grown up to assume the priestly character. It was awful to reflect how many sermons must have been written there. . . . There was in the rear of the house the most delightful little nook of a study that ever offered its snug seclusion to a scholar. It was here that Emerson wrote Nature; for he was then an inhabitant of the Manse. . . . When I first saw the room its walls were blackened with the smoke of unnumbered years, and made still blacker by the grim prints of Puritan ministers that hung around. These worthies looked strangely like bad angels, or at least like men who had wrestled so sternly with the devil that somewhat of his sooty fierceness had been imparted to their visages.

Here he was free to dream and to write. Here his first child was born—a daughter, whom he named Una in memory of the heroine of the first book of the *Faerie Queene*. Here he got, for the first time in his life, some experience in the intimacy of human contacts, both within his own family and among his neighbors. For Concord during the forties had more to offer than a river, surrounding woods, a lake, and Sleepy Hollow cemetery. There was Emerson, with whose optimistic Transcendentalism he was never fully in accord. "Mr. Emerson," he wrote in his journal for 1842, "is a great searcher for facts; but they seem to melt away and become insubstantial in his grasp." He admired Emerson as a poet of "deep beauty and austere tenderness," but added that he "sought nothing from him as a philosopher." Emerson, for his part, was attracted to Hawthorne as a person but complained that his books were "not good for any thing." The two men were diametrically opposed to each other in fundamental point of view. Emerson, the mystic sage, whose optimism led him practically to deny the existence of evil, found little to admire in Hawthorne's books, preoccupied as they were with the subject of human iniquities. And Hawthorne, who could not rid himself of his Puritanic prepossessions, wrote "The Celestial Railroad" to satirize the free and easy way to Heaven charted by the Transcendentalists. He preferred the "narrow but earnest cushion-thumper of puritanical times" to the "vaguely liberal clergyman." He wrote "Earth's Holocaust" to show that original sin was not a delusion; whereas Emerson, pushing his faith in natural goodness and self-reliance to the extreme, wrote, "If I am the Devil's child, I will live then from the Devil. No law can be sacred to me but that of my nature." Hawthorne's stories, almost as if they had been designed to refute this doctrine, repeatedly present characters who do just that. Ethan Brand, Rappaccini, Chillingworth, Judge Pyncheon, and dozens of others live selfishly—after themselves, and the Devil—until they become diabolical incarnations and end disastrously.

Hawthorne had passed, with the last generation or two of his family, from Calvinism to Unitarianism, but he did not go on to take the next step—to Transcendentalism. He recoiled, rather, back toward Puritanism. He had little respect for clergymen, theological writings, or the visible church. Indeed, his son Julian could not remember ever having seen his father in church. Yet he was by nature religious-minded—insisting, however, like the Unitarians, on his right as an individual to make his own creed. And in the formulation of that creed, he was impelled at numerous points to revert to the Puritanic doctrine in particulars. Unlike the Calvinists, he disclaimed any belief in a system of rewards and punishments as conventionally conceived, and he refused to regard Heaven and Hell as places of eternal bliss or damnation. Instead, he held that on the Judgment Day "man's only inexorable judge will be himself, and the punishment of his sins . . . the perception of them." His Day of Doom was not Michael Wigglesworth's, but simply "all future days, when we shall see ourselves as we are." Nevertheless, whether he gave them the conviction of his head or not, he continued using the old terms to designate the old religious quantities, such as Original Sin, Predestination, Atonement, and Redemption, lending them the sympathy of his imagination if not of his heart. If it came to choosing between Emerson and Bunyan, he preferred to take his stand with Bunyan.

Another Concord neighbor, that "awful Thoreau," as some people called him, provided Hawthorne with interesting, if not altogether satisfactory, contacts. While admiring Thoreau's skill as a boatman and as a naturalist, recognizing his "good sense and moral truth," and envying his sturdy independence and freedom from conventional restraints, there was something about Henry Thoreau that made him a little "terrific." He put him down as "a healthy and wholesome man to know," but he considered it a limitation in Thoreau that he "despised the world and all that it had to offer," and that he made one feel "ashamed in his presence of having any money, or a home to live in, or so much as two coats to wear, or of having written a book that the public will read."

There were other interesting, if odd, personalities in Concord: William Ellery Channing the younger, W. H. Channing, the volatile Alcott, the ethereal Jones Very, and visitors from Boston and from Brook Farm, some of whom Hawthorne felt he knew better than he cared to. From Margaret Fuller he continued to shy away. He could not bring himself to like her, and considered her typical of "the damned mob of scribbling women"—females who, like his sister-in-law, Elizabeth Palmer Peabody, were too much concerned with reform and masculine pursuits to suit his fancy. Although he did not enjoy equally all his Concord associates, they provided him in large measure with precisely those human contacts, agreeable and disagreeable, which he had missed during his earlier years; and they doubtless did much toward humanizing and maturing the man who was to publish between 1846 and 1852 eight separate volumes.

The first of these, Mosses from an Old Manse, appeared in 1846, the year he went back to his birthplace as surveyor of the Salem Custom House. During the three years that he served there he found it impossible to do any writing, so that his falling victim to the spoils system in 1849 was doubtless a good thing so far as his literary productivity goes. He set to writing with a fury. The story of how he was inspired by old records found in the Salem Custom House to write The Scarlet Letter (1850) is well known. The subject had long interested him, and the new manuscript materials supplied what was lacking to set his imagination going. Turning upon the deep-seated conflicts between impulse and conscience, between individual desire and the restraints of society, this old story of how sin affects the lives and characters of the chief participants in a triangular love affair enacted in the Salem of old Puritanical days ideally suited his fancy and inspired his best talents.

Before he published his next novel, Hawthorne was thrown much in the company of Herman Melville, during 1850 and 1851, while they found themselves neighbors near Lenox, Massachusetts. Given, as both

of them were, to taking an intellectually skeptical view of the doctrines of human progress rampant at the time, they each drew support from the other. This congenial association between two kindred spirits was especially salutary to Melville, whose Moby Dick was then being "broiled in the hell-fire of his brain." After his fruitless wanderings through the deserts of theological and philosophical speculation, Melville found it heartening to discuss his problems with Hawthorne, in whom he recognized one of those "thought-divers" who "compel a man to swim for his life." In Hawthorne he saw that same "deep, dark blackness" pervading him "through and through" that gnawed at his own vitals; and together they sat, often far into the night, talking "about time and eternity, things of this world and of the next, and books, and publishers, and all possible and impossible matters."

Hawthorne's next book, The House of the Seven Gables, appeared in 1851. More pictorial than The Scarlet Letter, it develops with the same restrained psychological intensity its moral—in this instance, the thesis "that the wrong-doing of one generation lives into the successive ones, and, divesting itself of every temporary advantage, becomes a pure and uncontrollable mischief." Following A Wonder Book for Boys and Girls (1851), he published in 1852 The Snow Image, The Blithedale Romance, a thinly veiled antireform novel, and a campaign biography of Franklin Pierce. Tanglewood Tales, another book for children, followed the next year, and before the year was out his old college-mate Pierce, now the fourteenth President of the United States, appointed him consul to Liverpool.

He resigned the consulship in 1856, but continued resident in England for a year longer, while traveling about a good deal and planning other novels, like The Ancestral Footstep, which was destined to remain incomplete. In 1857 he went to Italy, living first in Florence, and later in Rome, where he began The Marble Faun, subsequently completed in London and published in 1860, the year of his return to Concord. His European trip came too late to change him or to do him much good. Our Old Home appeared in 1863, but his best work was done. Like so many characters in his books, Hawthorne himself, too often, failed to find any proper endings or conclusions to life's problems. During his last years he was torn more than ever by the discords and conflicts that he saw all around him—not the least of which were the horrors of the Civil War. Not knowing in the least what the proper solution of such a catastrophe should, or would, be, he was inclined to believe that abolition, like every other species of organized or forced reform, was poorly adapted to serve the best ends. He was inclined to look upon slavery as "one of those evils which divine Providence does not leave to be remedied by human contrivances, but which, in its own good time, by some means impossible to be anticipated, but of the simplest and easiest operation, *when all its uses shall have been fulfilled*, it causes to vanish like a dream." His skepticism of human reason, progress, and perfectibility led him to the pessimistic conclusion: "There is no instance, in all history, of the human will and intellect having perfected any great moral reform by methods which it adopted to that end. . . . No human effort, on a grand scale, has ever resulted according to the purpose of its projectors. The advantages are always incidental. Man's accidents are God's purposes." "An abolitionist in feeling" rather than "in principle," he considered the war a horrible mistake, but knew not in the least how to avert it or how to settle its issues in any less costly way. Life, in the end, grew increasingly enigmatical and burdensome for him; and toward the last he felt that he had written himself out, and that, like Melville, he was going to pieces inwardly. His four last attempts to write another romance proved abortive; and Emerson, standing at the grave of his neighbor on May 23, 1864, and hearing the clods of earth falling on the coffin, felt that Hawthorne's untimely death was in the nature of a happy release.

EDGAR ALLAN POE (1809-1849)

Edgar Allan Poe, generally regarded the best exponent of romanticism in nineteenth-century America, remains to many an enigmatical figure. As in the case of Byron, people writing about Poe have found it difficult to write impersonally and objectively. At the one extreme are his defamers, beginning with his first biographer, the Rev. Rufus W. Griswold, who regard him as a perverse neurotic, a drunkard and drug addict, lacking both emotional stability and moral integrity. On the other side are his apologists, who relate all his difficulties to the malignity of his opponents, the hard circumstances which the times imposed on a literary aesthete, or the bodily and mental ailments that plagued him. And in between these two extremes all the gradations are represented by students bent on finding special psychoses, neuroses, frustrations, and other pathological, social, or economic causes to explain Poe's unique personality and his tragic life. Among them, they have built up about the figure of Poe a contradictory mass of fact and fiction that leaves the uninitiated bewildered.

The beginning student of Poe falls altogether too easily into the error of overestimating the influence upon Poe of alcohol and opium, especially since Poe, like other romanticists, sometimes indulged in that peculiar perversity which prompted him to let fall hints about himself that led people to consider him far worse than he actually was. But there is some truth in the observation of one of his critics who said that no greater injustice can be done to the memory of Poe than to acquit him wholly of the very vices that made his personality so fascinating and at the same time contributed so much to his genius.

The sensible view is to regard him as neither wholly angel nor devil, introvert nor pervert, but simply as a man with extraordinary literary and mental capabilities and equally large personal failings, who dedicated himself to literary pursuits, and who sought to make his livelihood by writing. Considering his weaknesses and the difficulties that beset the book business at the time, the wonder is rather that he wrote so much than that he wrote no more during his brief lifetime. While it may freely be admitted that between the few poems, stories, and critiques that measured up to his own strict literary ideals, there are dreary stretches of humdrum hack-work—the result often of the journalistic demands of meeting deadlines—there are, nevertheless, a score of superb poems, a like number of first-rate stories, and half as many pieces of fundamental criticism that nothing short of real literary genius could have produced. These deservedly live, whatever objections the moralist may raise to Poe's personal failings, and whatever shortcomings the critic may see in Poe's literary theory and practice. The seventeen volumes of his collected writings (in the standard Virginia edition) bear evidence that Poe drove ahead, through illness, frustration, poverty, despair, and plain hard luck, with a steadfastness that is truly amazing. The remarkable literary purposefulness and the energetic drive of the man are too often obscured by the legend of abnormality and oddity which a tradition of prejudicial special pleading, pro and con, as built round the more vital and essential Poe, who, of all the men of his generation, stuck most devotedly to his ideal of a literary life. In the year of his death, when the gold-rush fever affected less adventuresome spirits than his, he reiterated his faith, in a letter to his friend F. W. Thomas:

Depend upon it, Thomas, literature is the most noble of professions. In fact, it is about the only one fit for a man. For my own part there is no seducing me from the path. I shall be a *littérateur* at least, all my life; nor would I abandon the hopes which still lead me on for all the gold of California. Talking of gold and the temptations at present held out to "poor-devil authors" did it ever strike you that all that is really valuable to a man of letters—to a poet in especial—is absolutely unpurchasable? Love, fame, the dominion of intellect, the consciousness of power, the thrilling sense of beauty, the free air of Heaven, exercise of body & mind—these and such as these are really all that a poet cares for. . . .

His literary contemporaries, the major New England writers of the nineteenth century, differed from him in being not wholly dependent on their pens for a livelihood. Moreover, most of them were well-born and enjoyed a secure social status. And since they set the moral tone of what was expected of a literary man, not only in his productions but also ot his personal life, Poe's refusal to mix morality with aesthetics and his aberrations from the accepted code of conduct often caused his critics to pass strictures upon him which he would have escaped in a more liberal age. Poe was born a hundred years before J. E. Spingarn, speaking for a more generous attitude toward the poet and his poetry, told Americans that the poet's "only moral duty, as a poet, is to be true to his art, and to express his vision of reality as well as he can." That doctrine Poe understood perfectly, but no one else in the America of his day supported him in it. Instead, New England, with its moralistic inhibitions or reticences, sat as moral arbiter of taste and demanded conformity where Poe's firm conviction was that morality had no jurisdiction in the first place. Himself a Bostonian by birth, Poe grew bitter at the censorious proscriptions of the ingrained Puritanic temperament of the New England tradition, and spoke contemptuously of his native city as the "Frogpond." Striking out savagely at literary cliques of which he, a starveling journalist and a social outsider, was not and could never be a member—the type of literary fraternity which Holmes referred to with self-evident satisfaction as "Our Mutual Admiration Society"—Poe resolved to "make war to the knife against the New England assumption of 'All the decency and all the talent' which has been so disgustingly manifested in the Rev. Rufus W. Griswold's 'Poets and Poetry of America.' " They retaliated in ways that infuriated him all the more: the revered Longfellow at Craigie House chose to ignore his attacks altogether, and even the benign sage of Concord disposed of him with the glib phrase, "the jingle man." Poe's proud nature could stand anything better than to be brushed aside or to be ignored altogether. And so he pursued his solitary way, slashing about him and charging his trials and tribulations to the malignity of others, only to make himself thoroughly unhappy, while the mad world rushed past him heedlessly. He never attained to the wisdom of realizing that in many instances he was himself his own worst enemy, choosing instead to take whatever meager consolation he could find in such thoughts as he expressed in the following paragraphs from the *Marginalia,* written during the last year of his life:

I have sometimes amused myself by endeavoring to fancy what would be the fate of any individual gifted, or rather accursed, with an intellect *very* far superior to that of his race. Of course, he would be conscious of his superiority; nor could he (if otherwise constituted as man is) help manifesting his consciousness. Thus he would make himself enemies at all points. And since his opinions and speculations would widely differ from those of *all* mankind

—that he would be considered a madman, is evident. How horribly painful such a condition! Hell could invent no greater torture than that of being charged with abnormal weakness on account of being abnormally strong.
. . . This subject is a painful one indeed. That individuals *have* so soared above the plane of their race, is scarcely to be questioned; but, in looking back through history for traces of their existence, we should pass over all biographies of "the good and the great," while we search carefully the slight records of wretches who died in prison, in Bedlam, or upon the gallows.

The beginning of Poe's life, like the end, was attended by misfortune. Born in Boston, on January 19, 1809, of poor actor parents, he was left an orphan at the age of two, while his parents were playing in Richmond, Virginia. He was taken into the childless home of John Allan, a well-to-do tobacco merchant of Richmond, who became Poe's legal guardian, but never formally adopted him. Thus began the anomalous position by which Poe was reared in the indulgent atmosphere of Southern gentility, only to make the discovery some years later, after he had reached the height of his illusions as a Southern gentleman, that he was not and would never be really a member of the caste.

During 1815–20, while the Allans lived in England, Poe enjoyed the advantages of a good preparatory education in the Manor House School at Stoke Newington for several years; and on their return, he was sent to a good academy in Richmond. During the years between 1820 and 1826, favored treatment, special tutoring, and other privileges commonly accorded the lads of wealthy Southern gentlemen led Poe to assume and to demand the special favors belonging to the privileged. This was the period when he read widely in romantic poetry and developed a romantic attachment for Mrs. Jane Stith Stanard, the mother of one of his schoolmates, whose death in 1824 left him disconsolate, and to whom he later addressed the poem "To Helen" in commemoration of what he called "the first purely ideal love of my soul." Toward the end of the period he became "engaged" to Sarah Elmira Royster of Richmond.

While Poe was in his middle teens rifts were already developing between the practical-minded Allan and his artistically-inclined foster-son—quarrels which appear to have begun over Poe's waywardness of spirit and over his choice of a calling—quarrels which Mrs. Allan sought to assuage. During the calendar year of 1826, while Poe was at the University of Virginia, the letters between him and Miss Royster were intercepted by her parents, presumably because they had learned that Allan did not intend to make

Poe his heir. Miss Royster was accordingly bestowed upon a young man whose prospects were more promising, while Poe was left to nurture his hurt until it found expression in the romantic conceptions and Byronic disillusionments of such poems as "Tamerlane," "Dreams," "Spirits of the Dead," "A Dream within a Dream," and "Song," beginning, "I saw thee on thy bridal day." Allan's parsimony in failing to provide Poe with sufficient money for his fees and other necessities further complicated life for Poe. In desperation he took to drinking and gambling, only to make matters worse. If anything had been wanting to complete the rupture between Allan and his foster-son, it was supplied by Poe's ending his year at Charlottesville with accumulated debts in excess of $2,000—most of them representing gambling losses. When Allan refused to assume responsibility for these obligations, Poe, compelled to repudiate his debts "of honor," could not have returned to school and face his creditors even if he had wanted to. Other bitter quarrels followed when Poe refused to go to work as a clerk in Allan's counting house, and in March of 1827, Poe, in defiance of the code of his class, made his way to Boston and enlisted in the army as a common soldier. He was stationed for a time in Charleston, South Carolina, where he became familiar with the background of "The Gold Bug." On Mrs. Allan's death in 1829, Allan took Poe back into his good graces, secured his dismissal from the army (where Poe had risen to the rank of regimental sergeant-major), and helped him get an appointment to West Point, where Poe entered on July 1, 1830. Although he stood well in his classes, he found life at the Military Academy increasingly uncongenial, and by March of 1831 he had collected enough deliberately incurred demerits to effect his court-martial and dismissal. He went to Baltimore to live, chiefly at the home of his aunt, Mrs. Maria Clemm, and tried to make his livelihood as best he could by writing. If he still entertained any hopes of getting anything from Allan, those hopes were blasted by Allan's second marriage, in 1832. Having now the prospect of a direct heir, and having decided that Poe was a confirmed ne'er-do-well, Allan disowned him. In 1834, when Allan died, Poe discovered that he had not been left so much as a blessing.

Thus he found himself penniless, discouraged, generally ill-prepared, and with very few friends, to shift for himself. In 1827, shortly before enlisting in the army, he had published in Boston his first volume of verse, *Tamerlane and Other Poems, By a Bostonian*. This was followed in 1829 by *Al Aaraaf,*

Tamerlane, and Minor Poems, and immediately after his dismissal from West Point appeared a volume to which his classmates, expecting lampoons of their instructors and other tasty morsels, had subscribed—entitled simply *Poems*. These early volumes, redolent of the romantic notes inspired by Coleridge, Byron, Scott, and Moore, called some attention to his name, but brought him no material rewards. Accordingly he turned his attention to prose fiction as possessing better possibilities, but with little success until 1833, when the "MS. Found in a Bottle" won a $100 prize in a contest conducted by the Baltimore *Saturday Visitor*. For the rest, he drudged at hack-work, while trying desperately to find regular editorial employment where there was none to be had. Mary Devereaux, a pretty red-headed belle of the day, to whom he paid court, later described Poe as he appeared during his early Baltimore period:

Mr. Poe was about five feet eight inches tall, and had dark, almost black hair, which he wore long and brushed back in student style over his ears. It was as fine as silk. His eyes were large and full, gray and piercing. He was entirely clean shaven. His nose was long and straight, and his features finely cut. The expression about his mouth was beautiful. He was pale and had no color. His skin was of a clear, beautiful olive. He had a sad, melancholy look. He was very slender . . . but he had a fine figure, an erect military carriage, and a quick step. But it was his manner that most charmed. It was *elegant*. When he looked at you it seemed as if he could read your thoughts. His voice was pleasant and musical but not deep. He always wore a black frock-coat buttoned up, with a cadet or military collar, a low turned-over shirt collar, and a black cravat tied in a loose knot. He did not follow the fashions, but had a style of his own. His was a loose way of dressing as if he didn't care. You would know that he was very different from the ordinary run of young men.

Another characterization which fits this picture comes from the pen of John Pendleton Kennedy, then the commanding literary figure in Baltimore, who was attracted to Poe by the "MS Found in a Bottle" to befriend and support him and, in 1835, to secure his appointment as assistant editor of the *Southern Literary Messenger* in Richmond. Writing to Thomas W. White, the owner of the *Messenger*, Kennedy said:

Poe did right in referring to me. He is very clever with his pen—classical and scholar-like. He wants experience and direction, but I have no doubt he can be made very useful to you. And, poor fellow, he is *very* poor . . . The young fellow is highly imaginative and a little *terrific*. He is at work upon a tragedy [*Politian*], but I have turned him to drudging upon whatever may make money.

After five years of a hand-to-mouth existence in Baltimore, Poe was happy to find a haven and regular employment in Richmond. Following a secret marriage to his cousin, Virginia Clemm, the year before, a second, public ceremony took place in 1836, Virginia aged thirteen, Poe aged twenty-seven. Together with Virginia and her mother ("dear Muddy," as he called her, the guardian angel of the little family), he set out in Richmond upon a promising editorial career, rising, before the year was out, to the position of editor. Henceforth his life was intimately associated with journalism. His stories, poems, and critiques appeared in no less than forty-seven different periodicals, while he served in an editorial capacity for five magazines. Indeed, he was, for the rest of his life, a journalist, who early conceived the desire to found and publish a journal of his own that should rise above the common level. From 1836 onward almost everything he did can be related to this commanding ambition, and several times he came near attaining it.

His own poems and stories in the *Southern Literary Messenger* soon attracted attention to the magazine, and his trenchant, if too sharp, critical essays soon established it as the leading review in the South, while its subscription list rose, in a year's time, from seven hundred to nearly five thousand. Although he still lacked anything like a well-considered or consistent body of critical principles, his criticisms were, from the first, forceful and sometimes slashing in the manner of the Edinburgh reviewers. He made relentless war on mediocrity and rendered real service to the cause of American letters by enforcing strict and high literary standards, exposing "puffery" wherever he encountered it, attacking the "heresy of the didactic" in literature, and discovering plagiarism, even where there was none. In the end he ran into difficulties with White, who objected to Poe's severity as a critic and to his over-working the vein of horror in his stories. Poe's reply to White's objections to "Berenice" as being too terrible is illuminating as indicating that Poe was consciously schooling himself for the career of a journalist:

A word or two in relation to Berenice. Your opinion of it is quite just. The subject is far too horrible. . . . [But] the history of all magazines shows plainly that those which obtained celebrity were indebted for it to *articles similar in nature to Berenice*. . . . You ask me in what does that nature consist . . . in the ludicrous heightened into the grotesque; the fearful colored into the horrible; the witty exaggerated into the burlesque; and the singular heightened into the strange and mystical. . . . You may well say that all this is in bad taste. I have my doubts about it. . . . But whether the articles . . . are in bad taste is of

little purpose. To be appreciated you must be *read* and these things are sought after with avidity. . . . The effect —if any—will be estimated better by the circulation of the magazine than by any comments on its contents.

Although his friends claimed that Poe left the *Southern Literary Messenger* late in 1836 to accept a more lucrative and congenial position in New York, the truth seems to be that, having come to consider himself indispensable to the magazine and having grown imperious in his demands, Poe began to get lax in his habits and to absent himself from his desk during drinking sprees, whereupon White dismissed him. At all events, when he showed up in New York, early in 1837, no editorial position awaited him. But he wrote steadily, published a good deal in various periodicals, and in July, 1838, Harper's brought out *The Narrative of Arthur Gordon Pym*, a Crusoe-like sea story of the type for which there was a good deal of demand at the time.

In the summer of 1838 Poe removed to Philadelphia, where he lived for the next six years, and where he soon undertook the editorship of Burton's *Gentleman's Magazine*. Here the story of the *Southern Literary Messenger* repeated itself. Again finding himself successful, Poe's methods and habits provoked difficulties between himself and his employer, until Burton wrote him: "I cannot permit the magazine to be made a vehicle for that sort of severity which you think is so 'successful with the mob.' I am truly much less anxious about making a monthly 'sensation' than I am upon the point of fairness. . . . You say the people love havoc. I think they love justice."

At opposite poles in editorial policy, Burton and Poe parted company in the summer of 1840, for when Poe showed up several times more or less intoxicated, Burton fired him. But he was not long out of employment. In April, 1841, he became editor of *Graham's Magazine*, founded the preceding January. At no time was Poe's mind clearer or his pen surer than during this phase of his Philadelphia period. Thrilling stories and trenchant critical essays followed one another in rapid succession, while his articles on cryptography and autography attracted widespread attention. But in thirteen months Poe had once again outstayed his welcome. During 1843 he was associated for a while with the weekly *Saturday Museum*, and the next year he moved to New York, which remained his home until his death in 1849.

In the meantime he had published a collection of his stories under the title *Tales of the Grotesque and Arabesque* (1840), and in 1843 he had won a popular success and a $100 prize with the story of "The

Gold Bug." His first regular employment in New York was as assistant editor of the *Evening Mirror*, of which N. P. Willis was editor. It was in this periodical that Poe's "Raven" first appeared on January 29, 1845. The poem immediately laid hold of the popular fancy and met a success such as no other American poem had ever won. Even abroad, it made its mark, and Elizabeth Barrett Browning wrote, "This vivid writing, this power *which is felt*, has produced a sensation here in England. Some of my friends are taken by the fear of it, and some by the music. I hear of persons who are haunted by the 'Nevermore'; and an acquaintance of mine, who has the misfortune of possessing a bust of Pallas, cannot bear to look at it in the twilight."

Poe's position on the *Evening Mirror* was too frankly subordinate to last long, and in 1845, at about the same time that his *Raven and Other Poems* appeared, he changed over, with the best of feelings, to the weekly *Broadway Journal* as associate editor. He soon became the editor, and in October, 1846, he finally realized his ambition of becoming the owner of a periodical. But his best editorial labors and frantic efforts to borrow money were not enough to keep the declining *Journal* from dying on his hands during the first week of the new year.

The rest of the story is a sad one. After many changes of residence in New York City, the Poes moved to Fordham (now in the Bronx). In desperate straits, Poe was mortified to learn that a public appeal for charity was made in his behalf. In 1841 Virginia Poe had broken a blood vessel while singing, consumption had followed, and she remained an invalid until her death on January 30, 1847. Poe, distraught and disconsolate, fell ill, and resumed some of his bad habits, resorting now to opium as well as to other stimulants, while Mrs. Clemm labored heroically to save him. He pulled himself together to write such poems as "Ulalume" and in 1848 he finished *Eureka*, a "prosepoem," designed to explain the constitution of the universe in physical-metaphysical terms. For the rest, he did some lecturing, reading such essays of his as "The Philosophy of Composition" and "The Poetic Principle," which embodied his mature theories of poetry and prose fiction. In his almost hysterical eagerness for feminine sympathy, he became involved in sentimental relations with women like Mrs. Osgood, Mrs. Shew, and Mrs. Whitman, all of whom, however, broke their engagements with him when they realized that he could not keep his promises to correct his irregular habits.

Finally in 1849 it appeared that he was about to realize his ambition to found a journal on a sound financial footing. His earlier efforts in Philadelphia to establish *The Penn*, also called *The Stylus*, had come to naught, and the *Broadway Journal* never had a chance under his direction. But he clung to his aim. "Touching 'The Stylus,'" he wrote to Philip Pendleton Cooke, "this is the one great purpose of my literary life. . . . I wish to establish a journal in which men of genius may fight their battles, upon some terms of equality, with those dunces, the men of talent." Even "The Gold Bug" and "The Raven," his two greatest literary successes, appear to have been conceived and written especially to establish for himself a commanding reputation. Writing to F. W. Thomas, Poe said, " 'The Raven' has had a great 'run' . . . but I wrote it for the express purpose of *running*, just as I did the 'Gold Bug,' you know. The bird beat the bug, though, all hollow." Here speaks the journalist bent on writing something that will have a run, something that will draw attention to his name. With this purpose in mind, Poe's efforts at reputation-building sometimes turned out to be his best pieces; at other times, of course, his purposeful departures from his own high ideals, in order to write down to the level of the public taste, resulted in less felicitous productions. To Charles Anthon he confided in 1844:

Holding steadily in view my ultimate purpose,—to found a Magazine of my own, or in which at least I might have a proprietary right,—it has been my constant endeavour in the meantime, not so much to establish a reputation great in itself as one of that particular character which should best further my special objects, and draw attention to my exertions as Editor of a Magazine. Thus I have written no books, and have been so far essentially a Magazinist bearing, not only willingly but cheerfully, sad poverty and the thousand consequent contumelies and other ills which the condition of the mere Magazinist entails upon him in America. . . .

My sole immediate object is the furtherance of my ultimate one. I believe that if I could get my tales fairly before the public, and thus have an opportunity of eliciting foreign as well as native opinion respecting them, I should by their means be in a far more advantageous position than at present in regard to the establishment of a Magazine.

Finally, in 1849, when the well-to-do Edward Howard Norton Patterson appeared and it seemed that Poe had at last found a patron ready to back *The Stylus*, Poe's high hopes revived. Referring to his earlier efforts, he wrote:

I could see no reason why a Magazine, if worthy of the name, could not be made to circulate among 20,000 subscribers, embracing the best intellect and education of the land. This was a thought which stimulated my fancy and my ambition. The influence of such a journal would be vast indeed, and I dreamed of honestly employing that influence in the sacred cause of the beautiful, the just and the true.

Now that the dream was about to come true, he wrote to Patterson of his high hopes: "We must aim high—address the intellect—the higher classes—of the country (with reference, also, to a certain amount of foreign circulation) and put the work at $5. . . . Such a Mag. would exercise a literary and other influence never yet exercised in America."

This was written in April of 1849. Two months later he made a journey to Richmond to deliver some lectures en route and to settle some affairs of business, after which he planned to return to New York, when everything would be in readiness for the establishment of *The Stylus*. From that journey he never returned. In Richmond he became engaged to be married to Sarah Elmira Royster Shelton, then a wealthy widow. Late in September he started north to bring Mrs. Clemm to Richmond. In Baltimore he took to drink, fell into the hands of unscrupulous politicians, who, it is believed, drugged him, used him as a "repeater" at several of the polls of the election then in progress, and then abandoned him in the back-room of a tavern, which also served as an election place. He may also have been robbed and manhandled. It is possible that his death was caused by illness and delirium aggravated by drink. The circumstances attending his last days are far from clear. He died on October 7, 1849, at the age of forty. Two days after his death, there appeared in the New York *Tribune* a brief notice over the signature of "Ludwig," masking the name of the Rev. Rufus W. Griswold, whom Poe had known since his Philadelphia days, and whom he had trustingly appointed his literary executor. This notice of Poe's passing initiated the alternate vilification and glorification of his character that has gone on without abatement ever since:

> Edgar Allan Poe is dead. He died in Baltimore the day before yesterday. This announcement will startle many, *but few will be grieved by it.* The poet was known personally or by reputation, in all this country; he had readers in England, and in several of the states of Continental Europe; *but he had few or no friends;* and the regret for his death will be suggested principally by the consideration that in him literary art lost one of its most brilliant but erratic stars.

A professed aesthete and a meticulous craftsman, Poe left his mark on American verse with a notably small body of poetry. The range of his ideas is as narrow as his technical excellence is great. No poet who wrote so little rewrote that little so often, and so successfully. Killis Campbell's careful research in Poe reveals that of the forty-eight poems collected by Poe, no fewer than forty-two were republished at least once. Of the latter, all but one ("Sonnet to Zanthe") were subjected to some sort of verbal revision on republication. Six appeared in two different versions, thirteen in three different forms, nine occur in four different forms, eleven show five different readings, one ("Lenore") shows eight different renditions, and another ("The Raven") appeared in fifteen different forms. Three of the six poems that were published only once survive in manuscript versions that differ in some respects from the published version; while twenty of the forty-eight poems underwent a change of title, five of them changing title twice.

As a poet he adhered with remarkable consistency to his theory of verse as enunciated in his preface to the 1831 edition of his *Poems*: "Music, when combined with a pleasurable idea, is poetry." His earlier poems are illustrations of his faith that the writing of verse is almost exclusively a feelingful, emotional process, in which taste is the sole arbiter and beauty the only legitimate province. Subsequently he admitted the intellect and the moral sense to have at least collateral relations. As he progressed in his critical editorial work to seek for the unifying principles of art, unity itself became increasingly important—unity of interest, unity of impression, unity of form; and as he turned to the ratiocinative tales, his more ingenious concoctions, and finally to *Eureka,* in which he sought to explain the entire universe by the principle of unity rationally conceived, he attached increasing importance to the reason, ultimately concluding that the reason must play a complementary rôle to the poetic imagination. Still regarding poetry as "the Rhythmical Creation of Beauty," he came in the end to think of the more formal, rational principle as equally essential with the emotional and imaginative elements. The fusion of the deliberative and conscious processes with the intuitive and imaginative faculties he sought to illustrate in such poems as "The Raven" and "The Bells" and to explain in essays like "The Philosophy of Composition," "The Poetic Principle," and "The Rationale of Verse."

As a writer of prose fiction he left a body of sketches, short stories, and longer tales constructed on his strict principle that prose fiction must develop a single, predetermined effect. As in his poems, character and incident are subordinated to tone or mood, usually terror or horror, invested in a setting vaguely described as "the misty mid region of Weir." Except in his hoaxes, burlesques, and extravaganzas, which belong to a different order of writing, his stories all develop this singleness of impression. Whether his theme is death or revenge, the depiction of an unbalanced state of mind, or the ratiocinative unraveling of a mysterious plot, his purpose is to amuse and impress, to interest and harass, the mind of the reader. The third of the more notably early American short-story writers, Poe completed the threefold progression by which the short story developed. Irving, as the originator of the genre, more or less unconscious of any technique, was primarily concerned with telling a story of sufficient complication in its narrative to entertain the reader. Hawthorne added intellectual content to give it body or carrying power. Poe, notably in his review of the 1842 edition of Hawthorne's *Twice-Told Tales,* enunciated a technique which he believed the short story should follow. If, as has been said, Poe's narrow prescriptions of tone and methodology put the American short story into a strait jacket from which it was a half-century freeing itself, it is to be said, also, that his technique did much toward regularizing the form

and giving it a distinctive status among the accepted literary genres.

In literary criticism, the department in which Poe was most voluminous, most of his writing is represented by reviews, *i. e.,* the practical work of an editor and journalist. In the hurly-burly of the editorial room there was seldom time to dwell on fundamental literary considerations; yet occasionally he succeeded, even in such review articles as those on Hawthorne's *Twice-Told Tales* or Longfellow's *Ballads and Other Poems,* to discuss the basic principles of literature; while essays like "The Philosophy of Composition," "The Poetic Principle," and "The Rationale of Verse" contain an arresting statement of his rather narrow but highly influential critical philosophy. There are many who argue that as a poet his technical proficiency does not compensate for his lack of depth and dearth of ideas; there are others who feel that, as a short-story writer, he has been superseded by other more generous and gifted practitioners in that form; but there are few who deny his importance as the composer of the first body of valuable aesthetic criticism on this side of the Atlantic.

HENRY WADSWORTH LONGFELLOW (1807–1882)

Longfellow, during the nineteenth century, was in America what Tennyson was in England, and for much the same reasons. During the twentieth century both have suffered in their fame, chiefly because they seem "Victorian" to a sophisticated, hard-boiled, critical age of realism. Longfellow, especially, is damned for being reticent, sweet, serene, sentimental —"gentle" is the word. He contented himself with a vague form of hopeful moral idealism; modernity prefers a strident social propagandism. His New England reticence caused him to avoid certain themes as either irrelevant or unsuited to poetry; a later age insisted that if the poet is to be worth his salt, he must blink no fact of modern life, however harsh or distressing. The serene faith in goodness that is one of the most persistent notes of Longfellow's smooth verses is as insipid to critics of the latter day as the daring frankness and preoccupation with ugliness of many modern realists and naturalists would have been disgusting to him. Because he remained almost untouched by the pessimism and skepticism that followed in the wake of nineteenth-century scientific theory, preferring to reassert his faith in an abiding humanistic tradition and the Christian hope of human betterment, he has been put down as a shallow moralist and a superficial sentimentalist, lacking in vigor, depth, precision, and worth.

And, indeed, there is too much of seraphic faith, vagueness of thought, triviality of subject matter, sentimentality of feeling, dreaminess of mood, diffusion of idea, and obvious didacticism that no longer seems as essential to human well-being as it once did. But utterly to condemn him for the characteristics of his poetry which his own time found eminently satisfying, not to say edifying, while overlooking the lucid musicality of lyrics like "Hymn to the Night," the splendid pictorial simplicity of "A Dutch Picture," the superb narrative movement of *Hiawatha,* the idyllic repose of *Evangeline,* the vivid characterization of *The Courtship of Miles Standish,* the panoramic sweep of the *Christus* trilogy, the dramatic tension of "The Skeleton in Armor," the authenticity of his numerous sea poems, the high level of his sonnets, the competence of his translations from European literatures, and the dignified elevation of "Morituri Salutamus"—to ignore all these is to miss the fact that while he failed to equal the grandeur of a Homer or the sublimity of a Milton, he attained a versatility of form, a catholicity of art, an inviolability of taste that Americans could ill afford to have been without. There is no form or genre in which he did not write acceptably—not even the novel and the drama. His linguistic equipment, which included competence in a dozen foreign languages and a reading knowledge of eight others, enabled him to render a distinguished service for his provincial countrymen by translating for them some of the romance and beauty of Europe and European literature. It was through Longfellow, more than any other man, as Bliss Perry reminds us, that "the poetry of the Old World—the romance of town and tower and storied stream, the figures of monk and saint and man-at-arms, of troubadour and minnesinger, of artist and builder and dreamer—became the familiar possession of the New." He became the spirit incarnate of a cosmopolitan point of view in an emerging American art consciousness at a time when a wise selectivity was most desirable. His numerous excellent translations from all the important bodies of European literature, if he had written no original verse of his own, would entitle him to an honored place in the history of American letters and taste. He lacked profundity and originality, having, as Holmes remarked, "a receptive rather than an aggressive temperament"; his mind was acquisitive rather than creative. For his inspirations he read in books and turned toward the past, legendary and historical, instead of looking intently at the present or speculatively into the future. He never enlisted in what Emerson called "the soldiery of dissent." He had a mission, but it was a gentle one. "The natural tendency of poetry," he held, "is to give correct moral impressions, and thereby advance the cause of truth." This cause he sought to advance quietly and tastefully by his "sermons in verse," that avoided the unique, the bizarre, and the eccentric as faithfully as they dwelt on the sane, the normal, and the representative. He was as little the radical and rabble-rouser, on the one hand, as the pure aesthete or poet's poet, on the other. He wrote, not for the few, the

66

highly cultivated, but for all; and that he did so effectively is amply illustrated by the innumerable reprintings of "People's" and "Fireside" editions which were, and still are, called for. Even today, in Europe as well as in America, his currency remains unparalleled. In England alone twenty-four publishing firms have issued his works. Poems like *Evangeline* have received not one but several translations in German and in French. *Hiawatha* has achieved even a Latin translation. His writings are available in Russian, Hebrew, French, German, Italian, Spanish, Portuguese, Dutch, Swedish, Norwegian, Danish, Pennsylvania-Dutch, Yiddish, and Icelandic, and portions have appeared in the oriental languages. He remains, whether we like it or not, the representative American poet for the peoples of the world.

Although Longfellow came to be identified with the Cambridge-Boston fraternity of literary men, he was born in Portland, Maine, and did not go to live in Cambridge until he was in his thirtieth year. Like Bryant, he was descended from John Alden and Priscilla Mullens, and it was altogether fitting that he should write *The Courtship of Miles Standish*. Following a good preparatory education, he would doubtless have gone to Harvard, the alma mater of his lawyer father, if the latter had not become a trustee of Bowdoin College when his son came of college age. He passed the entrance examinations at fourteen, but pursued his freshman studies at home for a year, entering Bowdoin in 1822 as a sophomore and graduating in the class of 1825 with Hawthorne.

Two years before going to college he had written a poem on "The Battle of Lovell's Pond," which appeared in the Portland *Gazette*, and he continued to contribute essays and poems to various newspapers and magazines while he was a student at Bowdoin. Early in his senior year he asked for a year of postgraduate study at Harvard, where he proposed to add Italian to his Greek, Latin, and French, while devoting most of his time to "reading history" and "the best authors of polite literature" in preparation for the conduct of a "literary periodical." "I most eagerly aspire after future eminence in literature," he confided to his father; "my whole soul burns most ardently for it, and every earthly thought centers in it. . . . If I can ever rise in the world, it must be by the exercise of my talent in the wide field of literature."

Before this plan could be put in operation, the trustees of Bowdoin, struck by young Longfellow's translation of an ode of Horace and his position as fourth from the top in his graduating class, appointed him to the newly created professorship of modern languages. This post, carrying a stipend of $1,000, was too flattering for the lad of eighteen to turn down, especially since it provided an opportunity for him to go to Europe, for the offer was made with the proviso that he spend a year in Europe in further preparation for the position. His father agreed to finance him, and accordingly Longfellow set out in the spring of 1826 for Europe, armed with letters of introduction from George Ticknor and George Bancroft to professors in the German universities under whom they had recently studied. His approach to Europe was the same as Irving's. He was a romantic pilgrim entering hallowed ground; and although he was not to stay seventeen years, as Irving did, he managed to wheedle his father into letting him remain three years. During much of this time, he devoted more attention to sight-seeing and looking for the romantic and picturesque or diverting in France, Spain, Italy, and Germany, to writing at various literary works of a *Sketch-Book* sort, and to cultivating several romantic attachments to interesting young women whom he met in his travels, than to perfecting himself in the languages he was to teach at Bowdoin. But toward the end of his stay, he set resolutely to recoup lost time; and when he returned, in the summer of 1829, he had perfected his French, acquired a good command of Spanish and Italian, and learned enough German to write in fair idiom.

Shortly before his return he was outraged by the proposal of the college authorities to give him, not a professorship at $1,000 but a "tutorship" at $600. Disgustedly he wrote to his father that he would have all or nothing. Having traveled extensively in Europe and breathed the enlightened atmosphere of some of the most famous European universities, he had formed a contemptuous opinion of what passed for universities in America—"two or three large brick buildings—with a chapel, and a President to pray in it." If the Bowdoin affair terminated adversely (so he advised his father), he proposed to found a university of his own, the cornerstone of which would be a library, after the German pattern. "As soon as I return," he confided to his father, "I mean to proffer my humble endeavors to the execution of such a plan—and put my shoulder to the wheel. The present is just the moment: we must take the tide there is in the affairs of men."

The controversy over his rank and salary was compromised. He got the professorship at a salary of $800, with an additional $100 for serving as college librarian. His duties as librarian involved no manner of hardship, since the library was open only during the noon hour. But the haggling over the terms left a bad taste in his mouth. The young man, just attained to the maturity of twenty-two, but already up to founding a university of his own, found Bowdoin far short of his educational ideal, and the community of Brunswick execrably provincial in comparison with Paris, Rome, and Berlin. His marriage to Mary Storer Potter in 1831 brought him domestic happiness and release from the requirement of residing in the men's dormitory, where he was supposed to serve as proctor—a task that he considered onerous. Meanwhile a full professional career as teacher, editor of textbooks, scholar, poet, reviewer, and essayist kept him busy during his six years at Bowdoin. His chief literary production during this period was a collection of essays published originally in the *New England Magazine* (1831–33) and collected in the *Sketch-Book*-like *Outre-Mer: A Pilgrimage beyond the Sea* in 1833.

As early as January 4, 1831, he expressed his impatience with "this land of Barbarism—this miserable Down East"; and when, in 1834, he was offered the Smith Professorship of Modern Languages at Harvard to succeed Professor George Ticknor, he grasped the invitation eagerly as offering escape from his exile while affording an opportunity "to tread a stage on which I can take longer strides and spout to a larger audience."

As in the previous instance, the Harvard invitation carried the suggestion that he spend "a year or 18 months" in Europe at his own expense "for the purpose of a more perfect attainment of the German." So eager was he to be gone that he disregarded the advice of relatives and friends to delay the journey in deference to his wife's delicate health. Instead of proceeding directly to Germany, they spent the summer and fall traveling to the principal university towns of Norway, Sweden, Denmark, and Holland, in order that he might add what he called "new linguistic feathers to my cap." While he made good progress in the acquisition of these north-European languages, his wife was brought to the verge of death in October; at Amsterdam, by the premature birth of her child. Two months later, at Rotterdam, she took an unexpected turn for the worse and died. Distraught, he made the last arrangements for sending her body to America, and then pushed on, disconsolately and full of self-accusation, to Heidelberg, where he hoped that immersion in books might occupy his mind to the exclusion of all other thoughts.

Upon arriving at Heidelberg in December, 1835, he enrolled in the university, heard the lectures of the famous Heidelberg historians and philologists, and "buried himself in books,—in old, dusty books," working his way "diligently through the ancient po-

etic lore of Germany, from Frankish Legends of Saint George, and Saxon-Rhyme-Chronicles, and Nibelungen-Lieds, and Helden-Buchs, and Songs of the Minnesingers and Meistersingers, and Ships of Fools, and Reynard the Foxes, and Death-Dances, and Lamentations of Damned Souls, into the bright sunny land of harvests, where, amid the golden grain and the blue corn-flowers, walk the modern bards, and sing." While adding markedly to his academic attainments, he set about writing his first course of lectures on the European literatures. Under the stimulation of these studies, which made him thoroughly conversant with the spirit of German romantic song, his pent-up feelings and heartache found perfect reciprocation in the mood of Novalis, the young tragic poet of Germany who wept alone over the grave of his beloved in the twilight and composed "Hymns to the Night," very much like some of the *Voices of the Night* that were beginning to shape themselves in the mind of the young American poet, who also had loved and lost. The whole German *Sturm-und-Drang* literature accorded with his mood as he came to understand the language of German romantic sentiment and to accept the mystical communion which Novalis, for example, established with the spirit of his beloved in the holy solitude of night. This mood was soon to be supplemented by the sterner moralistic philosophy of Goethe, in whose doctrines of work and renunciation Longfellow sought an escape from the overpowering feelings of grief, purposeless reverie, indulgence in delicious sorrow, and romantic enervation. During the summer he made an extended tour through southern Germany, Switzerland, and Austria, which later furnished the materials for *Hyperion*, a prose romance into which he also wove, in thin disguise, his romantic attachment for Frances Appleton of Boston (ten years younger than himself), whom he met on this tour.

In December of 1836 he established himself in comfortable bachelor's quarters in Craigie House, Cambridge, and prepared for his academic duties, which began in January of the next year. Meanwhile he paid assiduous court to Miss Appleton upon her return to Boston. She had repulsed the arduous young widower's precipitous proposal in Switzerland, and she remained obdurate in Boston—a circumstance that goes far toward explaining the frustration, unrest, indecision, and inner conflict which he felt during his earlier Harvard career, and that accounts for much that is emotionally romantic and sentimentally melancholy in *Hyperion* as well as in his first two collections of poetry, *Voices of the Night* and *Ballads and Other Poems*. In this mood, he foolishly exhibited the pageant of his bleeding heart in the sentimentalized romance *Hyperion* in 1839, in the hope that it might soften the lady's heart. Announcing its forthcoming appearance to a friend, he wrote: "Next week I shall fire a rocket which I trust will make a commotion in that citadel. Perhaps the garrison will capitulate;— perhaps the rocket may burst and kill me." The rocket landed in the garrison on Beacon Hill without producing a capitulation, without any show of a white flag. Offended at Longfellow's indiscretion in thus publicizing his love for her, Miss Appleton's actions on their next meeting led Longfellow to record in his diary, "It is ended." However, he persevered, and in 1843, after seven years of ardent courtship, he won her. Craigie House, which came to the Longfellows as a wedding gift from her father, became their happy home, and there they lived together in complete happiness until her tragic death by burning in 1861.

In the meantime Longfellow's "Psalms" and "Ballads" were appearing in the newspapers. Many of them, like the several Psalms of Life, are the direct result of his efforts, under the stimulation of Goethe's philosophy, to gain control over his inward tumult, morbidity, and mournful retrospection by the exercise of renunciation, self-discipline, and a program of active work in the present instead of ineffectual longings for future promises or nostalgic regrets for the past.

Thus it is that Longfellow's first two collections of verse, *Voices of the Night* (1839) and *Ballads and Other Poems* (1841), are less the products of an Olympian calm and self-possession, supposedly natural to Longfellow, than of that peculiar need for self-expression which was inspired at one time by his own mixed feelings of love-sickness and irresolution and at the next by his immersion in the lyric poetry of Germany. Poe, reviewing these early productions, found the first of these notes generally admirable, but objected to what he called the "*recherché* spirit," or bookishness and didacticism—a tendency of mind, as he pointed out, resulting from Longfellow's immersion in the romantic literature of Germany.

Following another trip to Europe during 1842, the publication of *Poems on Slavery,* written during his return voyage, and his marriage in 1843, Longfellow turned more and more to a literary career, although he continued until 1854 to serve with marked distinction at Harvard, introducing his students to the best of the German, French, Spanish, and Italian literatures and, in 1845, publishing his *Poets and Poetry of Europe,* by which many Americans got their first acquaintance with modern European literary art other than English. He was for many years

the most distinguished American interpreter of the European literary spirit in America.

In 1843 he published his closet drama, *The Spanish Student,* followed by *The Waif: A Collection of Poems* (1845), *The Belfry of Bruges and Other Poems* (1845), and *The Estray: A Collection of Poems* (1847). *Evangeline,* representing the first of his longer narrative poems, established him as a national figure in 1847. The story was originally related by H. L. Conolly to Hawthorne and Longfellow with the recommendation of the narrator that Hawthorne make a story of it. As Longfellow recorded Conolly's account of the young Acadian couple it ran as follows:

On their wedding day all the men of the Province were summoned to assemble in the church to hear a proclamation. When assembled, they were seized and shipped off to be distributed through New England,—among them the new bridegroom. The bride set off in search for him— wandered about New England all her lifetime, and at last, when she was old, she found her bridegroom on his death-bed. The shock was so great that it killed her likewise.

Some time later, when it seemed that Hawthorne would not use it for a tale, Longfellow said to him, "If you really do not want this incident for a tale, let me have it for a poem." When *Evangeline* was done, and Hawthorne expressed his great delight in the poem, Longfellow replied, "This success I owe entirely to you, for being willing to forego the pleasure of writing a prose tale which many people would have taken for poetry, that I might write a poem which many people take for prose." This last reference alludes to the hexameter in which the poem is written, and to which there was critical objection in many quarters as unsuited to the English language. Others criticized the author for his dependence upon printed sources for his descriptions of regions which he had never seen, and still others thought he had relied too heavily upon such models as Voss's *Luise* and Goethe's *Hermann und Dorothea.* But it sold 5,000 copies in two months and, despite the objections of the learned and the envious, promptly made its way into the hearts of sentiment-loving Americans.

In 1849 appeared his novel, *Kavanagh,* of interest today chiefly because of the thesis that a great American literature is better developed through a judicious selection of the better motifs and characteristics of European art than by any exclusive attention to purely native themes. "Nationality," says Longfellow, "is a good thing to a certain extent, but universality is better." It is an argument for artistic cosmopolitanism as against nativistic provincialism. *The Seaside and the Fireside,* another volume of poems, appeared in 1850, and the next year he published his re-working of the old medieval story of *Der arme Heinrich* (The Poor Prince Henry), as originally told by Hartmann von der Aue. This he entitled *The Golden Legend*; it became eventually the second part of the trilogy, *The Christus*.

His position at Harvard was no more a sinecure than his professorship at Bowdoin had been. As he progressed in his increasingly successful poetic career, the "dull routine" of academic duties became more and more galling, chiefly because they distracted him from poetic pursuits. At the age of forty-three, reflecting that "Art is long, and time is fleeting," and that "few men have written great poetry after fifty," he decided that he could not go on until he reached fifty, for by that time he would be nothing more than "a fat mill horse, grinding round with blinkers on." Accordingly he resigned his professorship in 1854, to be succeeded by James Russell Lowell.

The first major work following his retirement was *Hiawatha* (1855), on a theme that had attracted him because of its epic qualities. Schoolcraft's books on the Indians supplied the material; the Finnish epic *Kalevala*, the rhymeless trochaic tetrameter measure; and his own narrative facility, the rest. While its action is not as close-knit as we normally expect of an epic, Hiawatha's central position as the son of his people, whose fate is bound up in his, lends it not only ethnic but also epic significance. Its theme is the history of a people, from their nomadic stage as hunters and fisher-folk, through primitive stages of agriculture and community life, the attainment of cultural solidarity as manifested by a common religion and a common fund of legend, until finally, becoming an oppressed people, their fortunes decline, their song becomes a memory, and their national heroism departs as Hiawatha disappears in the sunset. The poem was fiercely attacked in some quarters, parodied in others, and ridiculed by the critics, while Longfellow maintained his equanimity; and when his publisher protested that something must be done to stop "these atrocious libels," he asked, "By the way, Fields, how is *Hiawatha* selling?" When told that the sale was enormous, and that the presses could not run fast enough to supply the demand, he remarked quietly, "Then I think we had better let these people go on advertising it."

The Courtship of Miles Standish was another popular hit on its appearance in 1858. The income from his writings, which had been $219 in 1840, had risen to $2,000 by 1850, and thereafter often exceeded $3,000 annually. As Alexander Pope had been the first in England, so, just about a hundred years later, Longfellow was the first in America to make poetry a profitable business.

After the tragic death of his wife, Longfellow sought to forget his grief in the absorbing work of translating Dante's *Divine Comedy*, which was published during 1865–69. Meanwhile *Tales of a Wayside Inn*, a notable collection of verse tales obviously owing its inception and plan to Boccaccio's *Decameron*, was begun in 1862 and published in three installments, 1863, 1872, 1873. In 1868 he returned to his ambitious project, conceived as early as 1841: "to undertake a long and elaborate poem by the holy name of Christus, the theme of which would be the various aspects of Christendom in the Apostolic, Middle, and Modern Ages." *The Golden Legend*, published in 1851, formed the central part. In 1868 he published *New England Tragedies*, representing two episodes in the religious history of New England. It forms part III of *The Christus*. Three years later he completed the trilogy with *The Divine Tragedy*, a close metrical version of the gospel history, presenting successive scenes in the life of Christ. Thus *The Christus*, illustrating in its three parts, Faith, Hope, and Charity, came to represent what, in the sonnet "Mezzo Cammin" (written when he reached half man's allotted years of three score and ten), he had set himself as a goal:

> to build
> Some tower of song with lofty parapet.

He maintained his high poetic productivity to within two years of his death, publishing between 1873 and 1880 five volumes of verse, including many of his best sonnets, such poems of dignified repose and wisdom as "Morituri Salutamus," and his famous poem of farewell, "The Bells of San Blas," written in 1882, the last year of his life, and ending—

> Out of the shadows of night
> The world rolls into light;
> It is daybreak everywhere.

His last years were crowned with flattering honors, at home and abroad. Not the least appreciated of these was the gift from the school children of Cambridge of a chair made from the wood of the spreading chestnut tree of "Village Blacksmith" fame. Shortly after his death a memorial bust of Longfellow was placed in the Poet's Corner of Westminster Abbey, in recognition of his large participation in the general stream of life abroad and of his universal popularity. Longfellow's being the first American to be so honored is indicative of his fame in England. In America he came to hold a place in the people's mind so revered that, as Professor Odell Shepard remarked, "Criticizing Longfellow is like carrying a rifle into a national forest"; and Bliss Perry added, "One undertakes it with the hesitancy that a man would feel in making a purely aesthetic study of the Stars and Stripes."

That many of Longfellow's poems once highly esteemed are intrinsically meretricious seems obvious to the twentieth-century critic, and the conventional picture of the kindly grandfather, seated before the hearth, surrounded by adoring children, while reading to them in gentle accents is no longer as compelling as it once was. The trite advice of his Psalms of Life and the sentimental consolation to widows and orphans in "The Rainy Day," that "into each life some rain must fall," are aspects of Longfellow that we can afford to forget, but not his vigorous narrative poetry, his vivid characterization, his sonnets, his remarkable versatility, and, above all, the lucid simplicity of his lyrics. Though he lacked profundity, majesty, and sublimity, he was a master within the realms of homely affection, simple piety, spiritual aspiration, tender feeling, and refinement of thought and manners. But over and above these considerations is the fact that Longfellow, more than any other American poet, has spoken to the hearts of the common people, who have traditionally repeated his lines from childhood onward, until he has become vitally woven into the emotional and intellectual fabric itself of the American folk- and art-consciousness. Thus to become a part of a whole people is no mean achievement.

RALPH WALDO EMERSON (1803–1882)

Emerson holds a unique place in the opinion of the world as the spokesman of America, more particularly of the spirit of Americanism, compact of self-reliant individualism, enthusiastic progressivism, democratic liberalism, and practical idealism. Americanism was his natural heritage from a long line of ancestors who were not only ministers (though many of them were) but also merchants and farmers, bakers and coopers and distillers. Among them, they had shared all the experiences common to American pioneer life from early Puritan times onward; and Emerson, Boston born and bred, had every right to say that he "spoke also from Puritan experience." In times of war they had been patriots and soldiers, as, indeed, Emerson himself stood ready to become while he was still a grammar-school student of nine, when his class was called out to help throw up earthworks in Boston harbor for the defense of the city against the expected attack of the British during the War of 1812. He was nurtured by the expansive and nationalistic era that followed the second war with England, and his earlier writings, especially *The American Scholar* and *Self-Reliance*, voice the philosophy not only of individualism but of nationalism.

He watched the expansive westward movement of his country and, unlike his more provincial-minded neighbors, Hawthorne and Thoreau, he interpreted its progress hopefully. He repeatedly traveled westward on "hemisphere belting" lecture tours. While he found the exigencies of travel trying, every trip, whether to Missouri or Wisconsin or California, left him exhilarated and reconfirmed by the evidences of the "overflowing richness" of the new land, "whereby men should be great." He was less anxious that the "rapidity" of the American tempo should be "checked" than that it should be "guided" by intelligence and wisdom into its proper channels. Thus he absorbed the frontier, while seeking to evaluate its tremendous significance and uses in human and spiritual, instead of merely quantitative and material, terms.

Not that he was uncritically complimentary always. When the occasion arose, he could chide his countrymen in good round terms. He called the Fugitive Slave Law a damnable outrage, saying, "I will not obey it, by God!" and he strongly attacked the administrators of the law as week-kneed time-servers, called the State House of Massachusetts a playhouse, and the General Court, a dishonored body. Statesmen, he said, were "befriending liberty with their voices and crushing it with their votes." In the heat of his righteous indignation at a people who permitted things to be in the saddle, riding mankind, he charged that representative government had grown misrepresentative, the Union a conspiracy, and democracy and freedom only fine names for bilge water. He castigated New England's idol, Daniel Webster, as a compromiser of principle, and he glorified John Brown, while Brown was under sentence of death, as a "new saint awaiting his martyrdom," who, "if he shall suffer, will make the gallows glorious like the cross."

But these are instances of Emerson's wrath at particular abuses of his larger trust in his American ideal. In "The Poet" he declared that he was not blind to the "barbarism and materialism of the times," but pointed out that while "Banks and tariffs, the newspaper and caucus, Methodism and Unitarianism, are dull to dull people . . . they rest on the same foundations of wonder as the town of Troy and the temple of Delphi."

Our log-rolling, our stumps and their politics, our fisheries, our Negroes and Indians, our boats and our repudiations, the wrath of rogues and the pusillanimity of honest men, the northern trade, the southern planting, the western clearing, Oregon and Texas, are yet unsung. Yet America is a poem in our eyes; its ample geography dazzles the imagination, and it will not wait long for metres.

At the age of nineteen, he wrote on the first page of his journal, "I dedicate my book to the Spirit of America," more particularly to the present and the future of America, for, as he went on to say, "the dead sleep in their moonless night; my business is with the living." To the spirit of America he dedicated his essays, poems, and lectures—rebuking his generation when they forgot their high destiny in the grit and grime of money-making and land-getting, praising them when they elevated their eyes. For he believed with all his heart, and said so a thousand times, that spirit overlies nature, and that man has only one proper choice. No esoteric idealist, he never forgot that man must live on this earth, but he insisted on seeing the spiritual and the natural worlds in their proper relations—proper to man. "I have no hostility to Nature," he wrote, "but a child's love to it. . . . Let us speak her fair. I do not wish to fling stones at my beautiful mother, nor soil my gentle nest. I only wish to indicate the true position of nature in regard to man." Thus natural objects were only mediate things to him—not ultimate realities. Nature, to be sure, served many useful and noble purposes, even to hinting to man "the laws of right and wrong." "Every natural fact is a symbol of some spiritual fact." "The laws of moral nature answer to those of matter like face to face in a glass." "The axioms of physics translate the laws of ethics." "Every natural process is a version of a moral sentence." His choice of the ideal over the material, of mind over matter, as presenting the higher reality was considered and deliberate. "Be it [nature] what it may," he concluded in *Nature*, "it is ideal to me so long as I cannot try the accuracy of my senses."

This way of thinking made him what the philosophers call an idealist. But his idealism was subtle enough to accept both mind and matter, even while endeavoring, at various times during his life, to reconcile or identify the two with each other. An unhappy dualist, he sought throughout his life to unify his world—to make it monistic—to reduce the dualistic enigma of mind and matter to unity. To this end he searched the scientists from ancient to modern times no less than the idealistic philosophers from Plato to Kant and beyond. He sought to reconcile science and religion, or as he put it at one time, to make his "religion philosophical" and his "philosophy religious," and at another, "to square the head by the heart." In the process he rejected neither the natural nor the spiritual. He acknowledged "an occult relation between man and the vegetable. . . . They nod to me, and I to them." When his attempts at identifying the two failed, the mystic in him was content to believe in them both, imperfectly reconciled though they remained. But in the process, he alienated both the orthodox theologian and the strict scientist. Neither forgave him for what he conceded to the other. To the theologian he was a heretic, infidel, atheist; to the scientist, a transcendental dreamer, a mystical soothsayer, an impractical idealist.

These irreconciled elements in Emerson are not the only faults that men have found with Emerson. There are other inconsistencies that he did not bother to harmonize. He had no patience with what he called "foolish consistency." He declared, "I delight in telling what I think, but if you ask me how I dare say so, or why it is so, I am the most helpless of mortal men." And when it was suggested that such an unsystematic procedure would never beget a large following, he could say, "Very well, I do not wish disciples." He defied tradition and authority, and he wrote in the mood of the moment, from inspiration, leaving each utterance to take care of itself in its own place and time. Hence it often turned out that what he said in one connection contradicts what he said in another. Accordingly the seekers after paradox have found it an easy matter to make him out "conservative, or liberal, or radical, orthodox or infidel, whig or tory, moralist or amoralist, belligerent or pacifist, patriot or traitor." And, on the basis of single or isolated passages, he is all these, and more too.

What is more, he was careless in his methods of composition, throwing together passages from his voluminous notebooks for a lecture or an essay with what seemed in some cases reckless abandon. He liked striking, epigrammatic sentences. He cared little for the paragraph, and less for the larger structural units. He avoided connectives, qualifying words and phrases, and transitional devices. His friend Carlyle observed in a letter to Emerson, "Your sentences are very *brief*; and did not, in my *sheet* reading, always entirely cohere for me. Pure genuine Saxon; strong and simple. . . . But they did not, sometimes, rightly stick to their foregoers and their followers: the paragraph not as a beaten *ingot*, but as a beautiful square *bag of duck-shot* held together by canvas!" And his auditors sometimes observed, as did Lowell of one of his lectures, "It was as if, after vainly trying to get his paragraphs into sequence and order, he had at last tried the desperate expedient of *shuffling* them. It was chaos come again, but it was a chaos full of shooting stars." "His eye for a fine, telling phrase that will carry true is like that of a backwoodsman for a rifle; and he will dredge you up a choice word from the mud of Cotton Mather himself . . . it is like homespun cloth of gold. The many cannot miss his meaning, and only the few can find it." Speaking of a time when as a young enthusiast he first heard Emerson lecture, Lowell observed that while he and the other young people whom Emerson moved so profoundly came away uncertain about the precise meaning of anything Mr. Emerson had said, they came away feeling, "Thus saith the Lord." As a man of seventy, after he had gone to hear Emerson for forty years, Lowell wrote, "We do not go to hear what Emerson says so much as to hear Emerson."

But whatever difficulties Emerson the lecturer or the essayist presented to his followers, and however many conflicts he failed to settle in his own mind, he was consistent on one point. He believed implicitly in the moral principle as supreme and absolute. His God seemed to many people of doubtful divinity, but no one doubted Emerson's faith in goodness. Indeed, goodness and Godliness were very nearly synonymous with Emerson. However much his philosophical opinions changed (and they changed a good deal from youth to old age, even from day to day), he never relinquished for a moment his faith that the distinction between "Right and Wrong . . . is real and eternal." As a young man of twenty he declared:

Your opinions upon all other topics, and your feelings with regard to this world, in childhood, youth, and age, perpetually change. Your perceptions of right and wrong never change. . . . The mind may lose its acquaintance with other minds, and may abandon, without a sigh, this glorious universe; but it cannot part with its moral principle . . . If there is anything real under heaven, or in heaven, the perception of right and wrong relates to that reality. . . . It is the constitution of the mind to rely with firm confidence upon the *moral principle*, and I reject at once the idea of a delusion in this. This is woven vitally into the thinking substance itself, so that it cannot be diminished or destroyed without dissipating forever that spirit which it inhabited. Upon the foundation of my *moral* sense I ground my faith in the immortality of the soul, in the existence and activity of good beings, and in the promise of rewards. . . .

This is the central idea to which all other ideas of Emerson's are related, and the student who wants to see the larger consistency of Emerson's doctrine, by which the smaller inconsistencies are dwarfed into insignificance, must get hold of this central idea.

Emerson came quite naturally by his moral fervor. He was the son not only of Puritans but of a long line of Puritan (later Unitarian) ministers; and if this background had not been enough, there was his revered Aunt Mary Moody Emerson, who lived with the Emersons, and who repeatedly drilled him in the doctrines of self-reliance and moral righteousness. The essay on "Self-Reliance" concludes with two summarizing, climactic sentences: "Nothing can bring you peace but yourself. Nothing can bring you peace but the triumph of principles." These two ideas spring ultimately from what we are accustomed to call Puritan independence and Puritan righteousness. More immediately, Emerson derived them directly from Aunt Mary. She became what his father might have been to him if he had not died in Em-

erson's ninth year. She was his spiritual adviser; and even after he went to college, it was to her, rather than to his mother or to his brothers, that he wrote to bare his heart or to ask spiritual guidance.

Emerson's educational opportunities were excellent considering that when his father died in 1811, his mother was left in straitened circumstances. But the First (Unitarian) congregation, over which his father had presided, assisted Mrs. Emerson in her efforts to give her five sons a college education—as was customary under such circumstances. For the rest, relatives helped, and Emerson helped himself by waiting on table in commons and running errands for the president of Harvard. While his academic record was indifferent, he read to good purpose on his own initiative. He won two prizes with essays on philosophical subjects during his junior and senior years, and was chosen poet of his class in 1821.

For four years after graduation he tried teaching, chiefly in a girls' school under the direction of his brother William, while trying to decide whether to enter the ministry, as his mother fervently wished. Beset by doubts of his capabilities for a ministerial career and especially by indecision about his own faith, he finally decided, in 1825, to enter the Harvard Divinity School. Realizing that his reasoning faculty was "weak," and that theology was "from everlasting to everlasting debatable ground," yet willing to risk all, as he said, on the strength of his "moral imagination," he made the choice deliberately, adding, "In divinity I hope to thrive."

But during the first year of theological studies, his eyes and lungs failed, and the old doubts returned in a degree that made him fear for his mental balance. Sick in body and mind, he went south for the winter of 1826–27, ultimately settling in Saint Augustine, Florida. Here he slowly recuperated, while discussing his problems with a wealthy, cultivated young planter named Achille Murat, of French birth and rearing and of liberal and atheistical opinions. Emerson's characterization of his friend as "a sincere and consistent Atheist" is indicative of the torn state of mind of the young probationer in the church. Yet the tough fiber that was Emersonian held, and out of the "dark hours" in Saint Augustine came a reaffirmation of will to resume his theological studies.

In March of 1829 he became the colleague of the Rev. Henry Ware, Jr., of the Second (Unitarian) Church in Boston, and upon Ware's becoming a professor in the Harvard Divinity School shortly thereafter, he was left in sole charge of this influential church. His life seemed to be regulating itself, and he had every hopeful prospect when Ellen Louisa

Tucker, to whom he had become engaged in 1828, fell suddenly ill of consumption early in 1829 and the marriage had to be postponed until September. A year later he buried her. Meanwhile his favorite brother Edward had been reduced by a violent mental derangement to the state of a maniac. Under these stresses, Emerson's own health suffered. The strictures in his chest returned and he began to fear anew the "hereditary taint" of his family. His old doubts assailed him again. A strenuous course of reading in the sciences served only to aggravate his theological questioning. All his doubts came to a head in the summer of 1832 over the interpretation of rites and ceremonies in the church. He decided that he could not go on administering the Lord's Supper to his parishioners in the accepted way unless the congregation chose to agree with him and regard it as merely symbolic. Since they did not choose, he resigned, and shortly after preaching his last sermon, in which he stated the grounds of his dissent, he sailed for Europe. He had read the works of Landor, Coleridge, Wordsworth, and Carlyle; if he read them correctly, he concluded that they should be able to help him find answers for his questions. This unfrocking himself, abandoning the only profession for which he had been trained, and which promised a successful career, while striking out anew, at the age of thirty, with nothing more definite than a vague desire to write—this took courage, and it illustrates again his stiff-necked refusal to sacrifice principle for expediency.

Following a rapid tour of Italy, where he saw Landor, and a stop in Paris, where he haunted the natural museums, he visited Coleridge, Wordsworth, and Carlyle, and came away thoroughly disappointed in all but Carlyle. Coleridge, prematurely old at sixty-two, turned out to be "a short thick old man . . . anything but what I had imagined," and his visit to him was "rather a spectacle than a conversation, of no use beyond the satisfaction of my curiosity." Wordsworth, too, was a disappointment—lost by now in hopeless orthodoxy, his mind closed to all new currents of thought. Carlyle he warmed up to. Carlyle was hearty, genuine, and invigorating. But even in Carlyle he found a measure of disappointment; for however pleasant he found the Scotchman, he roundly evaded his questions—the questions Emerson had come specifically to get help on—questions regarding the ultimate worth of Christianity, the immortality of the soul, the free will of man. Emerson was left with the conclusion—the only possible conclusion—that these men could not help him, that nobody could help him, that he must help himself. It was ironical, he reflected, that he had traveled thousands of miles to find what had lain right within his own self all along. It was the great lesson of selfhood, of self-reliance, that he found at the end of his long and devious route.

Under the cheering impulse of this discovery, he began to put words together toward his first book, even before he started his return voyage. He bethought himself of his "penny Savings Bank," the notebooks, in which, since 1820, he had been recording all notable thoughts that had come to him. He began now to put the fragments together, and he was cheered to find the "fractions made integers by their addition." With self-reliance came articulation; and at the end of the first stint of writing those passages which ultimately formed the gist of *Nature*, he told himself in self-congratulatory mood, "I like my book about Nature." This was September 8, 1833. Three years were to elapse before the little booklet was to be done, for his decision to write not merely on "Nature" but also on "Spirit" threw many a metaphysical stumbling block into his way. It reopened the whole problem of mind *versus* matter, for the questionable solution of which (as he achieved it in *Nature*) he finally found help in the transcendental philosophy of Kant as interpreted to him by Coleridge's *Aids to Reflection* and Carlyle's essays.

German transcendentalism as promulgated by Kant was a philosophical analysis of the powers of the mind, an attempt to determine what could and could not be known by human understanding and reason. Kant's *Critique of Pure Reason* (1781) demonstrated that while the human understanding is capable of dealing reliably with sensory phenomena and demonstrable truths, the reason is powerless to reduce to absolute and verifiable knowledge such ultra-rational ideas as the soul has of God, of Immortality, and of Freedom. They remain ideas, beyond the realms of time and space. In his *Critique of Practical Reason* (1788) Kant went on to argue that within the realm of practice and on the basis of the assumption of moral necessity these ideas could be shown to have a practical validity, even if they could not be proved absolutely on purely logical or rational grounds. But this kind of practical "knowledge," he very carefully pointed out, rested on an assumption which itself remained unproved.

Emerson did not grasp fully the negative aspects of the Kantian criticism, but was led to believe, on the basis of what his English interpreters told him about the efficacy of the Kantian distinction between Understanding and Reason to prove the absolute validity of the Ideas of the Reason—what Kant had specifically demonstrated to be impossible. Although Emerson later made a disheartening attempt to read Kant himself, he knew nothing of him at first hand while he was writing *Nature*. Hence the confused point of view in that booklet between the sections on Nature and on Spirit, and his assertion of the reason's dominion over those areas which Kant had reserved to the realm of moral probability in terms of the "practically," rather than the "absolutely," true. In the summer of 1836, while putting the finishing touches to *Nature*, Emerson confessed that there still remained in his argument for the identity of Nature and Spirit "a crack . . . not easy to be soldered or welded"; and in the conclusion of the book he had to admit that he had presented nothing more than "a hypothesis" which still remained to be verified.

Yet the rumble of Kant's dialectic is clearly discernible in *Nature*. The Kantian tripartition of the mental faculties into Sensation, Understanding, and Reason supplied the epistemological terminology for the doctrines enunciated in *Nature* and the metaphysical groundwork for Emersonian transcendentalism generally. The application of this epistemological machinery is to be discovered chiefly in the careful subdivisions which Emerson made under the four Uses of Nature, each of which falls neatly into three sections depending on whether they are the object of the Sensation, the Understanding, or the Reason. But the attentive reader will discover that there was still something that eluded Emerson and that left him dissatisfied with his attempted identification of Nature with Spirit, matter with mind. For, in the section on "Spirit," this doctrine of transcendental idealism, as he understood it, is put down as being, "in the present state of our knowledge, merely . . . a useful introductory hypothesis." This indefinite and unsatisfying conclusion is owing in part to Emerson's inability to rid his mind of the old and familiar terminology of Berkeleian idealism even while he believed himself to be following the newer critical terminology of Kant; but it is owing chiefly to his failure to recognize the sharp distinctions drawn by Kant between practical and pure Reason, or between the provisionally and the absolutely true—between moral necessity and absolute certitude. The phrase, "in the present state of our knowledge," suggests that he still entertained hopes that the hypothesis might be proved to be something more than a mere hypothesis; but Emerson himself soon became dissatisfied with the strictly logical and critical method of transcendentalism, and the period during which he was under Kantian influence was relatively brief.

By the time he wrote "The Over-Soul," about 1839, Emerson had lapsed back into Platonic intuitionalism, a mode of thinking for which his mind was congenitally better suited. In that essay and in other essays of the period, like "Circles," he is the seer, whose faith perceived truth through revelation, intuitively by divination, immediately and unreflectively. This intuitive, or neo-Platonic, phase was followed by a period when he gave up technical philosophical questions and problems altogether, meanwhile contenting himself with writing essays and lectures on practical, common-sensical subjects, as illustrated by "Experience," "Politics," "Friendship," "Prudence," *Representative Men*, and reforms and reformers as he saw them eddying all about him in the New England of the forties. About 1850, he was attracted to Hegelianism as offering a philosophy consonant with the new nineteenth-century concept of "progressive development," and after 1859, when Darwin's *Origin of Species* gave the idea of evolution a new urgency, he renewed his quest for a philosophy that would embrace both the new science and his old religious or moral demands. But the theoretical and abstract methods of Hegel and the mental gymnastics demanded by the triadic development of the Hegelian dialectic were essentially alien to his mind. Though his friends among the St. Louis Hegelians and, later, among the Concord School of Philosophy, sought earnestly to instruct him, he never learned its techniques or entered into its spirit. Philosophy remained for him, he said late in life, "the eternal homesickness of the soul." He could neither get along with it nor without it; and however often he told himself that he was done with all metaphysical gibberish, he always returned to philosophy, to be plagued further by its inconclusiveness.

While these shifts and changes in Emerson's thinking on the technical problems involved in the processes of knowing are of real interest chiefly to the mature student of Emerson, they are indicative of one of the basic causes for the so-called contradictions among Emerson's ideas. It would be too much to expect that a man whose epistemological bases shifted so frequently should, during all the periods of his mental development, indite thoughts that would be infallibly consistent with each other.

When Carlyle first read *Nature*, he immediately recognized in it "the Foundation or Ground-plan," on which, he told Emerson, "You may build whatsoever of great and true you have been given to build"; and Emerson soon set to expounding its individual principles and following out its implications. In 1837 he delivered his lecture on "The American Scholar" before the Phi Beta Kappa Society of Harvard. Called by later critics the American Declaration of Intellectual Independence, it created no great stir at the time. The next year he delivered the "Divinity School Address" and earned for himself the reputation of a heretic. Striking out boldly at "the pale negations of Boston Unitarianism," he pleaded for a revitalization of Christianity that should be fresh, vivid, and personal. His enumeration of the defects of "historical Christianity" and his prescriptions for a reformation were taken by his auditors, some of whom were his old professors, as an attack upon them; and his one-time colleague, the Rev. Henry Ware, wrote to him demanding a particularization of the grounds and arguments on which Emerson brought his charges. It was on this occasion that Emerson wrote his famous letter refusing to give his reasons, explaining that he did "not know what arguments mean in reference to an expression of a thought," meanwhile maintaining his right to express his honest thoughts. In one sense it was Emerson's declaration of independence from the tyranny of philosophical method; in another, more immediate connection, it was a bland denial of the right of controversialists to draw him into polemical debate. Those who felt themselves to be the objects of his attack doubtless thought this an evasive and unfair trick, but it left them powerless, for Emerson steadfastly refused to be provoked into defending his pronouncements or into replying to the countercharges of his opponents, at the same time that it saved him from recriminatory wranglings and vexatious conflicts.

During the early thirties a series of deeply moving personal influences assailed his spirit. The death of his wife in 1832, his repudiation of the church in the same year, and the broadening experience of his first European journey in 1833 were followed in 1834 by the death of his brother Edward, and a year and a half later by the death of Charles—"my brother, my friend, my ornament, my joy and pride." In 1835 he moved into the Old Manse of Concord, the house built by his grandfather, to take what he felt at the time to be his proper place in the "quiet fields of my fathers." His going to Concord was the consummation of a desire expressed in 1823, in the poem which begins "Good-bye, proud world! I'm going home." Thither he brought in 1835 his second bride, Lydia Jackson. The next year he bought the house and plot of ground which was to be his home for the remainder of his days; and here, two years later, he held his first child in his arms. Truly, he reflected, life was running deep; it was both real and earnest, compounded of deep sorrows and abiding satisfactions. Under these humanizing experiences he was

stimulated to resume his writing, completing *Nature* in 1836, writing "The American Scholar" in 1837, the "Divinity School Address" in 1838, and a number of other essays, as well as lectures and poems. It was as if these soul-stirring events had been wanting to shock him into expression.

In 1836 he became the leading spirit in the formation of the Transcendental Club, which included such like-minded idealists as George Ripley, Theodore Parker, James Freeman Clarke, Elizabeth Palmer Peabody, Margaret Fuller, Amos Bronson Alcott, O. A. Brownson, W. H. Channing, and Frederic H. Hedge. He deliberated with them the plans that led to the Brook Farm experiment in communal living, but his deep-seated genius for pursuing his own individual way (as well as his family responsibilities) prevented his going there to live. During the first two years of the *Dial* (1841–42), he assisted Margaret Fuller in editing this noble experiment in journalism, and during the last two years of its existence he served as its sole editor. In 1841 appeared his *Essays, First Series*, followed three years later by the *Second Series*. Meanwhile he had been acquiring a commanding reputation as a lecturer, and his poems were adding to his renown. His first collection of *Poems* appeared in 1847, the year of his second trip to Europe. His lectures were enthusiastically received in England, and upon his return home he became the most renowned of the numerous lyceum lecturers. He made almost annually a wide sweep through the country, often as far west as the Mississippi, to spread his doctrine of idealism far and wide, even to the outposts of the frontier. In the meantime, he published three more of his more important books: *Representative Men* (1850), *English Traits* (1856), and *Conduct of Life* (1860).

During the years before the Civil War, the human issues involved overcame his dislike for organized reform until he was fairly drawn into the vortex to become one of the most impassioned disciples of abolition and, like Thoreau, a castigator of Northern expediency and lethargy no less than of Southern excess and injustice.

Following the war he regularly attended the dinners and participated in the conversations of the Saturday Club, which included Longfellow, Holmes, Agassiz, Whittier, Lowell, Dana, Motley, and Hawthorne, among others. By now Harvard had forgiven or forgotten the offense which the "Divinity School Address" had provoked in 1838; and accordingly, twenty-nine years later, he was invited to deliver another Phi Beta Kappa address. In 1867, too, he published *May Day*, a volume of poems. *Society and*

Solitude appeared in 1870, and in the same year he delivered a series of philosophical lectures at Harvard, published in 1893 under the title of *Natural History of the Intellect.*

In 1871, at the age of sixty-eight, he traveled all the way to California, thus realizing his ambition to know more fully the western frontier, which had been a constant source of stimulation to his optimistic philosophy. Later in the same year he revisited England, France, and Italy, journeying even as far as Egypt. On his return, he was welcomed by his townspeople into the new home which they had built for him after his former house had been destroyed by fire. He remained active to the end and published *Letters and Social Aims* in 1875. But thereafter his memory began to fade, and during his last public appearances as a lecturer he required the assistance of his daughter or a friend to help him keep his pages of notes in order. At Longfellow's funeral in 1882, only a month before his own passing, he looked intently upon the face of the dead poet, and then turned to a friend to say, "That gentleman was a sweet, beautiful soul, but I have entirely forgotten his name." His death came on April 24, 1882, of pneumonia, in his seventy-ninth year, and a few days later he was buried among his former Concord friends in Sleepy Hollow Cemetery.

Emerson has been variously interpreted and reinterpreted. There are those who like his essays and others who prefer his poems, Edwin Arlington Robinson, for example, considering him the greatest American poet. His poems, like his essays, have some stylistic and structural defects that a more meticulous craftsman would not have countenanced. Emerson cared little for prosodic perfection or melodic effects,

being intent primarily upon the idea he wished to convey. In the essay on "The Poet" he wrote, "It is not metres, but a metre-making argument, that makes a poem." He had a low opinion of pure literature; he believed that "the high poetry of the world from its beginning has been ethical, and it is the tendency of the ripe modern mind to produce it." In his verses, as in his essays, he is at his best in short passages, and the number of quotable lines is large. "Every poem," he said, "must be made up of lines that are poems." Hence the cryptic, epigrammatic nature of his poems.

Aware of his own deficiencies as a poet, he once remarked to a friend, "I feel it a hardship that—with something of a lover's passion for what is to me the most precious thing in life, poetry—I have no gift of fluency in it, only a rude and stammering utterance." Yet a surprising number of his poetic utterances—single lines, couplets, and quatrains—have become an intimate portion of the American people's poetic heritage.

Fundamentally, it is true that Emerson is Emerson, and that it makes little difference whether one reads his poems, his essays, or his lectures, or the sources of all three—his notebooks; they are all derived from that common storehouse, his voluminous journals, in which he preserved his thoughts, and out of which he extracted or selected the several ingredients that he combined and fused into the poetic wisdom that maintains for him a central place among American men of letters. His message of individualistic idealism, warning men that "things are in the saddle" and that they are riding mankind, in a way to debase the truly humanistic potentiality of man, remains as vital and stimulating today as it was to the men of his own day.

HENRY DAVID THOREAU (1817–1862)

The most distinguished spirit of the Transcendentalist Movement was Emerson. He was the high-priest of self-reliant individualism, saying "This is my charge plain and clear, to act faithfully upon my own faith, to live by it myself, and see what a hearty obedience to it will do." He was also the disciple of nature, leading a back-to-nature movement and counseling men to live in all simplicity, according to the examples and dictates of nature. Compared with Thoreau, however, Emerson was only the theorist; it was reserved for Thoreau to put his mandates into practice. He carried them to their natural and, in some instances, unnatural or extreme conclusions. Brook Farm was a practical application of Emerson's preachment about plain living and high thinking; but while he assisted in the planning of the communal experiment, he himself did not participate actively in the life of Brook Farm. Thoreau, on the other hand, experimented with life at Walden Pond in a very direct way, the difference between his procedure and that at Brook Farm being chiefly that he did it single-handedly instead of cooperatively. From first to last, Emerson urged men to live in Spartan simplicity, but he was himself enamored of the conveniences of housekeeping—too much so, thought his young friend Thoreau, who could see no sense in keeping a servant to do what one could do for oneself, much less seven servants, as Emerson's household at one time harbored, or supported. Emerson also repeatedly instructed men to live close to nature, but he seldom got much closer to nature than to dig abstractedly in his garden or to take á walk around Walden, either alone or in the company of a friend; but Thoreau actually lived for two years and two months in the woods with only the birds and the beasts for his companions. While Emerson had repudiated the church during his young manhood, supported the church in Concord with his money and kept a pew for his family; Thoreau declared his independence of all visible churches, and not only refused to give his money for their support but religiously stayed away from them, saying, "Men call me a skeptic, but I'm only too conscientious to go to church." Emerson fulminated against the institution of slavery and ranted at his government for condoning the evils of slavery, but Thoreau actively participated in helping fugitive slaves from stage to stage in the underground railway and went to jail rather than pay taxes in support of a government that carried on what he considered an unjust war with Mexico in order to extend the slave territory. Emerson, of course, had given hostages to fortune and to absolute independence; had the cares of a home and the responsibilities of a family. Thoreau had only himself to look after, and he was most careful to keep it so. He was free to come and go as he pleased, or to lead a one-man secession movement. He declared formally: "I cannot for an instant recognize that political organization as *my* government which is the *slave's* government also." "How does it become a man to behave toward this American government today?" he asked in 1849. "I answer, that he cannot without disgrace be associated with it." "My thoughts are murder to the State, and involuntarily go plotting against her." "I refuse her my allegiance, and express contempt for her courts."

Thoreau was Emerson's junior by fourteen years, and in the beginning he was Emerson's pupil. But it was not long before the zeal of the disciple outran the discretion of the master—in nothing so much as in Thoreau's fixed resolution to front life squarely, reduce it to its simplest elements, and discover what it really had to offer. It was his desire, he said, "to live deep and suck out all the marrow of life," "to drive life into a corner, in order to find out whether it was a mean or a noble thing." "I came into this world," he said, "not chiefly to make this a good place to live in, but to live in it, be it good or bad." And in the prosecution of that purpose, he concluded that he must choose wisely what he had to do and to determine what he must leave undone, for clearly a man "has not everything to do, but something; and because he cannot do *every* thing, it is not necessary that he should do *something* wrong." Accordingly, he deliberately chose, in this process of finding out how a man should live, to reduce life to its simplest essentials; and that, he was convinced, could best be done by studying intently the primal forms, the basic processes, and the fundamental laws of nature in their archetypal simplicity.

In the prosecution of that aim he cast off all superfluities of life, all artificialities of convention, and betook himself in all humility and earnestness to study the great fountainhead of simplicity and unity —nature herself. He made his boast, not the number of things he had, but the number of things he could afford to do without. So he proceeded, with unusual singleness of purpose, "to live as tenderly and daintily as one would pluck a flower," to make an art of living, consistently and according to the twin principles of the moral law of spiritual growth and the organic principle of natural development. Thus it is that one finds a remarkable unity of mood and of expression between the life and the writings of Thoreau—between his actions and his thoughts, in his expression of them. Indeed, Thoreau consciously cultivated this identity between the outward and the inward life, saying on one occasion:

> My life has been the poem I would have writ,
> But I could not both live and live to utter it.

In the pursuit of this ideal he allowed nothing to interfere or to throw him off his track, least of all the social conventionalities or the amenities of human intercourse. He had important work of his own to do that could not await the pleasure of others, though he insisted that it await his own pleasure. He refused to have his work degenerate into labor, and he never permitted his work to drive him. Like Whitman, he sauntered to his task and did as much of it as it pleased him to do. His demands were few, and a few days' wages served to keep him comfortably for many more. He believed with all his heart that most men foolishly allowed their jobs to enslave them. While men have allowed themselves to "become the tool of their tools," he was "convinced, both by faith and experience, that to maintain one's self on this earth is not a hardship but a pastime, if we will live simply and wisely," instead of piling "gewgaws upon the mantel piece." "Superfluous wealth," he pointed out, "can buy superfluities only." "Our life is frittered away by detail." Too many people come to the end of their days only to discover that instead of having lived, they have spent all of life merely preparing to live. Thoreau wanted to live every day, and that could be done only by choosing between what was important and what was unimportant, lest he waste his time. While most men complained that they had not enough time in which to do what was demanded

of them, Thoreau was seldom troubled by lack of time. Careful choosing between essentials and non-essentials left him so much time that in Walden he could say, "Time is but the stream I go a-fishing in." In Walden, too, he set down his motto: "Simplicity, simplicity, simplicity!"

An honest man has hardly need to count more than his ten fingers, or in extreme cases he may add his ten toes, and lump the rest. . . . I say, let your affairs be as two or three, and not a hundred or a thousand; instead of a million count half a dozen, and keep your accounts on your thumb nail. . . . Simplify, simplify. Instead of three meals a day, if it be necessary eat but one; instead of a hundred dishes, five; and reduce other things in proportion. . . .

If we stay at home and mind our business, who will want railroads? We do not ride on the railroad; it rides upon us. . . .

Why should we live with such hurry and waste of life? We are determined to be starved before we are hungry. . . . We have the Saint Vitus' dance, and cannot possibly keep our heads still. . . .

Cultivate poverty like a garden herb, like sage. Do not trouble yourself much to get new things, whether clothes or friends. Turn the old; return to them. Things do not change; we change. Sell your clothes and keep your thoughts. God will see that you do not want society. If I were confined to a corner of a garret all my days, like a spider, the world would be just as large to me while I had my thoughts about me. . . . Money is not required to buy one necessary of the soul.

Living simply and renouncing all luxuries as excrescences, he was free to cultivate his individualistic independence. "I would rather sit on a pumpkin and have it all to myself, than be crowded on a velvet cushion." And as for being kept from what was really important to him by the demands of making his livelihood, he could say, "It is not necessary that a man should earn his living by the sweat of his brow, unless he sweats easier than I do." He insisted that "the order of things ought to be reversed. The seventh should be man's day of toil; he should keep the other six for his joy and wonder."

Henry David Thoreau, the only one of the Concord writers who was a native of the village, was born there on July 12, 1817, the second son of John and Cynthia Dunbar Thoreau, of French descent. His father set up a pencil factory in Concord in 1823 and built up a profitable business. Henry received a good preparatory education, including a solid foundation in the classics, and proceeded to Harvard College in 1833, where he graduated in 1837. He earned part of his expenses by tutoring during the year and by teaching or peddling during the vacation periods. Like Emerson, he studied more on his own initiative than on the prescription of his professors, confessing that though he was for four years "a member of Harvard University," his heart and soul were "far away among the scenes of my boyhood," and that "those hours that should have been devoted to study have been spent in scouring the woods and exploring the lakes and streams of my native village." The story that he refused the bachelor's degree at the end of his four years saying, "Let the sheep keep their skins," is now known to be apocryphal, as are so many other colorful stories about Thoreau that are still current; but it was the kind of remark that he could have made. He did say that he preferred the chic-a-dee-dees to the D.D.'s; and when he heard someone boast that at Harvard they taught all branches of knowledge, he added drily, "Yes, but none of the roots." Education for him was a process of learning, of self-improvement, in which a college or professors could be only supplementary to contributory factors. Already at Harvard he began his intensive program of humanistic self-development, to which end he began, in 1837, his habit of elaborate journal-keeping. In this respect he followed his friend Emerson, and like him, subsequently turned to his journals for the immediate sources of what went into his books, essays, and lectures. In many respects Thoreau was more thorough than Emerson. For instance, he learned his Greek to retain it, and one of his great pleasures in later life was to translate from the Greek classics. Emerson contented himself for the most part with translations. He used encyclopedias, manuals, handbooks, short-cuts to knowledge or information; Thoreau was content with nothing short of the original sources.

Unlike most college graduates of his day, he did not enter professional life, although he taught school intermittently for a few years in Concord with his beloved brother John. However, no occupation held him long. He made pencils for a while in his father's factory, but suddenly he announced that having learned to make a perfect pencil, he was through with pencil-making. He saw no virtue in going on endlessly repeating a process whose possibilities he had already exhausted. There were other things he was ambitious to learn. So he worked at odd jobs for the most part—anything that offered not merely money but also experience. He could wield a hammer and saw expertly, mend fences or umbrellas, sharpen knives or make hay. Ten years after graduation he answered an inquiry from the secretary of his class in these terms:

I don't know whether mine is a profession, or a trade, or what not. . . . I am a Schoolmaster, a private Tutor, a Surveyor, a Gardener, a Farmer, a Painter (I mean a House Painter), a Carpenter, a Mason, a Day-laborer, a Pencil-maker, a Glass-paper-maker, a Writer, and sometimes a Poetaster.

Surveying his neighbors' lands was his most constant occupation, and he always had more requests for his services than he cared to fulfill. When he worked for pay, he delivered full services, rendered an exact account, and insisted on prompt payment; but he was careful not to engage himself for more labor than was needed to satisfy his financial demands for the moment. He was no disciple of Benjamin Franklin, bent on laying by a comfortable store of money: "Men say a stitch in time saves nine." So, observed Thoreau, "They take a thousand stitches today to save nine tomorrow." The time that he was called upon to devote to the management of his family's pencil-manufacturing business he gave conscientiously but nonetheless grudgingly.

About the time of his graduation Thoreau became intimately acquainted with Emerson, and recognized in him at once a man worth listening to. Emerson, on his side, reciprocated with a warmth of friendship that few people evoked in him. Thoreau became a confirmed transcendentalist, contributed poems, essays, and translations to the Dial and assisted Emerson in editing the periodical, and he lived in the Emerson house from 1841 to 1843, when he left for Staten Island, New York, to become the tutor in the family of William Emerson. It was during this period of discipleship that he developed certain Emersonian traits, even to imitating Emerson's manner of writing as well as speaking. The relationship has been overemphasized by critics like Lowell, who spoke of Thoreau as "the most remarkable . . . among the pistillate plants kindled to fruitage by the Emersonian pollen," while describing him in A Fable for Critics as an imitator straining to—

Tread in Emerson's tracks with legs painfully short.
How he jumps, how he strains, and gets red in the face,
To keep step with the mystagogue's natural pace!

As Thoreau's own personality and genius developed, he soon went beyond his mentor in such important particulars as his practice of individualism and his glorification of nature; and during the fifties there developed a coolness between them. It was not an open hostility; it was rather an unspoken mutual criticism, each of the other. Thoreau thought his friend too stiff and conventional, too ready to come to terms with the world, too much given to winning fame, gaining success, and wielding influence. He complained that he lacked friends who could wear a patch over the knee or trundle a wheelbarrow through the streets because they feared they would be out of character. He believed that men should develop a comprehensive character and rise above conventionalities; and with an eye on his respectable neighbor, he said, "It would be easier for them to hobble to town with a broken leg than a broken pantaloon." Emerson, for his part, complained that his young friend lacked ambition—that instead of putting his gifts to good use by "engineering for all America," he was content to be "the captain of a huckleberry-party." Moreover, there was, said Emerson, "somewhat military in his nature" that "wanted a fallacy to expose, a blunder to pillory"—that "required a little sense of victory, a roll of the drum." He delighted in opposition. He was a born protestant. "It cost him nothing to say No," said Emerson; "indeed he found it much easier than to say Yes. It seemed as if his first instinct on hearing a proposition was to controvert it, so impatient was he of the limitations of our daily thought. This habit, of course, is a little chilling to the social affections; and though the companion would in the end acquit him of any malice or untruth, yet it mars conversation." Emerson agreed with their mutual friend, Elizabeth Hoar, who said, "I love Henry, but I cannot like him; and as for taking his arm, I should as soon think of taking the arm of an elm tree." It was the same thing that Hawthorne had noticed. In 1848 he described Thoreau to Longfellow as a man "well worth knowing," a man "of thought and originality," but with "a certain iron-pokerishness, an uncompromising stiffness in his mental character," which, he added, might be "interesting" on occasions but "grows rather wearisome on close and frequent acquaintance." So Emerson observed:

If I knew only Thoreau, I should think coöperation of good men impossible. Must we always talk for victory and never once for truth, for comfort, and joy? . . . Always some weary captious paradox to fight for you, and the time and temper wasted.

Sensing a loss of the perfect accord that had once existed between himself and Emerson, Thoreau wrote in his journal for May 24, 1853, very much in the same vein:

Talked, or tried to talk, with R. W. E. Lost my time—nay, almost my identity. He, assuming a false opposition where there was no difference of opinion, talked to the wind—told me what I knew—and I lost my time trying to imagine myself somebody else to oppose him.

There was never an open break between them. They were, and remained, together on essentials; but each went his own way in particulars. This relationship between Emerson and Thoreau is typical of the general relationship among New England Transcendentalists, one to the other. They were all individualists—some more than others—but all individuals. The movement included too many people, each pursuing the bent of his own genius. A cooperative movement, like the Brook Farm Association, was destined to fail sooner or later. Emerson, for example, found all his risibilities quickening even at the word *association*; Thoreau felt that he would rather "keep a bachelor's hall in hell than go to board in heaven"; and Alcott's community at Fruitlands, as Emerson observed, "had only room for one."

With all his "iron-pokerishness," Thoreau was a man of tender feelings and fine sensitivity, nor was he devoid of the family affections, as has been charged. It is true that he never married, but not because he never loved a woman. There were several women in his life for whom he had a romantic attachment, notably Ellen Sewall of Scituate. But when he discovered that his favorite brother John was also in love with her, he quietly withdrew in his favor.

It was with this brother that he made a boat trip up the Concord and Merrimack Rivers and back to Concord in 1839—an excursion of ten days, which furnished many of the materials for his first book, *A Week on the Concord and Merrimack Rivers*, published ten years after the trip. It was the writing of this book which specifically prompted his decision in 1845 to build himself a cabin on some land owned by Emerson on the shore of Walden Pond. He needed a place where he could cogitate and write without interruption, and cabin life seemed ideally suited to the purpose. Besides this immediate object, he had, of course, the larger desire to put his theories of plain, simple living to the test—to see whether Carlyle had been right in saying that it was as easy to reach unity by deliberately reducing the denominator life's fraction as by constantly striving to increase the numerator. Thoreau took great pains to say what has been too often overlooked by his critics, namely, that the experiment was a personal one, and that he cared not in the least whether anyone followed his example. Indeed, he said pointedly that he did not recommend it to any but such as had a genius for it. He did not set out to prove that a hermit's life is better than social life. Bent solely on self-development, he was less interested even than was Emerson in reforming his fellow men. He did not allow the burdens of the world to rest very heavily on his shoulders; he had enough burdens of his own to remove. So he was not ambitious to remake the world. "I never assisted the sun materially in his rising," he said; "It was of the last importance only to be present at it." It was his purpose, for himself alone, "to improve the nick of time, and notch it on my stick too; to stand on the meeting of the eternities, the past and the future, which is precisely the present moment; to toe the line." If the experiment sufficed for him, that was all he required of it.

Indeed, he had no genius for philanthropy. "As for doing good, that is one of the professions which are full. Moreover, I have tried it fairly, and, strange as it may seem, am satisfied that it does not agree with my constitution. . . . What good I do, in the common sense of that word, must be aside from my main path, and for the most part wholly unintended." Philanthropy, he said, was bred of the stomach-ache, and he would have none of it. He wanted to leave others severely alone to pursue their proper way to heaven, as he wanted them to leave him alone. "If I knew for a certainty," he said in Walden, "that a man was coming to my house with the conscious desire to do me good, I should run for my life."

Like Emerson, he had a genius for trusting himself and going his own way, heedless of tradition or authority. In Walden he wrote, "I have lived some thirty years on this planet, and I have yet to hear the first syllable of valuable or even earnest advice from my seniors. They have told me nothing, and probably cannot tell me any thing, to the purpose. . . . The greater part of what my neighbors call good I believe in my soul to be bad, and if I repent of any thing, it is very likely to be my good behavior." Living thus, after his own plan and purpose, preferring truth to love, or money, or fame, and bearing constantly in mind that "goodness is the only investment that never fails," he could write during his last illness, "I *suppose* that I have not many months to live; but, of course, I know nothing about it. I may add that I am enjoying existence as much as ever, and regret nothing." When he was asked whether he had made his peace with God, he replied that he was not aware that he had ever quarreled with God; when Parker Pillsbury approached him on his deathbed about preparing himself for Heaven, Thoreau said, "If you don't mind, Mr. Pillsbury, one world at a time"; while Sam Staples, the constable who had once jailed him, and who was later to become his rod man, reported that he "never saw a man dying with so much pleasure and peace."

Thoreau's career as a lecturer, begun in 1838, gave him some local prominence, especially as the struggle over slavery advanced, and Thoreau's unflinching stand drew the spotlight. The most notable of his pronouncements inspired by the conflict over human liberty is his essay on "Civil Disobedience," originally published in 1849 as "Resistance to Civil Government" in Elizabeth Palmer Peabody's short-lived *Aesthetic Papers*. His lecture on "John Brown" is hardly less famous—a masterpiece of indignation and invective.

After *A Week*, he published only one other book during his lifetime—*Walden*, in 1854. Following his death in 1862, at the age of forty-five, there appeared a volume of essays collected from the magazines and called *Excursions* (1863), and Emerson prepared for the press *The Maine Woods* and *Cape Cod*, both in 1864, and *A Yankee in Canada* in 1866. The last three, like Thoreau's first published book, are the products mainly of trips which he had made to the regions named in the titles, although, like *A Week*, they contain not only descriptions and observations, but also Thoreau's thoughts on philosophy, religion, science, economics, and, in addition, they are "a mine of quotations from good authors." None of his volumes are, strictly speaking, books in the sense that they exhibit any close structure of organic organization or development. They are rather a brilliant miscellany of observation and experience, meditation and wisdom.

As a writer, Thoreau had his faults and his virtues. Aside from the originality of his thought, his books have what Emerson called the best merit of strengthening and fortifying the soul. Among his shortcomings are his lack of facility as a poet, a certain provincialism that expressed itself in his observation that he had "traveled a good deal in Concord," looseness of form in the larger structural units, and certain stylistic failings which he himself enumerated as a fondness for "paradox," for the "ingenious" expression, instead of the simple, direct one, "playing with words," "using current phrases and maxims," and "want of conciseness."

His books made no great stir during his lifetime. Of the 1,000 copies of *A Week* that were printed, 75 were given away and 219 were sold. When the publisher needed his storage space, he offered the remaining 706 copies to the author if he would haul them away. This Thoreau did promptly, and afterwards he boasted that he now possessed a library of more than a thousand volumes, over seven hundred of which he had written himself. He published only two volumes before he died; yet he stands today, despite his slender productivity, unqualifiedly as one of the five most challenging of the nineteenth-century American authors—with Hawthorne, Emerson, Melville, and Whitman. His collected writings number twenty volumes, but of these fourteen are journals, leaving only six so-called works; and fully half of the contents of these are of a "secondary" or "tangential" nature. Only *Walden* and the essays on "Civil Disobedience" and "Life without Principle" are widely known, but they are known well enough to make his place secure.

We are still undecided about which of his several qualities entitle him to the fame which is currently accorded him: whether it is the integrity of his mind, the challenge of his philosophy, the vigor of his idealistic attack upon materialism, the example of his life, or the expression of his ideas. Nor are we quite decided about how to interpret him. The first biographers and critics of Thoreau—Channing, Emerson, and Lowell—found him important as a poet-naturalist. Sanborn's *Life of Thoreau* in 1917 called attention to his stature as a transcendentalist. His critical attitude toward the growing industrialism of the United States and a machine age has given his writings a new urgency in the twentieth century. Questioning the premises of nineteenth-century material progress, he observed that "the most wonderful inventions of modern times" are an "insult" to nature.

Every machine, or particular application, seems a slight outrage against universal laws. How many fine inventions are there which do not clutter the ground? We think that those only succeed which minister to our sensible and animal wants, which bake and brew, wash and warm, or the like. But are those of no account which are patented by fancy and imagination, and succeed so admirably in our dreams that they give the tone to our waking thoughts?

Like Emerson, he charged that as man depends on his watch, he loses the skill to tell time by the sun; that he builds a coach, but loses the use of his feet. Accordingly he objected to the devastations wrought in nature by the railroads, observing that a few ride while many are run over; and he wanted to know, before constructing a telegraph line from Maine to Texas, whether Texas had anything to communicate to Maine. It is interesting to speculate on what he would have said about modern governmental controls and planned economies. Meanwhile, in another part of the world, his attack upon the tyranny of the state has been put to practice by Mahatma Gandhi, who read "Civil Disobedience" in 1907; and today millions of Orientals are motivated by Thoreau's doctine of passive resistance.

Thoreau has been variously received. His contemporary, Lowell, while raising a dozen objections, found in him "fine translunary things." Robert Louis Stevenson confessed that "this pure, narrow, sunnily-ascetic Thoreau . . . exercised a great charm" on him. Whittier considered *Walden* "capital reading, but very wicked and heathenish"; and Ludwig Lewisohn, admitting Thoreau's "singular excellence" as a prose-stylist, felt that he "left no complete book behind him," and called him at once "one of the bravest men that ever lived, but also a clammy prig." He is read today as he never was during his own lifetime; and it would seem that whatever the time or place, he will have his readers, who, whether they praise or blame him, will find his thoughts challenging.

JOHN GREENLEAF WHITTIER (1807-1892)

The name of John Greenleaf Whittier is usually associated with Longfellow, Lowell, and Holmes, Whittier's New England contemporaries, whom he deeply admired and numbered among his friends, especially the latter two. Certainly in their intellectual and moral heritage these men had much in common; but there was also a wide social and cultural gulf separating the folksy Quaker poet from the "Brahmins" of Boston and Harvard. Indeed, in his humble origin, his acquaintance with simple men through intimate and lifelong association, and his profound knowledge of the life and character of his region, he achieved in reality the ambitions which that much greater poet, Walt Whitman, could attain only in theory and vicarious dreams. (Like most common men of the period, too, Whittier was never able to understand or appreciate Whitman.)

Despite the fact that today Whitman's reputation is near the zenith and Whittier's hanging low on the horizon, the latter was not without poetic genius. But it was genius with a narrower range, more dependent upon ancestry, region, events of the times, and contemporary taste. His reputation has declined because most of the causes for which he fought have ceased to agitate the national consciousness, and the simple rural and village experiences to which he gave lyric utterance seem naïve and antiquated in the turbulent twentieth century. Nevertheless, Whittier is still a writer of importance for the modern student of American life and poetry. During the greatest crisis in the history of the Republic he hammered out poems as weapons for a moral crusade, and no other literary figures except possibly Lowell and Harriet Beecher Stowe exerted so wide an influence in the crusade against slavery. Of more permanent literary importance, however, are the simple lyrics about barefoot boys, country customs and superstitions (like "telling the bees"), and the cozy domestic pleasures of a snowbound farm home. Contemporary New Englanders took these songs to their hearts. And in modern times no one but Robert Frost has succeeded so well in capturing in poetic form the unsophisticated life of New England country folk.

Thomas Whittier came to America in 1638, with two uncles and a distant relative, Ruth Green, whom he later married. In 1647 they settled about five miles from the village of Haverhill, on East Meadow Brook. Of the ten children, five were boys, each over six feet in height. In 1688 the family moved to a new house about half a mile from the old, on the banks of a little stream called Country Brook. There for four generations the youngest son had stayed on at the old homestead, each marrying a farmer's daughter, until the bachelor poet inherited the ancient house and run-down farm.

These Essex County farmers early became Quakers and champions of religious freedom, another family inheritance which helped to shape the mind and character of the future poet. In 1652 two unlicensed exhorters, Joseph Peasley and Thomas Macy, were arrested for holding religious services in absence of the minister. They were probably suspected of being Quakers, a sect greatly abhorred by the orthodox Puritans, and they did later join the Society of Friends. A neighbor who protested the arrest was himself disfranchised and fined, an injustice which stirred other neighboors, including Thomas Whittier, to further protests. They, too, were disfranchised, Whittier until 1666. But this experience cemented the friendship of the Whittiers and the Peasleys, and in 1694 Thomas's son, Joseph, married Mary Peasley, daughter of the unlicensed exhorter—and later generations of Whittiers were loyal Quakers, down to the poet, who still used "thee" and "thou" to his friends.

From Thomas Whittier also came many of the stories and traditions about the Indians which the poet used in verse and prose. The frontier town of Haverhill remained on friendly terms with the Indians, who fished and hunted at their pleasure in the region until 1675, when friction arose between them and the settlers. Thomas Whittier, however, had received the Indians in his home on East Meadow Brook for many years, and he was never forced to seek protection for himself or his family in the houses which he had himself helped to fortify. During these Indian troubles he built his new house (1688) on Country Brook, and according to family tradition the savages in their war paint would pause while passing the house at night to look through the window at the firelight in the big open fireplace of the kitchen.

To this same frame house on Country Brook the forty-four-year-old father of the poet, John, brought his twenty-three-year-old bride, Abigail Hussey, in 1804. Here John Greenleaf Whittier was born in 1807, the second of four children. Perhaps the discrepancy in the ages of his parents explains in part why young John always turned to his mother rather than his father for sympathy in his literary ambitions. The family was poor, and only once in his youth did the future poet visit Boston, forty miles from Haverhill. On this occasion the country boy, though proud of his new homespun suit and "boughten buttons," was confused by the noise and crowds of the city and was glad to return to his quiet farm home.

In old age Whittier wrote to a correspondent regarding his youth:

. . . I found about equal satisfaction in an old rural home, with the shifting panorama of the seasons, in reading the few books within my reach, and dreaming of something wonderful and grand somewhere in the future. . . . I had at that time a great thirst for knowledge and little means to gratify it. The beauty of outward nature impressed me, and the moral and spiritual beauty of the holy lives I read of in the Bible and other good books also affected me with a sense of my falling short and longing for a better state.

In *Yankee Gypsies* Whittier tells how he first heard of Robert Burns, the poet who influenced him most in his early literary ambitions:

One day we had a call from a "pawky auld carle" of a wandering Scotchman. To him I owe my first introduction to the songs of Burns. After eating his bread and cheese and drinking his mug of cider, he gave us Bonny Doon, Highland Mary, and Auld Lang Syne. He had a rich full voice and entered heartily into the spirit of his lyrics.

At the age of fourteen Whittier's schoolmaster, Joshua Coffin, lent him a volume of Burns' poems, and he began at once to learn the Scottish dialect. The poet later remembered this volume as "about the first poetry I had ever read—with the exception of the Bible, of which I had been a close student,—and it had a lasting influence upon me." After reading Burns the farm boy began to make rhymes himself and to live "in a world of fancy."

Young Whittier also became acquainted with an American imitator of Burns, a homespun poet living in Windham, New Hampshire, named Robert Dinsmore. The debt to Dinsmore was repaid gracefully in a memorial essay, "Robert Dinsmore," in Whittier's *Prose Works:*

He tells us of his farm life, its joys and sorrows, its mirth and care, with no embellishment, with no concealment of repulsive and ungraceful features. Never having seen a nightingale, he makes no attempt to describe the fowl; but he has seen the night-hawk, at sunset, cutting the air above him, and he tells of it. Side by side with his waving corn-fields and orchard-blooms we have the barnyard and pigsty. Nothing which was necessary to the comfort and happiness of his home and avocation was to him "common or unclean."

Whittier recalls that "the last time I saw him, he was chaffering in the market-place of my native village, swapping potatoes and onions and pumpkins for tea, coffee, molasses, and, if the truth be told, New England rum." Though the prim Quaker poet never equaled Dinsmore in earthiness, his tolerant admiration of the rum-drinking New Hampshire farmer-poet reveals his warm humanity.

The young poet's sixty-year-old father was unimpressed by his son's rhyming, but other members of the family were proud of him, and in 1826 his sister sent one of his juvenile poems, "The Exile's Departure," to the editor of a near-by paper, the New-buryport *Free Press.* The editor happened to be William Lloyd Garrison, who a few years later became widely known as the leader of the most radical faction of the Abolitionists. He printed the poem on June 8 and declared editorially of the unknown author that this "poetry bears the stamp of true poetic genius, which if carefully cultivated, will rank him among the bards of the country." After learning the identity of the youthful bard, Garrison visited the Whittier home and finally persuaded the father to permit his son to attend the newly-founded Haverhill Academy. Whittier worked his way through a six-months term in 1827, taught school during the following winter, and in the spring of 1828 returned to the Academy for another term. Thus ended the poet's formal education—a few scattered months in a country school and about a year at the "academy."

In 1827-28 Whittier printed about a hundred poems and a number of prose articles in the Haverhill *Gazette.* At this time some of his poems appeared in the Boston *Statesman,* and many were reprinted in other newspapers. Thus he was beginning to be known while still a schoolboy. It is not surprising, however, that these productions were imitative and mediocre. He extravagantly admired Moore, Willis, Bryant, and especially the sentimental and didactic Mrs. Hemans. In his adolescent love affairs he also liked to play a Byronic rôle.

Despite the popularity of Whittier's poems among newspaper readers throughout the country, he could not yet earn even a meagre living with his poetry. Having first gained a hearing, and even a certain amount of fame, through newspapers, it was natural that he should turn to journalism for a livelihood. On January 1, 1829, he became editor of the *American Manufacturer* in Boston, at the salary of $9.00 a week. The policies of this undistinguished journal were anti-Jackson, pro-Clay, and of course for protective tariff and the mercantile interests. In his editorials Whittier tried to appeal to the "young mechanics of New England." In August, however, he was called home by the illness of his father, who died the following June. During this time he had to take charge of the farm. For six months he edited the Haverhill *Gazette*, and then became editor of the *New England Review* in Hartford, Connecticut, a magazine which had become well known as a pro-Clay organ. But in less than a year Whittier had to return home again to settle his father's affairs, and after unsuccessfully attempting to edit the magazine by correspondence, he became so seriously ill that he was forced to resign.

From Hartford in 1831 Whittier published his first book, *Legends of New-England*, containing seven prose sketches, dealing mainly with Indian and local subjects. These strike the modern reader as an anemic imitation of Hawthorne, typical of magazine stories and articles of the 1830–40's. Like most American writers before the Civil War, he was trying to prove that his native country was not deficient in the elements of poetry and romance—meanwhile unconsciously transplanting English and European romanticism.

This romanticism was also partly responsible for Whittier's rebellious, Byronic mood of the early 1830's, though disappointment in love (a judge's daughter had repulsed him in Hartford) and poor health were also responsible. "I cannot look upon the world with kindness," he wrote to a friend, "however much I desire to do so. It has neglected, it has wronged me, and its idle praise is little less repulsive to me than its loud and open rebukes." In this frame of mind, in contrast to his later serenity, Whittier was greedy for fame and in 1832 began to dream of making a name for himself in politics. This was no idle fancy, either, for his friends seriously considered him for Congress; but he was then not quite twenty-five, the legal age for holding the office, and before his next birthday arrived conditions were unfavorable for his candidacy.

Had Whittier not soon found a cause in which he could forget his personal ambitions, he might have become—as he seemed so near doing in 1832—an opportunistic politician; but, instead, in 1833 he became an active participant in the then unpopular Abolitionist movement. The New England Anti-Slavery Society had been founded by Garrison the previous year, and had started the *Liberator* as the official organ, but Whittier had not joined at once. There were at this time many reform movements in America, and the leaders were often—though not always —crude, semi-educated, impractical, and fanatical. Churches, colleges, and the refined elements of society found these leaders annoying and increasingly alarming. It took courage to join the ranks of the Abolitionists when Whittier did, and for a man with frail health he showed remarkable fortitude on several occasions when he and his antislavery friends were threatened by angry mobs. But while Garrison often endangered the success of the great cause of Abolition by his championship of women's rights and other reforms, Whittier remained the practical politician, working through local committees and organizations. In this manner he made his influence felt in the halls of Congress. Meanwhile he himself was twice elected to the Massachusetts Legislature, but he soon overtaxed his strength and was forced once more into retirement.

In 1836 Whittier sold the old farm and bought a modest house in Amesbury, a near-by village where his family had attended the Quaker church. To this quiet village he moved his mother and sister, and there, except for short intervals, he lived and worked during most of his remaining life. In 1837 he helped edit the *Emancipator* and the *Anti-Slavery Reporter* in New York. In 1838 he edited the *Pennsylvania Freeman* in Philadelphia, and was present though unharmed when a mob burned Pennsylvania Hall, a sumptuous building recently erected with funds raised by subscription.

In 1838 Whittier brought out an edition of his *Poems*, placing first antislavery poems, "The Yankee Girl," "The Slavery-Ships," and "The Hunters of Men." No other American abolitionist was as successful in wielding a poem like a pikestaff. But his moral and patriotic zeal were stronger than his aesthetic or critical judgment. In an editorial in the *Freeman* in 1838 he could write of the "Psalm of Life," which he had seen printed anonymously:

It is seldom that we find an article of poetry so full of excellent philosophy and common sense. . . . These nine simple verses are worth more than all the dreams of Shelley, and Keats, and Wordsworth. They are alive and vigorous with the spirit of the day in which we live—the moral steam enginery of an age of action.

During the 1840's Whittier found it difficult to support his mother, sister, and himself at Amesbury, but between frequent attacks of dyspepsia and migraine headaches he managed to give a few abolitionist lectures, write frequent letters to friends and politicians in the interest of the cause, and sell poems to various newspapers and magazines. The inflexible Garrison faction grew increasingly hostile toward Whittier because of his practical reasonableness, but he continued to write for other antislavery publications. In 1847 he became corresponding secretary of the *National Era*, an abolition magazine in Washington.

These experiences broadened the poet until in 1848 he could advise his friend Charles Sumner to abandon party lines in order to work for "the great party of Christian Democracy and Progress. . . . Why try to hold on to these old parties, even in name? . . . Let your emancipated friends now rise to the sublime altitude of men who labor for the race, for humanity." But party leaders could not share these liberal sentiments. After the "Free Soil" elements were purged from the Democratic Party, it became proslavery. About this time the Whigs lost out, and in 1856 the new Republican Party had a weak candidate. Consequently, Whittier became less hopeful of reforms through the regular parties. But in 1848 he was still known mainly for his propaganda writings, as Lowell indicated in "The Fable for Critics": /

> Our Quaker leads off metaphorical fights
> For reform and whatever they call rights,
> Both singing and striking in front of the war,
> And hitting his foes with the mallet of Thor; . . .

Abolition and reform are prominent in all the collections of verse which Whittier published between 1843 and 1855: *Lays of My Home* (1843), *Voices of Freedom* (1846), *Poems* (1849), *Songs of Labor* (1850), *The Chapel of the Hermits* (1853), and *The Panorama* (1856).

Whittier never actually lost faith in reform, and in 1859–60 he took great interest in Garibaldi's struggle for freedom in Italy; but in the 1850's he began to turn his attention more to reminiscence and personal experience, as in "To My Old Schoolmates" (1851) and "The Barefoot Boy" (1855). One of his

earliest major poetic themes had been New England legend and history—such as the juvenile *Mogg Megone* (1836) on the early border strife with the Indians and the more successful prose in *The Supernaturalism of New England* (1843). During this decade he returned to the local scene for some of his most interesting poems, such as "The Garrison of Cape Ann" and "Skipper Ireson's Ride" in 1857, and "The Prophecy of Samuel Sewall" and "The Double-Headed Snake of Newbury" in 1859.

After the founding of the *Atlantic Monthly* in 1857 Whittier's financial worries decreased, for he was invited to become a regular contributor, and he had already attained sufficient prestige to command a good price for his poems. One of the first which he contributed to *The Atlantic Monthly* was "Skipper Ireson's Ride," though without the dialect, which editor James Russell Lowell, who fancied himself an expert on dialect, persuaded the country-bred poet to add. Association and correspondence with the *Atlantic* coterie brought Whittier into more intimate contact with the leading New England writers of his generation. He and Dr. Holmes, for example, developed a mutual admiration for each other's writing. Whittier enthusiastically predicted in 1858 that "The Chambered Nautilus" was "booked for immortality."

As the fateful Civil War drew nearer, Whittier, who had fought relentlessly for two decades against slavery, became increasingly pacifistic. Perhaps his Quaker background was beginning to tell, at the very time when he was turning from outward events to his inner experiences and memories for poetic inspiration. On December 2, 1859, he wrote to a friend regarding John Brown's raid on Harpers Ferry: "What a sad tragedy to-day in Virginia! I feel deep sympathy for John Brown, but deplore from my heart his rash and insane attempt. It injures the cause he sought to serve." On another occasion he declared: "It is worse than folly to talk of fighting Slavery, when we have not yet agreed to vote against it. Our business is with poll-boxes, not cartridge-boxes; with ballots, not bullets." When war finally came, he was passively devout, as in the prayerful "Thy Will Be Done" and the Lutheran hymn "Ein feste Burg ist unser Gott." As George Rice Carpenter says, "The verses wrung from him in these bitter years were not the warrior's shout, but the wail of the stricken woman, the prayer of faith and resignation that breathed submission to the will of Heaven and trust in the outcome of the right."

In the 1860's the retiring old bachelor in the tiny village of Amesbury returned time and again in his poems to the moral of "Maud Muller," *i.e.*, the social barrier hindering marriage between the rich and poor. In "Amy Wentworth," "The Maids of Attitash," and "Among the Hills" we can see that the poet did not remain a bachelor by inclination, and his imagination dwells as lovingly on "what might have been" as if there had been a Beatrice in his life. How much family affection meant to him we can also see in the classic "Snow-Bound" (1866), published two years after the death of his dear sister, Elizabeth.

In his old age Whittier's income more than supplied his simple needs. "Snow-Bound" alone brought him $10,000 in royalties. He was so well known and so popular that famous men visited him on his birthday, and the day was observed by school children. Public and academic honors were also heaped upon him. In 1858 he was elected by the Legislature to membership on the Board of Overseers of Harvard College. In 1860 Harvard conferred an honorary Master of Arts degree upon him, and six years later he was made an honorary Doctor of Laws. In 1869 he became a member of the Board of Trustees of Brown University.

After his sister's death in 1864, the poet's niece, Elizabeth Whittier, kept house for him in Amesbury until in 1876 she married Samuel T. Pickard, who later wrote the authorized biography of Whittier. From this time until his death in 1892, he divided his time between the Pickards and some cousins at Danvers. For a generation after this event, his reputation remained high, though it slowly declined as the fame of Lowell and Holmes also ebbed away. But he did not really belong to their genteel world, and perhaps his popularity with the readers of the early *Atlantic Monthly* was an indication of his retreat from the life of the common people which he knew better than the affable Dr. Holmes or the distinguished editor of the *Atlantic*. When he relaxed the fight for human rights, he sought refuge, like Mark Twain, in boyhood memories and fond dreams of the past. Today most of his fighting songs for the lowly and drown-trodden have lost their original significance, and only the personal lyrics of the fifties and sixties have retained their somewhat diminished charm. Yet enough is left for the sympathetic student to see that John Greenleaf Whittier had native poetic genius and deserved in his own day to stand with the great.

OLIVER WENDELL HOLMES (1809–1894)

In the ripe years of his life Oliver Wendell Holmes thought the Saturday Club, which met at the Parker House for a six-hour dinner when Emerson came to Boston from near-by Concord, represented "all that was best in American literature," adding, not unmindful of the fact that he, himself, occupied an honored seat with the best-known contemporary writers and editors of New England: "Most of the Americans whom educated foreigners cared to see . . . were seated at that board." Between the publication of the *Autocrat* essays in the first numbers of the newly founded *Atlantic Monthly* in 1857 and the death of the genial Dr. Holmes in 1894, few Americans would have challenged his right to sit with the most famous literary men of his generation, but the twentieth-century critics of the "genteel tradition" succeeded for a while in whittling his reputation down to that of a pleasant wit and second-rate poet of Harvard class reunions and dining room celebrations for the contributors to the *Atlantic Monthly*.

Of course everyone knew that Dr. Holmes held an M.D. degree and lectured on anatomy at Harvard, but these facts were regarded either as the quaint eccentricity of this poet-essayist or as further evidence of his astonishing versatility. Even Holmes' early biographers seemed to share this attitude. During the past two decades, however, various scholars, critics, and biographers have discovered that Dr. Holmes was a distinguished pioneer in medical science. An eminent professor of psychiatry has found in the "medicated" novels anticipations of Freud and psychoanalysis. The latest biographer, Eleanor M. Tilton, denies the Freudianism, but insists on balancing the scientist against the man of letters. As a result of these reinterpretations of Holmes, he is now correctly recognized as an amateur in letters; but as a wit, humanist, medical reformer, and literary personality he occupies a truly unique position in the cultural history of America.

Oliver Wendell Holmes was born in Cambridge, Massachusetts, August 29, 1809, on the day preceding the annual Harvard commencement, then a community celebration resembling the opening day of a State Fair. In years to come Holmes would enliven commencements by many a poem, song, or speech in the long life which he made a perpetual circus. There was nothing suggesting a circus, however, in his eminently respectable ancestry, which included many of the old and well-known families of New England. His father, the Reverend Abiel Holmes, pastor of the First Congregational Church of Cambridge and amateur historian, was born at Woodstock, Connecticut, where the Holmes family had settled in 1686. He had graduated from Yale, and his first wife, Mary Stiles, was the daughter of Ezra Stiles, president of Yale, where Calvinistic orthodoxy still flourished. Mary Stiles Holmes died childless in 1795, and Abiel Holmes married Sarah Wendell, the only daughter of a well-to-do Boston merchant.

The fourth of the Reverend Holmes' five children (one died young) was named Oliver Wendell. While "Wendell" was still a schoolboy his two older sisters married, Mary Jackson to Dr. Usher Parsons, who had been a Navy surgeon with Commodore Perry in the Battle of Lake Erie, and Ann Susan to Charles Wentworth Upham, a Unitarian minister at Salem. The younger brother, John, was lame, and never married but remained at home to care for his parents.

Sarah Wendell Holmes, having grown up in liberal, Unitarian Boston, was by nature cheerful and sympathetic with her children, though she loyally attempted to teach them the religious doctrines of her Calvinist husband. Abiel Holmes was kindly and perhaps less austere than some of his deacons, who involved him in a bitter quarrel which split his congregation into two factions, the more conservative of which seceded and built a new church in which it installed the Reverend Holmes. These quarrels and the severe theology of his father made Oliver Wendell Holmes a lifelong foe of religious orthodoxy. "To grow up in a narrow creed and to grow out of it," he declared in maturity, "is a tremendous trial of one's nature." *Pilgrim's Progress* seemed to him "like the hunting of sinners with a pack of demons for the amusement of the Lord of the terrestrial manor."

At school young Holmes was "moderately studious," especially fond of reading stories. His father's library of two thousand volumes contained mainly sermons, history, and biography, though the English classics were also represented. The boy acquired the fondness for books which he later extolled in his *Autocrat* essays, but he never became the wide reader that his fellow townsman, Lowell, did. Perhaps he was too much inclined to depend upon his quick brain, thinking, in his own words, that he had "drawn a prize, say a five-dollar one, in the grand intellectual life-lottery." However, he disliked another quick-witted school-mate, Margaret Fuller, and remembered with distaste, years later, that he had learned the word "trite" from her comment on a theme which he had written. Holmes prepared for Harvard, with special attention to Latin and Greek. He had more fun with a magnifying glass which his father bought for him, played the flute, bought cigars and smoked them a little at a time, keeping the stub in an old pistol barrel, into which his mother and sisters would never think of looking. It has been suggested that the cigars may have influenced his father to send him, at the age of fifteen, to Andover, a preparatory school very strict in Calvinistic orthodoxy, before entering him at Harvard. After a miserable year at Andover, Holmes left this "doctrinal boiler" for Harvard, the "rational ice-chest."

No great intellectual awakening took place during Holmes' years as an undergraduate at Harvard. He was convivial, but studied enough to graduate about midway in rank in the class of '29, a class which would become famous, partly through the achievements of Holmes. For a year he studied law halfheartedly, then found his true profession in medicine. To a friend he wrote: "I know I might have made an indifferent lawyer,—I think I may make a tolerable physician,—I do not like the one, and do like the other." Perhaps he might have done better at law if he had not found more enjoyment in writing poems for an undergraduate magazine, the *Collegian*. "In that fatal year," he declared, "I had my first attack of author's lead poisoning," and never recovered. He experienced something like real fame when he published, September 16, 1830, "Old Ironsides" after hearing that the Navy was planning to scrap the frigate *Constitution*, built in 1797. The poem was widely reprinted and helped to save the ship.

In 1832, while still a medical student, Holmes began the series of essays which would lead him to real fame a quarter of a century later. This was, of course, *The Autocrat of the Breakfast-Table*, two numbers of which were published in the short-lived *New England Magazine*. Twenty-five years later Holmes revived this project in the *Atlantic Monthly* with this opening sentence: "I was going to say when I was interrupted." What had interrupted him in 1832 was his absorption in medical studies. At that time, and until many years later, the medical course at Harvard consisted only of two four-month terms. If Holmes had wished merely to secure a degree and a license to practice, he might have done so without great effort or expense. But his ambitions were higher than that. He wished to learn everything possible about medical science. Consequently, he enrolled both in the Harvard Medical School and in a private school taught by Dr. James Jackson and other leading physicians of Boston. Having learned all that America had to offer, Holmes persuaded his parents, who were far from wealthy, to send him to Europe for further study in Paris.

When Holmes sailed from America on March 30, 1833, he had two purposes in mind, one scientific and the other humanistic. At that time Paris led the world in medical progress, and it was typical of Holmes that he wanted contact with the best minds in the field. And like most intellectual Americans of his generation, he also wanted to see Europe. He loved Paris at first sight, and quickly acquired sufficient facility in the French language to feel at home with the French people. He alarmed his parents by his enthusiasm for the theatre, and also by his refusal to economize, declaring that "economy, in one sense, is too expensive for a student." His plans for self-development included "a certain degree of ease," such as "a tolerably good dinner, a nice book when I want it, and that kind of comforts." He also needed money for travel and with difficulty persuaded his father to finance a second year in Europe. While abroad he visited England, Scotland, Italy, Holland, Switzerland, and Germany, enjoying in each the scenery and historical sights. In England he attended the Epsom races and declared, "Every New England deacon ought to see one Derby day to learn what sort of world this is he lives in. Man is a sporting as well as a praying animal." At the opera he saw Princess Victoria, then fifteen, and the royal family. With American irreverence he commented on William IV: "The King blew his nose twice, and wiped the royal perspiration repeatedly from a face which is probably the largest uncivilized spot in England."

But Holmes did not waste much time in sightseeing and having fun. He attended the best lecture courses at the École de Médecine and spent many hours in the wards and hospitals. From the best teachers, especially Pierre Louis, he acquired ideas far in advance of contemporary American medical knowledge. He wrote his parents that he had learned three principles in Paris: "Not to take authority when I can have the facts; not to guess when I can know; not think a man must take physic because he is sick." Holmes returned to America in December, 1835, bringing with him a hatred for homeopathy and similar delusions, Louis' technique for keeping written case records (then unknown in the United States), and the conviction—while Pasteur was still a schoolboy—that the bounds of medical knowledge would soon be extended by microscopic research.

Back in Cambridge, Holmes was granted the M.D. degree by Harvard and licensed to practice medicine in Massachusetts. But his poetic talent was recognized more quickly than his scientific ability. In 1836, one year before Emerson's great "American Scholar" address on a similar occasion, Holmes gave the Phi Beta Kappa poem at the Harvard commencement. He called the composition "Poetry: A Metrical Essay," and in it he presented, as he later remarked, "the simple and partial views of a young person trained after the schools of classical English verse as represented by Pope, Goldsmith, and Campbell, with whose lives his memory was early stocked." In most of the poems which he wrote throughout his life this neoclassical influence and taste was apparent, though he did later study and lecture on the romantic poets of England. With the brashness of youth and his infectious self-confidence, the neophyte physician recited from memory this "metrical essay" and some other verses for an hour and ten minutes, with frequent interruptions for applause. He loved applause and could seldom resist the opportunity to provoke it by public exhibitions of his wit and poetic facility. His effervescent energy and resonant voice more than compensated for his slight physique and five feet three inches of stature, and perhaps his boyish appearance contributed to his personal charm on the rostrum.

It is characteristic of Holmes, too, that his first honors in medicine were won by his pen. He wrote two dissertations in 1836, one for his M.D. degree, on acute pericarditis, and one for the Massachusetts Medical Society, on intermittent fevers in New England. The latter won a Boylston Prize at Harvard. The following year Dr. Holmes won two Boylston prizes with a dissertation on neuralgia and one on direct exploration in medical practice. The three prize-winning essays were collected into a book in 1837, Holmes' first published volume of prose. The book seems to have made a favorable impression on the medical profession in New England.

Dr. Holmes made some attempt to establish a general practice, but with slight success. Probably he was not temperamentally adapted to the life of a practitioner. His official biographer, J. T. Morse, thought his levity was a handicap:

When he said that the smallest fevers were thankfully received, the people who had no fevers laughed, but the people who had them preferred some one who would take the matter more seriously than they thought this lively young joker was likely to do.

Another witness, the minister, Dr. W. E. Channing, reported that once when he took Dr. Holmes with him to visit an invalid lady, she rose up in bed and demanded, "Dr. Channing, why do you bring that little boy in here? Take him away! This is no place for boys!" Still another witness, Dr. David W. Cheever, demonstrator for Holmes' lectures on anatomy, thought that he was "too sympathetic to practice medicine," adding:

. . . he soon abandoned the art for the science, and always maintained the same abhorrence for death and tenderness for animals. When it became necessary to have a freshly killed rabbit for his lectures, he always ran out of the room, left me to chloroform it, and besought me not to let it squeak.

It was natural, therefore, that Dr. Holmes should turn to teaching. With three other young physicians he founded Tremont Street Medical School, which was affiliated with Harvard in the awarding of degrees. He taught several courses, but most significant was the use of the microscope, something new in American medical schools of the time. For a few months in 1839–40 he served as Professor of Anatomy at Dartmouth College, returning to Cambridge and Boston between the short terms.

Some of the older physicians were no doubt irritated by Holmes' attacks upon the superstition and quackery of the profession. In 1842 he read a paper to a medical group on "Homeopathy and its Kindred Delusions," and declared, "I firmly believe that if the whole *materia medica, as now used,* could be sunk to the bottom of the sea, it would be all the better for mankind—and all the worse for the fishes." The following year he wrote a paper on "The Contagiousness of Puerperal Fever" which is still read by students of nursing and medicine. He was not the first to advance the theory that "child-bed" fever was being spread by the physicians themselves, who carried the infection on their persons and instruments, but he was the first in America to assemble the evidence and to campaign for asepsis before bacteria had been discovered. He republished his essay in 1855 under the title, *Puerperal Fever as a Private Pestilence*, for which he wrote an introduction in which he declared sarcastically for the benefit of his critics, "I had rather rescue one mother from being poisoned by her attendant, than claim to have saved forty out of fifty patients to whom I had carried the disease."

Meanwhile Dr. Holmes felt sufficiently prosperous to choose a wife, an event which he had been considering for some time, with a combination of humor and shrewdness. On June 15, 1840, he married Amelia Lee Jackson, daughter of Charles Jackson, Associate Justice of the Supreme Court of Massachusetts, and niece of Dr. James Jackson, Holmes' best-loved American teacher. In the days when the place of a wife was thought to be in the home, Amelia Jackson made a perfect partner for her husband. They had three children, the eldest being Oliver Wendell Holmes, Jr., who became Associate Justice of the Supreme Court of the United States. There was one daughter, Amelia, and a second son, Edward Jackson, who graduated from the Harvard Law School and served as private secretary to Charles Sumner, but died at the age of thirty-eight. Like his father, he suffered from painful attacks of asthma. A biographer of the Associate Justice has probably exaggerated the antagonism between the father and his eldest son, though there were undoubtedly conflicts between the small, extroverted "Autocrat" and his tall, reserved, philosophical namesake.

In 1847, Dr. Holmes was appointed professor of anatomy and physiology at Harvard and from '47 to '53 he served as Dean of the Medical School. After 1871 he taught anatomy only until his retirement in 1882. As a lecturer he was unquestionably the students' favorite of the entire faculty. He lectured at the most unfavorable hours of the day, in a dreary, poorly-ventilated amphitheatre, but his showmanship, his wit, and his love of his subject never failed to hold attention. To quote Dr. Cheever again, "he was never tired, always fresh, always eager in learning and teaching it. In earnest himself, enthusiastic, and of a happy temperament, he shed the glow of his ardent spirit over his fellows. . . ." Some of his more serious students, however, thought his performances were superficial, and he admitted himself that "I do not give the best lectures that I can give. I should shoot over their heads. I try to teach them a little and to teach it well." Though not himself a great original discoverer, he was, nevertheless, a thorough

scholar of medical knowledge, past and present, and was always one of the first to detect and expose sham and dishonesty in the medical profession.

But in literature he was an amateur, and never pretended to be anything else. He wrote many poems, usually on the spur of the moment for some public occasion, such as the inauguration of a Harvard president, the laying of a cornerstone, or the anniversary of an agricultural fair. Some of these "occasional" poems, especially the Rabelaisian specimens recited at medical dinners, were never gathered into his collected *Poems*. But they can hardly be a great loss. Even in his collected verse he succeeded only a few times in blending the right combination of humor and sentiment to achieve a universal appeal, as in "The Last Leaf," "My Aunt," or the more satirical "Deacon's Masterpiece." Many of his poems are still enjoyable, but they are likely to mislead the modern reader into thinking that Holmes was more genteel and sentimental than he actually was. This is the danger of ignoring Holmes the scientist, as most critics did until recent years.

Of course in reality Holmes was both a genteel "Brahmin" (his own designation for the Cambridge-Boston intellectual group to which he belonged) and a scientist. This double nature is apparent in his career as lyceum lecturer. The lecture platform became a thriving business in the 1840's and '50's, and Holmes's fondness for hearing his own voice any time, anywhere, combined with a remarkable store of information and a gift for witty aphorism, made him almost inevitably one of the most successful performers. His subjects ranged from "History of Medicine" and "Homeopathy and Its Kindred Delusions" to "Love of Nature" and the romantic poets of England. In the forties audiences wanted to be educated, but in the next decade they became more blasé and preferred entertainment. Dr. Holmes was equal to any shift in popular taste. As Miss Tilton says, "being a form of talk, a kind of extended conversation, the lecture allowed Holmes freedom for his pinwheel mind." Consequently, the subject was not particularly important to him. He declared that "as the head is all the better for an occasional shampooing, so the mind needs to be rubbed down with the generalities of humor." Like all really entertaining talk, his lectures were provocative rather than thorough, but sometimes he could toss off an observation that a serious critic might elaborate into a useful chapter or a book, as when he remarked:

Wordsworth's power never passed beyond his own personality, and he merely described men and things as he found them. He cannot be illustrated, because he only adds quality to pre-existent objects, and creates nothing.

Though Holmes, with his faith in reason and science, always preferred the neoclassic to the romantic writers, he gradually warmed up to the Lake School, and Keats he thought the "most truly poetic poet of the century." But he was blind to extremists of all kinds. In Thoreau he could see only a "nullifier of civilization, who insisted on nibbling his asparagus at the wrong end." Abolitionists irritated him. In an early poem, "The Hot Season," he wrote:

> The abolition men and maids
> Were tanned to such a hue,
> You scarce could tell them from their friends,
> Unless their eyes were blue.

The pacifist he dismissed contemptuously in "The Moral Bully" as:

> A timid creature, lax of knee and hip,
> Whom small disturbance whitens round the lip . . .

In 1846 James Russell Lowell protested in a letter against Holmes's conservatism and the Doctor good-naturedly replied that "in a little club of ten physicians, I rather think I occupy the extreme left of the liberal side of the house." In the medical profession Dr. Holmes was undoubtedly "radical," but in all other fields he was likely to be somewhere right of center. In 1850 he congratulated Webster on his "compromise" speech of March 7. In 1855, the year he aroused the indignation of conservative physicians by reprinting his essay on puerperal fever, he became the object of bitter vituperation from Horace Greeley and most of the Northern reformers when he criticized the abolitionists and prohibitionists in a speech in New York. When the Union was threatened, however, Holmes became thoroughly aroused, and throughout the war he supported the North with fiery poems and oratory, especially after his older son hastily left Harvard to accept a commission in the Union Army. And in 1862 after seeing the battlefield at Ball's Bluff, on his famous trip to find his wounded son, Holmes was convinced "that the disease of the nation was organic, not functional, calling for the knife, and not for washes and anodynes."

Before the outbreak of the Civil War Holmes began the one work on which his literary reputation still chiefly rests, the series of essays which he called *The Autocrat of the Breakfast-Table* (1857–58), followed by similar works called, respectively, *The Professor at the Breakfast-Table* (1859–61) and *The Poet at the Breakfast-Table* (1870–72). When the

Atlantic Monthly was founded in 1857, Holmes was one of the first writers whom the new editor, James Russell Lowell, invited to contribute. Holmes made a wise choice in returning to the literary device which he had experimented with twenty-five years earlier in the *New England Magazine*, the monologue of the garrulous talker at the boardinghouse breakfast table. This loose device enabled him to exploit his natural gifts and ride the hobbies and prejudices about which he had talked and argued spiritedly for many years in classroom, lyceum hall, and private groups—such pet topics as pseudo-science, moral bullying, vulgarity, and the uselessness of syllogistic reasoning. The monologue was often almost embarrassingly personal, fully justifying the subtitle used when the essays were published in book form—"Every man his own Boswell." The book sold 10,000 copies within three days, remarkable for the time, and not bad for any age. Dr. Holmes was the most popular American author of the year, and England was almost equally enthusiastic.

In *The Professor at the Breakfast-Table*, which began to appear in the *Atlantic* in January, 1859, Holmes exploited himself less and paid more attention to his fellow boarders. Miss Tilton believes these facts indicate that "Holmes wanted to write a novel, didn't dare try it right away, but thought he'd practice a little." He created a character, Little Boston, whom he used as a vehicle of satire, and also as a means of introducing a heroine, so that the essays began to take on some of the characteristics of a story. Through these essays Professor Holmes also experimented with some of the ideas which he would later develop in his novels, especially the harm done by religious fanaticism. Meanwhile he was meeting serious opposition to a lyceum lecture on "The Chief End of Man," in which he outraged the orthodox by suggesting that the main purpose of human life was to develop the whole man, not merely the spiritual. As an observant and intelligent physician he could see the damage that had been done to health and personality by the moral repression of Calvinism. Thus, despite his social conservatism and literary gentility, he anticipated the revolt of a later age—without the slightest understanding that Walt Whitman, for whom he had no great respect, was already attempting a similar revolt.

Dr. Holmes wrote his three novels, not because he was trying to create works of art, but to inculcate certain observations about life which he had been mulling over in lecture and essay for some years. His novels were extremely awkward in technique and silly in ideas. Nothing could be sillier than the plot of *Elsie Venner* (1861), though the ideas which he was trying to convey were far from ridiculous or trivial. The novel tells the tragic story of a young girl who acts and thinks like a snake because her mother was bitten by a snake before the daughter's birth. Certainly Dr. Holmes, the foe of pseudo-science, did not believe in prenatal influence (as he indicated in a preface), but he used this superstition merely as a symbol of those forces independent of volition which he later described in "Mechanism in Thought and Morals":

The more we examine the mechanism of thought, the more we shall see that the automatic, unconscious action of the mind enters largely into all its processes.

. . . . .

Our dwellings are built on the shell-heaps, the kitchen-middens of the age of stone. Inherited beliefs, as obscure in their origin as the parentage of the cave-dwellers, are stronger with many minds than the evidence of the senses and the simplest deductions of the intelligence.

Thus in *The Guardian Angel* (1867), the personality of Myrtle Hazard is the psychic battleground of drives and phobias inherited from her ancestors. And the spiritual concern of the pious minister for her soul is less spiritual than perhaps even he himself realizes. At last she finds the love of the right man. She is "saved" in a deeper sense than most readers of the day were prepared to understand. Similarly, in *A Mortal Antipathy*, Maurice Kirkwood is cured of his neurotic fear of women resulting from a traumatic shock which he received in childhood when a pretty female cousin dropped him. Whether or not Dr. Holmes actually anticipated Dr. Freud, he was obviously exploring realms of human experience untouched in his day not only by the moralist but even by the psychologist for half a century. And it is an ironical paradox that the man who fought all his life against the "determinism" of his Calvinistic father should have ended by embracing a scientific determinism no less rigid. But therapeutically there was a vast difference, for Holmes believed that crime and abnormality should be cured by scientific treatment, not avenged by a vindictive society.

Nineteenth-century American readers, however, who bought "Household" and "Cabinet" editions of his poetical works had little or no understanding of Holmes the explorer of new frontiers of mind and experience. It was the genial humorist that England, too, hailed on his second trip, in 1886, when he was greeted by royalty, the prime minister, and British authors, and was granted honorary degrees by the universities of Oxford, Cambridge, and Edinburgh. Back in America, other honors were heaped on him, until, sitting quietly in his library, October 7, 1894, "He simply ceased to breathe." In his copy of Montaigne, Holmes had underscored a sentence which might serve as his literary epitaph:

I make no doubt but that it shall often befall me to speak of things which are better, and with more truth, handled by such as are their crafts-masters.

JAMES RUSSELL LOWELL (1819–1891)

In his maturity James Russell Lowell was fully aware of the good fortune which he inherited in being born into the community of Cambridge, Massachusetts, at "Elmwood," in the first quarter of the nineteenth century. And to some extent he was also aware of the handicaps which the birthright entailed.

Elmwood was a spacious old house, three-story, Georgian-style, built in 1767 by the Lieutenant-Governor of the province, Thomas Oliver, whom the citizens of Cambridge forced to abdicate in 1774. After serving as a hospital for wounded soldiers during the Revolution and later as Governor's Mansion, the house was bought by the Reverend Charles Lowell a year before the birth of his sixth child, James Russell. There, on "Tory Row," the boy spent a delightful childhood. Many years later on Lowell's return to America after his career as Minister to Great Britain, a friend suggested that he settle in Washington, D. C., but he replied warmly that he had "but one home in America, and that is the house where I was born, and where, if it shall please God, I hope to die." On another occasion, however, he commented that the house "was born a Tory and will die so. . . . I often wish I had not grown into it so."

On his father's side James Russell Lowell was descended from an old New England family, with several generations of Harvard graduates, ministers, lawyers, bankers, and, recently, industrialists. The poet's grandfather, John Lowell, a graduate in law from Harvard, was said to be responsible for abolishing slavery in Massachusetts. Charles Lowell, father of the poet, spent three years of study abroad after receiving his Harvard degree and then became a popular Boston minister. His published sermons show little depth of thought, but contemporaries testified that his radiant personality and musical voice never failed to impress an audience. In both religion and politics he was conservative, and later regarded abolitionism as eccentric.

In 1806 the Reverend Charles Lowell married Harriet Traill Spence, whose Tory family had originally come from the Orkney Islands. In contrast to the stable practicality of the Lowells, the Spence family was reputed to be negligent. Mr. Greenslet characterizes the poet's mother in this sympathetic manner: ". . . Mrs. Lowell possessed much of the wild beauty of the people of those windy northern isles, and her mind showed an irresistible tendency toward their poetic occultism. This tendency became irretrievably fixed in a visit which she made to the Orkneys in company with her husband early in their married life. Thenceforward until 1842, when her tense brain became disordered, she was a faerie-seer, credited by some with second sight." Her love for crooning old ballads in the twilight must have made an early impression on her imaginative son, for throughout his life dreams and intuitions impressed themselves upon his consciousness with the strength of "visions."

The youngster's imagination seems also to have been stimulated by his sister's reading him the *Faerie Queene* as a bed-time story. As soon as he could read books for himself, he was turned loose in his father's well-stocked library of three or four thousand volumes, and books thus became his early companions. His childhood, however, was not abnormally precocious. He led a wholesome life with his brothers and sisters and other Cambridge playmates. His father often took him on long drives in a chaise through eastern Massachusetts and southern New Hampshire. Looking back on his youth, he wrote to a friend in 1876, "I . . . received my earliest impressions in a community the most virtuous, I believe, that ever existed."

Lowell was prepared for college by attending first a "dame school" and then a boarding school, receiving at the latter excellent training in Latin. Without unusual exertion, he was able to excel because of his natural aptitude for languages. When he entered Harvard in 1834 the college had only two hundred students. The president was Josiah Quincy, whose eccentricities Lowell later recalled sympathetically in "A Great Public Character." The curriculum heavily stressed Greek, Latin, and mathematics, but these did not interfere with young Lowell's friendships, his wide though desultory reading, and his writing for the student magazine. In fact, his student life was so erratic that he was suspended (or "rusticated") to Concord for the last two months before his graduation in August. The final indiscretion which brought about this penalty seems to have been, as Greenslet daintily expresses it, "ambrosial jubilation" on the day he was elected class poet. He was permitted to write the poem but not to read it himself at commencement. Though naturally chagrined, Lowell spent his exile in Concord pleasantly, reciting his lessons to the Reverend Bargillai Frost and accepting the hospitality of Emerson and Thoreau, whom he ungraciously ridiculed in the poem he was writing.

For the modern student the chief significance of this class poem, a satire on contemporary ideas, is that it shows the bent of the young poet's mind. As one biographer has remarked, "From Aristophanes down the satirists have been Tories, and have turned their points against innovation rather than against tradition." In this first serious literary effort Lowell attempted in heroic couplets to ridicule the fermentation of new ideas in America, from Emerson's Transcendentalism to abolition and vegetarianism, though he shared the sympathy of the romanticists for the mistreated Indian. In a few years, after he, too, had turned reformer, Lowell would develop his satire into a propagandistic weapon rivaled in effectiveness only by the righteous anger of Whittier or the pathos of Mrs. Stowe. Yet, even in this humanitarian reform, he would remain part "Tory."

For two years after his graduation from college Lowell was so despondent over an unsuccessful love affair and his inability to decide upon a congenial vocation that he contemplated suicide: "I remember in '39 putting a cocked pistol to my forehead and being afraid to pull the trigger." He enrolled in the Harvard Law School, however, received his degree in 1840, and for two years attempted to apply himself to the practice of law, but the attention which his first volume of poems received in 1841 encouraged him to give up this profession for literature and journalism.

During these crucial years the callow satirist of 1838 was being transformed into a humanitarian by his compelling desire for affection. In a letter he confessed:

I go out sometimes with my heart so full of yearning toward my fellows that the indifferent look with which even entire strangers pass me brings tears to my eyes.

He began to sympathize with the abolitionists and to become interested in the plight of the oppressed of all lands. Consequently, when in 1840 he met Maria White, a delicate young poetess of strong moral and humane sensibilities in near-by Watertown, he fell rapturously in love and began to flower at once as poet and reformer. Miss White's friends, who called themselves the "Band," read De Quincy, Coleridge, Keats, and Tennyson, believed in temperance and abolition, and frolicked in literary games of fantasy and mysticism. The "Band" enjoyed the reflected glory of the exalted romance between the two poetic souls, and Maria passed James' love letters around for the whole group to read. However silly these diversions may seem to the modern reader, there can be little doubt that Maria White and her friends gave Lowell the stimulation and encouragement which he needed to arouse his mind and emotions and develop his talent.

A Year's Life and Other Poems (1841) was the first literary product of Lowell's courtship and engagement. Perhaps the excessive "spirituality" of these poems betrays the poet's immaturity, but in control of form they are remarkably competent, especially the sonnets. His "Ode" (written in 1841) contains his theory of poetry. In these romantic reflections on the age when the poet was "holy man" and "seer," who embraced the "universal sorrow of mankind," Lowell conceives the poet's function to be that of

> Humbling the tyrant, lifting up the lowly,
> And sending sun through the soul's prison bars.

He anticipates Whitman (or perhaps more accurately, echoes Shelley) in calling for a new poet-messiah to redeem mankind.

The success of this first book encouraged Lowell to think that he could support himself by writing. After publishing verse in the Southern Literary Messenger and Graham's Magazine, he began in 1842 writing essays on the Elizabethan dramatists for the Boston Miscellany. The following year he became co-editor of an ambitious but short-lived magazine, the Pioneer, which was discontinued after the third number, leaving Lowell $1,800 in debt. One of his essays in the Pioneer, however, reveals the former satirist of Emerson as now believing that:

True poetry is but the perfect reflex of true knowledge, and true knowledge is spiritual knowledge, which comes only of love, and which, when it has solved the mystery of one, even the smallest effluence of the eternal beauty, which surrounds us like an atmosphere, becomes a clue leading to the heart of this seeming labyrinth.

In another editorial he joined the controversy over a national American literature by demanding not a national but a natural literature.

After the Pioneer fiasco Lowell went back to Elmwood, where he prepared a new edition of Poems (copyrighted 1844). His interests had broadened since his first volume, especially on moral and political issues. Most reviewers were again flattering, but Margaret Fuller was an exception. She called the *Poems* "absolutely wanting in the true spirit and tone of poesy" and said the verse was stereotyped. "His interest in the moral questions of the day," she declared, "has supplied the want of vitality in himself; his great facility of versification has enabled him to fill the ear with a copious stream of pleasant sound." Such frankness hurt, and Lowell never forgave the critic.

The success of his second book enabled Lowell to marry Miss White. They went almost immediately to Philadelphia, where he was to join the editorial staff of the *Pennsylvania Freeman,* an abolitionist journal. There for a while they were very happy in their "little room in the third story (back)," but Lowell soon found the editorial policy of the *Freeman* tame and lost interest in his work. During the autumn of 1844 he was busy preparing his first book of criticism for publication, *Conversations on Some of the Old Poets* (printed in December, 1844, but dated 1845). Lowell's lifelong method as a critic is described by himself in his treatment of George Chapman:

Our object is to cull out and give to our readers the most striking and beautiful passages in those of his plays which are accessible to the American critic, adding a few explanatory notices and criticisms of our own.

After a little over a year in Philadelphia Lowell lost his position, and the young couple returned to Elmwood, where they again occupied third-floor rooms. There in four years four children were born to them, two of whom died. Their happiness was also clouded by the fact that by this time the poet's mother had completely lost her sanity and his sister's mind had also become disordered. Meanwhile Lowell wrote with undiminished vigor for the moral crusades to which he had given his allegiance and talents. Not content with merely attacking the slaveholders, he preached complete racial tolerance and equality:

It has always seemed to us that abolitionists could in no way more usefully serve their holy cause than by seeking to elevate the condition of the colored race in the free states, and to break down every barrier of invidious distinction between them and their privileged brothers.

In his unrelenting fight against slavery, the South which supported it, and politicians like Daniel Webster who were willing to compromise, Lowell offended many of his Harvard friends and even his own conservative father. But the first series of *The Biglow Papers,* which he began writing in 1846 (published

in book form in 1848), was immediately successful. The war with Mexico was unpopular in New England with a fairly large group, which saw in the conflict only the attempt of the slaveholding states to extend their territory and political power. Lowell's first attempt to dramatize his opposition to the Mexican war through the dialect rhymes of a back countryman named Hosea Biglow met with such instant approval that he continued to air his views through nine satires in this medium.

For productivity and the expression of the many sides of his mind and talent Lowell never equaled again this marvelous year, 1848, during which he published forty articles and four books, concerned with reform, literary criticism, witty ridicule, and lyric feeling. But he was not yet altogether sure of himself, and marveled at his own double nature:

I find myself very curiously compounded of two utterly distinct characters. One half of me is clear mystic and enthusiast, and the other humorist.

The "mystic and enthusiast" wrote *The Vision of Sir Launfal,* a moral and sentimental fable in which a knight dreams he sets out in youth to seek the Holy Grail and returns a broken old man to find Christ in the guise of a beggar at his own door. This poem and *A Fable for Critics* were included in the second series of *Poems,* one of the four books. The *Fable* represents the other side of the poet, that of humorist and critic. Despite the personal spleen and bias, it was, on the whole, just, though only the genteel authors like Irving and Dr. Holmes escaped the satirist's animus. Margaret Fuller and Thoreau, neither of whom was blind to the narrowness of the Cambridge tradition, were soundly cudgeled. But many of his judgments have stood the test of time. And with rare objectivity the satirist described himself as unable to climb Parnassus with the bundle of didacticism on his shoulders:

The top of the hill he will ne'er come nigh reaching
Till he learns the distinction 'twixt singing and preaching.

The next two years saw the beginning of a change in Lowell's life and writing. Another daughter was born in July, 1849, and died in the following February. The next month his mother died, and in December, 1850, his only son, Walter, was born. During these family events Lowell continued to write prose and verse for the *Anti-Slavery Standard,* for which he was now corresponding editor at the salary of $900 a year. But he was beginning to find the company of the fanatical abolitionists increasingly uncongenial, and he was dropped from the editorial staff in 1852. Probably he did not care, for he was weary of reform and wanted to devote his time and energy to poetry. To a friend he wrote:

My poems have thus far had a regular and natural sequence. First, Love and the mere happiness of existence beginning to be conscious of itself, then Freedom—both being the sides which Beauty presented to me—and now I am going to try more *wholly* after Beauty herself. Next, if I live, I shall try to present Life as I have seen it.

As a first step in carrying out this resolve Lowell decided to see Europe, a part of his education which had been neglected. After selling enough land to finance two years abroad he set sail in July, 1851, with his wife, his son and daughter, and a nurse and milch goat for the children. While he was away his father suffered a paralytic stroke and Walter died, but the Lowells refused to return home until they had seen the places they had planned to visit. The poet felt most at home in Rome and believed that the Americans were the modern Romans. After traveling in Switzerland, Germany, and France, the Lowells took in the Cathedral towns of England, then sailed for America in October on the same ship with Thackeray and Clough. But the Elmwood to which they came back was a gloomy place, with the father helpless and his mind almost destroyed; and after the loss of three children, Lowell realized that his wife did not have long to live. She died in 1853.

The death of his wife was the severest shock that Lowell had yet received from life, and he sought relief in work. About 1854 he entered a new phase in his intellectual development. Though he continued to write poetry, this might be called his prose period. *Fireside Travels* (1864) is not the equal of some of his books of criticism, but it contains one of his most charming essays, "Cambridge Thirty Years Ago," and the anecdotal "Leaves from My Italian Journal" is dramatic and vivid. Especially interesting in the latter is the attitude of the descendant of American Puritanism toward the Roman Church:

She is the only church that has been loyal to the heart and soul of man, that has clung to her faith in the imagination, and that would not give over her symbols and images and sacred vessels to the perilous keeping of the iconoclast Understanding. She has never lost sight of the truth, that the product of human nature is composed of the sum of flesh and spirit, and has accordingly regarded both this world and the next as the constituents of that other world which we possess by faith.

In style this prose is simple, clear, and pleasantly rhythmical, though the author's exuberance is not always sufficiently controlled. His metaphors also tend

toward an enthusiasm bordering on mysticism, as in the opening sentences of "A Moosehead Journal":

I knew as little yesterday of the interior of Maine as the least penetrating person knows of the inside of that great social millstone which, driven by the River Time, sets imperatively agoing the several wheels of our individual activities.

Here, as in the famous "Ode Recited at the Harvard Commemoration" of 1865, we find the same faults and virtues in poet and prose writer: great sincerity and facility of expression but an emotionalism that diffuses itself in prolix diction.

This prose seems, however, to have been well adapted for success in public delivery. In 1854-55 Lowell began a series of lectures on the English poets at Lowell Institute in Boston. His discursive style, his irrepressible whimsicality, and his beautiful reading voice captivated his audience. Three weeks after beginning these lectures he was appointed Professor of French and Spanish Languages and Literature and Belles-Lettres at Harvard, the position which Longfellow had held. Like his predecessor, Lowell went to Germany for study before assuming the duties of his position. He returned in August, 1856, and a little over a year later married his daughter's governess, Frances Dunlap, a devoted friend of his first wife. This fortunate marriage gave Lowell's home the atmosphere of tranquillity and encouragement which he needed for success and happiness as professor, lecturer, and author. He was not a specialized scholar, though he knew several languages and spent many years in studying Old French; above all else, he was an interpreter of literature. He believed that—

True scholarship consists in knowing not what things exist, but what they mean; it is not memory but judgment.

In a lecture published after his death he stated what he considered to be the benefits of studying *belles-lettres*:

I believe that the study of imaginative literature tends to sanity of mind, and to keep the Caliban of common sense, a very useful monster in its proper place, from making himself king over us. It is a study of order, proportion, arrangement, of the highest and purest Reason. It teaches that chance has less to do with success than forethought, will, and work.

When the *Atlantic Monthly* was founded in 1857, Lowell became the first editor, at a salary of $2,500 —later $3,000. With the support of Holmes, Emerson, Whittier, Longfellow, and a few contributions from Thoreau and Howells, this magazine quickly acquired the greatest prestige of any literary periodical in America. Although Lowell often found the editing monotonous and irksome, he performed his duties with distinction. Some of his contributors thought, however, that he edited manuscripts too freely. Thoreau was furious because Lowell deleted from "Chesumcook" the sentence about a pine-tree: "It is as immortal as I am, and perchance will go to as high a heaven, there to tower above me still." But such concessions to orthodoxy no doubt increased the prestige of the magazine with the genteel audience for which it was chiefly edited.

For some years after his withdrawal from the ranks of the abolition propagandists Lowell took a less active interest in politics; but as the national crisis approached a climax, he became one of the ablest political essayists in the country. In 1858 he exposed the deception of the American Tract Society (in an essay by this title), which had disingenuously become the helper of slavery. Lowell was most indignant, however, over the compromising, temporizing, and appeasing of the Southern slave owners by an irresolute national government. In "The Election in November" (1860) he branded the government as "an organized scramble, and Congress a boy's debating club with the disadvantage of being reported." He believed that the politicians were thwarting popular government. In "E Pluribus Unum" (1861) he declared that "the moral bankruptcy at Washington is more complete and disastrous than the financial . . ." One reason for Lowell's impatience with all attempts to save the Union by compromise was that he thought not in terms of politics, economics, or expediency but moral principles. In fact, his conception of right government is that of his theocratic New England ancestors:

Every human government is bound to make its laws so far resemble His that they shall be uniform, certain, and unquestionable in their operation; and this it can do only by a timely show of power, and by an appeal to that authority which is of divine right, inasmuch as its office is to maintain that order which is the single attribute of the Infinite Reason that we can clearly apprehend and of which we have hourly example.

Perhaps only an idealist, more at home in his study than in the untidy world which Lincoln knew, could have seen all these issues so clearly in black and white, but he was undoubtedly right in his firm belief that political problems are not to be solved by appeasement of antidemocratic forces, and this was the foundation of his political thinking, then and later. In one of his most moving poems of the period, "The Washers of the Shroud," he sensed intuitively the possibility of national disaster, but he contributed

his own support to the preservation of the Union by reviving Hosea Biglow. This second series of *The Biglow Papers* was even more popular than the first. It is a bit ironical that the pacifist of the first series should now be so militant, but Lowell was never actually a pacifist, only an opponent of the extension of slave territory. The second *Biglow Papers* are also superior to the first in being less dramatic and more lyrical—some numbers, in fact, being entirely concerned with folk-experiences and not propagandistic at all. The price of the war was brought home to Lowell by the death of two of his nephews, Lieutenant James Jackson Lowell and Brigadier General Charles Russell Lowell, and he poured both his personal and his vicarious grief into the "Commemoration Ode."

Lowell's growth as an essayist was greatly facilitated by his opportunity to edit the *North American Review* in 1864. Although he had freely published his own writings in the *Atlantic*, the *North American* afforded him more space for the expression of his thoughts in prose. In 1866, therefore, he published two of his best critical studies to date, "Carlyle's 'Frederick the Great' " and "Swinburne's Tragedies," and the following year he produced "Rousseau and the Sentimentalists," an essay which anticipated Irving Babbitt's *Rousseau and Romanticism* (1919) and perhaps had some influence in starting the American New Humanism movement of the 1920's. Lowell's essay, however, is fairer and less doctrinaire than the humanists' condemnation of Rousseau, arch enemy of moderation, restraint, and tradition. In a more famous essay, "On a Certain Condescension in Foreigners" (1870), Lowell, with truly prophetic foresight, reminded the British that their harsh critical manners were alienating friends in the United States whom they might need in the future, while he advised his countrymen, as Irving had done in 1819 in "English Writers on America," not to be so thinskinned. In other essays, notably "Chaucer," Lowell furnished chapters for his best critical volume, *Among My Books* (1870).

The remaining two decades of Lowell's life were the most momentous and distinguished, but they belong more to political than literary history. He spent 1872–73 in Europe, then returned to teaching. But the corruptions of the Grant administration drew him into politics. He helped form an "Independent" wing of the Republican party to defeat the nomination of Blaine for the Presidency and as a consequence became a delegate to the Republican convention in Cincinnati. Then he was named a presidential elector, and in the deadlock between Hayes and Tilden that followed the national election, Lowell's vote helped to decide the dispute in favor of Hayes. In 1877 he declined his appointment as Minister to Austria but accepted for Spain, where he became nearly as popular as Washington Irving had been. In 1880 he was transferred to the Court of St. James and quickly became probably the best loved ambassador the United States had ever had in Great Britain. In constant demand as a public speaker, Lowell strove unceasingly, and always with remarkable success, to increase the consciousness of kinship between the two countries. The faculty and students of St. Andrews petitioned him to accept the rectorship of the University, and he was also offered a professorship at Oxford. He was appointed to many honorary positions, such as the Presidency of the Birmingham and Midland Institute. His inaugural address, "Democracy," was an eloquent apologia for American political theory; but in admitting defects in its operation, he offended some of his compatriots. In 1884 the Republican party lost the presidential election, and the following year, after his wife died, Lowell was quite willing to return to America. For several years after his return he lived at Deerfoot Farm, at Southborough, usually spending his summers in England, which he loved and which loved him. In 1889 he moved back to Elmwood, and his wish to die there was fulfilled.

During these last years Lowell was less a party man than ever. He found himself constantly in disagreement with the Republican party. He had more in common with the more liberal Democrats, and particularly admired Cleveland, but in 1888 he ably defended "The Place of the Independent in Politics." Lowell was increasingly disillusioned by American politics in action, not only because of the bribery and collusion in government, but, like Henry Adams, by the decline of culture and gentlemanliness in the

men elected to office. Christ he called in "Democracy" the "first true gentleman" and "the first true democrat." This simple statement is indicative of Lowell's thinking in both politics and religion. Without actually opposing contemporary science, he greatly feared the effect of Darwinism on morals. In the epilogue to his lecture-essays on the old dramatists, which stands at the end of his collected works, he voiced a conservative fear which time has turned into prophecy:

But I have my own suspicion sometimes that the true age of flint is before and not behind us, an age hardening itself more and more to those subtle influences which ransom our lives from the captivity of the actual, from that dungeon whose warder is the Giant Despair.

The permanence of James Russell Lowell's literary achievement lies in his intuitive flashes of truth, worth, and goodness, rather than in any enduring brilliance of expression or treatment. He confessed his distrust of "the poetic temperament," with "its self-deception" and "unblessed magic," and he wrote no single poem so lasting as the best of Emily Dickinson, whom he did not know, or Walt Whitman, who impressed him as a crude barbarian not to be taken seriously. But the spirit of his poetry is that of a man who loves both nature and humanity with a deep devotion. His criticism has been overpraised by the American Humanists, who fit him into their own dogmatic strait jacket. In their attempt to make him the greatest American critic, they give him more credit for judgment and consistent principles than he deserves. But as Lowell carries his readers with him on his rambling, whimsical, and observing tours of the great books and great authors of several languages, he is a cultivated and enthusiastic guide to aesthetic beauties and moral values of the world's best literature, and this function alone entitles him to high rank in American criticism.

HERMAN MELVILLE (1819–1891)

Herman Melville is another nineteenth-century American author whose reputation has fluctuated violently. In the 1840's his stories of adventure in the South Seas were widely read and admired both in this country and in England, though some readers were offended by his severe treatment of Christian missionaries and his account of the exploitation of simple Polynesians by capitalistic countries. Even these disapprovals, however, contributed to Melville's literary notoriety, and he was generally regarded as a promising author. But the implied criticism of his age and civilization suddenly developed into bitter satire and obscure allegory which both enraged and baffled Melville's readers. Within a few years he had so small an audience that in 1857 he stopped trying to publish his prose and turned to the writing of poetry mainly for himself. He never again tried seriously to compete in professional letters, with the result that he died in literary obscurity.

The obscurity was not complete, however, for Melville had loyal friends in New York who wrote appreciative articles about him and his work at the time of his death, and a small cult grew up in England, composed at first of such men as Edward Carpenter, Theodore Watts, and Robert Buchanan, and later of Robert Louis Stevenson, J. M. Barrie, and John Masefield. In America, Melville was still read by a few people who praised him by word of mouth until Carl Van Doren finally read *Moby Dick* around 1912 and joined the band of enthusiasts. In an interesting "Foreword" to the Readers Club edition of *Billy Budd*, *Benito Cereno*, and *The Enchanted Isles*, Professor Van Doren has described some of the events which followed his discovery of Melville:

I compiled the first detailed bibliography of Melville (1917) and encouraged Raymond Weaver to undertake the first biography (1921). What is called the Melville revival in America may be said to have begun with the Melville centennial in August 1919, which Weaver celebrated by an article in the *Nation*, of which I was literary editor, and Frank Jewett Mather, later in the month, by two articles in the *Review*. Within two or three years, particularly after Weaver had published his biography and had edited, in England, a collected Melville in sixteen volumes, everybody was reading Melville or claiming to

have read him. Throughout the decade of the 1920s Melville was the subject of many swarming enthusiasms. During the 1930s he came to be a favorite subject of many scholarly investigators. In 1921 I had roused questions by writing that nobody knew American literature who did not know Melville. In 1940, revising the book in which this statement had appeared, I dropped it as now too obvious.

The disillusionment which led Melville to jettison his popularity in the 1850's by his ironical probings at the very roots of existence proved congenial to the equally disillusioned post-war generation of the 1920's. During this time Melville was probably overrated, but two decades of continued research and critical appraisal have confirmed his position as a major figure in American literature.

Herman Melville was born August 1, 1819, in New York City, in a comfortable home at No. 6 Pearl Street. He was the second son and third child of Allan and Maria Gansevoort Melville. Several of the Melvilles had led colorful lives. Herman's grandfather, Thomas Melville, had been a major in the Revolutionary army and was a successful businessman in Boston, a quaint character who still wore a cocked hat and knee-breeches, as Oliver Wendell Holmes' poem about him, "The Last Leaf," indicates. An uncle, John de Wulf, had crossed Russia in winter by dog-sled. Herman's great-uncle, who had disgraced himself by failing in business in Paris and marrrying a Frenchwoman, now lived near Pittsfield, Massachusetts, like an aristocrat in exile. On his mother's side, the Gansevoorts were apparently more prosperous, though perhaps even more conventional than the Scotch Presbyterian Melvilles, being orthodox members of the Dutch Reformed Church. Biographers have regarded the proud, shallow Mrs. Glendinning in *Pierre* as a caricature of Herman Melville's mother, but actually very little is known of her.

More is known about the father, Allan Melville. He started out in business with his father in Boston, went to Albany after his marriage in 1815, then moved to New York the year of Herman's birth, where he throve for a while as an importer of French silks, gloves, hosiery, perfumes, and other elegant luxuries. In 1824 he bought a comfortable house on

Bleecker Street, then a suburb. In a lecture to young men he voiced his own conviction that "money is the only solid substratum on which man can safely build in this world." He had traveled in Europe, spoke French with one of his servants, and enjoyed the good things that money could buy. Lewis Mumford conjectures that "in Herman Melville's earliest years, nothing ever conveyed a sense of danger or physical stress."

But Allan Melville's good fortune did not last. The economic depression of 1826 ruined his New York business. He tried in 1830 to re-establish himself in Albany, but died in 1832 of pneumonia, perhaps aggravated by worry and a sense of failure. The oldest son, Gansevoort, started a cap and fur store in Albany, and Herman, after a term or two in Albany Academy, went to work at fifteen, first as a clerk in his uncle's bank and later as clerk in his brother's store. He spent another year on his uncle Thomas Melville's farm, and in 1837 went to sea on a merchant ship bound for Liverpool.

Herman's confidence in the world and his personal pride suffered an irreparable shock over the reversal in the Melville fortune. *Redburn*, the story of the disillusionment of an innocent young man similar to the author, is not entirely autobiographical, but some of the nostalgic sentiments expressed by the chief character for his lost youth probably came from Herman Melville's own memories, *e.g.*:

But I must not think of those delightful days, before my father became a bankrupt, and died, and we removed from the city; for when I think of those days, something rises up in my throat. . . . I was a poor friendless boy, far away from home, and voluntarily in the way of becoming a miserable sailor for life. And what made it more bitter to me, was to think of how well off were my cousins, who were happy and rich, and lived at home with my uncles and aunts, with no thought of going to sea for a living.

There seems little doubt that at least one reason for Melville's emotional turbulence was his disappointed youth, for he also wrote in *Redburn*:

Talk not of the bitterness of middle-age and after life; a boy can feel all that, and much more, when upon his young soul the mildew has fallen; and the fruit, which with others is only blasted after ripeness, with him is nipped in the first blossom and bud. And never again can such blights be made good; they strike in too deep, and leave such a scar that the air of Paradise might not erase it.

But disappointed ambition was not the only reason for Herman Melville's becoming a sailor. During his youth American ships were famous for their speed, fortunes were being made in trade with the Orient and in the whaling industry, and writers as diverse as Lord Byron and R. H. Dana were romanticizing faraway places and adventures on the ocean. There were also home influences stirring the imagination of young Melville, for both his father and his Uncle Thomas liked to talk of their experiences abroad. Probably again Herman Melville was writing from experience when his hero in *Redburn* confessed:

As years passed on, this continual dwelling upon foreign associations, bred in me a vague prophetic thought, that I was fated, one day or another, to be a great voyager; and that just as my father used to entertain strange gentlemen over their wine after dinner, I would hereafter be telling my own adventures to an eager auditory. And I have no doubt that this presentiment had something to do with bringing about my subsequent rovings.

If we can judge from the internal evidence in *Redburn*, Melville's trip to Liverpool gave him his first concrete experience with the brutal aspects of human nature, such as the cruel discipline and degraded mores aboard a merchant ship and his observations of numbing poverty in a great seaport like Liverpool. But this trip lasted only a few months, between spring and autumn of 1837. After his return home he taught school at intervals for three years in Pittsfield, Massachusetts, and Greenbush (East Albany), New York, but he also became disillusioned about the American system of common-school instruction, and on January 3, 1841, signed on at New Bedford for a whaling trip to the South Seas on the *Acushnet*. This trip, he later declared, was the only Yale and Harvard he ever knew, and that it was both educational and exciting there can be little doubt. He rounded the Horn, visited the "Enchanted Isles" (Galapagos group), and deserted ship with a companion on July 9, 1842, at Nukuhiva, in the Marquesas Islands, where he lived for a month with cannibals in the Taipi valley. He escaped from the Taipi, was rescued by an Australian whaler, and reached Tahiti. After more adventures, he left Tahiti aboard another whaler, the *Leviathan*, which probably carried him to Japan, and later to Honolulu, where he spent several months before joining the U.S. frigate *United States*, on August 17, 1843. This vessel returned home the following year, and Melville was discharged in Boston on October 14.

Melville kept no diary or notes during these eventful years and probably did not think of the literary possibilities of his experiences until after he had returned home. Then to refresh his memory and stimulate his imagination, he read all the books he could find on the South Seas and its inhabitants, mostly factual and unliterary accounts by explorers and sea captains. His first book, *Typee* (1846), was based, therefore, both on his own observations and the experiences of other travelers, though the first-person narrative led many readers to regard the story as a true account until C. R. Anderson traced down Melville's printed sources.

Typee is still good reading, with its unaffected narrative of the escape of the author and his friend Toby from the ship, of their perilous descent through a waterfall into an unknown valley, and the suspense created by their uncertainty as to the identity of the inhabitants, whether they will be the friendly Happars or the cannibalistic Typees. They are the Typees, and they prove to be cannibals, but the narrator is held in a sort of Garden of Eden captivity. In fact, one purpose of the book seems to have been the depiction of a primitive Utopia. The childlike savages are clean, unselfish, beautiful, and happy. And Fayaway is one of the most captivating heroines in all fiction, though undoubtedly a bit shocking to many readers in 1846:

Fayaway and I reclined in the stern of the canoe, on the very best terms possible with one another; the gentle nymph occasionally placing her pipe to her lip, and exhaling the mild fumes of the tobacco, to which her rosy breath added a fresh perfume. Strange as it may seem, there is nothing in which a young and beautiful female appears to more advantage than in the act of smoking.

But she was still more charming on another day, when

. . . she disengaged from her person the ample robe of tappa which was knotted over her shoulder (for the purpose of shielding her from the sun), and spreading it out like a sail, stood erect with upraised arms in the head of the canoe. We American sailors pride ourselves upon our straight clean spars, but a prettier little mast than Fayaway made was never shipped a-board of any craft.

It is little wonder that *Typee* was both scandalous and successful, and that the author would try to repeat his first literary achievement with a similar one. The second book, *Omoo* (1847), continues the adventures of the same author-hero in the Pacific after his escape from the Taipi valley. In suspense and narrative skill it resembles *Typee*, but the difference is in Melville's critical attitude toward the exploitation of the Polynesians by the so-called civilized nations, and especially by Christian missionaries. Observing that "the Tahitians can hardly ever be said to reflect: they are all impulse," and that "anything like a permanent religious impression is seldom or never produced," he decided that "there is, perhaps, no race upon earth, less disposed, by nature, to the monitions of Christianity, than the people of the South Sea." The moral and social patterns of Western civilization were not suited to these tropical people.

Despite the fact that missionary societies strongly disapproved of *Omoo*, and that church papers condemned it in vigorous editorials, the book sold well, and Melville's future as a man of letters seemed assured. He married Elizabeth Shaw, daughter of Chief Justice Lemuel Shaw, of Boston, and settled in New York at 103 Fourth Avenue. In New York he was befriended by Evert and George Duyckinck, editors of the *Literary World*, and prominent in the social and literary life of the city. Intellectually they were mediocre, and within a few years Melville outgrew them, but in the first critical years of his authorship their friendship and professional advice were a great help and stimulation to him.

Melville followed up the success of *Omoo* by publishing what at first appeared to be another romance of adventure in the South Seas, *Mardi* (1849), but on more careful scrutiny this book turned out to be a highly complicated allegory and satire. Critics still do not agree on the interpretation of the allegory, though the pursuit of the blue-eyed maiden, Yillah, by the hero, Taji, is reminiscent of the adventures of the Red Cross Knight in Spenser's *Faerie Queene*. Yillah was evidently intended to be a spiritual symbol akin to Spenser's Una, though having lost her, Taji never finds her again, and at last in an act of abdication turns his prow into the racing tide.

The satire of *Mardi*, however, resembles *Gulliver's Travels*. Various islands visited by Taji represent the nations of Europe and America. Vivenza, for example, is the United States, and Great Britain is designated as Dominora, ruled by King Bello (John Bull?). American jingoistic pride is thus ridiculed in Chapter CLVIII:

The throng that greeted us upon landing were exceedingly boisterous.

"Whence came ye?" they cried. "Whither bound? Saw ye ever such a land as this? Is it not a great and extensive republic? Pray, observe how tall we are; just feel of our thighs; are we not a glorious people? Here, feel of our beards. Look round; look round; be not afraid; behold those palms; swear now, that this land surpasses all others. Old Bello's mountains are mole-hills to ours; his rivers, rills; his empires, villages; his palm-trees, shrubs."

Despite the conviction of the inhabitants that everyone in Vivenza is a sovereign-king, the visitors observe in "The Great Central Temple" (Capitol) a man with a collar round his neck, and the red marks of stripes upon his back . . . in the act of hoisting a tappa standard—correspondingly striped." And a voice from the gods warns these freedom-proud people that theirs is "the best and happiest land under the sun . . . not wholly, because you, in your wisdom, decreed it: your origin and geography necessitated it." Freedom, itself, "is more social than political. And its real felicity is not to be shared. *That* is of a man's own individual getting and holding. It is not, who rules the state, but who rules me."

In the midst of this satire we also find a conviction which would soon lead Melville to the brink of intellectual annihilation:

And though all evils may be assuaged; all evils can not be done away. For evil is the chronic malady of the universe; and checked in one place, breaks forth in another.

But before taking up this theme in, respectively, his masterpiece (*Moby Dick*) and perhaps his greatest failure (*Pierre*), Melville turned his attention to a pot-boiler, *Redburn* (1849). The nature of this work has been indicated above, a semiautobiographical account of Melville's youthful trip to Liverpool as a green sailor. On December 14, 1849, he wrote to Evert Duyckinck: ". . . I hope I shall never write such a book again—tho' when a poor devil writes with duns all round him . . . what can you expect . . . but a beggarly 'Redburn'!"

Although *Redburn* is far from being one of his best works, it was not as bad as Melville thought. It is still of interest today; moreover, it may be said to have marked a turning point in Melville's intellectual life. On his way to London, for which he sailed in October, 1849, to arrange for the English publication of *White-Jacket*, Melville wrote in his diary: "This time to-morrow I shall be on land, and press English earth after the lapse of ten years—*then a sailor*, now H. M. author of *Peedee*, *Hullabaloo*, and *Pog-dog*." And earlier in the year he had written Evert Duyckinck, apropos Emerson, "I love all men who *dive* . . . the whole corps of thought-divers, that have been diving and coming up again with blood-shot eyes since the world began."

Before beginning his "thought-diving" in earnest, Melville published *White-Jacket* (1850), a sea-story based in part on his knowledge of life aboard a man-of-war. There was already at this time great agitation in Congress for laws to alleviate the cruelty of naval punishment—especially flogging—for minor offenses, and Melville both capitalized on the public interest in the subject and contributed to the popular demand for reform.

After his return to the United States in January, 1850, Melville moved his family to "Arrowhead," near Pittsfield, Massachusetts. Hawthorne lived only a few miles away, at Lenox, and the two authors became intimate friends. Some biographers have blamed Hawthorne for not responding more warmly to Melville's friendly advances, but recent evidence indicates that Hawthorne was more sympathetic and responsive than Lewis Mumford and Raymond Weaver believed. In fact, probably no other person encouraged and stimulated Melville's intellectual growth as much as Hawthorne. At the time they met, on August 5, 1850, each author had recently discovered the works of the other. Hawthorne was reading all of Melville's published romances, and Melville was writing a long review of *Mosses from an Old Manse*, which the Duyckincks printed, under a pseudonym, in their *Literary World* on August 17 and 24. Melville was especially attracted by the "dark" side of Hawthorne and compared his handling of tragic themes to Shakespeare's "short, quick probings at the very axis of reality." While Melville was at work on *Moby Dick* he declared that "Hawthorne has dropped germinous seeds into my soul."

In the months immediately preceding Hawthorne's removal from Lenox in November, 1851, Melville wrote his new friend long letters which provide intimate and revealing glimpses into his mind during this crucial period. In June he confessed: "What I feel most moved to write, that is banned,—it will not pay. Yet altogether, write the *other* way I cannot. So the product is a final hash, and all my books are botches." Even as he worked on the "Whale" Melville had a conviction that "Though I wrote the Gospels in this century, I should die in the gutter." When he thought of fame, he resented going down to posterity as the "man who lived among the cannibals!" But despite this mood of bitter discouragement and resentment, Melville was aware of a quickening growth of his mind and talent:

My development has been all within a few years past. . . . Until I was twenty-five, I had no development at all. From my twenty-fifth year I date my life. Three weeks have scarcely passed, at any time between then and now, that I have not unfolded within myself. But I feel that I am now come to the inmost leaf of the bulb, and that shortly the flower must fall to the mould.

This was Melville's mood before *Moby Dick* reached the public, but in November, after the book had been published both in England and the United States, he experienced a new surge of hope when he received Hawthorne's "joy-giving and exultation-breeding letter" of praise: "A sense of unspeakable security is in me this moment, on account of your having understood the book. I have written a wicked book, and I feel spotless as the lamb."

Like *Mardi*, *Moby Dick* is another story of an epic

search for the unattainable. A half-crazed old sea captain, Ahab, whose leg has been bitten off by the fabulous White Whale, Moby Dick, turns a whaling expedition into a personal quest for revenge, eventually destroying his ship and everyone on it except the author-narrator, Ishmael. To Ahab the White Whale is the "monomaniac incarnation of all those malicious agencies which some deep men feel eating in them, till they are left living on with half a heart and half a lung." This strange voyage in search of a monster who personifies demoniac forces in nature is so obviously symbolical, and is developed with such a variety of symbolisms, that many readers have regarded it as an outright allegory, but in a letter dated January 8, 1852, Melville denied to Mrs. Hawthorne that he had consciously written an allegory. The question is too complicated for discussion here, but it will repay further study. The important fact is that Herman Melville himself was now, with all his energies, probing "at the very axis of reality."

The following year (1852) he continued the probing, with what now amounted almost to fanaticism, in another symbolical story, Pierre. There can be little doubt that this book reflects Melville's own spiritual confusion, but it is probably less autobiographical than Redburn. The hero is Pierre Glendinning, gentle born, adored by his proud widowed mother. He loves and is engaged to Lucy Tartan, an almost ideal mate for him. But Pierre discovers that a mysterious, dark-haired girl, Isabel, who lives in poverty near by, is in reality his illegitimate half-sister. To make amends for his father's wrong and to protect his mother, Pierre decides to support her in the city under the pretense of having eloped with her. In the city Pierre struggles to write the kind of novel Melville dreamed of writing, but everything goes wrong. The mother dies of wounded pride, Pierre is goaded into committing murder, and he and Isabel finally take poison. This melodramatic plot, with the implication of incest, so shocked the few American readers who had survived Moby Dick that presently Melville had practically no audience whatever.

But the author seems not to have realized his plight immediately. Through 1853–56 he contributed stories and essays to Putnam's Monthly Magazine and Harper's New Monthly Magazine, but these fugitive pieces did not pay enough to live on. On December 10, 1853, a fire at Harper's destroyed his entire stock of books, and since there was not sufficient demand to justify the expense of reprinting them, Melville's literary reputation seemed almost on the point of vanishing. However, he did not give up the struggle for several years. In 1855 he published Israel Potter, a story of the American Revolution which he rewrote from a chapbook version published originally in 1824. It is the account of an American soldier captured by the British, who spent nearly half a century in Great Britain living a hand-to-mouth existence. The following year Melville published The Piazza Tales, a collection of stories which might have redeemed his reputation if it had not already sunk so low. This book contained the brilliant novelette, "Benito Cereno," and "The Encantadas; or, Enchanted Isles," both of which had appeared in Putnam's in 1854 and 1855 respectively. The latter work, impressionistic essays on the mysterious Galapagos Islands, shows a strong influence of Sir Thomas Browne and other seventeenth-century writers who were favorites of Melville. For the modern student The Piazza Tales contains some of Melville's most interesting prose. But this period of writing culminated in 1857 with the publication of the author's most angry satire, The Confidence Man, a bitter indictment of the shams of the society in which Melville had failed to find a market for his talents.

Meanwhile his family had increased to two sons and two daughters, whom Melville could not support without the help of his wife's family or his own relatives. For three years he tried giving lectures on Roman statuary and the South Seas, but this was not sufficiently lucrative or congenial. In 1860 he sailed to San Francisco with his brother Thomas, who was captain of a clipper, returning by way of Panama. He attempted, without success, to secure a consulship from President Lincoln. In 1863 he moved his family back to New York City, and three years later he was appointed District Inspector of Customs, a position which he held for nearly twenty years.

For two decades, while Melville supported his family by his work at the customs house, he wrote very little. During the Civil War he had written some war poems, which he had published in 1866 as Battle-Pieces and Aspects of the War, and he continued to write poems for his own amusement. His most ambitious poem, Clarel, a long narrative of a trip to the Holy Land and speculations on theology and philosophy, was published at the expense of his uncle, Peter Gansevoort, in 1876, but attracted little attention, and is hardly ever read today except by the most devoted Melville admirers. Although some critics have tried to find beauties in Melville's poems, to most readers they are prosy and flat. They do, however, reveal the author's continued interest in certain fundamental ideas and indicate the curve of his mental development.

When Melville died on September 28, 1891, he

left in manuscript a novelette, *Billy Budd*, which was not published until 1924, though written around 1888–91. Artistically, it is perhaps Melville's most unified and consistent story. *Moby Dick* and *Pierre* are turgid, rambling, and often erratic in style— especially *Pierre*. As tragic as either of these works, *Billy Budd* is without their rhetorical eccentricities. It is the story of a simple but incorruptible sailor whose very innocence involves him in a crime for which officers who love him as a son are forced by the code of the articles of war to hang him. But he dies blessing the captain who had condemned him to death. The English biographer, John Freeman, says that whereas "*Moby Dick* ends in darkness and desolation . . . *Billy Budd* ends in a brightness of escape, such as the apostle saw when he exclaimed, 'O death, where is thy sting?' " Freeman, sees a reflection of Melville's own serenity and final reconciliation to life in Billy's transfiguration:

The hull, deliberately recovering from the periodic roll to leeward, was just regaining an even keel—when the last signal, the preconcerted dumb one, was given. At the same moment it chanced that the vapoury fleece hanging low in the east was shot through with a soft glory as of the fleece of the Lamb of God seen in mystical vision; and simultaneously therewith, watched by the wedged mass of up-turned faces, Billy ascended; and ascending took the full rose of the dawn.

But Melville did not choose to end his story here.

He felt compelled to add three more short chapters, though well aware of his literary offense:

The symmetry of form attainable in pure fiction cannot so readily be achieved in a narration essentially having less to do with fable than with fact. Truth uncompromisingly told will always have its ragged edges; hence the conclusion of such a narration is apt to be less finished than an architectural finial.

In one of these epilogue chapters the *Indomitable* is attacked by the *Athéiste*, "the aptest name . . . ever given to a warship." The allegorical implications are reminiscent of the humanitarian attitudes of the author of *Typee, Omoo, Mardi*, and *White-Jacket*. And in the distorted account of Billy Budd's "crime" that survived we have the irony of *Pierre*. To judge by a note that Melville crossed out in the manuscript, he once planned to end with Chapter xxv: "Here ends a story not unwarranted in this incongruous world of ours—innocence and infirmity, spiritual depravity and fair respite." To heighten the irony in his presentation of the ways of "this incongruous world," Melville added still another chapter, in which even the sailors who worshipped Billy, treasure a chip of his gibbet as "a piece of the Cross," assume his guilt and embalm his memory in a traditional ballad of the condemned murderer. Truly, Herman Melville was never reconciled to the morality of this incongruous man-of-war world of ours.

WALT WHITMAN (1819–1892)

During his lifetime Walt Whitman was the most controversial figure in American literature, and the violence of the disputes which raged around him has left permanent imprints upon his reputation. Both his outraged enemies, who were shocked by his treatment of sex and his unconventional prosodic experiments, and his small band of fanatically loyal defenders (W. D. O'Connor, Dr. R. M. Bucke, John Burroughs, and Horace Traubel especially), who regarded him as a prophet of a new religion, contributed to the formation of myths, legends, and false interpretations of both the man and his work which still distort biographical and critical interpretations of one of America's most original and most influential poets.

Walt Whitman was born May 31, 1819, in a farmhouse still standing today at West Hills, Long Island. His father's family came to America from England in the seventeenth century. In the new country some were clergymen and some farmers, but none of them were particularly successful. The poet's father, Walter Whitman, tried farming on Long Island and carpentering in Brooklyn, and apparently worked hard, but never earned more than a meager living. Walter Whitman married Louisa Van Velsor, the daughter of a jolly, comparatively prosperous Dutch farmer. Neither had much education, but Walter read Tom Paine and subscribed to a "free thought" journal edited by the socialists Frances Wright and Robert Dale Owen. Both Walter and Louisa Whitman were sympathetic with a radical branch of Quakers led by Elias Hicks, though neither was a member of any church.

Young Walter, whom the family called "Walt" to distinguish him from his father, was the second of nine children, and the only one who had more than mediocre ability. Indeed, the youngest son was an imbecile and the oldest died a lunatic. The poet who represented himself as "Well-begotten and rais'd by a perfect mother" was either idealizing or unconsciously attempting to compensate for his shabby origin, which probably contained a strain of degeneracy. These details, ignored or minimized by all the earlier biographers (who sought the aid of the poet himself in collecting and interpreting the biographical facts), are important for two reasons: (1) they throw light on the poetic process of sublimation in *Leaves of Grass* and (2) they emphasize both the genius and the effort required by the poet to overcome his handicaps.

In 1823 the Whitmans moved from West Hills to Brooklyn, then a country town of seven thousand population. There Walt attended public school for a few years, the only formal education he ever had. By 1831–32 he was working in printing offices and learning the trade. After four or five years of employment in printing offices in Brooklyn, rural towns, and New York, he taught school for a few years in several small schools on Long Island, "boarding round" at the homes of his students. Meanwhile he began to contribute to several New York journals and magazines, writing sentimental stories and poems in the tradition of the time. He also took an active part in politics as a "Free Soil" Democrat.

For two years (1846–47) Whitman edited the Brooklyn *Eagle*. In January, 1848, he was discharged because of political disagreement with the owner. In February he left for New Orleans to join the editorial staff of the newly organized *Crescent*, but in less than three months he resigned again and returned to Brooklyn by steamer up the Mississippi and across the Great Lakes. In 1905 Henry Binns created a story of a romance in New Orleans between Whitman and a high-bred Creole woman, and later biographers have embroidered the conjecture, but no evidence has ever been produced to support it. Many have thought that the poet's "soul" was first awakened in this romantic setting, but this, too, is an hypothesis. All we know for sure is that Whitman returned to Brooklyn in June of 1848 and became editor of the *Freeman*, a position which he held for a year. After this, except for an interlude in 1857–59 when he edited the Brooklyn *Times*, he turned from journalism to other fields.

For the years when Whitman was formulating his new theory of poetry and experimenting with techniques to express it, we have scanty information. From 1851 to '54 he worked intermittently at the carpenter trade in Brooklyn with his father, but it was his inner dream-life, not his daily goings and comings, which was important during these years, and all we know about that are the fragmentary notes and tentative poems in the manuscripts and juvenile publications which Emory Holloway has preserved in the *Uncollected Poetry and Prose* and *Pictures*. From these, and other materials printed by Clifton J. Furness in *Walt Whitman's Workshop*, we can see that Whitman spent these years in writing orations and cultivating a rhetorical style which finally became the reiterative, parallelistic strophe form of *Leaves of Grass*.

On or near July 4, 1855, the first edition of this famous book appeared in a thin quarto volume of ninety-five pages, bound in green cloth stamped ornately with a design of leaves, roots, and flowers. The book was printed by some friends of the poet in Brooklyn, and he set some of the type himself. The author's name did not appear on the title page; and as a frontispiece he used a photograph of himself, bearded, in shirt sleeves, wearing a large black hat, standing in a slouched posture. This was

Walt Whitman, an American, one of the roughs, a kosmos,
Disorderly fleshly and sensual . . . eating drinking and
    breeding,
No sentimentalist . . . no stander above men and women
    or apart from them . . . no more modest than immodest.

In this first edition the young poet was self-consciously posing in a rôle which he had not yet learned to play with professional skill. But despite the posing, he was sincere and profoundly earnest in his intention to become a great national poet by making his own life into a poem. Emerson had declared that the poet is "representative" and "stands among partial men for the complete man." Walt Whitman intended to be that "complete man" and to record in a new, indigenous style his own life-experiences as representative of nineteenth-century American democracy, with all its vitality, materialism, expansiveness, and spiritual aspirations. This program for himself and his nation he tried to explain in a long preface in rhapsodic prose, segments of which he later incorporated into one of his major poems, "By Blue Ontario's Shore." After the preface came twelve unnamed poems, the first being the embryonic "Song of Myself." Another, the fourth, later called "The Sleepers," used a stream-of-consciousness imagery many years before the term was known to literary criticism. Perhaps the most finished lyric, and the most autobiographical poem in the book, was the now famous "There Was a Child Went Forth."

Few if any copies of the first edition of *Leaves of Grass* sold, but Whitman generously sent copies to reviewers and eminent authors. Most recipients either ignored the book or unmercifully ridiculed it, but Emerson, to whom Whitman had hopefully sent a copy, impulsively replied that he found it "the most extraordinary piece of wit and wisdom that America has yet contributed" and greeted the young poet "at the beginning of a great career." With this encouragement, Walt Whitman ignored the abuse and incomprehension from almost every other person who had taken the trouble to read his poems (Whittier burned his copy), and he promptly set about preparing a new edition. The second edition appeared in 1856, augmented by twenty new poems, a tactless printing of Emerson's letter without permission, and a boastful reply to the "Master." Despite these gaucheries, however, the new edition showed marked growth in poetic feeling and lyric power. The evolution of *Leaves of Grass* had begun and would continue until the last years of the poet's life, fulfilling the prophecy of the 1855 Preface.

The third edition of *Leaves of Grass* was brought out in 1860 by a reputable Boston publisher, Thayer and Eldridge, but the following year the firm went into bankruptcy and the plates were acquired by a dishonest publisher who issued many pirated copies, some of which are still on the market. The student of Whitman will find this edition one of the most interesting and revealing. The poet had not abandoned his expansive program announced in 1855 and amplified in 1856. He still, as in "Starting from Paumanok," wrote from "an American point of view" and intended to "trail the whole geography of the globe, and salute courteously every city large and small." But to his national and cosmic themes he had added a personal theme of love and companionship.

In 1855 and '56 Whitman had regarded sex as suitable for poetic treatment because he believed all phases of nature to be equally good, but his insistence on sex in the 1860 *Leaves* probably sprang from some inner need for self-expression and assurance. In a section called "Enfans d'Adam" (renamed "Children of Adam" in 1867) he treated sex philosophically, under the imagery of pantheistic transmigration, as in "To the Garden the World":

. . . here behold my resurrection, after slumber,
The revolving cycles, in their wide sweep, having brought
    me again.

But in another section, called "Calamus," the poet advanced his theme of "great companions." It is not difficult today, in the light of modern psychology, to see in the symbolism of these "Calamus" poems the search for an ideal companionship which the poet had never known in reality. His "new City of Friends" was a compensatory dream.

Some of the poems in the 1860 edition of *Leaves of Grass* reflect an unhealthy state of mind, a contradiction of the rôle which Walt Whitman assumed in 1855 as the poet of joy and robust vitality. Perhaps his failure to gain recognition for his first two editions of the *Leaves* and his unsatisfied longing for love and companionship were turning his mind inward, making it morbidly introspective. But in the emotions aroused in him by the outbreak of the Civil War, which threatened the unity of the nation that he had dedicated himself to celebrate in song, Whitman found a personal release and a sublimation for his psychological hungers and his pent-up energies. He went down to the battlefields of Virginia to find his wounded brother George, and he stayed to nurse the sick and comfort the dying.

Out of Whitman's experiences during the war years came the marvelous lyrics, *Drum-Taps*, published as a pamphlet in 1865 and added to *Leaves of Grass* in 1867. Some of the poems were written before Whitman visited the battlefield, and in them we catch the sound of marching feet and share the excitement of young men setting out on a crusade. In a section of "The Wound-Dresser" added in a later version the poet has recorded the biography of his own emotions during the war period:

(Arous'd and angry, I'd thought to beat the alarm, and urge relentless war,
But soon my fingers fail'd me, my face droop'd and I resigned myself,
To sit by the wounded and soothe them, or silently watch the dead;) . . .

For a decade, from 1863 to 1873, Whitman lived in the national capital, working as a volunteer in army hospitals, then as clerk in the service of the Government. His first clerkship was in the Indian Bureau of the Department of the Interior, but he was discharged in about six months because the Secretary of the Interior had allegedly discovered that his employee was the author of what the Secretary thought was an indecent book (meaning the sex poems in the third edition of *Leaves of Grass*, which Whitman was then revising for the fourth edition). Whitman's friends, especially the impetuous William Douglas O'Connor, came hotly to his rescue and the poet was appointed to a similar clerkship in the Attorney General's office, a position which he held until paralysis in 1873 incapacitated him. Not content

with securing a new position for his friend, O'Connor published a highly eulogistic vindication called *The Good Gray Poet*, the first contribution to Whitman hagiography.

During these years Walt Whitman continued to revise and add to the ever-growing volume of poems, *Leaves of Grass*. The death of President Lincoln inspired his best poem, "When Lilacs Last in the Dooryard Bloom'd." So completely did the poet transmute the grief of himself and his nation into the perennial symbols of the lilacs, the fallen star, the resurrection of nature in springtime, and "memory of him I love" that the elegy acquired universal meaning. On the death of another great wartime President during a springtime crisis eighty years later, this deeply moving poem was recited over the radio with perfect appropriateness. Swinburne called it "the most sonorous nocturne ever chanted in the church of the world."

While in Washington, Whitman also published *Democratic Vistas* (1871), regarded by most critics as his best prose work. This long essay was an amplification of the faith in a democratic utopia first announced in the 1855 Preface. Whitman still believed that a new invigorating democratic art and literature could bring to fruition in "these States . . . the moral political speculations of ages, long, long, deferr'd, the democratic republican principle, and the theory of development and perfection by voluntary standards, and self-reliance." But he warned that his earlier prophecy had not yet come true and that "society in these States, is canker'd, crude, superstitious, and rotten. . . . Our New World democracy . . . is, so far, an almost complete failure in its social aspects . . ." *Democratic Vistas* is a combination of lofty idealism and plain-spoken realism.

Although Whitman still had only a very small following in the United States, his poetry and prose began to win recognition abroad during the Washington decade. The fourth edition of *Leaves of Grass* (1867) was reviewed promptly in England by William Rossetti, who the following year edited a well-selected volume of poems which introduced Whitman favorably to British readers. As a result other English authors began to befriend the neglected American poet. *Democratic Vistas* was translated into Danish, and Whitman gradually became known on the continent, first in Germany, France, Scandinavia, then Italy, Spain, and other countries.

In February, 1873, Whitman suffered the paralytic stroke which forced him to abandon Washington— in fact, to be a semi-invalid for the remainder of his life. This was an ironic fate for the "caresser of life," the poet of glowing health and physical vigor, "muscle and pluck forever." In his discouragement Whitman wrote "Prayer of Columbus," in which he pathetically identified himself with the "batter'd, wreck'd old man." After his paralysis Whitman was a different poet, but what his poetry lost in gusto it gained year by year in poise and serenity. For several years he went in summer to a farm at Timber Creek, in New Jersey, where in secluded rest, mild outdoor exercise, and patient recording of his little experiences with nature, the crippled old man partially regained his health and acquired an emotional and intellectual poise which he had never known before. This poise may be seen not only in his numerous old-age photographs but also in the later Leaves, in the parts of Specimen Days devoted to his later life, and perhaps in the annual addresses on Lincoln which he began in 1879 to give on the anniversary of the assassination. Nearly everyone who knew Whitman after 1860 testified to his magnetic personality, but in old age his charm seems to have become almost hypnotic. After he settled in his own cottage on Mickle Street, in Camden, New Jersey, many famous men visited him, and few went away unimpressed by the remarkable man they had met.

In 1881 occurred Whitman's second unfortunate experience with Boston publishers. James R. Osgood and Company published the seventh edition of Leaves of Grass, but the district attorney, urged by the Society for Suppression of Vice, threatened prosecution unless the book was withdrawn from the mails or some of the sex poems expurgated. The poet refused to expurgate a single line, and Osgood returned the plates. But Whitman immediately secured a new publisher in Philadelphia—first Rees Welsh and Company and then David McKay.

The seventh edition of Leaves of Grass (all imprints by the three publishers from the same plates) may have been intended for the final version. At any rate, Whitman made in it his final revisions of text, his last change of titles, and arranged the poems in a sequence which has been kept in all authorized editions down to the present time. Poems written after 1881 were inserted in appendices or newly created sections tacked on to the seventh edition. Whitman thought he was arranging his work in a scheme which would reveal his poetic intentions and symbolize his life-experiences, but it is doubtful whether he clarified as much as he obscured. For the student who cannot study each edition in order of publication, the best plan is to read the poems in chronological order, the arrangement found in most anthologies and selected editions.

Whitman's second book of prose, Specimen Days, appeared in 1882. It is his most directly autobiographical work, being a collection of entries in notebooks, extracts from diaries, journalistic pieces, personal essays, etc. The book begins with a brief autobiographical sketch apparently written at this time. Then come the war memoranda, taken, the author says, from "verbatim copies of those lurid and bloodsmutch'd little note-books" which he kept with him constantly in Washington during his experiences in the war hospitals. Many of these accounts give intimate and realistic glimpses into the war and the suffering which it caused. They should be read along with Drum-Taps.

The third part of Specimen Days reveals still another side of Whitman's life, that of the nature lover and half-paralytic recuperating at Timber Creek, taking sun baths, making amateurish botanical and ornithological observations, and scribbling down his impressions on the spot. The mood is that of serene, healing repose. It is a relief to see the poet basking in this Indian Summer atmosphere after the feverish search for "companions" in the "Calamus" period and the exhausting excitement of the years in Washington.

In another old-age book, November Boughs (1888), containing sixty-four poems and one of Whitman's best prefaces, "A Backward Glance O'er Travel'd Roads," we see the spiritual gains which these later years brought the poet. Both the lyric fire of the earlier poems and the self-assertiveness of the 1855 and '56 prefaces have given way to calm reflection and reminiscence. In "A Backward Glance" he frankly admits that "I have not gain'd the acceptance of my own time, but have fallen back on fond dreams of the future." He is content, however, that "I have had my say entirely in my own way, and put it unerringly on record—the value thereof to be decided by time." Leaves of Grass was always an experiment anyway, "as, in the deepest sense, I consider our American Republic itself to be, with its theory" of freedom and equality. He is satisfied that he has "positively gain'd a hearing."

It was with great difficulty that Whitman prepared November Boughs for the press, for early in June of 1888 he suffered another paralytic stroke which made any kind of exertion almost impossible and kept him "house-tied" through 1889. But in 1891 he was sufficiently improved for a birthday dinner in Camden, which was attended by many friends and admirers. The roster of speakers and the senders of congratulatory messages included a long list of the most distinguished names in the United

States and Great Britain. Walt. Whitman had not yet won a secure position in American literature, and would not for perhaps half a century, but he was a famous man, providing good "copy" for newspapers. He died on March 26, 1892, and was buried in Harleigh Cemetery, Camden, where a tomb had been prepared under his own direction. Hostile critics have exaggerated the cost of this monument which the poet erected to himself, but his lifelong struggle for recognition against almost overwhelming opposition is undoubtedly reflected in his final effort to perpetuate the fame which he knew he deserved. The world was slow in discovering that Walt Whitman was right, though eventually it did.

Today it is not difficult to understand why Whitman was shocking and unintelligible to American readers in the heyday of Longfellow, Whittier, and the genteel poets. There was, and still remains, much crudity in some of the poems of Leaves of Grass, though in a more unconventional, more informal age these crudities are less of an obstacle to appreciation of the poet's other positive merits, such as his all-embracing love, his cosmic amplitude, his strong, democratic world sentiment. His subject matter was also difficult for readers before the age of realism, not only his physiological themes but also his exploitation of his own ego as a symbol. In the opening lines of the first edition the poet announced:

I celebrate myself,
And what I assume you shall assume,
For every atom belonging to me as good belongs to you.

But most readers still thought that the "I" in the poems meant Walt Whitman. Sometimes it did; more often it was generic.

Probably, however, Whitman's "organic" style was still more misunderstood, though Coleridge had defined the theory of such a style many years earlier:

The organic form . . . is innate; it shapes, as it develops, itself from within, and the fulness of its development is one and the same with the perfection of its outward form. Such as the life is, such is the form. Nature, the prime genial artist, inexhaustible in diverse powers, is equally inexhaustible in diverse forms;—each exterior is the physiognomy of the being within,—its true image reflected and thrown out from the concave mirror;—and even such is the appropriate excellence of her chosen poet.

The average reader in Whitman's day, accustomed to rime and meter, could find no recognizable form in Whitman's long free verse lines, with his reiteration of words and phrases, long catalogs of names, scenes, and activities ranging over the whole globe, and his parallel grammatical structure. Whitman's style reminded a few readers of the verse structure in Old Testament poetry, and this was a significant comparison, for the parallelism of Leaves of Grass is reminiscent of this primitive prosodic device, i.e., the repetition of thought (clauses, etc.) provides a verse technique, as rime and meter do in conventional verse. (For fuller explanation see American Prosody and Walt Whitman Handbook, listed in "Selected Bibliography.") The modern reader, accustomed to the symphonic impressionism of Debussy, the "expanding ego" of the expressionists, the stream-of-consciousness of Joyce and his followers, has little difficulty understanding Whitman's "organic" style. But if the techniques of Joyce, Proust, and Thomas Wolfe have helped to make Whitman coherent, these writers in turn are intelligible partly because Whitman wrote as he did. His experimental style is one of the major links between him and modern art.

Readers have also been conditioned to Whitman's thought and form by the numerous critics who have interpreted his literary intentions and achievements. He has been translated and discussed in critique and biography in France, Germany, Italy, Spain, Russia, Scandinavia, India, Japan, and Latin America. A great body of critical—and in some countries imitative—literature has grown up around his name. Of all American writers, Mark Twain is probably most loved abroad, and Poe most admired in Latin countries, but no other poet of the United States occupies today a surer position in world literature than Walt Whitman, who prophesied in "Salut au Monde!":

My spirit has pass'd in compassion and determination
     around the whole earth,
I have look'd for equals and lovers and found them ready
     for me in all lands, . . .

SIDNEY LANIER (1842–1881)

"The life and song of Sidney Lanier are so intimately related, and the frustrations that beset his ambition for achievement as an artist so poignant," writes Professor Charles R. Anderson, the general editor of the Centennial Edition of Lanier's collected *Works*, "that the tendency has been to lose the poems in the poet." This fact constitutes the first problem for the modern student of Lanier. A poet should be judged on the basis of his literary merit, but even today the story of Lanier's gallant and tragic struggle against ill health, poverty, and other handicaps dwarfs the poems.

Another difficulty for many readers of Lanier is the extent to which his thought and expression were permeated by the region and culture in which he grew up. Though the South may have colored Poe's sensitive imagination, his poems and stories are as easily appreciated by a Northern or a Western as a Southern reader. But Lanier's sentiment, his luxuriant diction, his vicarious feudalism, and his justifiable self-pity are Southern. Some years ago Gamaliel Bradford expressed it in this way in *American Portraits:*

He was a Southerner, always a Southerner. He loved the South, and the South loved and loves him. And in his day the spur of that glorious spirit, ever toiling, ever hoping, giving up all material success for the long pursuit of an ideal, was the very stimulus that the young men of the South needed above all others. Who shall say that the young men of the whole country do not need and cannot profit by it now?

Though Sidney Lanier later shared to the fullest extent the Southern dream of a new Athens, in which every street would be lined with statuary and every hamlet would have its Plato, the town in which he was born, Macon, Georgia, was neither aristocratic nor feudal like the great plantations around Charleston. It was, in fact, a thriving commercial town, a stop-over for the stagecoaches from New York to New Orleans and the chief cotton market in Middle Georgia (Atlanta developed later).

Family legend has it that the Laniers were of Huguenot origin, but we first find the American branch living in Virginia, with large estates and ample income. The poet's grandfather migrated from Virginia to Georgia, where he became a prosperous hotel proprietor. The father of the poet, Robert Sampson Lanier, graduated from Randolph-Macon College, studied law, and attempted to practice in Macon. He seems not to have been outstandingly successful as a lawyer, but his family apparently lived comfortably before the War of Secession. He married Mary Jane Anderson of Virginia, of Scotch Presbyterian ancestry, a lover of poetry and music. With their three children, Sidney, Clifford, and Gertrude, they were almost idyllically happy. The family devotion was so strong, indeed, that Aubrey Starke, author of the definitive biography of the poet, thinks it may have been an unhealthy influence.

In Lanier's youth Macon had no public schools, and he first attended a private one-room school, then Bibb County Academy. At home he absorbed the rudiments of music and quickly learned to play almost any instrument. The violin was his favorite, but his father, believing that playing it overstimulated his delicate nervous system, encouraged him to play the flute. For his flute-playing he gained the reputation of a child prodigy. Meanwhile he eagerly devoured the romances of Scott, Bulwer, Froissart, Geoffrey of Monmouth, and Malory. Froissart, whom he later edited for boys, always remained a favorite. This taste for feudal romance and chivalry was typical of the whole South before the Civil War, but Lanier was so deeply impressed that he never ceased to think of himself as a Christian knight, and the imagery of chivalry permeates his mature poetry and prose.

At the age of fifteen Lanier entered Oglethorpe University, a Presbyterian college at Midway, two miles from Milledgeville, then capital of Georgia. After taking examinations, he was admitted as a sophomore. Although he spent much time in playing his flute and in serenading young ladies, he did well in his studies, especially in mathematics. He also extended his reading, becoming acquainted through Carlyle with such German romantic writers as Jean Paul and Novalis, who encouraged him in his fondness for reverie and trancelike day-dreaming. Possibly these moods of extreme sentiment influenced his father to withdraw him from college for a year at the end of his junior year. But after clerking for twelve months in the Macon post office, Lanier returned to Oglethorpe in 1859. Meanwhile Professor James Woodrow, who had studied under Agassiz at Harvard and taken a Ph.D. at Heidelberg, had joined the faculty, and he exerted a profound influence on young Lanier. Professor Woodrow's field was natural science, but he was also deeply interested in literature and religion. Lanier's own interest in science, and its relation to other fields, was undoubtedly first awakened by this gifted teacher—whose own attempts to reconcile science and religion brought him into conflict with Presbyterian orthodoxy and resulted in 1888 in his being tried by the General Assembly of the Presbyterian Church and convicted of heresy.

After his graduation in 1860 Lanier was appointed a tutor in Greek, and he decided to prepare for his new duties by taking a vacation at his grandfather's summer resort in the mountains of eastern Tennessee. The scenery and the delightful experiences of this summer were to be utilized later in his immature novel, *Tiger-Lilies*. How successful Lanier was in teaching Greek we do not know, for the accounts of this year emphasize only his continued enjoyment of music and his experiments in writing poetry. His brother Clifford remembered the poems as "Byronesque, if not Wertheresque" and "tinged with gloominess." Lanier also began collecting notes for an ambitious poem on the Jacquerie rebellion in fourteenth-century France, a project on which he worked, off and on, for many years but never completed. More important, during this year of tutoring Greek the young poet-musician was taking stock of his talents and trying to decide upon his career. He knew his "natural bent" to be music and was confident that his musical talent was "extraordinary": "But I cannot bring myself to believe," he confided to his notebook, "that I was intended for a musician, because it seems so small a business in comparison with other things which, it seems to me, I might do. Question here: 'What is the province of music in the economy of the world?'"

This divided mind in the choice of a career haunted Lanier until the last few years of his life, when he fortunately found means of combining his interests and his talents. At Oglethorpe the choice was mainly between science and music, for Professor Woodrow had fired him with the desire to take a Ph.D. at Heidelberg, as he had done. Later the choice was between poetry and music. But whatever he did, music was never absent from his life.

The outbreak of hostilities between the Northern

and Southern states decided Lanier's activities for the duration of the war. Like most young men North and South, he responded eagerly in the spring of 1861 to the popular state of mind which he later described with a tinge of ironic disillusionment in *Tiger-Lilies*:

An afflatus of war was breathed upon us. Like a great wind, it drew on and blew upon men, women, and children. Its sound mingled with the solemnity of the church-organs and arose with the earnest words of preachers praying for guidance in the matter. It sighed in the half-breathed words of sweethearts conditioning lovers with war-services. It thundered splendidly in the impassioned appeals of orators to the people. It whistled through the streets, it stole in to the firesides, it clinked glasses in bar-rooms, it lifted the gray hairs of our wise men in conventions, it thrilled through the lectures in college halls, it rustled the thumbed book-leaves of the school-rooms.

"Who could have resisted," the author asks, "the fair anticipations which the new war-idea brought?" Certainly an emotional and patriotic young man like Sidney Lanier could not. He promptly joined the Confederate Army and marched off to war with his beloved flute in his knapsack. At first he had light picket duty and lived like a gay troubadour, entertaining the camp with his music, making love to responsive young ladies, and confident, as he bitterly confessed after the war, that the South could whip five Norths. But at Drury's Bluff, near Richmond, he experienced the horrors of battle, and in the Mounted Signal Service he fought at Chancellorsville.

On a furlough in the spring of 1863 Lanier met Mary Day, daughter of a Macon jeweler, originally from the North but now loyal to the Southern cause. Miss Day had studied music in New York, and Lanier naturally found her congenial, though he continued for a time to court and serenade other young ladies. Back in camp, he helped to pass the time by translating German poems and composing verses of his own. Though he continued his music for recreation, he was now thinking of poetry as his major vocation. To his father he wrote a surprisingly acute analysis of his own defects as a poet:

I have frequently noticed in myself a tendency to a diffuse style; a disposition to push my metaphors too far, employing a multitude of words to heighten the patness of the image and so making it a *conceit* rather than a metaphor, a fault copiously illustrated in the poetry of Cowley, Waller, Donne, and others of that ilk.

In 1864 Lanier was transferred from the Signal Service to blockade running and was captured on November 2. Just before the vessel was surrendered, the Captain tried to persuade him to don an English officer's uniform in order to avoid imprisonment, but Lanier refused to disguise himself. He was sent to Point Lookout, Maryland, a horror hole comparable to the worst Confederate prisons, and there he nearly died of hunger, exposure, and disease. Almost the only cheer in the prison was this gallant soldier's wonderful flute music. Father Tabb, who was in the prison, heard it and became the musician's lifelong friend. Finally, almost more dead than alive, he was released and on March 15, 1865, stumbled into Macon. In April Macon surrendered to the Union army, and the war was over. But from the effects of his exhaustion in military service and his illness in prison Lanier never entirely recovered.

After partially regaining his health, Sidney Lanier now began the long, discouraging struggle against poverty. In September he became a tutor on a plantation nine miles from Macon, but in a short time he was forced to resign on account of his health, and his physician advised his going to Mobile Bay. He seems to have inherited a constitutional weakness for tuberculosis of the lungs, and this disease was now his chief enemy. In January he felt strong enough to assume the light duties of clerk at the Lanier-owned Exchange Hotel in Montgomery, Alabama, where Clifford was then employed. There the two brothers worked on their novels, Clifford on *Thorn-Fruit* and Sidney on *Tiger-Lilies*. These black days of "Reconstruction" were especially discouraging to a man whose great ambition was to produce literature. To a college friend who had gone North, Sidney Lanier wrote, "There's not enough attrition of mind on mind, here, to bring out any sparks from a man." But he succeeded in publishing a few poems in one of the better New York magazines, the *Round Table*. In the spring of 1867 he resigned his position, and after a brief rest in Macon, went to New York to arrange for publication of *Tiger-Lilies*. It was finally published by one of the leading firms, Hurd and Houghton, but at least partly at the author's expense—or rather that of his wealthy cousin in the city, Mr. J. F. D. Lanier.

Sidney Lanier himself soon outgrew *Tiger-Lilies*, branding it in 1869 as "a foolish book . . . of a foolish boy." As a work of art it is, indeed, silly, but it is important in the understanding of Lanier's mental development. It begins with an allegorical preface, and the first book is excessively "romantic" in the Novalis-Richter vein of the German Romantic tradition, the author's obvious source. The story tells of friendship at first sight, of a beautiful German maiden who had fled to the Smoky Mountains (with a maid and plenty of money) after her seduction by

an American in Germany, of a duel at a masquerade ball between her former and her present lover, of an Indian lover who guards her like a good angel, and of other improbable things. The best part of the romance is the second half, based at least to some extent on the author's own war experiences. Even here the literary allusion and quotation is excessive, the atmosphere is heavy with chivalry, the humorous adventures are derived from the picaresque novel; and the style is quaintly "poetic," abounding in Elizabethan conceits, puns, and florid metaphor. The only half-way convincing character is a mountaineer who speaks in untutored dialect. The other characters are mere personifications, but the main themes of the book are Beauty and Love, and the two are joined by music, for the novel ends with the transcendental conclusion that "music means harmony, harmony means love, and love means—God!"

Most Southern reviewers of *Tiger-Lilies* were highly laudatory, though the book won Lanier no money and little fame. There seemed small prospect of his earning a living with his pen. Consequently, he turned to teaching, becoming principal of an academy at Prattville, Alabama, toward the close of 1867. In December he married Mary Day, after a four-year courtship. The following month he suffered his first hemorrhage of the lungs, and in May the school closed because most parents of the students could not pay the tuition. These were truly "The Raven Days" both for the poet and the defeated Confederacy:

> O Raven Days, dark Raven Days of sorrow,
> Will ever any warm light come again?
> Will ever the lit mountains of To-morrow
> Begin to gleam across the mournful plain?

But no matter how discouraging the outlook, Lanier never gave way to despair. Even in 1868 he could dream of making his life itself a song:

> His song was only living aloud,
> His work a singing with his hand!

With no prospects of gaining a livelihood by poetry, music, or teaching, Lanier resigned himself to studying law in his father's office, and for five years he stuck doggedly to the legal profession. He continued, however, to write a few poems. "Nirvâna" (fall of 1869) expresses his resignation. Two years later we find him writing dialect poems, humorous in language, serious in the purpose of teaching the South how to meet its economic problems. But the hemorrhages returned, and Lanier was advised to spend the winter of 1872–73 in Texas. The most devoted husband and father imaginable, he was almost unbearably homesick and began in Texas, perhaps for the first time, to realize the hopelessness of his struggle. To his wife he wrote, "Ineffable poems—of music and words—torment me." And on January 10, 1873, "I have not yet dealt so much as a good sword-stroke in life." But he was not idle. He spent hours with Chaucer and Shakespeare, and under their influence began to devalue his two early favorites, Morris and Tennyson. He also took an interest in the life and history of Texas and wrote some "Letters from Texas" for the New York *World* (which earned him a mere pittance) and a long essay, published in the *Southern Magazine*, on "San Antonio de Bexar." Lanier's health improved in Texas, and possibly he might have been cured if he had remained, but with returning health came reviving ambition.

In September, 1873, Lanier went again to New York, seeking a market both for his literary productions and his music, but his hopes now rested especially on his music. He heard Theodore Thomas' concerts in Central Park Garden and hoped to secure a position as flutist in Thomas' orchestra, the most famous at that time in America, but failed even to meet the director. On his way to New York he had stopped in Baltimore, where Asger Hamerik was organizing the Peabody Orchestra. Lanier was offered a position with this orchestra as first flutist for sixty dollars a month. He played with the Peabody for several seasons, returning each spring to his family in Georgia, being unable to support his wife and children in Baltimore. During these years he found time to experiment with composition, his most successful and characteristic efforts being the tone poems for flute solo, "Black-Birds" and "Swamp-Robin." As Philip Graham says in his study of Lanier's musical compositions, "he sought to turn his music into poetry exactly as he tried to make his verse into music."

During the summer of 1874 at Griffin, Georgia, Lanier became interested in the cultivation of corn in the South instead of the soil-exhausting and price-fluctuating cotton and began the composition of his first major poem, "Corn." For the form he used the Cowleyan ode, with his own experimental tone-poem diction, but he aimed to create not merely pleasing sounds and images but also to criticize the agrarian economy of the South. His economics were sound and his diction lyrical, but their incongruity is likely to jar on the modern ear. The *Atlantic Monthly* and *Scribner's Magazine* rejected the poem but *Lippincott's* published it in February, 1875. Gibson Peacock, editor of the Baltimore *Evening Bulletin*, liked it so much that he launched a campaign for the poet and became his steadfast friend. Through Peacock,

Lanier also became acquainted with the actress Charlotte Cushman and the *literati* of Baltimore.

During the following spring Lanier wrote his most ambitious poem, "The Symphony." Again we find the tone poem and the didactic message combined. The poet attempts to imitate the sounds of the various instruments and then to combine them in orchestral effects. He was contemplating the theme as early as 1868 in the uncompleted novel in verse, "The Jacquerie," to be derived from Froissart and Michelet, perhaps the latter influencing him to take the side of the people and the former arousing his chivalric sympathy. In the fourteenth century, Lanier declared, "Trade arose & overthrew Chivalry," but "it is *now* the *gentlemen* who must arise & overthrow Trade." The idea of a modern chivalry had always appealed to the romantic and religious Lanier. In 1865 he asserted: "The days of chivalry are not gone, they are only spiritualized. . . . In these times, the knight of the nineteenth century fights, not with the trenchant sword, but with the trenchant soul."

By "Trade" Lanier meant such effects of industrialism as he had observed in West Virginia rolling-mills with the "blaring furnaces" where the sweating men labored "with only enough time betwixt tasks to eat in and sleep in,—far too little to wash in!"; and the contrast in Baltimore between the prosperous merchants and "the all-wanting, anything-grasping folk who are rogues by birth and by necessity and who suffer, suffer, throughout life." Lanier's hatred of trade, therefore, is not so much aristocratic scorn of tradesmen as Christian sympathy for the oppressed. Professor Anderson says, "As in the earlier [*i.e.,* "The Jacquerie"] so in the later poem the evil effects of trade were to be overcome not by economic reforms but by chivalry, in the most idealistic Christian interpretation of that code of unselfish service."

> And ever to solve the discords true—
> Love alone can do.

Feeling that music symbolizes the generous heart of God and the immortal longings of the Soul (Lanier's deepest conviction), he ends "Trade" with the cryptic line:

> Music is Love in search of a word.

Early in 1875 the president of the Atlantic Coast Line Railway employed the rising poet to write a guidebook to Florida. Lanier eagerly accepted the assignment because it would pay him a living salary for three months, and in the spring he left for Georgia and Florida to gather material. The book was published in the fall by Lippincott under the title

Florida: Its Scenery, and History. In a final chapter Lanier recommended the climate of Georgia and Florida "for consumptives," but he could not afford to stay long enough to prove its curative value for himself. With all his conscientious effort, *Florida* remained hack-work, but it did his growing reputation no harm. He met Bayard Taylor and other New York *literati*, and Miss Cushman invited him to Boston, where he met Longfellow and Lowell. During the winter of 1875–76 he played, as usual, with the Peabody Orchestra.

The new year brought the beginning of Lanier's harvest, both the good crop and the bad: in literature he began to receive heart-warming recognition, but continued exertion beyond his strength brought failing health and a foreshadow of the inevitable end. First, he was commissioned, through the recommendation of Bayard Taylor, to write a cantata for the Philadelphia Centennial. He completed it in January, Dudley Buck delightedly set it to music, and the performance was given in May. Against Lanier's wishes the words were published without the music, and though some critics liked it, others found the diction obscure and even unintelligible, and there was a considerable newspaper controversy, which hurt the poet more than he would admit to his friends but at least made his name familiar to the nation. During the spring he published another piece of hack-work, "Sketches of India," in *Lippincott's*. Then in the summer the overwork and excitement took its toll. He became dangerously ill. "Clover" reflects the near-despair to which he was reduced. In November Lippincott and Company printed an edition of ten of his poems which had received magazine publication, and "Corn" and "The Symphony" were widely praised by the critics. But Lanier was in no condition to enjoy his triumphs. In December he went to Tampa to recuperate.

With a new, if temporary, lease on life Lanier returned North the following summer, seeking employment from June to September in Baltimore, Washington, New York, and Philadelphia, finally resigning himself, as usual, to engagement for another season with the Peabody Orchestra. In October he was at last able to move his family to Baltimore, and for the moment the outlook seemed brighter. During the next four years, with his health even more precarious than before, he managed to turn out a prodigious amount of work, most of it experimental and more promising than actually successful, but much of it valuable pioneering. To take the least important first, he edited juvenile versions of Froissart, King Arthur, the *Mabinogion*, and Percy. He continued to play with the orchestra and sometimes to give private concerts. In "The Marshes of Glynn" he demonstrated his genius for religious poetry. Here and in his short lyrics, not in his economic tone poems, we find the best of Lanier the poet.

But Lanier was also working feverishly in several other—but related—fields, as if stimulated by a premonition of his early death. In the spring of 1878 he began lecturing on literature at the Peabody Institute, and the following year was employed by President D. C. Gilman of the newly established Johns Hopkins University to give public lectures, the first series being on Shakespeare, the second on Chaucer and Shakespeare, and the final one on the "English Novel." These lectures were given outside the regular curriculum, resembling what would later be called adult education courses.

Even before his appointment at Hopkins, Lanier was studying and writing on "The Physics of Poetry" and had already planned a book on prosody. In 1880 he managed to finish his *Science of English Verse*, a book in which he attempted to reconcile the laws of poetry and music and to establish a theory of prosody on a scientific basis. Later prosodists have usually agreed that he did not entirely succeed, but he made a positive contribution even by his attempt, and if he had lived to revise his book, his achievement might have been greater. Only by the utmost exertion of his strong will could he get through his lectures on the English Novel. In the spring of 1881 he fled hastily to the mountains of North Carolina, which had become a famous resort for consumptives, but the end could be postponed only a few months. It came on September 7, near Tryon.

Since most of Lanier's literary criticism was not published until after his death, it is appropriate to make a posthumous summary of his theories. His poetic doctrine is to be found mainly in *Music and Poetry* (1898), *Retrospects and Prospects* (1899), *Shakespeare and His Forerunners* (1908), and here and there in *The English Novel* (1883). The foundation of his poetics is his attitude toward music. To him music is the finest of all the arts, being freest "from the weight and burden of realism," and is the means by which "man relates himself . . . to the infinite." He calls upon music to lead him out of "this labyrinth of the real, the definite, the known, into . . . the region of the ideal, the infinite, the unknown . . . ." But the "mission of music is not merely to be a quietus and lullaby to the soul of a time that is restless with science." It is not so much an "escape" as a means of carrying "our emotion toward the Infinite." Poetry can accomplish this end less successfully than music, but the more musical—and "ideal"—the poetry, the more nearly it can produce the divine rapture of true music.

This theory of music led Lanier to regard the relation of prose to verse as "not the relation of the formless to the formal" but "the relation of more forms to fewer forms." His own poetry is sufficient proof that he did not wish to preserve conventional formalism, though he regarded form as the essence of poetic merit. In fact, he elevates Form to a philosophical plane:

. . . Science is the knowledge of these forms . . . Art is the creation of beautiful forms . . . Religion is the faith in the infinite Form-giver . . . Life is the control of all these forms to the satisfaction of our human needs.

The form of art, therefore, is moral as well as aesthetic, and it is not surprising that in his specific judgments he makes morality the touchstone of greatness:

. . . I think it clearly demonstrable that in all . . . [the profligate] artists there was a failure in the artistic sense precisely to the extent of the failure in apprehending those enormous laws of nature whose practical execution by the individual we call morality. You can always see where the half-way good man was but the half-way artist.

These theories sometimes led Lanier into erratic judgments. Despite the fact that he liked the sanity and vigor of *Leaves of Grass*, he felt compelled to condemn the work as poetry because he did not recognize a form in Whitman's apparent formlessness. And in his lectures on the novel, he placed George Eliot ahead of all other novelists because of her conception of Love as the organic idea of moral order, and he admired Bulwer-Lytton because his "gentleman is always given as a very manful and Christian being." On the other hand, he could read none of the novels of Richardson, Fielding, Smollett, and Sterne "without feeling as if my soul had been in the rain, draggled, muddy, miserable." He even compared their works to gunpowder, nitroglycerine, and poison, and confessed that "if I had my way with these classic books I would blot them from the face of the earth." And it is not surprising that the editor who expurgated Malory for schoolboys could not stomach Zola and "naturalism." But his high conception of the functions of the artist, and his insistence on judging the work in its relation to life, still give his critical theory a universality and importance that cannot be denied. His theory is important also to the student, for we find in it both the limitations and the strength of Sidney Lanier as a literary master.

EMILY DICKINSON (1830–1886)

Today Emily Dickinson is almost universally recognized as one of the literary giants of nineteenth-century American literature, but when this frail little lady died in 1886 only a few of her unpublished poems were known to a small group of friends, and the general public had no knowledge whatever of her existence. Three poems had been published anonymously, but of course they attracted little attention. Hundreds of better ones had been accumulating for half a lifetime in her quiet home in a small New England village. The manuscripts were disorganized, many well-nigh illegible, for she had done nothing to make publication easy or likely. But fortunately most of them were finally more or less deciphered and printed, though the circumstances and methods of much of the editing have not yet given us a complete or an accurate text. One of the greatest evidences of her genius is the fact that despite the piecemeal, erratic publication of her poems, Emily Dickinson's reputation has steadily grown since the appearance of the first collection of her verse in 1890. During the past decade several books with new poems and information have appeared to increase her literary stature, and it is now safe to predict that her reputation will continue to increase. To appreciate this prediction we need to know not only the story of her growth as a poet but also the story of the editing of her poems.

Emily Dickinson was born December 10, 1830, in the little town of Amherst, Massachusetts, in a comfortable brick house on Main Street built by her grandfather, a lawyer and town leader who had staked his own fortune on the founding of Amherst College. Her father, Edward Dickinson, followed closely in his father's footsteps, serving as trustee and treasurer of the college until his death in 1874, engaging in a lucrative law practice, becoming a member of the State Legislature and Senate and finally of Congress. All sources of information testify to his upright character and success as a citizen and politician, but the biographers do not agree on his personal qualities as a father. His family was devoted to him, but some biographers think he was puritanical and bigoted. His younger daughter, Lavinia, claimed late in life that he prevented his two girls from entertaining young men in their home, though Emily's letters do not corroborate this accusation. Mrs. Millicent Todd Bingham, who as a neighbor knew the Dickinson home when she was a young girl, does not remember that he ever smiled. But Professor George F. Whicher, who has taught for many years at Amherst College and has talked with people who remember the Dickinson family, thinks the Squire was no more stern than other fathers of the time, and that he was a friendly and likable man.

The town was far more conservative than Unitarian Cambridge, and many vestiges of Calvinistic Puritanism still lingered, as they did in many a remote New England village. Card games and dancing were frowned upon; there were few concerts, and no theatres. Going to church was one of the main social amusements, and the Dickinsons regularly attended the Congregational Church, though Edward Dickinson did not join until 1850, during an old-fashioned "revival." One of the most serious purposes of the College was to send out missionaries to all parts of the world, a purpose which strongly influenced the town itself. Squire Dickinson was not an anachronism as he walked impressively with shiny beaver and gold-headed cane down the streets of Amherst.

Of Mr. Dickinson's wife, Emily Norcross, there are few records. Emily said cryptically that she did "not care for thought," and all indications are that she was an intellectual nonentity, completely dominated by her strong-minded husband and her clever children. During her last years she was an invalid, and Emily devotedly helped take care of her.

Squire Dickinson's only son, Austin, grew up to resemble his father, whose place he took in the community and the college. To strangers he also had an austere appearance, but all members of his family adored him, though when he and his father were together they quarreled. After teaching in Boston and taking a law degree at Harvard, he returned to practice law in Amherst. But in his marriage to Susan Gilbert, daughter of a too convivial tavern keeper, he brought misery upon himself and his sisters, who lived next door, where he often fled, in Emily's words, from the "Vesuvius at home."

Concerning Lavinia the testimony is confusing. She is said to have been an attractive child; but as the years passed, she lived only for her garden, her cats, and Emily, whom she worshipped. Spinsterhood apparently soured her countenance and embittered her mind. Mrs. Bingham remembers her as a neurotic old hag, but Professor Whicher, more charitably, thinks she was not without charm even in her old age.

Emily herself, though older than her sister, seems to have been the pampered pet of the family. Even though Austin and Lavinia thought her a genius, they always protected her like a child, and perhaps they delayed her emotional maturity. To judge by her portrait, she retained a certain girlish charm into her womanhood, but she is said never to have been pretty —with the possible exception of her red hair and brown eyes. Perhaps as a schoolgirl she attempted to compensate for her physical deficiency by cultivating her wit and her gift of verbal expression. Her schoolmates remembered her especially for her fun-loving sociability, her satirical literary compositions, and her clever letters. There are no indications, however, that she was abnormal or maladjusted. In her juvenile letters she speaks often of death, but the religious atmosphere which surrounded her childhood reminded her of the seriousness of life and the need of preparing for the world to come. She attended the Academy founded by her grandfather and was then enrolled for a year at Mount Holyoke Seminary, rigorously presided over by the famous woman educator, Mary Lyon, who combined training of the mind with saving of the soul. Emily attempted to "find grace," and at times became deeply disturbed that she could not, but she remained, in her own words, "one of the lingering bad ones." She always liked her teachers and did well in her studies, both in the Academy and Seminary, but was frequently absent from the classroom on account of poor health. Her father decided that she was not strong enough for a second year in college, and Emily returned to the protection of her home in Amherst, where she spent the remainder of her life except for a couple of months in Washington and Philadelphia while her father was in Congress and, later, two prolonged visits to Boston to have her eyes treated.

To all outward appearances Emily Dickinson lived in Amherst as quietly as a nun, becoming gradually more shy and reserved until she finally became a complete recluse. During the last fifteen years of her life she dressed entirely in white, saw no one except members of her own family and occasionally an intimate friend, sought diversion only in her garden, and assiduously worked on her poems. Probably in 1863

she suffered something like a nervous breakdown. In a letter to a cousin with whom she corresponded regularly she alluded to "a snarl in the brain which don't unravel yet, and that old nail in my breast pricked me. . . ." The following year she wrote to another correspondent, "I work in my prison and make guests for myself."

What experiences or emotional shocks brought about this retirement from the world and focused Emily Dickinson's attention so almost exclusively upon the private drama of her mind we can only conjecture from the evidence of her poems and her letters, but at least the outlines of her spiritual biography are beginning to emerge. In 1862 she wrote to T. W. Higginson:

When a little girl, I had a friend who taught me Immortality; but venturing too near, himself, he never returned. Soon after, my tutor died, and for several years my lexicon was my only companion. Then I found one more, but he was not contented I be his scholar, so he left the land.

Biographers have sought for years to supply names and dates for these tantalizing allusions. There now seems little doubt that the friend who taught her "Immortality" but ventured too near himself was a young man who studied in her father's law office during the winter of 1847–48, Benjamin Franklin Newton. Ten years older than Emily, he was more widely read, and introduced her to stimulating literature, smuggling books to her of which her father disapproved. The following winter he returned to his home town, Worcester, where he married in 1851 and died two years later. Whether or not Ben Newton meant anything else to Emily Dickinson, it was probably he who gave her confidence in her poetic ability. In another letter to Colonel Higginson, from whom she had sought literary criticism, she confessed:

Your letter gave no drunkenness, because I tasted rum before. . . . My dying tutor told me that he would like to live till I had been a poet, but Death was much of mob as I could master, then.

The same year that Ben Newton died another young man who had actually been Emily Dickinson's teacher, Leonard Humphrey, also died, and several of the poems which refer to the "two I lost" probably express her grief of this period. Isolated from literary circles and competent judges of her own productions, Emily was always hungry for companionship with minds capable of tutoring her own, as in her turning to Higginson for advice.

Neither of these "tutors" of Emily Dickinson's youth, however, was responsible for the great crisis of her life, which apparently reached a climax some time in 1862. This lover—and the language of many of the poems is unmistakably that of love—was the "atom preferred to all the lists of clay," the "fugitive, whom to know was life." But it was a love "in vision and in veto." In the spring of 1862 she referred to him as having "left the land," and on April 25 of the same year she wrote to Colonel Higginson of "a terror since September, I could tell to none."

Various biographers have advanced candidates 'for the rôle of the lover. Lavinia, perhaps in an attempt to counteract some of the wild gossip circulating in Amherst, told a romantic story of Emily's infatuation with a classmate, George Gould, disapproved by Squire Dickinson, and Genevieve Taggard has elaborated this conjectural romance. But the known facts do not corroborate the hypothesis. Another biographer, Josephine Pollitt, has argued that the man was Major Edward B. Hunt, husband of Emily's friend, Helen Hunt, though Major Hunt is known to have had a marked dislike for Miss Dickinson. Mrs. Bianchi attempted to treat the problem in vague and confused imagery, but without shedding much light. Professor Whicher has given the most convincing solution in his identification of the man as Reverend Charles Wadsworth, a distinguished Presbyterian minister in Philadelphia whom Emily met in May, 1854, during her trip to Washington and Philadelphia. Still grieving over Ben Newton's death, she probably sought spiritual guidance from Reverend Wadsworth. At any rate we know that she was greatly impressed by this famous pastor and carried on a correspondence with him. He visited her in Amherst some time in 1860, and there may have been a second visit. In the spring of 1862 he accepted a church in California and "left the land" by ship, the sea route by way of Panama still being the easiest means of travel between the Eastern Seaboard and the West Coast. Emily's "terror," however, had been with her since the previous September, though nothing is known of the specific details. That the distinguished clergyman was philandering seems improbable, and he may have been entirely unaware of his emotional effect upon his young friend in Amherst. When he met her in 1854, he was forty and Emily twenty-three years old, a considerable discrepancy in age. Moreover, the Reverend Wadsworth was married to a congenial wife. Nothing remained for his young lover but to hide her pain and find such relief as she could in her poems. Professor Whicher says that "Emily Dickinson's friendship with Wadsworth, unlike her earlier friendship with Ben Newton, was not primarily an intellectual affair. It taught her all that

a woman can learn who gives herself spiritually and imaginatively to the man of her choice, and more than she needed to know of suffering."

One cannot say that Emily Dickinson's hopeless infatuation for someone she could never marry made her a poet, for she was a poet before she met Reverend Charles Wadsworth; but, as a poet, she did gain much from the experience. Her agonizing frustration and self-pity passed into more objective analysis of her own states of mind until she was finally able to dramatize her experience in symbols of universal significance. Mental suffering taught her also to see with magnified intensity the simple beauties of nature in her own backyard. At times she could declare, "I find ecstasy in living; the mere sense of living is joy enough." She might, in fact, be called the poet of ecstasy, for her poems are nearly all ecstatic—either with joy or pain. And she was not unaware of or indifferent to the suffering of others. War she called "an oblique place," and she was almost prostrated with grief over the casualties of Amherst men on the battlefield. Her actual contact with the life of the nation during the fateful years of the Civil War was remote, but her own moods during the sixties and seventies were often analogous to those of the country at large.

It has often been thought that Emily Dickinson's own private tragedy prevented her from publishing, but actually, like almost every creative artist, she longed for an audience, and her failure to find one in her own lifetime was due more to her short-sighted advisers than to her own inclinations. She sent poems and solicited criticism from Col. T. W. Higginson, one of the popular authors and critics of the day, from Samuel Bowles, owner of the Springfield *Republican*, from Josiah Holland, associated with Bowles and first editor of *Scribner's Magazine*, and from Thomas Niles of the prominent Roberts Brothers publishing firm. All recognized Emily Dickinson's originality and claimed to enjoy her poetry, but they thought it too fragile and eccentric for the literary public of the day. What chiefly bothered them were her liberties in style and grammar. Colonel Higginson patiently corrected what he regarded as her vagaries, but Emily could not be instructed. Even after her death, when her poetry had been rescued from oblivion by Mrs. Todd, Higginson was still puzzled:

The impression of a wholly new and original poetic genius was as distinct on my mind at the first reading of these four poems [sent to him for criticism] as it is now, after thirty years of further knowledge; and with it came the problem never yet solved, what place ought to be assigned in literature to what is so remarkable, yet so elusive of criticism. The bee himself did not evade the schoolboy more than she evaded me; and even to this day I still stand somewhat bewildered, like the boy.

All one can say is that Emily Dickinson was unfortunate in turning to the men she did for advice. Since her poems quickly found an audience in 1890, they probably would have earlier.

The one person who did try to persuade Emily to give her poems to the world was her childhood friend, Mrs. Helen Hunt (later Mrs. Jackson). In the early 1870's she returned to Amherst and tried to counteract the advice of the Higginsonian "tutors," but without success. Exactly what went on during the many hours while she was closeted with the timid poetess we do not know, but presumably it was not without Emily's permission that Mrs. Hunt used her experiences in the last of the Saxe Holm stories, "Esther Wynn's Love Letters," which describe letters and poems revealing "the whole soul of a woman" like Emily Dickinson, and in the anonymous *Mercy Philbrick's Choice*. To people who knew Emily Dickinson, the novel seemed almost like the work of the poet herself. An anonymous writer to the Springfield *Republican* on July 25, 1878, suggested that the author was not Helen Hunt Jackson, as generally supposed, but another Amherst writer. Mrs. Mabel Loomis Todd, however, after a thorough investigation, decided that Emily did not write *Mercy Philbrick's Choice*, a conclusion supported by the internal evidence of style. But it is significant that Emily's friendship for Mrs. Jackson did not waver after the publication of these two apparently fictionized versions of her own biography. In 1878 Mrs. Jackson also published one of Emily's poems, "Success is Counted Sweetest," in an anthology, *A Masque of Poets*, though not without tampering with the diction. Possibly she hoped that interest in this poem would encourage her friend to stop concealing her genius. But if so, the stratagem failed, and Mrs. Jackson soon turned her attention to the American Indian, the subject for which she is best known.

Emily Dickinson's brother and sister and her few intimate friends knew that she had been composing poems for years, but after her death in 1886 Lavinia seems to have been astonished at the number of manuscripts which her sister had left. Many of the earlier poems had been tied together in little bundles of half a dozen sheets, but later compositions had been scratched down hurriedly with pencil on odd scraps of paper and tossed helter-skelter into a pile. Emily had left no instructions whatever for the disposition of these literary remains, but Lavinia was determined to publish them as quickly as possible. She herself knew nothing whatever of editorial matters and realized that she must have assistance. To whom could she turn?

Next door was her sister-in-law, Susan Gilbert Dickinson. However, the fact that for years Austin had been fleeing from his own home to sanctuary with his sisters would not dispose Sue to help a member of the detested house. Despite this fact, Lavinia did apparently broach the subject to Mrs. Austin Dickinson, but aside from the family feud, Susan had literary ambitions for her daughter, Martha, and she thought that if anyone in the family was to be known as a poet, it should be her own daughter. Martha herself had written satirical skits about her "queer aunt Emily." Obviously no help could be found in this direction. Lavinia appealed to Colonel Higginson, but he pleaded lack of time, omitting to explain his lack of faith in the financial success of an edition of Emily's poems.

Finally, however, Lavinia discovered a potential editor in Mrs. Mabel Loomis Todd, the brilliant wife of a young instructor in astronomy at Amherst College. Mrs. Todd, realizing the work involved in deciphering, copying, and arranging the poems, was reluctant to accept so arduous a task, but she finally consented to undertake it with the assistance of Colonel Higginson. Consequently, in 1890 the first volume of *Poems by Emily Dickinson* was published by Roberts Brothers in Boston. Colonel Higginson wrote a Preface in which he stated that the selection of Miss Dickinson's poems was "published to meet the desire of her personal friends, and especially of her surviving sister." Probably no one was more surprised than he that the public liked them too. Mrs. Todd, therefore, began at once preparing a second selection, which was published the following year. Since the chronology of the poems was unknown, and could be only vaguely guessed at from the style of handwriting or the kind of paper used, Mrs. Todd arranged them by theme, about the only unity possible, and all later editors have loosely followed this precedent. The order in the first edition was: Life—Love—Nature—Time and Eternity. The editors made a few emendations, particularly to satisfy Colonel Higginson, but Mrs. Todd strove for as much accuracy as possible.

The sales of the two collections of *Poems* made a volume of letters seem desirable. With considerable difficulty, Mrs. Todd managed to secure enough letters for two volumes, which were published in 1894. Then she brought out a third collection of *Poems* in 1896. The *Letters* also contained 102 poems, and the total published in 1896 (including those during Emily's lifetime and one released by Sue from manuscripts which Lavinia did not know she had) was 555. Then suddenly all publication ceased, until Martha Dickinson Bianchi, the niece who had written the satirical skits of her "queer aunt," brought out in 1914 a collection called *The Single Hound*. The story back of this hiatus in the publication of Emily Dickinson's remarkable literary remains was unknown to the public until 1945, when Mrs. Millicent Todd Bingham, daughter of the first editor, gave the surprising details in *Ancestors' Brocades*. For her hundreds of hours of work in editing the three collections of *Poems* Mrs. Todd received no compensation whatever, all royalties having gone to Lavinia Dickinson. Emily's brother, Austin, understanding the labor involved and Lavinia's greedy attitude, gave Mrs. Todd a small strip of land as a token payment. His sister signed the transfer of title, but after Austin's death in 1895 she chafed over the loss of family property. In 1898, perhaps under the instigation of her malicious sister-in-law, Lavinia brought suit to recover this insignificant piece of real estate. Stories were spread of intimacy between Mrs. Todd and the late Mr. Dickinson and the whole town took sides in the legal battle. At the trial in 1898 Lavinia gave conflicting and inconsistent testimony, but she won the lawsuit. Mrs. Todd, understandably, felt that she had been betrayed, and she promptly locked up the copies of the poems which she had made for future editions. Lavinia, who more than anyone else longed to have them published, knew no one to whom she could turn for further help. She herself died the following year, promising her friends that she would hide the poems where Sue could never find them.

It is most unfortunate that these ugly stories of jealousy and hatred are entangled with the biography of Emily Dickinson, but one cannot understand the confused text of her poems without knowing something of how it became so confused—and some critics also think that the charged atmosphere in which the poet herself lived may explain many of the puzzles in her own life. After Lavinia's death, Austin's family became the heirs of the manuscripts. No more poems were printed, however, until Susan Dickinson died in 1913. The following year her daughter, Martha (now Mrs. Alexander E. Bianchi), began a new series of publication. After *The Single Hound* in 1914 came *Life and Letters* in 1924. The copyright on Mrs. Todd's edition had lapsed and Mrs. Bianchi renewed it in her own name, and then unpardonably garbled the text. In 1924 Mrs. Bianchi also published what she called *Complete Poems*, though they were not complete (even of poems hitherto published), and in 1929 she added another volume of *Further Poems*, supposedly recently discovered. Readers began to wonder how many poems still remained unpublished, and a partial answer came in 1936 with a new volume called *Unpublished Poems*. Some critics even asked whether all these "new" poems were genuine, but Mrs. Todd told her daughter that *Further Poems* were. Her daughter wondered how she knew that these poems were genuine, and that many had not been correctly printed. Mrs. Todd finally unlocked the copies of the manuscripts which had been in her possession before the lawsuit started, and her daughter began to learn for the first time why publication had ceased in 1896. Before Mrs. Todd's death she had managed to edit the *Letters*, restoring names deleted by request of the recipients and adding some passages which had also been withheld from the original edition. Mrs. Todd's revised and corrected *Letters of Emily Dickinson* was published in 1931 and is now the only authentic edition.

Mrs. Bingham found among her mother's copies of the original manuscripts several hundred poems which, for all Mrs. Bianchi's activities, had never been published. These she presented in 1945 in one of the finest collections we have, *Bolts of Melody*, containing 666 poems, including some fragments. Whether all of Emily Dickinson's poems are now in print is not known. Mrs. Bingham does not think so. Moreover, the manuscripts which Mrs. Bianchi used are not available to scholars for checking with the versions that have been printed. We probably have, therefore, the bulk of Emily Dickinson's total production, but unorganized, much of it unverified for accuracy, and most of it undated. In addition, the quality is uneven, but it will be time for sifting after a full and accurate text has been established. All members of the Dickinson family are now extinct, and perhaps in the course of time it will be possible for lovers of poetry to study Emily Dickinson as they are now able to study Chaucer or Spenser in reliable texts.

A final note needs to be added about Emily Dickinson's form. Early readers found her inaccurate rimes and irregular lines puzzling. After *The Single Hound* appeared, Miss Amy Lowell's circle of free verse poets championed Emily Dickinson as a forerunner of their own experiments. But we now know that some of the unconventional structure in the Bianchi texts was due to incompetent editing. Emily's manuscripts must be a trial to any editor, and some of them are worse than that—especially those of the poet's later years, when she often wrote with a pencil on scraps of paper of odd sizes and shapes. Neither the punctuation (or lack of it) nor the line divisions are a safe guide to the pattern of the poem. On careful examination it will be discovered that the majority of the poems are in iambic meter, usually riming *abab* or *abcb*. Some of the poems which Mrs. Bianchi printed in irregular form can be rearranged in this conventional form, with obvious gain in clarity. It is true, however, that Emily was often satisfied with a faint approximation of a rime instead of a full rime, and it is particularly noticeable that the more ironic poems seem to strike something like a discord in the rime. There was probably a psychological reason for her variations from convention, as with John Donne or Gerard Manley Hopkins, both of whom she resembles at times. Like Donne she wrote in a time of intellectual contradiction, pulled one way by faith and another by contemporary actuality. Emily Dickinson lived through the age of Emersonian optimism into the age of pessimism of Mark Twain and Henry Adams. Her links with Emerson were recognized by her earliest readers, but she also had much in common with Mark Twain, in her exaggerated metaphors, her ironic humor, and her keen sense of human frailty. Like Henry Adams, too, she sensed, in her own frustration, the shadow of a world tragedy. Despite her limited experience, Emily Dickinson was also a spokesman of nineteenth-century America.

NOTE: Since the above essay was written Thomas H. Johnson has edited from the manuscripts, now in the Houghton Library at Harvard University, an authoritative edition: *The Poems of Emily Dickinson*, Harvard University Press, 1955. In *Complete Poems of Emily Dickinson* the same editor gives his transcriptions in one volume, without manuscript variants or notes: Boston, 1960.

SAMUEL LANGHORNE CLEMENS (1835–1910)
(Mark Twain)

No other major American writer has had more extensive and varied experience with the life, the regions, and the different levels of American society than Samuel Langhorne Clemens, known to the world as "Mark Twain." He was born in a frontier town on the banks of the Mississippi River, grew up as journeyman printer, became a steamboat pilot on the river during the flush times before the Civil War, served for a few weeks as a soldier on the Confederate side, then migrated to mining towns in Nevada, where he prospected for gold and shared the feverish dreams of immediate and vast wealth which haunted practically everyone in the West. There he became professional journalist, humorist, and lecturer—activities which eventually brought him not only the wealth which he had failed to find in Nevada mines, but also world fame, and in old age the rôle of national oracle.

Meanwhile the slovenly, semicultured, frontier humorist married a refined and wealthy girl in the East, where he spent most of the second half of his life. He founded a large publishing house, invested a fortune in an unsuccessful typesetting machine, finally went bankrupt, and then, at the age of 56, set out gallantly on a lecture trip around the globe in order to pay off every cent of indebtedness (for which he was no longer legally responsible). He not only succeeded in this determination but also created a new fortune, so that in his final years he was worth several hundred thousand dollars.

But financial success and millions of admirers did not bring Mark Twain lasting happiness or peace of mind. He was always irritated by stupidity, even his own, and infuriated by worldly sham and hypocrisy. In old age his many disappointments, especially the death of loved ones, brought him to the brink of despair and confirmed the pessimistic philosophy which had been growing on him since his youth. It is no wonder that a life so varied and contradictory and a personality equally puzzling have exercised the biographers. To his contemporaries, though most of them loved him, he was merely a literary clown. Before his death, however, a few critics like William

Dean Howells realized that he was a writer of major stature. Later came the psychological analysis of his genius. To Van Wyck Brooks he was a thwarted literary artist, frustrated by the crudity of his frontier background and later by the artificial refinement of his wife and New England culture. To Bernard DeVoto, an authority on the history of the frontier, Mark Twain drew his vitality from the Mississippi and the West. The controversy is still far from settled, though recent biographers and critics lean more toward DeVoto than Brooks.

Some of the contradictions in the remarkable life of Mark Twain might be traced back to his ancestry. Both his father and his mother were English in origin, and on both sides there was lingering pride in remote aristocratic pretensions. His father believed himself descended from a Clemens who sat as a judge in the trial of Charles I, and Mark Twain liked to believe that "he did what he could toward reducing the list of crowned shams of his day." His mother's family, the Lamptons, thought themselves descended from the family which inhabited the castle of Lampton, in Durham, for nine hundred years, though her son declared that he "never heard her refer in any way to her gilded ancestry when any person not a member of the family was present, for she had good American sense." But these stories indicate that a conviction of inner superiority persisted, a compensation for these Americans struggling for existence in a frontier economy. Such dreams led one of the Lamptons, the original of Colonel Mulberry Sellers in *The Gilded Age*, to live constantly in a world of fantastic illusion, and even the mature Mark Twain was forever hatching new schemes which he expected to make him a millionaire.

John Marshall Clemens was born in Virginia in 1798. When he was seven years old his father was killed, and the family moved to Kentucky, where the mother remarried. In 1823 John married Jane Lampton, reputed belle of the community. A respectable Virginian would choose a profession instead of a trade, and John chose law, which he attempted to practice in Gainsborough, Tennessee, on the Cumberland River. There his first child, Orion, was born in 1825. Then John moved to Jamestown, where he became circuit clerk of the county court, but he was soon reduced to keeping a general store. While in Tennessee he managed to scrape together $500, with which he bought 75,000 acres of land, believing thereby he had insured the future wealth of his children. Eventually the land was worth all that John Clemens predicted—and more—for in addition to the valuable timber and fertile soil which it contained, both coal and oil were discovered on it—but not until long after it had passed out of the hands of the Clemenses.

After several moves, John Clemens left Tennessee in 1835 for a small frontier town on the Mississippi River—Florida, Missouri—where his brother-in-law, John Quarles, owned a farm and a general store, descriptions of which have been preserved in the lyric prose of Mark Twain's *Autobiography*. There Samuel was born November 30, 1835, a seven-months baby, not expected to live. Four years later the family moved to another town up the river, Hannibal, where John Clemens died in 1847, leaving a wife with four children. The oldest, Orion, had learned the printing trade, and he tried, without much success, to support the family with his printing office and a weekly newspaper, employing at one time his two brothers, Sam and Henry. In his brother's office Sam learned to set type, got his first experience at writing for the public—some of his experiments being crude satires on a rival editor—thereby laying the foundation of his later success as journalist and author. From 1853–56 he worked as journeyman printer in St. Louis, New York, Philadelphia, Keokuk, and Cincinnati, and occasionally got letters and humorous sketches published in various papers.

While employed again by his brother, who had moved to Keokuk, Sam decided—or later thought he had—to take a trip up the Amazon River. After finding a fifty-dollar bill which no one claimed, he set out —but, curiously, by way of Cincinnati, where he stopped to work in another printing office. In the spring of 1857 he started by boat toward New Orleans, but before arriving there he was fired with the ambition to be a steamboat pilot, and Horace Bixby reluctantly accepted him as an apprentice. Later in *Life on the Mississippi* Mark Twain described the nightmare of learning to pilot a large boat through the ever-shifting channels of the river. Traffic on the Mississippi was booming. The pilots could earn as much as four hundred dollars a month. Samuel Clemens also enjoyed the glamour and the authority of being a pilot. But all this ended when the Union army blockaded the river, and after the war steamboats could not meet the competition of the railroads.

For a few weeks Sam marched around his county with an informal company of amateur soldiers loyal to the Confederate side, but the group soon disintegrated. Meanwhile Orion, who had campaigned for Lincoln, was appointed Secretary for the Nevada Territory. Sam went with him by stagecoach to Nevada, a rugged trip which Mark Twain later narrated, with burlesque exaggeration, in *Roughing It*. In Nevada the brothers quickly caught the gambling fever of the mining towns, but after spending all his savings Sam finally accepted a position on the Virginia City *Enterprise*. Ostensibly he was a reporter, but he was expected to specialize in the kind of hoax, broad farce, and violent humor which delighted a rough masculine community. In this employment Samuel Clemens adopted the pen-name "Mark Twain," which was to become famous within a few years.

Forced to leave Nevada because he had foolishly challenged an editor to a duel, thereby violating a newly enacted law, he went to San Francisco, where he found employment as a reporter on the *Morning Call*. There he was also associated with Bret Harte and Artemus Ward, whom he had met in Nevada. Reporting proved irksome, but Mark Twain enjoyed contributing to two literary magazines, *Golden Era* and the *Californian*, each edited for a time by Bret Harte. In 1865 "The Jumping Frog" yarn was published in New York and was reprinted and quoted throughout the country. Suddenly he was famous.

After a visit to Nevada, in 1866, he made a trip to Hawaii, then known as the Sandwich Islands, for the Sacramento *Union*. On his return he gave his first public lecture in San Francisco, with such success that he would never again need to depend entirely on journalism for a livelihood. His Missouri drawl, his engaging personality, and the dramatic tricks of humorous delivery which he had learned from Artemus Ward, all contributed to his becoming one of the most popular speakers in America's history. On the stage, or in the uninhibited flow of his imaginative conversation, the full power of his genius made itself manifest. Some critics think there was a considerable leakage between his oral and written expression. But even his literary style, as he himself explained in his *Autobiography*, grew out of his knowledge of oral speech.

After a whirlwind lecture success in California, Mark Twain decided in 1867 to visit his family by way of the Isthmus of Nicaragua, Key West, and New York, meanwhile writing travel letters for the

Alta Californian. This trip was a turning point in his life. In New York City a visit to the Holy Land on the *Quaker City* was being highly advertised, and the *Alta Californian* readily agreed to send Mark Twain along as a reporter, permitting him also to write some letters for New York papers. These accounts, revised, formed the substance of Mark Twain's second book, *The Innocents Abroad,* published in 1869. Both the letters and the book were almost phenomenally successful, partly because they were genuinely funny and partly because the author's aesthetic taste and common-sense skepticism were on the cultural level of most of his readers. Having seen no art except chromos and cheap paintings, he found little to admire in the old masters. Consequently he ridiculed them with the same raucous humor which he had turned against the sham sentiments and pious hypocrisies of his fellow passengers. Some ministers and church members were offended, but most of his readers, who had no more respect for the past and ancient civilizations than he, were highly amused. In many ways *Innocents Abroad* was truer than its author could have realized.

One of the passengers aboard the *Quaker City,* Charles Langdon, from Elmira, New York, showed Mark Twain a picture of his sister, Olivia, and he immediately fell in love with the image. Back in New York, he secured an invitation to visit the wealthy and conservative family, which was at first shocked by his unconventional manners, but he married Olivia on February 2, 1870. Mark Twain thought a married man should settle down, and, with Mr. Langdon's help, bought a third interest in the Buffalo *Express.* As a wedding gift the generous father also gave his daughter and son-in-law a fine house in Buffalo. But nothing went right. The first child, a boy, was born prematurely, and Olivia was ill for a long time. Mark Twain soon became bored with his routine editorial duties, and the Clemenses were thoroughly unhappy. Selling his interest in the paper at a loss, Mark Twain moved his family to Hartford, Connecticut, where he brought out his third book.

In this book, *Roughing It,* he attempted to capitalize on his trip to Nevada as he had done with the excursion on the *Quaker City.* He could recall few of his experiences, however, until he borrowed Orion's diary; then he freely invented and drew upon the tall-tale humor which he had heard in the West. The book is notable, however, because it shows how completely Mark Twain had mastered the most effective trick of successful humor, that of making himself the supreme ass of the asinine human race. This rôle he

played with increasing mastery until his final bitter and satirical assaults on the very conditions of human existence.

Meanwhile joy and sorrow were coming in quick contrast. In the spring of 1872, the second child, Susan, was born, and a few weeks later the boy, Langdon, died. Perhaps the loss of his son turned the father's thoughts to his own boyhood days in Missouri, for at this time he began planning the story which three years later was published as *Tom Sawyer,* probably the best-loved account of boyhood life in all literature (rivaled only by *Huckleberry Finn*). In 1872 Mark Twain went to London to copyright *Roughing It,* to prevent English publishers from pirating the book. In England his personality captivated nearly everyone he met, and he was lionized like an international celebrity, which indeed he was already becoming.

The following year the Clemens family again settled down in Hartford, and Mark Twain collaborated with Charles Dudley Warner, a neighbor and friend, on *The Gilded Age,* a title which has given a name to a period in American history. The collaborators attempted to satirize the social and economic evils of the scandalous reconstruction years following the Civil War. But the story was melodramatic, and the satire was scattered in too many directions to be effective. This is one of Mark Twain's least successful books; yet it does contain one unforgettable character, Colonel Mulberry Sellers, an American Mr. Micawber, though actually modeled on James Lampton, a cousin of Mark Twain's mother.

In the same year, 1873, the whole family went to England, but Clemens brought Olivia and Susan back when Olivia became homesick, then returned to complete the necessary residence for an English copyright of *The Gilded Age.* This trip, like the former, was a continuous round of personal triumphs. Home again in 1874, he gave more lectures, completed *Tom Sawyer* in 1875, and collaborated with Bret Harte on a play, *Ah Sin,* which failed on the stage. Like his friend Howells, he never learned to write for the theatre, though he tried several times.

Perhaps the only time in his life when Mark Twain ever failed as a lecturer was his attempt to burlesque the literary reputations of the leading New England authors on the occasion of Whittier's birthday dinner, December 17, 1877. Though intending no offense, the humorist took personal liberties with reputations and idiosyncrasies which did not amuse the Boston "Brahmins."

During the 1880 decade Mark Twain published five major works: *A Tramp Abroad* (1880), based on a walking trip through the Black Forest and Switzerland; *The Prince and the Pauper* (1882), a story of mistaken identity in Tudor times; *Life on the Mississippi* (1883), a hodge-podge of reminiscences, tall tales, and serious essays on the life and region of the Mississippi River, parts of which had been published in the *Atlantic Monthly* in 1875; *The Adventures of Huckleberry Finn* (1884), that companion romance to *Tom Sawyer*; and finally *A Connecticut Yankee in King Arthur's Court* (1889). All these works reveal the author's characteristic literary weaknesses and virtues. In all, the unity of plot and structure is uneven. One of the best stories in *A Tramp Abroad* is "Baker's Blue Jay Yarn," an American tall tale, having nothing to do with Europe. The confused identity of *The Prince and the Pauper* is a melodramatic motif from the Victorian novel, though the device appealed to Mark Twain because it suggested to him man's irresponsibility for his actions, a device used again in *The Tragedy of Pudd'nhead Wilson* (1894) and anticipating the essay "What is Man?" The first half of *Life on the Mississippi* contains some of Mark Twain's finest writing, but the latter half is padded with newspaper clippings and odds and ends. Halfway through a book, Mark Twain usually bogged down—an observation which applies even to *Huckleberry Finn*. And in some ways the author of the *Connecticut Yankee* had grown very little intellectually since *Innocents Abroad*. He had little understanding of institutions, and his characters, no matter what the century or country, were simply Americans whom he had known in Missouri, the West, or Eastern cities. His view of the world was in some aspects always provincial.

But perhaps it is not important that structurally *Huckleberry Finn* is a poor novel. It has vitality, inventiveness of a rich imagination, and by some kind of literary magic it transfers living speech to the printed page. The same is true of *Life on the Mississippi*. And all these books contain penetrating social criticism, from the realistic portrayal of squalor and degeneration on the lower Mississippi to political autocracy and ecclesiastical humbug in Europe.

The 1890 decade was a critical one for Mark Twain. His publishing house, after making huge profits in the 1880's, was now running heavily into debt. This, the money he was spending on the Paige typesetting machine, and the $35,000 a year required for living expenses, were driving him to financial ruin. In 1891 he decided he could live more cheaply abroad than at home and settled his family in Berlin. He was too worried to write anything of consequence. In 1894 a new business manager settled with his credi-

tors for fifty cents on the dollar, but Mark Twain insisted on paying off every cent of his indebtedness. As one means of raising the money he undertook a world lecture tour, though his health scarcely seemed equal to the trip. Leaving Jean and Sue in America, he set out with his wife and Clara, traveling to Australia, India, and finally returning to England. In every country he was greeted like a hero. The trip was a great success. But in August Susan died of meningitis, and he soon learned that his youngest daughter, Jean, was an epileptic. About this time his brother Orion also died. Early in 1898 he was informed that the proceeds of his lecturing and the sale of his book about the trip, *Following the Equator*, had freed him from debt. But he was too bitter over his personal losses to enjoy the good news. During these years of suffering he produced two serious works, both in defense of women who he thought had been wronged. One was his *Defense of Harriet Shelley* and the other *Personal Recollections of Joan of Arc* (1896). His feeling for Joan of Arc was a mystic adoration, and he published the work anonymously for fear that the public would not read it with sufficient seriousness under his name.

In Vienna, in 1898, he gave expression to his bitterness by working on his would-be philosophic essay, "What is Man?" (printed in 1906), which expounds a theory of extreme determinism that he had been developing for years. The argument was that man is responsible for nothing he does. His actions are the outcome of his "make" and his conditioning. It has been called Calvinism without God. He also completed his most brilliant and most pessimistic short story, "The Man that Corrupted Hadleyburg." He worked, too, on the longer story finally published after his death as *The Mysterious Stranger*, one of the bitterest fables ever written in the guise of a children's story.

From England Mark Twain viewed the Boer War with mixed feelings. He sympathized with the Boers, but declared prophetically that "England must not fall; it would mean an inundation of Russian and German political degradation which would envelop the globe and steep it in a sort of Middle-Age night and slavery which would last until Christ comes again."

World affairs increasingly depressed him. He greeted the new century with this bitter toast:

I bring you the stately nation named Christendom, returning, bedraggled, besmirched, and dishonored, from pirate raids in Kiao Chou, Manchuria, South Africa, and the Philippines, with her soul full of meanness, her pocket full of boodle, and her mouth full of pious hypocrisies.

In October, 1900, Mark Twain sailed for home. To avoid living in the house where Susan had died, he rented a house in New York. He had already been given two honorary degrees by Yale, and in 1902 Columbia and the University of Missouri similarly recognized him. But these new honors were dimmed by his wife's illness. In desperation he took her to Italy, where she died in 1904. This new grief increased his gloom. Some critics have thought she repressed his art by her Victorian standards of propriety, but Mark Twain was certainly not aware of such an influence, and probably it did not exist.

Mark Twain's pessimism could hardly have deepened with the years, but he became a male Cassandra on the stage of the world. He opposed the imperialistic attitudes of the United States. He objected to the settlement of the Russo-Japanese War: it should have been permitted to continue until there was a revolution in Russia overthrowing the Czarist regime. The crime and degradation of lower East Side New York saddened him. He heaped sarcasm upon the head of the exhibitionist Theodore Roosevelt. Many of these heated accusations and maledictions have been collected by Bernard DeVoto under the appropriate title of *Mark Twain in Eruption.*

But it would be a mistake to think that Mark Twain got no enjoyment out of his last years. Always somewhat of an exhibitionist himself, he began at seventy to dress entirely in white, winter and summer, and he took delight in the sensation which his appearance created in public. He occasionally attended banquets and could still sway an audience with his racy language. Reporters interviewed him almost daily. He was, in fact, a sort of philosophical oracle, as Will Rogers was later. But the personal grief continued. Jean died in 1907, and he himself became seriously ill with angina.

Samuel Clemens was born during the appearance of Halley's comet, and he had long predicted that he would die when the comet returned. Like so many other curious happenings in this remarkable life, his prophecy came true on April 21, 1910.

The color, the drama, and the consummate acting in Mark Twain's literary life have often led to a misunderstanding of his mind and character. Although Van Wyck Brooks may have exaggerated the crudity of the social environment of his youth, Mark Twain did live close to the frontier—if not in Missouri, certainly in Nevada Territory and the mining camps—and there he acquired habits, mannerisms, and professional humorous devices which later became his stock in trade as a writer. It is difficult

at times to separate the man from the rôle, but, like all really great humorists and satirists, Mark Twain was above all else a moralist. A moralist is at heart profoundly serious, and so was Mark Twain more often than his public realized. He once remarked that he was not, in fact, a humorist at all, but that he merely told the truth and people, not being familiar with truth, thought it was funny. This was an accurate observation on his art, for his chief literary characteristic was telling the truth—of course as he saw it—so boldly, so uncompromisingly, that he shocked the reader. In this respect he was a realist, like Stephen Crane and Theodore Dreiser, whom he anticipated. The main difference between Mark Twain and Dreiser, for instance, is that Dreiser does nothing to disguise his seriousness, to make it appealing.

Even Mark Twain sometimes discarded his cap and bells when he talked or wrote on his one most profound conviction, his belief that man is merely a puppet whose strings are manipulated by forces beyond his knowledge or power. In expressing this deterministic doctrine, he may become so serious that he is boring, as in "What is Man?" But his accounts of how he became a writer by accident are always enlivened by anecdote and paradox. Some critics have attributed this dogmatic pessimism to Mark Twain's philosophical ignorance, but the majority of professional philosophers of the late nineteenth and early twentieth century adopted some variety of determinism. In denying free will to man Mark Twain anticipated the bulk of twentieth-century sociological, educational, and, to a large extent, even ethical theory. Economic depressions, unemployment, and world wars have not given modern men confidence that they are the masters of their own fate or captains of their souls. To those individuals who still believe that each man is personally responsible to a just God for everything he does or fails to do in this life, Mark Twain should have some appeal, too, for no writer has more vigorously condemned selfishness, dishonesty, and intolerance. Though he did not belong to a church, he supported worthy causes, and was the intimate friend of the Reverend Joseph Twitchell, in Hartford, Connecticut. His book on Joan of Arc contains proof that he was not without reverence for a saintly character.

The reader of Mark Twain's *Autobiography* will also discover that he had the sensibility of a poet. The memorable odors of spring woods, of growing things on the farm in a Missouri summer, and of the appetizing foods heaped up at a country dinner, all come back to the old man dictating at random his life of the past, and they are conveyed to the reader with the fresh vividness that only the master of style can achieve. Nor is this aesthetic quality absent from earlier works, such as *Tom Sawyer* and *Huckleberry Finn*, those poetic images of perpetual youth. Even in *The Mysterious Stranger*, a fable of childhood so bitter that the author left it to be published post- humously, there is a tender compassion for human suffering probably unsurpassed in any literature. Whether as clown, satirist, amateur philosopher, or romancer of youth, Mark Twain wrote as an artist, not always with uniform success, but constantly test- ing the value of words and the rhythm of speech, oral and written.

WILLIAM DEAN HOWELLS (1837–1920)

William Dean Howells published nearly forty novels, many of them widely read, and was probably the most influential literary critic in the nation for over a quarter of a century. It is an odd fact, therefore, that to the present day there is no book-length biography of him. This neglect is even more surprising when one considers this typically American success story of a poor boy from the backwoods of Ohio, whose formal education scarcely extended through grammar school, who at the age of twenty-four became United States consul in Venice and a few years later the respected friend and associate of the leading writers of New England at the time when Boston was the literary capital of America.

The omission, however, is a significant aspect of the biographical story itself. Howells himself was fully aware of the literary possibilities of his personal experiences and published in all seven autobiographical books: *A Boy's Town* (1890), *My Year in a Log Cabin* (1893), *My Literary Passions* (1895), *Literary Friends and Acquaintance* (1900), *My Mark Twain* (1910), *New Leaf Mills* (1913), *Years of My Youth* (1916), and *Eighty Years and After* (1921). To this list could be added the "Pony Baker" stories, and in other stories and essays Howells obviously drew heavily upon personal history, especially the travel books, such as *A Day's Pleasure and Other Sketches* (1876). Anyone who set out to write a biography of Howells during his lifetime, therefore, would have had to compete with the author himself, who had already exploited the materials. Moreover, only Howells himself was capable of intimate presentation of the emotions and inner life of his childhood. *A Boy's Town* has never been as greatly admired as *Tom Sawyer*, but as a picture of life in a certain place and epoch it is more literal and, therefore, valuable as history.

During the height of William Dean Howells' public reputation, his autobiographical works were widely read, but the number of his readers has declined so rapidly since his death that today these books are far from well known. This decline explains why biographers have neglected his life since his death. Some of his work still lives, however, and literary historians have never underrated his influence on the theory known in literary criticism as "realism." Howells is undoubtedly of major historical importance, and the biographies and reappraisals of his life and works will come yet.

The Howells family was originally Welsh, manufacturers of cloth in Wales, whence the author's grandfather came to America in 1808. After business experiments in New York, Virginia, and Ohio he finally settled in the latter state at Hamilton, where he kept a combination drug and book store. His son, William Cooper Howells, married Mary Dean, whose father was Irish and mother Pennsylvania "Dutch."

William Cooper Howells was sociable, idealistic, and impractical. He tried a number of occupations, from painting houses to editing small newspapers, but was never successful at any, and found it difficult to support his eight children. His father was Methodist, but, after a period of religious skepticism, he became a follower of Swedenborg. From 1837–40 he lived at Martin's Ferry, where William Dean was born. Then he moved to Hamilton—the "Boy's Town"—where he edited a Whig newspaper until Taylor was nominated for president. A rabid champion of Free Soil, Howells sold his paper rather than support Taylor. Then followed another unsuccessful newspaper experiment in Dayton, from 1848–50, succeeded by a still more rash venture, an attempt to manufacture paper on the Little Miami River. This project failed within a year, but it provided the future writer with materials for his two books, *My Year in a Log Cabin* and the thinly veiled autobiographical story, *New Leaf Mills*.

The Howells family had few books, but William Dean learned to spell in the printing office, and in setting type acquired a facility in handling words which turned him, first, to journalism, and then to literature. In 1851–52 father and son went to Columbus, Ohio, where the son worked in a printing office and the father reported the sessions of the Legislature. Between intervals of publishing other small newspapers, one in Ashtabula and another in Jefferson, they returned again to Columbus in 1856–58, this time William Cooper Howells as clerk for the

Legislature and William Dean as reporter for a Columbus paper.

These years in Columbus were fruitful ones for young Howells. From 1858–61 he was successively exchange editor and editorial writer for the *Ohio State Journal*. He met other people with literary interests, including Miss Elinor C. Mead of Vermont, his future wife, and he apparently read a great deal. He had already taught himself to read French, Spanish, and Italian, and had received instruction in German. He began contributing to the *Atlantic Monthly* and the *Saturday Press* in New York. With his friend, J. J. Piatt, he published his first volume of poems, called *Poems of Two Friends*. These writings attracted sufficient attention for William Dean Howells to be invited to write a campaign biography of Abraham Lincoln.

This biography was written from notes collected by someone else, and it probably had small literary merit, but it is said to have been widely read in the West, and President Lincoln was sufficiently grateful to appoint the twenty-four-year-old author to the consulship of Venice, at a salary of $1,500 a year. The first thing that Howells did with the proceeds from his book was to visit New England, where Lowell, who had accepted some of his verses for the *Atlantic*, introduced him to leading authors of the region. Hawthorne wrote, in a note of introduction to be carried to Emerson, "I find this young man worthy." In *Literary Friends and Acquaintance* Howells has given a charming account of his impressions of the region and the famous men whom he visited on this trip.

In 1861 Howells sailed for Italy, where he served four years as consul in Venice. On December 24, 1862, in Paris, he married Miss Mead, who had come to Europe with her brother, a sculptor. Their first child was born in Italy. This period of the Civil War in America was a happy time for the Howells family. William Dean studied Italian literature, did considerable traveling and sightseeing, and recorded his fresh and untutored impressions in essays which won him a secure place in American letters after his return home. The success of *Venetian Life* (1866) prepared the way for *Italian Journeys* (1867). He was most interested in people, avoided the kind of effusions over architecture and the past usually found in travel books, and gently poked fun at some of the Byronic and romantic associations which had become trite. He was another "Innocent Abroad," no less independent than Mark Twain, but more sympathetic and urbane. These books contributed to the growth of Howells' literary talent, and the later records of his travels are still readable: *Tuscan Cities*

(1886), *London Films* (1905), *Certain Delightful English Towns* (1906), *Seven English Cities* (1909), and *Hither and Thither in Germany* (1920).

On his return to America in 1865, Howells was employed for a year in New York by E. L. Godkin, editor of the *Nation*, at a salary of $40 a week. The following year he was offered an assistant editorship on the *Atlantic Monthly*, and he moved to Cambridge, where he lived for twenty years. In 1872 he became the editor, a position of considerable prestige and influence. In 1886 he moved to New York and took over the department called "Editor's Study" in *Harper's Magazine*, which he wrote until 1891. After occupying other editorial positions he returned to *Harper's* in 1900 to write the "Easy Chair" until his death. These were years of steady success, adequately remunerative, and increasingly rewarding in personal associations and literary prestige. Yale, Harvard, Columbia, and Oxford Universities conferred honorary degrees upon this self-educated author, and Harvard, Columbia, and Johns Hopkins offered him professorships in English and Comparative Literature.

But despite the fact that Howells was largely self-educated, his intellectual progress followed a consistent curve from his youthful admiration of Goldsmith, Irving, and Cervantes—especially Cervantes—to his mature theory of "realism," which he advocated as a critic and attempted to practice in his own novels. As a boy his romantic longing for foreign lands made Irving's *Conquest of Granada* and *The Alhambra* appealing to him, but in the end he found the common sense of eighteenth-century rationalism more permanently satisfactory. The satirical Cervantes, also, turned him against romanticism. Later he recalled that at fourteen he wrote pastorals in imitation of Pope and "was growing more literary and less human," but Shakespeare, and especially Falstaff, quickly humanized him: "There I found a world appreciable to experience. . . . There I found joy and sorrow mixed, and nothing abstract or typical, but everything standing for itself and not for some other thing." Dickens also increased Howells' democratic sympathies: "His view of the world and of society . . . was instinctively sane and reasonable, even when it was most impossible."

Lowell's critical essays aroused Howells' interest in major poets, though he failed to share Lowell's enthusiasm for Spenser. Chaucer, however, he found like Cervantes, warmly human in his satire. In his youth Howells admired most Tennyson and Longfellow, perhaps because they were both didactic, for he was tone-deaf and probably never appreciated their prosodic music. And though he learned to read Heine in German, even this great lyricist taught him mainly that "the expression of literature" must not be "different from the expression of life." In nearly everything he read, in fact, Howells found increasing evidence that that literature is best which most nearly expresses life. In Italy he studied the eighteenth-century dramatist, Carlo Goldoni, in whom he discovered the foundation of a "realistic" theory of literature.

Howells' first literary ambition, however, was to be a poet. While in Columbus he submitted some verses to Lowell, who accepted them for the *Atlantic Monthly* after making sure that they were not plagiarized from Heine's works—then one of Howells' "literary passions." In all, Howells published five books of poetry, from the collaboration, *Poems of Two Friends* (1860), to the mature works, *No Love Lost, A Romance of Travel* (1869), *Poems* (1873—revised in 1885, 1901), *Stops of Various Quills* (1895), and *The Mother and the Father; Dramatic Passages* (1909). Some poems were also included in *The Daughter of the Storage* (1916). But despite his continued interest in poetic expression, Howells never got beyond a weak imitation of Longfellow, Tennyson, and Heine. Longfellow's hexameters especially had a fatal fascination for him, resulting in facility without substance. When his verse approached originality, it became prosy, for prose was his natural medium of expression.

Howells himself was slow to discover his ability in the two genres for which he was especially gifted, criticism and fiction. In fact, it is doubtful that he ever fully appreciated the importance of criticism, though it was the attempt to exemplify his literary theories that produced his many novels, and his critical influence finally surpassed his other literary achievements. As late as 1910 he declared in *Essays in Criticism* that "the critical faculty is lower than the imitative." Critics lag behind creators; they have "condemned whatever was, from time to time, fresh and vital in literature. . . . Every literary movement has been violently opposed at the start." Perhaps Howells did not fully realize that as the American exponent of a new literary movement he was, in the process of aiding and explaining the basic ideas of the movement, creating a substantial body of critical writing, first in book reviews in the *Atlantic* and then in collected essays and books of criticism.

This theory, as finally clarified in *Criticism and Fiction* (1891), reflected the age in its dependence on science. Literature, he thought, was "a plant which springs from the nature of a people, and draws its forces from their life." Like the botanist, the critic should be a dispassionate classifier, placing "a book in such a light that the reader shall know its class, its function, its characteristics." From the Spanish novelist, Valdés, Howells borrowed the metaphysical doctrine (akin to Walt Whitman's cosmic democracy) that "all is equally grand, all is equally just, all is equally beautiful, because all is equally divine." Consequently, declares Howells, "Let not the novelists, then, endeavor to add anything to reality, to turn it and twist it, to restrict it." Or again, in life the realist finds nothing insignificant; all tells for destiny and character; nothing that God has made is contemptible. He cannot look upon human life and declare this or that thing unworthy of notice, any more than the scientist can declare a fact of the material world beneath the dignity of his inquiry.

The most active years of Howells' campaign for uncompromising realism were from 1886 to 1892, while he conducted "The Editor's Study" for *Harper's*. During this time he championed Zola, whom most American critics were denouncing as filthy and immoral, and he greatly admired Turgenev. But he saw in Zola a moral force exposing vice and degeneration for clinical treatment, and it was Tolstoi whom Howells found most congenial: "He has been to me the final consciousness, which he speaks of so wisely in his essay on Life. . . . The supreme art in literature had its highest effect in making me set art forever below humanity." This doctrine culminated in a book which Howells called *Literature and Life* (1902), a book containing a phrase and a point of view which has profoundly influenced the teaching of literature in American schools for a generation.

After 1892, when Howells took over the editorship of *Cosmopolitan Magazine* and later (1900–20) in his "Easy Chair" department for *Harper's*, he was less aggressive in the fight for "realism." This was due partly to a sense of failure: romanticism still flourished, as the popularity of Robert Louis Stevenson testified. Also Howells had not realized that a theory and literature which had grown out of the life of the times might not be immediately accepted by the people of that time (as with Whitman, whom Howells also did not understand or appreciate). But his own disposition, and his experience with the gentler aspects of American experience, resulted in his accepting as typical a reality which seemed tame to such later realists and naturalists as Jack London, Frank Norris, and Theodore Dreiser. Furthermore, he held the Victorian belief that "morality penetrates all things," and hoped that "the time will come when the beast-man will be so far subdued and tamed in us that the memory of him in literature will be left to perish." Unable to put into practice his own doctrine that the novelist should in no way restrict the truthful presentation of reality, Howells would even permit the expurgation of objectionable passages in the classics. He thought that French and Russian novelists dealt with subjects that "decent" Anglo-Saxons should not, and he even censured Tolstoi. He believed that America did not have the sex problems treated in French and Russian fiction. His squeamishness concerning sex may explain why he could never admire Flaubert.

This Victorian conception of decency, however, was not inconsistent with Howells' purpose as a novelist, which was, he explained as early as 1872 in his Preface to *Their Wedding Journey*, to present man not in his "heroic or occasional phases," but "in his habitual moods of vacancy and tiresomeness." Consequently, we find in this and Howells' later novels characters who are intentionally commonplace and bourgeois. They are not far removed from the ignoramus whom Ring Lardner was later to satirize with the bitterness of hatred, but Howells, with sympathetic tolerance, wished "to think his shallow and feeble thoughts, to be moved by his dumb, stupid desires, to be dimly illumined by his stinted inspirations, to share his foolish prejudices, to practice his obtuse selfishness."

In his earlier fiction Howells' theory restricted him in many ways. His presentation of common, average characters, while embracing a large fraction of humanity, excluded the exotic, the abnormal, or the picturesque. He tried to avoid statistically improbable coincidence, contrived plot, and dramatic endings. He wished to write "from the beginning forward, and never from the ending backward," as Poe, with his emphasis upon literary effect, tried deliberately to do. Life, Howells argued, has no endings, and the novel, a transcript of life, should be true to the final unfinished page.

The author should also keep himself out of the story and not, like Thackeray, "stand about in his scene, talking it over with his hands in his pockets, interrupting the action, and spoiling the illusion in which alone the truth of art resides." But this detachment did not prevent Howells from drawing upon his own experience and emotions in creating his stories. In fact, his choosing a slice of life for literal treatment necessitated his choosing a slice fairly closely related to his own life. Furthermore, his sympathetic identification of himself with common humanity prevented criticism and satire, though the reader may become impatient with the shallow thought or boresome triviality of his characters' speech.

In *Their Wedding Journey* (1872) Howells made an easy transition from writing travel sketches to fiction. There is no plot; it is simply a detailed narrative

of two commonplace people on a honeymoon to Niagara, Montreal, and Quebec. The couple, Isabel and Basil March, are as average as Howells' theory could demand, and there is nothing subtle or "literary" about their impressions. In a chapter found only in editions prior to 1887 we are given a glimpse of the Marches' marriage twelve years later. The idealistic expectations of the honeymooners have evaporated, especially for Isabel. Marriage has become a drab monotony. But in the sequel, *Their Silver Wedding Journey* (1899), disillusionment has given way to a not unhappy resignation. Mr. and Mrs. March appear many times in subsequent novels, always as representatives of average domestic life. Howells is almost polemical in his insistence that love at first sight or "they-married-and-lived-happily-ever-afterward" is not common enough in reality to be truthful in fiction.

Howells' women are likely to be stubborn, illogical, and sometimes hysterical; his men mildly self-centered, egotistical, and unable to comprehend the baffling complexity of women. Their relationships, and still more the contacts between different social strata, provide the main substance of these early novels. The product is a mild comedy of manners, faintly reminiscent of Jane Austen—a sort of Cambric tea version. In *A Modern Instance* (1882), however, Howells treated the theme of an incompatible marriage with greater boldness. The husband sinks into complete moral degeneration, while the wife is so insipid that the modern reader is not likely to have much sympathy for her, or for the conscience-racked New Englander who feels damned because he had loved her in silence before she was divorced.

The Howells novel which has best survived the test of time is *The Rise of Silas Lapham* (1884). Here we have another comedy of manners, but the story is most memorable for the strength of character which enables Lapham to rise above his economic misfortunes. As a wealthy capitalist he was egotistical, narrow, loud, vulgar, and antisocial. It is primarily a character study, but the story also reveals Howells' growing interest in economic and social problems.

Many critics have thought that Howells underwent a great change of social outlook after he moved to New York just before his fiftieth birthday. Some have attributed his increasing concern with social injustice to his having moved away from Cambridge and the conservative influence of the *Atlantic Monthly*. Howells himself gave Tolstoi credit for having brought him "the knowledge of myself in ways that I had not dreamt of before, and began at last to discern my relations to the race, without which we are nothing." But recent investigation has brought to light other influences besides Tolstoi. One of these was the American Socialist leader, Laurence Gronlund, whose speeches and writings brought Howells into sympathetic contact with Marxian philosophy. Another source was the Norwegian novelist, Björstjerne Björnson, whom Howells befriended in Cambridge, and whose democratic books he praised in reviews in the *Atlantic Monthly*. Henry George, Edward Bellamy, and other American reformers also caused Howells to take up the study of politics, economics, and sociology, and as early as 1872 he had introduced a department on "Politics" into the pages of the *Atlantic*. National events, too, like the trial following the Haymarket riot in Chicago in 1886, the streetcar strike in New York, and the general industrial strife of the times, aroused Howells' sympathy for labor.

In *Silas Lapham* the ethics of capitalism is a secondary motif, but *Annie Kilburn* (1888) treats the problem specifically. Annie returns from abroad with the intention of using her wealth to alleviate the suffering of the poor, but she learns from Mr. Peck, whose belief in social equality we may assume to be Howells' own, that money "can sometimes create a bond of gratitude . . . but it can't create sympathy between rich and poor. . . . Because sympathy— common feeling—can spring only from like experiences, like hopes, like fears. And money can't buy these." In *A Hazard of New Fortunes* (1889) the setting is New York during the streetcar strike. All metropolitan classes except the destitute are represented in this sociological study. *April Hopes* (1888) presents what had come to be a favorite theme with Howells, the conflict between puritanism and social democracy. The point of view of *The Quality of Mercy* (1892) is that of a pessimistic determinism which reminds one of Mark Twain's "What is Man?" The hero is a millionaire robber, but he "isn't the disease; he's merely the symptom. . . . He was a mere creature of circumstances—like the rest of us! His environment made him rich, and his environment made him a rogue."

The most penetrating treatment of these economic, social, and ethical problems is found in Howells' utopian romance, *The Traveler from Altruria* (1894). The conversations between Mr. Homos, the visitor from utopian Altruria, and representatives of American society contain such penetratingly ironic commentaries on the shams and pretences of the free enterprise system that one wonders why Howells' contemporaries were not scandalized. This mystery is particularly puzzling in view of the fact that in his

later novels he continued to hammer away at the abuses satirized by the Altrurian. But perhaps Howells was too kindly and sympathetic to make a deep impression as a satirist, despite the irony of this book and *Through the Eye of the Needle* (1907).

The man who began his career by disliking Thackeray never learned to hate strongly enough to rival the great satirists. Farce was more suited to his temperament, and he wrote nearly two dozen light dramas, beginning with *The Parlor Car* (1878) and ending with *Parting Friends* (1911). He particularly liked to build a comedy around an absurd episode in a sleeping car, an elevator, a depot, a smoking car, or to poke fun at some foible like feminine rodent-phobia, as in *The Mouse-Trap* (1889). Many of these were produced on the professional stage, but they have been most successful in private theatricals. *The Mouse-Trap* was played in London by an all-star cast, including Ellen Terry, and was warmly praised by George Bernard Shaw. These little dramas are still interesting; they reveal a side of Howells which his novels and criticism do not.

Still another curious side of this author who started out to be an unflinching realist is his later interest in dreams, telepathy, and psychic phenomena, as in *The Shadow of a Dream* (1890), *Questionable Shapes* (1903), and *Between the Dark and the Daylight* (1907). These lead one to suspect that he was familiar with the *Proceedings* of the Society for Psychical Research. Since there was during the period of these books considerable popular curiosity about such subjects, we have in Howells' treatment of the theme another indication of his close contact with contemporary thought, fads, and events. This fact marks Howells as a perennial journalist.

Journalism, in fact, is the key to Howells' weaknesses and virtues as a writer. He not only learned to write in printing and newspaper office, but he remained all his life so alert to the contemporary scene that he wrote always for a contemporary audience. Not only his comedy of manners transcribed from observations of people whom he saw on steamer, in railway station, or on the streets of Boston and New York, but his themes of domestic life and his theses echoing the doctrines of the socialistic and economic reformers were as contemporary as the morning newspaper. This generalization applies also to his aesthetic taste and the literary style which his generation thought the last word in refinement and "purity," a word often used to characterize his style. The great writers—like Melville, Whitman, and Henry James—are often almost unreadable to their own generation, while the author whose style is most congenial to his contemporaries may be inane to a later generation. Perhaps Howells' clarity and simplicity have contributed to his decline in reputation. Critics have not had to struggle with his meaning and been stimulated to explain him, as they have with Melville, Whitman, and James. But this neglect of Howells is undeserved, and it is regrettable, for neither his portrayal of average human nature in American democracy nor his criticism of the hypocrisies which thwart democracy is out of date. His influence, however, has not been lost, for later realists, naturalists, and social critics have picked up the themes and the theories where Howells dropped them, and in their sharper-edged style his thoughts still live; nevertheless, the student will find it rewarding to go back to the source in Howells' own writings.

HENRY JAMES (1843–1916)

Few men in the history of American literature have been so fortunate as to inherit both wealth and the genius to use it for the enrichment of the thought and art of the nation, but the Jameses were the lucky exception. William James, the psychologist and philosopher, and his younger brother, Henry, were doubly fortunate in their inheritance, for it included not only financial independence but also a remarkable father who aided and stimulated the development of his gifted sons in every way he could.

The James who made possible the brilliant careers of the philosopher and of the novelist was also named William, an Irishman who came to Albany in 1793 with little except ability, and left, at his death in 1832, an estate valued at three million dollars. His son Henry, father of the William and Henry known to fame, rebelled against his father's Presbyterian theology and his philosophy of success. Instead of going into business, he studied theology, traveled, and after his marriage in 1840 to Mary Walsh gave all his attention to raising a family and writing books on theology which he published at his own expense. In England in 1844 he studied the French socialist, Fourier, and had a mystical experience which might be called a "conversion" to Swedenborgianism, though his strongly independent interpretations were never accepted by the Swedenborg Church.

The Jameses took a house at 21 Washington Place in New York City, where their two oldest sons, William and Henry, were born in 1842 and '43. Mr. James lectured on his religious ideas and won the friendship of Emerson, Thoreau, Margaret Fuller, Theodore Parker, Bronson Alcott, and other prominent writers and thinkers, who visited the James home. Three other children were born inside four years, Wilkinson, Robertson, and Alice, and their father began his original experiments in education. The future novelist had already been taken to Europe at the age of one and a half years, and in 1849 Mr. James wrote to Emerson that he was thinking of returning to Europe so that the boys could "absorb French and German and get a better sensuous education than they are likely to get here." This plan was carried out in 1855, and the family spent three years abroad, except for a brief period in 1858. Mr. James kept moving his sons around from schools and tutors in Paris, Geneva, and London and seemed to fear that they would settle upon one subject or ambition before they had sufficiently experimented with their talents and interests. William was gifted in drawing and painting, and Henry struggled to imitate him, but in this as in many other activities he was never able to keep pace with his versatile brother.

When William announced his intention of making a profession of art, his paradoxical father moved the family from Paris to Newport, Rhode Island, so that his son might study with William Hunt. But William soon had a new ambition, and in 1861 entered the Lawrence Scientific School, the first step on his road to psychology. Henry, not to be outdone, entered the Harvard Law School in 1862 after he had suffered a "physical mishap." The exact nature of this accident is still unknown but Henry later referred to it ambiguously as "an obscure hurt" and at least once as an injury to his back. It prevented him from enlisting with his brothers "Wilky" and "Rob" in the Union Army, and this depressed him, but he was no doubt easily turned from law, for he had already decided that he wanted above all else to write stories.

From 1864 to '69 the James family lived in Boston and Cambridge, favorable locations for a young writer to begin his first experiments. In 1864 Charles Eliot Norton, editor of the *North American Review*, accepted from Henry a review of Senior's *Essays on Fiction*, which appeared in the October number. It is perhaps significant that this first publication was a criticism, not a story, for no other American author of fiction ever learned his craft more deliberately and methodically. Apparently Norton liked this first critical essay, for presently Henry James was reviewing the popular novels of Miss Prescott and Mrs. Seemuller—authors of the "best sellers" of the day. Through these reviews we learn that, at this period, James liked Scott, Reade, Mérimée, Balzac, and disliked Richardson, Fielding, and Smollett. Scott was evidently a favorite, though the young critic advised Miss Prescott and Mrs. Seemuller to study Mérimée and Balzac. He accused these sentimental lady novelists of immorality, *i.e.*, untruthfulness to life.

Henry James published his first story, called feebly "The Story of a Year," in the March, 1865, *Atlantic Monthly*. The subject was the psychological adjustments of a soldier and the girl he had left behind when he went to war, but the plot was overcrowded and poorly coordinated. The story gave little promise of his later skill. But he continued to learn while he reviewed books for Norton and for E. L. Godkin, editor of the weekly *Nation*, published in New York. He wrote essays on Arnold, Balzac, and probably other authors (all these essays have not yet been authoritatively identified). The following year he was attracted by the art and thought of George Eliot, a novelist whom he always rated high. In 1866 he admired her for her truth and understanding of character, but especially for her humanity, which, he declared, colored "all her other gifts—her humor, her morality, and her exquisite rhetoric." It was probably his admiration for George Eliot that led him to condemn French realism, though he still aspired to be the American Balzac when he met William Dean Howells later in the year.

The friendship which developed between James and Howells, six years his senior and then assistant editor of the *Atlantic Monthly*, undoubtedly meant a great deal to both men. Howells had not read Balzac when they met in 1866, but he had admired the depiction of Italian life in the plays of Goldoni, and he could appreciate James' demand for truth in fiction. Probably his talks with James no less than the books he was reading influenced Howells in working out his own theory of realism. But apparently at this time Howells' own influence on his younger friend was romantic. At any rate, James' next two stories, "The Story of a Masterpiece" and "The Romance of Certain Old Clothes," were highly colored and impressionistic. Perhaps these experiments taught James something about finish and style, but he had not yet discovered his own particular forte.

During the first four years of his career as a professional writer of fiction and criticism James lived in New England and his attention was focused on America. Howells pronounced him "gifted enough to do better than any one else has yet done toward making us a real American novel," and this appears to have been James' own highest ambition. In going to Europe, therefore, in 1869 he was not trying to escape from his own country, as some critics have believed, but was simply attempting to complete his education. William had spent two years in travel and study abroad and Henry wanted to take his turn.

The period of 1869–75 was, as Cornelia Kelley says in *The Early Development of Henry James*, "his Wanderjahre. He went forth into the world to look, to listen, and to learn."

On the 1869 trip James visited England, Italy, and France. He later described his emotions and experiences in *The Middle Years*, but the enthusiasm for England which he expressed in this book was that of his mature years, when he completed the work. From the spontaneous ejaculations in the letters which he wrote to his family at this time we learn that he was at first depressed by London, though he soon became absorbed by his discovery of England's past, as his "passionate pilgrim" did in the story by this name which he published in the *Atlantic Monthly* in 1871. Italy, however, thrilled him immediately. In Rome he exclaimed, "At last—for the first time—I live!" He was also observing people as well as scenery, and fellow Americans whom he met were so unappreciative of the beauties which stirred him to exclamation that he felt disillusioned with them. From Florence he wrote his mother:

A set of people less framed to provoke national self-complacency than the latter it would be hard to imagine. There is but one word to use in regard to them—vulgar, vulgar, vulgar. Their ignorance—their stingy, defiant, grudging attitude toward everything European—their perpetual reference of all things to American standard or precedent which exists only in their own unscrupulous windbags—and then our unhappy poverty of voice, of speech, and of physiognomy—these things glare at you hideously.

But he admitted that, "on the other hand, we seem a people of *character*, we seem to have energy, capacity and intellectual stuff in ample measure." These two attitudes toward Americans soon appeared in James' stories. In fact, his observations of his countrymen abroad constituted his first authentic fictional material and before long he became something of a specialist in the field of international relations of character and manners.

After spending two more years in Cambridge, James returned to Europe in the spring of 1872 to write travel sketches for the *Nation* and the *Atlantic Monthly* and to store up new impressions. A few weeks in Paris convinced him that both the French novel and drama were morally rotten. He was impressed by Swiss scenery, he detested Germany, and he became an expert critic of Italian art. Out of his increased knowledge of people and artists he wrote between 1873–74 three of his best stories to date: "Madame de Mauves," "The Madonna of the Future," and "The Passionate Pilgrim." The first is a story of French and American morality, the second of an artist who wasted his life preparing to paint a masterpiece, and the third of an American who inherited an estate in England but was denied his patrimony when he arrived to claim it. The latter story has often been cited as evidence of James' own homesickness for the culture of an old and aristocratic nation, but a close reading will reveal that he was as critical of English as of American mind and character. He was interested in dramatic contrasts rather than polemics of superiority.

Henry James' own attitudes, however, were becoming increasingly antinationalistic and cosmopolitan. This was undoubtedly one factor in his major decision in 1875 to live in Europe, a decision which has probably caused more biographical and critical discussion in America than any other action of his life. Even in his own family there was hostility toward his self-expatriation. William never seemed to understand why his brother needed to live abroad in order to become a writer of fiction. And in general the nationalistic critics have regarded Henry James' "deracination" as a tragic mistake. Van Wyck Brooks based his biography, *The Pilgrimage of Henry James* (1925), on the thesis that the novelist thwarted his own genius by alienating himself from his own country: "In this alien world [Europe], with which his relations were so tenuous, he drifted further and further from life itself." Five years later Parrington, in his *Main Currents*, declared in discussing James that "It is not well for the artist to turn cosmopolitan, for the flavor of the fruit comes from the soil and sunshine of its native hills." Edith Wharton, no rabid nationalist but an intimate friend of James and a disciple of his art, asserted in her autobiography, *A Backward Glance* (1934), that he left America because "he was never really happy or at home there," and he found that he could work better in Europe. Mrs. Wharton added that "Henry James was essentially a novelist of manners, and the manners he was qualified by nature and situation to observe were those of the little vanishing group of people among whom he grew up, or their more picturesque prototypes in older societies."

After he made his momentous decision, James went to live in Paris, where he made the acquaintance first of Turgenev, who introduced him to Flaubert. He became intimate with Renan and with Daudet. He was also acquainted with Zola and Maupassant. Though he found living in Paris interesting and pleasant, eventually he settled in London. In 1877, after seven weeks in Italy, he wrote to his family, "I have just come back, and am on my way to London, whither I gravitate as toward

the place in the world in which, on the whole, I feel most at home." The following year he wrote to William, who had apparently suggested his returning to America to live in Washington, "I know what I am about, and I have always my eyes on my native land."

Evidently he did know what he was about, for in the next few years James published the following books: *Roderick Hudson* (1875–76), *The American* (1877), *Daisy Miller* (1878–79), *Hawthorne* (1879), *Washington Square* (1880–81), *The Portrait of a Lady* (1881). *Roderick Hudson* was Henry James' first important novel, and it reveals the kind of material which he could handle successfully. Roderick Hudson is a young Boston sculptor who is taken to Europe by a rich young protégé, Rowland Mallet, with the hope that Europe will develop his genius. But the result is that Europe destroys Roderick's creativeness and brings to the surface his innate weak character. A central situation in the novel is the relationship between Rowland and Roderick. Probably the author sympathized with both, with Rowland the passive spectator of life, and with the artist that Roderick might have been. James was himself still uncertain of his own artistic strength, but there are some indications in the story that he identified himself more with the vicarious participator in life, Rowland. *Roderick Hudson* is not one of James' great novels, but it is a good introduction to the subjectivity of his stories—his projection of his own fears, problems, and ambitions into imaginative creations.

These books of the 1870's also confirm the duality of American character which James had observed in the letter to his mother written in Florence. Newman, the retired millionaire in *The American*, goes to Europe to find the best in life. With the crude forthrightness which had won him success in American business he attempts to woo and marry a charming girl of one of the oldest houses in France, only to find himself thwarted by the treachery of her aristocratic family. His strength of character is revealed when, revenge within his grasp, he chooses acquiescence and renunciation. *Daisy Miller*, too, treats this duality in another way, but with a subtlety which misled many American readers when the story first appeared and aroused sufficient controversy to carry this work into the "best seller" class, a success which the author never repeated. Daisy's instinctive and unconventional conduct shocks a fastidious American who reminds one of James himself, but her complete innocence and sincerity are revealed after her death, and her innocence far outweighs her lack of decorum.

Many contemporary readers, however, thought *Daisy Miller* was a satire on American girls.

In his biography of Hawthorne, still a valuable critical study, James continued to explore the contrasts between America and Europe. "For myself," he says, "as I turn the pages of his journals, I seem to see the image of the crude and simple society in which he lived. I use the epithets, of course, not invidiously, but descriptively . . ." James enumerates the "items of high civilization" absent:

No sovereign, no court, no personal loyalty, no aristocracy, no church, no army, no diplomatic service, no country gentlemen, no palaces, no castles, no manors, nor old country-houses, nor parsonages, nor thatched cottages, nor ivied ruins . . . no literature, no novels, no museums . . .

But he adds that "The American knows that a good deal remains," and James is not unappreciative of the strictly native qualities which produced so indigenous a literary phenomenon as Hawthorne.

In *Washington Square* (1881), and later in *The Bostonians* (1886), James attempted to use American materials, having lived as a youth in New York and a young man in Boston, but his genres and scenes can hardly be called typical—though the relatives of one old lady in Boston thought the book caricatured her. In 1881, however, James achieved his first major success in *The Portrait of a Lady*, another story of an incorruptible American pitted against morally decadent Europeans. In the beginning of the novel Isabel Archer is immature, but suffering develops in her poise, tolerance, and wisdom. In the crisis she is one of those Americans who has "character, . . . energy, capacity and intellectual stuff in ample measure."

A considerable part of the years 1881–83 James spent in the United States, first on a visit in the winter of '81–'82, during which time his mother died, and he returned again in the following December to be with his dying father. After these severe personal losses he did not revisit his native land again for twenty years. Back in London, he published a collected edition of his novels and tales in fourteen volumes (1883). This edition serves as a convenient milestone in James' literary progress, for he was about to begin new experiments. He himself seems to have been conscious of the passing of an epoch in his life, for he began keeping a notebook on his trip to America in 1881, and during the next few years felt a compulsion to "sum up" his experiences. These notebooks, used by Matthiessen in *Henry James: The Major Phase*, indicate how completely the novelist was now living for his art. "Not

at any point in his 'summing up,' " says Matthiessen, "is there a sign of a major intellectual or emotional event, or of any intense human relationship, save in the moving pages which describe the death of his mother." His whole desire was

To live *in* the world of creation—to get into it and stay in it—to frequent it and haunt it—to *think* intensely and fruitfully—to woo combinations and inspirations into being by a depth and continuity of attention and meditation—this is the only thing.

From 1889 to '95 James tried passionately to write dramas, but none of his plays were successful, and after he was hissed from the stage in London at the first-night performance of *Guy Domville* he gave up his theatrical ambitions. Some critics have thought that James' fiction gained in scenic detail and characterization from his interlude with the drama, but actually he denuded his novel increasingly of scenic detail until eventually he was using the equivalent of stage props only, and his characters were revealing themselves, as on the stage, by what they say and do. In the later novels, in fact, they do little; they talk a great deal; they cerebrate constantly.

His tales of the unappreciated or misunderstood literary and artistic genius also belong to the dramatic years. "The Figure in the Carpet" and "The Next Time" came soon after the failure of *Guy Domville*. To the 1890–1900 decade belong also ten of the eighteen "ghostly tales" that he wrote, including that perennially controversial work, "The Turn of the Screw," which the critics cannot agree to classify definitely as either a story of the supernatural or a psychiatric study.

Matthiessen thinks that 1895 was the turning point in James' career. Earlier critics agree, too, that a great change took place in his writing about this time, though most of them have thought it a degeneration into obscurity and an almost pathological subtlety. Even William James protested against his brother's later style, demanding brutally in 1907, "Say it *out*, for God's sake . . . and have done with it." But recent critics have reversed this interpretation. Matthiessen calls the period of *The Wings of the Dove* (1902), *The Ambassadors* (1903), and *The Golden Bowl* (1904) James' "major phase." Clifton Fadiman says that "those who care passionately for our English speech find in the precision, the exquisiteness, the close workmanship of James's prose a relief from the careless, uncleanly, and hyperthyroid jargon which currently passes muster for sound writing." It was in the later novels and stories that James strove hardest for precision and nuance.

The style had to be subtle and complex because he was attempting with increasing intensity to explore the depths of both the conscious and unconscious mind. "Seen in the light of what Freud has taught us," Fadiman comments, "James suddenly demonstrates an extraordinary perception of the hidden and even sinister drives of men and women." Thus the later critics link James with Joyce, Proust, and Mann —with the great modern novelists.

The ironical story in *The Wings of the Dove* indicates this modernity, a psychiatric treatment of love, selfishness, and awakened shame. *The Ambassadors*, too, is "modern" in its emphasis on the fulness of experience. Strether, who goes to Paris to rescue a young New Englander from an affair with a married woman, finds the young man much improved by the *liaison* and himself stays in Paris, now advising the young man:

Live all you can; it's a mistake not to. It doesn't so much matter what you do in particular so long as you have your life. If you haven't had that what *have* you had?

This theme reappears time after time in the later stories, as in "The Beast in the Jungle" (1903), the story of a man who wasted his life waiting for something marvelous to happen to him, and "The Jolly Corner" (1909), the account of an expatriate like James who comes back to his old home and meets the ghost of the person he might have been if he had not gone abroad to live. In both these short stories there is also a faithful woman who spends her life in sterile waiting for the man to settle his fate.

It is easy to see in these stories a ghost of James himself. *The Golden Bowl* is less obviously subjective, though equally modern in its psychology. It is perhaps the most "patterned" of all James' major novels, elaborately symmetrical in structure and highly symbolical in style. The plot is a quadrangle between father, daughter, and their ill-chosen mates. The chief point of the story is the unspoken understanding—a marriage of minds—between father and daughter.

In 1904 James made a ten-month visit to America after having lived abroad for nearly twenty years. He traveled to California and to Florida, and his discovery of the scenery and life of his own country stirred him almost as deeply as Italy had on that memorable trip thirty-five years earlier. Part of these belated observations he presented in 1907 in *The American Scene*, a book of sketches neglected until its republication in 1946 with a valuable introduction by W. H. Auden. James intended to cover his trip to the West in a separate book, which was never published. In reviewing the Auden edition of *The American Scene* Edmund Wilson said that the book shows "an incisiveness, a comprehensiveness, a grasp of political and economic factors, that one might not have expected of James returning to Big Business America." Other critics, however, continued to find this book overly fastidious in style and thought.

In 1907 also appeared the New York edition of *The Novels and Stories of Henry James*, in twenty-four volumes—posthumously increased to twenty-six with the addition of his two unfinished works. James carefully prepared the text himself, revising his stories as usual, explaining his purposes and literary theories in a preface for each volume. Though these prefaces were written in old age, they are singularly consistent with the theories he first expressed in book reviews (which need to be collected and republished). Indeed, in these final prefaces he drew extensively upon his reviews and notebooks.

One proof of the perennial vitality of the literary genius of Henry James is the fact that he continued to experiment (though the experiments also reveal his increasing dissatisfaction with twentieth-century civilization). Frustration often leads to fantasy, and *The Sense of the Past* (published, like *The Ivory Tower*, posthumously in 1917) is a time-fantasy. Ralph Pendrel travels back to the early nineteenth century (about 1820, *i.e.*, to the past of James' father and grandfather), and changes places with a young American who looks to the future, just as Ralph looks to the past. This Wellsian device gave James an opportunity for ironic contrast but showed his inability to deal imaginatively with the impressions of his travels in 1904. *The Ivory Tower* also indicates his old-age interest in the younger generation, but he was never able to finish the story. He tried in vain to recapture the confident mood of his productive years. In a note he prayed: "Let me fumble it gently and patiently out—with fever and fidget laid to rest—as in the old enchanted months." But the "old enchanted months" were gone forever.

When war broke out between England and Germany in 1914 Henry James was tragically shocked. He wrote in a letter:

The plunge of civilization into this abyss of blood and darkness by the wanton feat of these two aristocrats is a thing that so gives away the whole long age during which we have supposed the world to be, with whatever abatement, gradually bettering, that to have to take it all now for what the treacherous years were all the while really making for and *meaning* is too tragic for words.

This tortured utterance gives the key to much of James' modern significance, for in retrospect it is easy to see in the pathetic futility of many of his prim characters the author's own foreboding of a vanishing civilization. His autobiographical books, *A Small Boy and Others* (1913), *Notes of a Son and Brother* (1914), and *The Middle Years* (1917), reveal his desire for order and decency in life, but in the social and political world in which he lived these were deteriorating. Looking back on Western civilization after two world wars, we now recognize the pent-up violence that was straining for release in social upheaval. Henry James, with his clinical interest in human motives, was unconsciously a social prophet, as Stephen Spender has brilliantly demonstrated in *The Destructive Element* (in which James is the central literary figure). The novelist, of all artists, deals most intimately with human nature, and James, through his endless probing into the motives of such people as he knew, disclosed the stresses and the weaknesses of the social structure of his generation.

Probably every reader of Henry James has definite impressions of his personality after reading his stories, but it is not likely that two readers have quite the same impressions. Indeed, even James' friends and contemporaries give conflicting testimony. They do not agree on why he found life in England more congenial than in America, and it is not certain he himself knew. Stories like "The Jolly Corner" suggest that he may have struggled to answer this question to himself. In recent years psychological critics have attempted to trace the origins of James' fictional motifs and his highly individualized style to certain frustrations of his life, such as his inability to rival his older brother's intellectual brilliancy, and possibly the mysterious injury which kept him from participating in the Civil War with his younger brothers—thus giving him a feeling of shirking his responsibility. His closest friends understood that his dignified bearing and meticulous manners cloaked an inner insecurity. William James, despite a certain intellectual gulf between himself and the novelist, deeply loved his younger brother, and probably, as one of the foremost psychologists of his generation, understood Henry's character and personality better than anyone else. After visiting Henry in London in 1889, William wrote back to his wife in America this acute observation:

> Harry is as nice and simple and amiable as he can be. He has covered himself, like some marine crustacean, with all sorts of material growths, rich sea-weeds and rigid barnacles and things, and lives hidden in the midst of his strange heavy alien manners and customs; but these are all but "protective resemblances," under which the same dear old, good, innocent and at bottom very powerless-feeling Harry remains, caring for little but his writing, and full of dutifulness and affection for all gentle things. . . .[1]

Until a future biographer brings forth a more convincing explanation, this must stand as the best clue to what Henry James was really like behind his ambassadorial dignity and his "alien manners and customs."

[1] From *The Letters of William James* by Henry James. Copyright 1920 by Henry James. Reprinted by permission of Paul R. Reynolds & Son.

HENRY ADAMS (1838–1918)

Henry Brooks Adams was born February 16, 1838, "under the shadow of the Boston State House," as he expressed it in the *Education*. Although he admitted that "probably no child, born in the year, held better cards than he," he seems to have become more and more convinced as he matured that these cards handicapped him in the game of life. But he himself admitted when he was seventy that, "as it happened, he never got to the point of playing the game at all; he lost himself in the study of it, watching the errors of the players," but his temperament and his point of view were at least in part inherited, and the study of his ancestry throws more light on his mind and character than is true of most authors.

Henry Adams was the direct descendant of three generations of as brilliant and distinguished men as America has produced: John Adams, the second President of the United States; John Quincy Adams, who followed in his father's footsteps to the Presidency; and Charles Francis Adams, one of the nation's most successful foreign ministers. But despite this eminence, John Adams was defeated by Thomas Jefferson; John Quincy Adams was beaten by the rough-and-tumble frontier politics of General Jackson; and Charles Francis Adams failed to win the Vice-Presidency in 1848 on the Free Soil ticket. Each of these three men championed a lost cause. Thus despite the unparalleled combined success of the three generations, the Adamses seem to have been more conscious of their defeats than their victories, and Henry Adams was often morbid over the fate which assigned him a passive rôle in national affairs.

The Adamses were usually small-boned and short of stature, but Henry was two or three inches shorter than his brothers, the result, he thought, of a severe attack of scarlet fever at the age of three. Whether or not this illness permanently affected his physique, he was undoubtedly nervous, irritable, and restless, and these traits may have stimulated his mental faculties, as they sometimes do. He seems, also, to have been acutely influenced by his environment. "The chief charm of New England," he wrote in the *Education*, "was harshness of contrasts and extremes of sensibility—a cold that froze the blood, and a heat that boiled it—so that the pleasure of hating—one's self if no better victim offered—was not its rarest amusement." In winter he lived in Boston with his parents, in summer at his grandfather's eighteenth-century home in Quincy, seven miles away. Thus for Henry, "Town" came to mean "winter confinement, school, rule, discipline," while Quincy meant "liberty, diversity, outlawry, the endless delight of mere sense impressions."

After he grew up, Henry Adams continued to feel a close affinity with the eighteenth-century world of his grandfather. John Quincy Adams had believed with naïve faith that God acted according to fixed natural laws, that through science and reason man could learn these laws and by means of them build a perfect society, eliminating war, slavery, and social evil. But science produced the cotton gin, which made slavery profitable, and the construction of railroads and canals multiplied speculators and landjobbers. It seemed to him that human greed and rapacity would destroy the Republic which his generation had founded with high idealism. He died a disillusioned and embittered old man, as his father, John Adams, had before him, after similar disappointments. Thus the boy, Henry Adams, inherited his double nature and came, as his own character and intellect matured, to look upon the world as an ironic paradox.

Association with his father, grandfather, and their distinguished visitors probably contributed more to the education of Henry Adams than the schools that he attended. His father gave him a writing table in the library, and there he studied his Latin while men like Charles Sumner, the boy's hero, talked politics and the affairs of the world. In this library, stocked mainly with eighteenth-century books, the boy read history, essays, and poetry. Of the more or less contemporary authors, he enjoyed Dickens, Thackeray, and Wordsworth, and his father read Tennyson aloud. But best of all was the table talk, never surpassed, he later recalled, by any conversation which he heard in Europe or America.

Of his formal education, Henry Adams was always contemptuous. He hated Mr. Bixwell's school in Bedford Street. In 1854 he entered Harvard, but he was bored by his four years there and always looked upon the time as wasted: "It taught little, and that little ill." After his graduation he decided to study law in Germany—why Germany it is difficult to understand. But his parents gave their consent and he sailed in November, 1858, on the best ship available. At the University of Berlin he attended one lecture, discovering to his surprise that he could not understand the language well enough to follow the lecturer. Besides, the Germanic system of higher education depressed him. Harvard, he decided, "was instinct with life as compared with all that he could see of the University of Berlin." Consequently, instead of studying law he spent two years of pleasant travel and amusement on the continent. Music interested him for the first time, and he began his observation and study of cathedrals. As James Truslow Adams says, "He was, indeed, to receive a marvellous training, but it was not one leading to late nineteenth-century power." The result, however, was something better than "power": "It was to lead to one of the greatest contributions any one man of letters has made to American intellectual life."

When Henry Adams arrived back home after his two years in Europe, his father had been elected a member of Congress. The family promptly moved to Washington, and Henry went along as his father's secretary. But the stay was brief. On March 18, 1861, Charles Francis Adams was appointed Minister to England, and again Henry went along as his father's secretary. Many prominent people in England sympathized with the Confederacy, and the new Minister's primary task was to keep Great Britain neutral. At times British antagonism to the Union was so intense that Henry believed his family was surrounded by enemies, though he may have been overly sensitive; but eventually Charles Francis Adams was acknowledged by the British themselves as one of the most popular and successful Ministers the United States had ever sent them. Henry was exhilarated by his father's brilliant achievement. The course of his own life was probably deeply effected by these years in England, which lasted until 1868, when the family returned to America. He had made friends, associated with eminent writers and statesmen, and learned to cherish the British Isles, even the climate, he said.

Two years before Mr. Adams resigned his Ministry the family began discussing Henry's future. The young man was now twenty-eight, and the idea of returning to Harvard to study law did not appeal to him, though his grandfather had done so after seven years of service abroad as secretary, first to the United States Minister to Russia, and then to his father in

London during the peace negotiations of 1813. Henry believed his father agreed with him that "for the law, diplomacy had unfitted him; for diplomacy he already knew too much." No doubt the family as well as Henry himself set a rather high evaluation on the young man's talents and a suitable career for him. Meanwhile Henry, perhaps more by natural inclination than conscious planning, had already taken steps in preparation for a literary career. He read prodigiously—De Tocqueville, Mill, Comte, Darwin, Sir Charles Lyell, and similar writers. He also began writing for the North American Review, with journalism now definitely his goal, though perhaps only a stepping stone to other things. For his first article he chose Captain John Smith and the Pocahontas legend as a subject likely "to break as much glass, as any other stone that could be thrown by a beginner." His factual, scholarly debunking of this cherished legend may not have been as sensational as Adams hoped, but it did rankle in the minds of Virginians for many years. Perhaps more important was his long review of Lyell's Principles of Geology (published in the North American Review, October, 1868), which introduced this epoch-making work in America. He also wrote some informative articles on British banking.

Three months after he returned to America Henry Adams set out for Washington, where he intended to launch himself as a professional journalist and make a name as an expert on national affairs. He arranged to send correspondence to the Nation in New York and his heavier articles to the North American Review. Washington was then little more than a village, and within a short time he knew everyone of importance. He soon felt himself to be an expert on behind-the-scene politics. In April, 1869, he published in the North American Review "The Session," intended to be the first of "a permanent series of annual political reviews," and a second "Session" covered 1869–70. But when President Grant announced his cabinet, Henry Adams decided it would be useless to stay in Washington, because, "after such a miscarriage, no thought of effectual reform could revive for at least one generation. . . ."

Obviously, this descendant of John and John Quincy Adams had higher aims than simply a career in journalism. But before giving up journalism, he had one more card to play. Jay Gould and Jim Fisk had nearly wrecked the country with their manipulation of the stock market. Henry Adams and his brother Charles Francis Adams had painstakingly collected material for an exposé of financial corruption, and Henry now took to England a courageous revelation of "The Gold Conspiracy" which he hoped to publish in the influential Edinburgh Review. Both the *Edinburgh* and the *Quarterly Review*, however, were afraid of libel suits, and the article finally appeared in the *Westminster Review*. American journals pirated the essay on a large scale, and in the next presidential campaign Grant's opponents distributed copies by the thousand. But Henry Adams decided to give up his journalistic ambitions. He later blamed his family for opposing his return to Washington, though probably he was already tired of this uncertain road to national influence, his real goal.

The new career which opened to him in 1870 was an academic one, for which he had few obvious qualifications and apparently at first little inclination. But his family had decided that a professorship at Harvard would give him the opportunities which he needed to develop his abilities and gain recognition, and, fortunately, Henry's brother-in-law, Professor E. W. Gurney, was chairman of the Department of History at Harvard. An assistant professorship was first offered to him by President Eliot while he was in England trying to sell his "Gold Conspiracy" article, but Henry declined. After his return, however, he was offered an assistant professorship in medieval history combined with the editorship of the *North American Review*. This position Henry Adams accepted. The editorship was perhaps more wearisome than he had expected, but he quickly developed into a stimulating and even popular teacher of history. He conducted his course as a seminar, and he and his students enjoyed exploring the subject together.

During his seven years on the Harvard faculty Henry Adams matured rapidly. On a trip to Colorado in 1871 he met Clarence King, a geologist educated at Yale, but now, in Adams' words, "saturated with the sunshine of the Sierras." King became one of Henry Adams' closest friends, especially later in Washington. A second beneficial influence on the young Harvard professor was his marriage in 1872 to Marian Hooper, the daughter of an eminent Boston surgeon and heiress to a considerable fortune. Granted a year's leave of absence, Professor Adams took his bride to Europe for a year. Marian Hooper was a charming young lady of refinement and taste, and socially the match was thought to be exceptionally fortunate.

After the honeymoon trip Henry Adams returned to teaching for a few years, but he became so dissatisfied that in 1877 he and Mrs. Adams moved to Washington, though they maintained a summer home at Beverly, Massachusetts. One excuse for going to Washington was to be near the Congressional Library, and Henry did make good use of it for the next decade. In 1877 he published *Documents Relat-*

ing to New England Federalism, 1800–1815, a subject of personal interest because of the rôle which John Quincy Adams had played in the Federalist controversy, but the editor refrained from comment except for a short introduction. The book exerted a valuable influence in demonstrating to history students the importance of original sources. Two years later Adams collected *The Writings of Albert Gallatin* in three volumes and added a lengthy *Life* in a fourth volume. In 1882 he published a biography of John Randolph.

But probably Henry Adams' main reason for settling in Washington can be found in the novel, *Democracy*, which he published anonymously in 1880. It is the story mainly of a corrupt politician who thwarts the ideals on which the Republic was founded (the same old theme that haunted the latter days of John and John Quincy Adams), but of greater autobiographical interest is the heroine, a widow, Mrs. Madeleine Lee. She had forsaken New York society in order to establish at the national capital a salon where she could "see with her own eyes the action of primary forces; to touch with her own hand the massive machinery of society." She wanted "power," the word which occurs so many times in Henry Adams' letters before his wife's death. All witnesses agree that Mrs. Adams did not resemble the aggressive Mrs. Lee, but perhaps her husband wished that she did. This supposition is strengthened by the events following the publication in 1884 of a second novel, *Esther*, under the pseudonym "Frances Snow Compton." Esther is believed to have been the portrait of Mrs. Adams—or it might be better to say a caricature. In the story Esther is torn between her love for a clergyman and her loyalty to her sceptic father, and loyalty wins over love and religion. Some critics have thought that Esther's desire "to get out of life rather than suffer such pain, such terror, such misery of helplessness" after her father's death may have given Mrs. Adams the suggestion of escape from her own anguish.

Although the situation could not have been entirely parallel, Mrs. Adams did become despondent after her father's death and on December 6, 1885, committed suicide by taking cyanide. Henry Adams could not have been more crushed by his wife's death if he had thought himself guilty, and possibly he did. He spent the remainder of his years as if he were doing penance. As literature his two novels are dismal failures, but they raise many curious questions about the spiritual biography of Henry Adams and are, therefore, of special interest to the student of his life.

In the spring following his wife's tragic death Henry Adams interrupted his historical studies and writing and took a long trip to Japan with his good friend, John La Farge, the painter. While on this trip Adams conceived the idea of a memorial statue which he later had the famous sculptor, Augustus Saint-Gaudens, erect at Mrs. Adams' grave in Rock Creek Cemetery, Washington. The recumbent figure, which soon became a renowned piece of American sculpture, was one of the first evidences of Henry Adams' interest in Oriental mysticism. In his instructions to Saint-Gaudens, Adams asked him to study pictures of the frescoes in the Sistine Chapel at Rome and of Chinese statues, especially of Buddha, but he left specific plans entirely to the sculptor. The finished bronze has puzzled many observers. Saint-Gaudens called it "the Mystery of the Hereafter . . . beyond pain and beyond joy." Adams called it "The Peace of God," and said that its meaning would be obvious to any Asiatic. James Truslow Adams' comment is that "from the love of Adams and his wife, from the brooding peace of the East to which Adams fled after his tragedy, there has arisen amidst the most frantic life of incessant activity that the world has ever seen, the figure of eternal calm beyond desire." For Henry Adams the figure was truly symbolic, for he spent the remainder of his life searching for spiritual peace and philosophical unity.

Despite his grief, Adams managed to finish his ambitious work, a *History of the United States during the Administrations of Jefferson and Madison*, published between 1885 and 1891 in nine volumes. As usual with his books, this had a personal meaning for him, because in it he was able to defend his grandfather's break with the Federalist party. But the work has been justly praised for its comprehensiveness and its integrated exposition of the political and social ideas of the period. Through his research and studies Adams was beginning to see history in terms of energy.

His *History* finished, Adams continued his restless travels, usually contriving to spend his summers in Europe. During the financial panic in 1893 his brothers, Brooks and Charles Francis, called him back to Boston, fearing bankruptcy, but they weathered the storm. Then Henry resumed his travels, visiting the Chicago Exposition, going in 1894 to the West Indies for the winter, to Yellowstone for the summer, and after pretty well covering American railway routes, visiting Mexico. He was in the latter country when the American Historical Association, to which he had been elected president, held its annual meeting. Not being able to deliver the presidential address in person, he mailed back a long essay on "The Tendency of History," in which he urged teachers of history to search for a mathematical law for social phenomena.

An extensive study of scientific writings had convinced Henry Adams that thought was simply a form of energy, and that the laws of physics could be applied to social science. Brooks Adams was working on his book, *Civilization and Decay*, a forerunner of the Oswald Spengler theory of the disintegration of Western civilization, and Henry originally intended his essay as a preface to his brother's book, which he regarded as not sufficiently philosophical. What he wanted to do was to make history a science: "Any science of history must be absolute, like other sciences, and must fix with mathematical certainty the path which human society has got to follow." But it was not until 1909 that he evolved a formula which he believed valid. In "The Rule of Phase Applied to History," he used "the law of squares" to illustrate the ever-increasing acceleration of man's control over energy. For example:

Supposing the Mechanical Phase to have lasted 300 years, from 1600 to 1900, the next or Electric Phase would have a life equal to $\sqrt{300}$, or about seventeen years and a half, when—that is, in 1917—it would pass into another or Ethereal Phase, which, for half a century, science has been promising, and which would last only $\sqrt{17.5}$, or about four years, and bring Thought to the limit of its possibilities in the year 1921. It may well be! . . . but even if the life of the previous phase, 1600–1900, were extended another hundred years . . . the Ethereal Phase would last till about 2025.

In the "Atomic Age" these predictions are not as absurd as they appeared in 1909.

Before publishing his theory of "phase" applied to history, Henry Adams had reached other conclusions more important in his development as a writer. Even in his attempt to discover scientific law for human history he decided that society was already on the retrograde. But eventually convinced that "chaos is the law of nature; order the dream of man," he began searching for the period in civilization when man attained most order, unity, and spiritual poise. The answer, he concluded, was the thirteenth century in Europe, especially France, during the height of the worship of the Virgin. The book which this conclusion led him to write, *Mont-Saint-Michel and Chartres* (privately published in 1904), has frequently been regarded as Henry Adams' homage to the Virgin, to whom he wrote a prayer which was found in his wallet after his death; but however well it may have filled a personal need, this work is too subtle and ironical to be entirely the product of a religious conversion. As one result of his years of studying medieval history and literature, and visiting year after year the great cathedrals of France, Adams chose Mont-Saint-Michel and Chartres as two symbols of medieval unity and energy, the one of military power during the time of the Norman conquest and the other of the spiritual and social power of the Virgin. This book is remarkable also for the author's integration of the multifarious aspects of the two ages—religion, politics, art, literature, and social customs.

Since Adams was beginning to develop a thesis, however, he probably found more unity in these medieval periods than ever existed in reality. The thesis was his theory of the increasing chaos of society. Believing his own age to be near complete disintegration (in 1903 he declared: "My figures coincide in fixing 1950 as the year when the world must go to smash"), his imagination seized upon the remote thirteenth century as the antithesis of everything which he feared and detested in the twentieth century. *Mont-Saint-Michel and Chartres* was, therefore, only one act of the drama. The final act was another symbolical book, Henry Adams' own spiritual autobiography, which he wrote in the third person as *The Education of Henry Adams*. The use of the third person enabled him to assume an ironic detachment that strengthened his didactic purpose. It is not a true autobiography. The *Education* is the record of incessant failure. Every good intention and high ideal leads to frustration in the book. But Henry Adams' life included triumphs as well as some failures, and his mood was not habitually morose and pessimistic, as his many exuberant letters to his friends testify. The *Education* is a masterpiece of analysis and condemnation of intellectual chaos, but it is more didactic than personal.

From the third-rate novels to the masterly *Education*, all the writings of Henry Adams record the development of one of the most sensitive and astute minds in the history of American literature. Some of the bitter irony in these writings is the heritage of the frustrated Adams family, but this heritage enabled the historian-philosopher to foresee events and understand modern dilemmas with such clarity and accuracy that one might almost call him an inspired prophet. For example, in 1897 he predicted in a personal letter: "For the last generation, since 1865, Germany has been the great disturbing element of the world, and until its expansive force is decidedly exhausted, I see neither political nor economic equilibrium possible." In 1901 he called Germany a "powder magazine," declaring, "All her neighbors are in terror for fear she will explode, and sooner or later, explode she must." Unlike most of his countrymen, Adams was not surprised when war finally broke out in 1914. In 1904 he also wrote prophetically: "I am half crazy with fear that Russia is sailing straight into another French revolution which may upset Europe and us, too."

Today the dangers of scientific progress are obvious, but probably few Americans believed in 1902 "that science is to wreck us, and that we are like monkeys monkeying with a loaded shell; we don't in the least know or care where our practically infinite energies come from or will lead us to." Since the invention of the atomic bomb Americans hear almost hourly an echo of the opinion which Adams expressed nearly half a century ago: "Some day science may have the existence of mankind in its power, and the human race commit suicide by blowing up the world." With this danger now apparent, the modern student should find especially rewarding the study of a man who had the wisdom to write the chapter on "The Virgin and the Dynamo" in the *Education* early in the destructive twentieth century.

STEPHEN CRANE (1871–1900)

At the public Library in Newark, New Jersey, a memorial tablet bears these words:

Inscribed to the memory of Stephen Crane, born in Newark, November 1, 1871. He attained, before his untimely death, June 5, 1900, international fame as a writer of fiction. His novel, "The Red Badge of Courage," set a model for succeeding writers on the emotions of men in battle. His verse and his delightful stories of boyhood anticipated strong later tendencies in American literature. The power of his work won for him the admiration of a wide circle of readers and critics.

Memorial inscriptions are often exaggerated, but this one unveiled November 7, 1921, made no claims not soon to be corroborated by many men of letters both in England and America, for the 1920's brought a revival and growth of Crane's literary reputation. Carl Van Doren, for example, stated in the first issue of a new magazine, *American Mercury* (January, 1924), that "modern American literature may be said, accurately enough, to have begun with Stephen Crane thirty years ago." By this time it was becoming apparent that Crane was modern in his "realism" (or, as some said, his "naturalism") as well as in the quality of his writing; he not only anticipated writers like Dreiser, Anderson, and Hemingway, but to a large extent he created a style for them. Thus the works of Crane, written in the final years of the nineteenth century, afford a convenient and proper starting point for the study of twentieth-century American literature.

Stephen Crane was the fourteenth child of the Reverend Jonathan Townley Crane, D.D., pastor of the Central Methodist Church in Newark, New Jersey. He was named for an ancestor who had signed the Declaration of Independence and served in the Continental Congress. The Reverend Jonathan Crane, originally Presbyterian, had revolted at the doctrine of infant damnation while a student at Princeton and had found, he thought, a more humane theology in the Methodist Church. Stephen's mother, Mary Helen Peck, the daughter and sister of Methodist ministers, was a fitting wife for her ministerial husband. Her youngest son wrote of her:

My mother was a very religious woman but I don't think that she was as narrow as most of her friends or her family.

. . . After my father died, mother lived in and for religion. We had very little money. Mother wrote articles for Methodist papers and reported for the *(New York) Tribune* and the *(Philadelphia) Press.* . . . My brother Will used to try to argue with her on religious subjects such as hell but he always gave it up. Don't understand that mother was bitter or mean but it hurt her that any of us should be slipping from Grace and giving up eternal damnation or salvation or those things.

Even as a child Stephen's health was precarious, and his parents watched over him anxiously. He suffered from frequent colds, and his father would leave his study, and sometimes even his pulpit, to nurse him. This slight, blond boy was the pet of the family. But his mother taught him to endure pain or disappointment without crying and to rely upon his own strength and courage. His brothers took him swimming and marveled that he seemed to have no sense of fear. In 1879 Dr. Crane, thinking that the inland climate might be better than coastal New Jersey for Stephen's health, secured an appointment to a church at Port Jervis, New York.

In this pleasant town beside the Delaware River Stephen began his first attendance at school, roamed the countryside with his brothers, and grew rosy-cheeked. But this happiness was interrupted the following year when his father suddenly caught pneumonia and died. Mrs. Crane, almost without resources, experienced great difficulty in supporting her large family, which she moved back to New Jersey, then returned to Port Jervis, and in 1882 settled at Asbury Park, New Jersey, where Stephen attended school for the next six years. He learned easily and did well in every subject except mathematics, though he probably cared more for outdoor activities than books—he was passionately fond of horseback riding all his life. But he was also reading, observing, and storing up memories. The Civil War especially interested him. He read about it, heard veterans talk of it, and was impressed by their realistic, unglorified accounts. In 1883 he saw a white girl stabbed by her Negro lover, and he pedaled his bicycle away in terror, but refrained from mentioning the experience to his mother. Mrs. Crane herself was busy fighting vice (such as selling alcohol to schoolboys) and attending religious conventions. She had many lecture engagements, too, and Stephen remembered her strong, rich voice and dignified bearing. She always spoke impromptu, words never failing her. Asbury Park was becoming an important summer resort, and her son Townley established a news bureau for "Shore News." In the summer of 1888 he employed his youngest brother to interview new arrivals and report the social news.

In January, 1888, Stephen Crane registered in the preparatory department of Claverack College and Hudson River Institute, three miles from Hudson, New York, a combined preparatory school and college of respected reputation. The school had been founded in 1854 and flourished until the end of the century. During Crane's two and a half year attendance, students were enrolled from fourteen states and several foreign countries. One of its publicized features was its military training, to promote "an erect carriage and dignified bearing, quickness and promptness of movement besides being an agreeable and health-giving exercise." In later years Crane, who never respected formal education, remembered that he was awkward at military drill, but the record indicates otherwise, for in 1890 he had become first lieutenant of the company that won first prize in the annual parade, and at the end of the year he was promoted to the rank of captain. More important than his military proficiency, this record also indicates his leadership. He distinguished himself still more, however, in baseball, the school magazine reporting that "Crane, catcher, was tendered the office of captain," though for some reason he declined. Some of his own writing was published in this school magazine, called *Vidette*, and its simplicity and clarity plainly foreshadowed his mature style.

In the fall of 1890 Crane entered Layafette College, at Easton, Pennsylvania, instead of returning to Claverack College. He remained at Lafayette, however, only one term, and the records for his residence there are meager. We do know that he played baseball, joined a fraternity, and was taking a scientific course. There is also a record of his grades for this term: algebra 60, French 88, elocution 92, and theme writing 0. A fellow student remembered an attempt to haze Freshman Crane. For some reason (possibly his grades) he transferred in January, 1891, to Syracuse University, then a Methodist institution. He registered, as at Lafayette, for a scientific course, but soon changed, with his mother's permission, to *belles-lettres*. His main ambition was now to become a writer, and he was already, in a small way, a journalist, for he was the Syracuse correspondent for the New York *Tribune*, wrote special articles for the Detroit *Free Press*, and did some reporting for the local newspaper office.

At Syracuse, Crane was an erratic student, for he seemed to be happy only when playing baseball, at which he starred, and was elected captain of the team. He is said to have shocked the faculty by saying that he disagreed with St. Paul's theory of sin and refused to meet Miss Frances E. Willard, ardent reformer and prohibitionist, at the home of one of the professors. His mother wrote him to be good, independent, and honest, and he at least followed two-thirds of the advice. Independence and honesty became, in fact, two guiding principles of his life. American writers of the day he called insincere, and according to his biographer he preferred Tolstoy to any other contemporary abroad. Perhaps his mother's simple Christianity influenced his evolving literary theory and taste more than he realized. Suddenly in the spring his mother died after attending a woman's congress in Boston, and in June Stephen turned his back on college forever. Perhaps he did not desire to be a financial burden to his brothers, but, with his impatient and independent spirit, he probably realized by this time that no college could help him to become the kind of writer he wanted to be.

In the fall, after Crane left Syracuse, he experienced his first and perhaps his only love affair. Somewhere he met a tall, attractive brunette, Helen Trent, an unsuccessful singer trained in Europe but then living in New York as a companion to an invalid lady of means. In his off-hours of erratic reporting for various newspapers he frequently visited her or wrote her brief notes. She was already engaged and was alarmed by the emotions and the ideas of this precocious nineteen-year-old boy, but she also found a certain fascination in his shocking talk, and she postponed telling him of her engagement. Probably, too, he desperately needed someone to whom he could pour out his thoughts and ambitions. He said the Bowery was the most interesting place in the world, and Miss Trent lectured him on going into such naughty places. She was astonished also that he thought a Negro could be handsome, that he pronounced American religion "mildewed," that Buddhism interested him, and that he believed it was all right for a certain actress with a cottage on the New Jersey beach to go swimming at dawn without a bathing suit. After a hansom ride on Fifth Avenue with Miss Trent, he wrote her:

You have the most beautiful arms I ever saw. You never should have to wear dresses with sleeves. If I could keep your arms nothing else would count. It would not matter if there was nothing else to hope for in the world or if there was no more world. In dreams, don't you ever fall and fall but not be afraid of anything because somebody safe is with you? I shall be here tomorrow. I must get back to Ed's [his brother's] house now.

When he called the next day, Miss Trent told him that she was soon to be married in London. Crane gasped, wheeled, and left. But the love poems in *The Black Riders* testify to the importance of this frustrated romance. One poem, especially, reveals his tragic feeling:

> Should the wide world roll away,
> Leaving black terror,
> Limitless night,
> Nor God, nor man, nor place to stand
> Would be to me essential,
> If thou and thy white arms were there,
> And the fall to doom a long way.

It would be a mistake, however, to attribute Crane's knowledge of terror and doom entirely to frustration in love. During that autumn of 1891 he was making such a clinical study of life in the Bowery as Zola was advocating in his essay on "The Experimental Novel." These observations made Crane something of a determinist before the word became popular in literary circles. Shortly before Christmas, according to his own account, he finished a short novel about the sordid life of a girl in the Bowery. It is the story of a drunken mother, a son brutalized by his environment, and a pretty daughter early seduced, then driven into the streets by her mother and thus forced into suicide. The book ends ironically with the mother's crying "I'll fergive her!" after hearing of her daughter's death in the river. In the original version the characters were not named; they were merely types of humanity left derelict on the stream of a thoughtless society, but Crane finally named the story *Maggie: A Girl of the Streets*. He had no other purpose in writing it, he said, "than to show people to people as they seem to me." But no publisher would touch it. Richard Watson Gilder read the manuscript and began criticizing the grammar. "You mean that the story's too honest?" Crane asked, and Gilder truthfully agreed. Finally Crane borrowed money to print it himself. He asked his brother what was the stupidest name he could think of, and he replied Johnson or Smith; so Crane used the pseudonym of "Johnston Smith." Eleven hundred copies in paper covers were delivered to him, and the book was priced at fifty cents. By January, 1893, only a hundred copies had been sold, and the critics had ignored the work. In February Crane lost his position with the *Tribune*, and he attempted to support himself by free-lancing. That year he nearly starved, but finally *Maggie* came to the attention of Hamlin Garland, who liked it so well that he sent a copy to William Dean Howells and helped Crane sell some sketches to the *Arena*. Howells was equally enthusiastic and began trying to find a publisher. He invited Crane to dinner and read Emily Dickinson to him.

To be appreciated by the critic who had first praised Tolstoy in America and had defended Zola was perhaps stimulating, if not remunerative, for Crane began almost immediately to read everything he could find on the Civil War in preparation for a new story. He came to feel, however, that nothing of any value had been written on the subject. He knew Zola's *La Débâcle*, and possibly may have derived unconscious hints from it, but what he was mainly interested in was the emotions of an average man during the horrors of war, and he had to rely upon his knowledge of human nature and his own imagination. He called the book ironically *The Red Badge of Courage*, but it was more about fear than courage. Henry Fleming, a farm boy plunged into battle with no experience or faith to guide him, is hero and coward by turns, but Crane presents him without credit for either. He is merely a bundle of human sensitivity stumbling through experience as best he can. But Crane described the emotions so convincingly that the story became a sensation. He sold it for less than a hundred dollars to Irving Bacheller's Syndicate, and it was printed in convenient installments for the Philadelphia *Press*, then mailed to other newspapers. When Crane visited the *Press* office the printers, some of them war veterans, crowded around to congratulate him, and letters of praise came in from all parts of the country.

On the basis of the newspaper success of *The Red Badge* before book publication, Bacheller employed Crane to make a trip to Mexico by way of the Western states to collect material for stories and sketches. Crane's visit to Chicago was spoiled by meeting children on the street dressed like Little Lord Fauntleroys, a fad started a few years earlier by Mrs. Frances Hodgson Burnett in her famous book for children. Always a foe of sentimentality, Crane particularly hated *Little Lord Fauntleroy*. One of his favorite books was *Life on the Mississippi*, which he thought Mark Twain's best, and he was eager to see the great river. In Lincoln, Nebraska, he tried to stop a fight, suffered from a blizzard, and got an idea for a story from the sight of a hotel painted a revolting shade of blue. He was disappointed in New Orleans, perhaps because the food gave him indigestion, but he loved

San Antonio and Texas in general. (Miss Willa Cather thought his Texas story, "The Bride Comes to Yellow Sky," one of his best.) But if he loved Texas, he adored Mexico. There he was chased by bandits, much as he has described in "Horses—One Dash," and met exciting characters like the 'Frisco Kid and the New York Kid of "The Five White Mice." These stories owe something to the synthetic glamour of Western romance, but they are always original in the point of view, the impressionistic imagery, and the deliberately flat ending: the prospective gun-battle terminates in anticlimax; the tourist thinks he is facing death but suddenly finds himself safe. The Swede does get himself killed in "Blue Hotel" but not because the cowboy, the saloon-keeper, or the gambler wants to fight. Crane's endings are the antithesis of O. Henry's, as commonplace as average life, but framed in the author's ironic detachment.

Appleton bought *The Red Badge* while it was being syndicated, but Crane's travels delayed the publication of the book until October 3, 1895. Within a few months it had become a "best-seller," though at first England seemed more enthusiastic than America. H. G. Wells remembers that *The Red Badge* came as "a record of an intensity beyond all precedent," and Ford Madox Ford says, "One awakened one morning in the nineties in England and *The Red Badge of Courage* was not; by noon of the same day it filled the universe. There was nothing you could talk of but that book. And by tea-time, as it were, this hot blast of fame had swept back across the Atlantic and there was nothing they could talk of in New York and its hinterlands but that book."

Even though we grant that the story was, and is, a masterpiece, the excitement it created may have been due to some extent to the fear of war throughout the world during the closing years of the nineteenth century. National rivalries and frictions were increasing, and there was threat of war on every continent. Perhaps the common man in many a country was wondering how he would stand the test of actual battle, and in Henry Fleming, who doubted his own courage, the average man may have unconsciously found a reflection of himself. Fleming learned, too, that he could not judge others by their words; reality he could experience only in himself. This fundamental truth about human nature was not prevalent in fiction before Crane. And he was in no way more modern, more apperceptive, than in his repeated attempts in his writings to explore the reality concealed by verbal habits. In the disintegration of cultural patterns and the withering of communal faith man

was becoming lost in his own intellect, an easy prey for degenerating doubt and withering scepticism. Crane had no remedies for these social and psychological diseases; but with clinical efficiency he searched out and recorded the symptoms.

When he explored his own inner experience, however, as he did in his first book of poems, *The Black Riders* (1895), he revealed a state of mind which the average man could not understand. In fact, few men or women anywhere could. Of course Garland, to whom the book was dedicated, was an exception, and so was Howells; but the public, which still admired Longfellow and was just then enchanted with Fitzgerald's rendering of Omar Khayyam, could find neither poetry nor sense in Crane's free verse lines packed with dissonance and satirical disenchantment. Perhaps they were like the man in the poet's vision:

> I saw a man pursuing the horizon;
> Round and round they sped.
> I was disturbed at this;
> I accosted the man.
> "It is futile," I said,
> "You can never—"
>
> "You lie," he cried,
> And ran on.

In mood and epigrammatic style these poems resemble the lines of Emily Dickinson more than any other nineteenth-century poet, but the imagery (though not of the sample quoted above) reminded a few critics of French symbolism. When asked if he admired Stéphane Mallarmé, Crane replied, "I don't read much about Irish authors." Indeed, his poems were about as little derivative as any verse could be, but they anticipated "imagism" and much of the best American free verse. *War Is Kind* (1899) showed considerable development in rhythm and phrasing, and the two books entitle Crane to serious consideration as an important poet, but his fiction still outweighs his verse in popularity. One of the central themes in his poetry, the strength of the gods in contrast to the puny weakness of man, links him with Thomas Hardy. It is also significant that one of his warmest admirers in England was Joseph Conrad, who was equally appreciative of the sorry plight of man in a disinterested universe.

Since Crane had won his success with a war story, both he and the public seemed to expect him to rush to every battlefield that presented itself during the blustery end of the nineteenth century. In the fall of 1896 "filibustering" ships were secretly carrying munitions to revolutionary forces in Cuba. William Randolph Hearst engaged Crane as correspondent for the New York *Journal*, and Crane boarded a dilapidated ship in Florida. Wrecked off the Florida coast, he and three members of the crew rowed for several days and nights—an experience unforgettably described in a story called "The Open Boat." But Crane's health, never robust under favorable conditions, was, in the opinion of his brother William, permanently injured, and his experiences the following spring certainly did not improve it. In March he wrote to his brother:

I have been for over a month among the swamps further South [of Jacksonville], wading miserably to and fro in an attempt to avoid our derned U. S. Navy. It can't be done. I am through trying. I have changed my plans and am going to Crete.

The *Journal* agreed to this shift in Crane's plans and accordingly employed him to report the Graeco-Turkish war, already in progress. He went by way of England, where he secured another contract to write for the *Westminster Gazette*, was lionized in British literary circles—though he antagonized some by his acid comments on R. L. Stevenson, then quite the rage—and tried in France to pick up enough French to help him report the war in Greece. He seemed to be shocked to discover that this fracas was being carried on in foreign tongues. From Switzerland he wrote:

I now know that I am an imbecile of rank. If nobody shoots me and I get back alive through those Indians in London I will stay home until there is a nicer war in Mexico where it does not matter what you talk so long as you can curse immoderately. Willie Hearst has made a bad bargain.

That it was, indeed, a bad bargain became more apparent in Greece, where he declared disgustedly that observing the war was "like trying to see a bum vaudeville show from behind a fat man who wiggles." Out of his experiences, however, he did write one superb sketch, "Death and the Child," told from the point of view of an infant watching with incomprehension from a hill the bloody fighting in the valley below. In Athens Crane, ill with dysentery, was nursed by Cora Taylor, an attractive, vivacious woman, who became his common-law wife, after a notorious career in Jacksonville. She had fallen in love with him, perhaps in a maternal way, and had followed him to Greece. There are no indications that Crane ever loved her as he thought he did Helen Trent, but he was devoted to her in his own way, and he could not have found a more loyal wife. They returned to England, where they made their home in a picturesque old town, Limpsfield, in Surrey, near London.

There they recklessly entertained friends and spongers alike. Among their friends were Rupert Brooke, Robert Bridges, Joseph Conrad, Ford Madox Ford, and Henry James, who lived only a few miles away.

When the Spanish-American war finally began, Crane could hardly wait to report it. Upon arriving in New York, he was employed by the *Journal* and the *World*. He visited the troops in Guantanamo, Santiago, Havana, and Puerto Rico. Half crazed with fatigue and fever, he took unnecessary risks, and his companions thought he was trying to get himself killed. Of course under these conditions the reporter could not do his best work, and he returned to New York a broken man. He seemed not to care what happened to him and delayed rejoining his wife in England, but finally he did go back and was temporarily revived by his many loyal English friends. He rented an old manor house, repaired a few rooms so that he and his wife and his many dogs could live in them, and once more settled down to work. He employed a man to take care of his favorite horses, Hengist and Horsa, took daily rides, and was perhaps the happiest he had ever been. Even after hemorrhages of the lungs warned him that his remaining days were limited, his friends found him cheerful, though pressed for money and having to drive himself to turn out the work he did. On New Year's Eve, 1900, he gave a lavish party for his friends, who worried more about his health than he did. In May he was persuaded to go to the Black Forest, but in June he passed quietly away at night, several months short of his thirtieth birthday. Many stories had been circulated about him before his death, and they continued afterward, delaying for many years an appreciation of his genius in America. Gossipers whispered that he drank too much, smoked too much, that he used morphine. His biographers attribute most of these stories to jealousy and malice and to the fact that he was indifferent to public opinion and often said things which could be misunderstood. Illness and fatigue, of course, also gave him a dissipated appearance. But the friends who knew him best thought him one of the kindest, most generous and sincere men they had ever known.

Of one excess he was guilty: he wrote too many books, and the quality of his writing suffered as a consequence. But he seemed to have a premonition that he would not have many years in which to write, and he drove himself without mercy. Some of his later works, however, are almost as good in their own way as anything he wrote. *The Third Violet*, a study of lovers unable to probe beneath the words which conceal their real emotions for each other, is a psychological achievement. *The Monster*, the story of a small-town physician's loyalty to a Negro who was horribly disfigured while saving his employer's small son, was the most penetrating revelation of small-town bigotry and inhumanity before *Main Street*. And the *Whilomville Stories* (1900) should be known as classics in the literature on childhood. They were, in fact, probably the most truthful accounts of child psychology that had ever been presented in fiction, surpassing the better known efforts of Mark Twain and Booth Tarkington in truthfulness. But, as with all Crane's best efforts, these simple narratives have a deeper meaning: as one critic has noticed, underneath the comedy of children playing at life is the cruel tragedy of tribalism. Crane's fictitious characters mirror not the smiling face of social life in the "gay nineties" but the hidden fears secretly gnawing at the vitals of the supposedly civilized people. By his uncompromising realism he was unconsciously prophetic of the "blood-baths" of the twentieth century.

INDEX

Principal Names and Titles

Adams, Brooks: *Civilization and Decay,* 146
Adams, Henry, xliii, xliv, 143–47; Works: *Democracy,* 145; *Education,* 143; *Esther,* 145; *History of the United States,* 146; *Mont-Saint-Michel and Chartres,* 146; "The Virgin and the Dynamo," 146
Adams, J. Q., xxxi
Alcott, Bronson, xxxvi
American Renaissance, xxxiii–xxxvii
American Transcendentalism. *See* Transcendentalism
Anderson, Sherwood, xlviii
Antinomianism, xvii

Bianchi, Martha, 123, 124
Bierce, Ambrose, xliii–xliv
Boone, Daniel, xiii
Brackenridge, Henry Hugh, xxx
Bradford, William, xxi
Bradstreet, Anne, xxii
Brooks, Van Wyck, 1
Brown, C. B., xxx
Bryant, William Cullen, 41–45; Works: "The Ages," 45; "The Embargo," 41; "The Flood of Years," 45; "Inscription for the Entrance to a Wood," 43; *New York Post* (editor), 42–43, 44; "O Fairest of the Rural Maids," 43; "The Poet," 43; "The Prairie," 44
Byrd, William, xxiii

Cabell, J. B., xlviii–xlix
Calhoun, John C., xxxix
Calvinism, xv, xxiii–xxiv
Cargill, Oscar, xi
Carnegie, Andrew, xliv
Cather, Willa, xlviii
Clemens, Samuel Langhorne, 125–30; Works: *Autobiography,* 126; *Connecticut Yankee,* 128; *Defense of Harriet Shelley,* 128; *Following the Equator,* 128; *The Gilded Age,* 127; *Huckleberry Finn,* 127, 128; *Innocents Abroad,* 127; *The Mysterious Stranger,* 128, 130; *Personal Recollections of Joan of Arc,* 128; *The Prince and the Pauper,* 128; *Roughing It,* 127; *Tom Sawyer,* 127; *The Tragedy of Pudd'nhead Wilson,* 128; *A Tramp*

Abroad, 127; "What Is Man?" 128, 129
Colonial Literature, xxi
Cooke, John Esten, xlii
Cooper, James Fenimore, 34–40; Works: *Deerslayer,* 36; *The American Democrat,* 37–38; *Home as Found,* 38; *Homeward Bound,* 38; *A Letter to His Countrymen,* 37; "Leather-Stocking Tales," 36; *Lives of Distinguished Naval Officers,* 39; *Monikins,* 38; *Notions of the Americans,* 37; *Pathfinder,* 36; *Pioneers,* 35; *The Prairie,* 36; *Precaution,* 35; *Redskins,* 39; *Satanstoe,* 39; *The Spy,* 35
Cotton, John, 3
Crane, Stephen, xlvi, 148–153; Works: *The Black Riders,* 150, 151; "Death and the Child," 152; *Maggie,* 150; *The Red Badge of Courage,* 150–51; *The Third Violet,* 152; *War Is Kind,* 151
Crèvecoeur, Hector St. John, xii, xxiii

Deism, 18–19, 28
Dewey, John, xlv
Dickinson, Emily, xlvi, 119–24; Works: *Bolts of Melody,* 123; *Letters,* 122–23; *Poems* (1890–96), 122; *The Single Hound,* 123
Dreiser, Theodore, xlvii, l
Dunlap, William, xxix

Edwards, Jonathan, xviii, xxv, 7–13; Works: *A Faithful Narrative,* 10; "Farewell Sermon," 16; *Freedom of the Will,* xviii, 7, 11–12; *God Glorified,* 9; *Original Sin,* 12; *Personal Narrative,* 12; "Sinners in the Hands of an Angry God," 9; *Treatise Concerning the Religious Affections,* 10, 12, 13
Eliot, T. S., xlix
Emerson, Mary Moody, 74
Emerson, Ralph Waldo, xii, xxxv, 72–78; Works: "The American Scholar," 72, 76; *Conduct of Life,* 77; *English Traits,* 77; *Essays,* 77; *Letters and Social Aims,* 78; *The Natural History of Intellect,* 78; *Nature,* 75; *Representative Men,* 76; "Self-Reliance," 72; *Society and Solitude,* 77–78
Expansion (Western), xxxvii ff.

Federalist, The, xxv
Franklin, Benjamin, xxv–xxvi, 14–22; Works: "Articles of Belief," 18; *Autobiography,* xxiii, 14, 19; "Bagatelles," 22; *Dogood Papers,* 15, 21; *Experiments in Electricity,* 21; *Poor Richard's Almanac,* 14, 20; "Rules for Reducing a Great Empire," 21; *The Way to Wealth,* 20
Freneau, Philip, 29–33; Works: "The American Village," 29; "Beauties of Santa Cruz," 30; "The British Prison Ship," 30; "The House of Night," 32; "The Indian Burying Ground," 32; "The Jamaica Funeral," 30; "The Memorable Victory," 30; *National Gazette* (editor), 30–31; "The Prophet Jonah," 29; "The Power of Fancy," 32; "Pyramids of Egypt," 29, "The Wild Honey Suckle," 32
Fuller, Margaret, xxxvi

Garland, Hamlin, xliii
George, Henry, xliii
"Gospel of Wealth," xliv
Great Awakening, 10–11

Hamilton, Alexander, xxvi, xxviii
Hartford Wits, xxviii
Hawthorne, Nathaniel, 52–58; Works: *Blithesdale Romance,* 55; "The Celestial Railroad," 56; *The House of Seven Gables,* 57; *The Marble Faun,* 55, 57; *Mosses from an Old Manse,* 55, 56, 57, 105; *Notebooks,* 55; *Our Old Home,* 57; *Twice-Told Tales,* 54, 55; *Wonder Book,* 57
Higginson, Col. Thomas W., 121
Holmes, Oliver Wendell, 90–95; *Autocrat of the Breakfast Table,* 93; "The Deacon's Masterpiece," 93; *Elsie Venner,* 94; *Guardian Angel,* 95; "The Last Leaf," 93; *A Mortal Antipathy,* 95; "My Aunt," 93; *Poet at the Breakfast Table,* 93; *Professor at the Breakfast Table,* 93; *Puerperal Fever as a Private Pestilence,* 93
Howells, William Dean, 131–36; Works: *Annie Kilburn,* 135; *Atlantic Monthly* (editor), 132; *A Boy's Town,* 131; *Essays in Criti-*